Mar r
Ma .000

The Chartered Institute of Marketing/Butterworth-Heinemann Marketing Series is the most comprehensive, widely used and important collection of books in marketing and sales currently available worldwide.

As the CIM's official publisher, Butterworth-Heinemann develops, produces and publishes the complete series in association with the CIM. We aim to provide definitive marketing books for students and practitioners that promote excellence in marketing education and practice.

The series titles are written by CIM senior examiners and leading marketing educators for professionals, students and those studying the CIM's Certificate, Advanced Certificate and Postgraduate Diploma courses. Now firmly established, these titles provide practical study support to CIM and other marketing students and to practitioners at all levels.

The Chartered Institute of Marketing

Formed in 1911, The Chartered Institute of Marketing is now the largest professional marketing management body in the world with over 60,000 members located worldwide. Its primary objectives are focused on the development of awareness and understanding of marketing throughout UK industry and commerce and in the raising of standards of professionalism in the education, training and practice of this key business discipline.

Management Information for Marketing Decisions 1999–2000

Tony Hines

Published on behalf of
The Chartered Institute of Marketing

BUTTERWORTH HEINEMANN

OXFORD AUCKLAND BOSTON JOHANNESBURG MELBOURNE NEW DELHI

I would like to thank my wife Janice for her support in my hermitage in our study.

Butterworth-Heinemann
Linacre House, Jordan Hill, Oxford OX2 8DP
225 Wildwood Avenue, Woburn, MA 01801-2041
A division of Reed Educational and Professional Publishing Ltd

A member of the Reed Elsevier plc group

First published 1999

British Library Cataloguing in Publication Data
A catalogue record for this book is available from the British Library

ISBN 0 7506 4365 X

Composition by Genesis Typesetting, Laser Quay, Rochester, Kent
Printed and bound in Italy

PLANT A TREE
BTCV British Trust for Conservation Volunteers
FOR EVERY TITLE THAT WE PUBLISH, BUTTERWORTH-HEINEMANN WILL PAY FOR BTCV TO PLANT AND CARE FOR A TREE.

Contents

A quick word from the Chief Examiner

I am delighted to recommend to you the new series of CIM workbooks. All of these have been written by authors involved with examining and marking for the CIM.

Preparing for the CIM Exams is hard work. These workbooks are designed to make that work as interesting and illuminating as possible, as well as providing you with the knowledge you need to pass. I wish you success.

Trevor Watkins,
CIM Chief Examiner,
Deputy Vice Chancellor,
South Bank University

How to use your CIM workbook

The authors have been careful to structure your book with the exams in mind. Each unit, therefore, covers an essential part of the syllabus. You need to work through the complete workbook systematically to ensure that you have covered everything you need to know.

This workbook is divided into twelve units each containing the following standard elements:

Objectives tell you what part of the syllabus you will be covering and what you will be expected to know having read the unit.

Study guides tell you how long the unit is and how long its activities take to do.

Questions are designed to give you practice – they will be similar to those you get in the exam.

Answers give you a suggested format for answering exam questions. *Remember* there is no such thing as a model answer – you should use these examples only as guidelines.

Activities give you the chance to put what you have learnt into practice.

Exam hints are tips from the senior examiner or examiner which are designed to help you avoid common mistakes made by previous candidates.

Definitions are used for words you must know to pass the exam.

Extending activity sections are designed to help you use your time most effectively. It is not possible for the workbook to cover *everything* you need to know to pass. What you read here needs to be supplemented by your classes, practical experience at work and day-to-day reading.

Summaries cover what you should have picked up from reading the unit.

A glossary is provided at the back of the book to help define and underpin understanding of the key terms used in each unit.

Introduction

The rationale for changing the title of this examination was based upon the fact that management information is an input to the marketing decision making process. Therefore a title that more clearly reflected this was deemed to be more appropriate. *Managing Information for Marketing Decisions* says exactly what this subject area is focused upon without ambiguity. The weightings in the new syllabus reflect the changing emphasis of the paper. *Marketing research* has been reduced by 20 per cent to 20 per cent. This is because the focus for the revised syllabus is on the outputs from the marketing research process and how they are applied to provide information that supports decision making. Although it is still important for candidates to understand the ways in which marketing research data has been collected the paper will not in future be testing how the data has been collected or the techniques used to collect data. It will however expect candidates to know and understand those tools and techniques in order that they may comment sensibly on the limitations of data used by organizations when making marketing decisions. The book still contains explanations for the tools and techniques as background knowledge and also recognizing that there are currently two sets of readers – those completing their studies following the old syllabus and those new to the subject who will be studying the new syllabus. Questions set for the new syllabus will be more focused upon the application of marketing research.

Financial information for marketing decisions has remained at a weighting of 40 per cent and is now the single largest element of the area. This reflects the significant emphasis on the importance of understanding financial implications in the marketing decision-making process. From secondary and primary research carried out with a wide variety of marketing professionals it is clear that this aspect of their work has grown as competitive environments have become more intense. A number of existing area have been expanded to recognize their growing importance in the field and new areas have been added to the syllabus. Activity based costing has been expanded to cover activity based management and its significant role in improving marketing decisions. The sections on pricing decisions has been expanded to recognize the variety of marketing contexts in which prices are set particularly in setting appropriate transfer prices for internal or external movement of goods and services. Finally, in the context of retail marketing decisions it is important to know and understand the key concepts of direct product profitability (DPP), channel, category, product and market profit and cost analysis. Sections within the book now cover these new areas.

A completely new section has been added to the syllabus, *Management information systems – basic concepts* (10 per cent). A knowledge and understanding of the important role that information plays in supporting decision making in marketing. This new element has been introduced as a consequence of feedback from tuition centres and the general lack of awareness evidenced through the examination papers when questions have addressed this area as part of other areas of the syllabus where it was necessary to explain marketing information as part of a management information system. It is fundamental to the subject area and its importance has been fully recognized in the new syllabus by having its own section with a 10 per cent weighting attached. The fundamentals that must be understood to set the context for any MIS or MkIS system are:

- Identification of the component parts of management information systems (MIS) and a marketing information system (MkIS).
- Demonstration through application of basic management information concepts on how information is gathered, stored and retrieved to support marketing decisions.
- The ability to recognize and recommend improvements to the MIS or MkIS.
- The ability to recognize the importance of context in suggesting system improvements to the MIS or MkIS.

Information and communication technology supporting marketing decisions (20 per cent).

This is an area of growing importance. When the syllabus was first introduced five years ago many of the topics covered within this area seemed to many candidates developments that would take place at some future date. For example, five years ago fewer than 5 per cent of general retailers in the UK had set up their own website to either test the market or to attempt to sell their products directly to consumers. Recent estimates refer to over 80 per cent usage of an Internet site by general retailers for the purpose of test marketing, listing catalogues or attempting to sell goods and services directly to consumers. This is only one aspect of development, there are, of course, many others. The growing importance has been recognized by raising the weighting for this area by 10 per cent to 20 per cent of the syllabus. It maybe that in another five years this area has developed so much that it becomes an examination in its own right? The box below provides details of the focus for the area in the current syllabus.

> Knowledge of the developing information and communication technologies and how they can be used to support decisions taken in marketing and management. In particular how ICTs are changing the ways in which data sources are accessed, processed, analysed and evaluated. Students will be expected to know current terminologies, e.g. hardware, software, networks (Internet, Intranet and Extranet), CD ROM, e-mail, multimedia, databases, data warehousing, datamining and Ecommerce.

Forecasting information for marketing decisions (10 per cent).

This is the final area of the syllabus and its weighting remains unchanged at 10 per cent. However, I have tried to make what is examined or examinable much clearer and appropriate examples are listed below.

It will be necessary for students to know the range of forecasting methods and tools that are available to develop forecasts, e.g. time series analysis, econometric forecasting, sales forecasts, decision trees, delphi technique and critical path analysis.

Specific areas of application

From the underpinning knowledge students will need to:

- Prepare financial forecasts based on sales forecast data.
- Use decision trees to analyse the marketing options available.
- Prepare a critical path based upon forecast data.
- Prepare financial plans based upon forecast data.
- Distinguish between a forecast and a budget.

All in all the revised syllabus recognizes the growing importance of specific areas to marketing professionals in their work. In this respect you should find the topics of interest as well as challenging but most of all rewarding for your personal development as you aspire to take on increasing responsibilities through the progress of your own career.

Unit 1

The nature of management information for marketing decisions

Objectives

After reading this unit you should be able to:

- ❑ Know the differences and be able to distinguish between data and information; and between information and intelligence.
- ❑ Recognize the various levels of marketing and sales information for strategic, tactical and operational decisions.
- ❑ Define and distinguish between the terms marketing research and market research.
- ❑ Identify the main sources of marketing research data. (*Note* Specific techniques will be discussed later.)

Study Guide

This introductory unit is designed to prepare you for the studies ahead. You will be introduced to all the areas of study at a basic level. There are also some very important concepts that you need to understand before proceeding further. For example: definitions of data and information and definitions of marketing research and the distinction between marketing research and market research.

You should allow 2–3 hours to work through this first unit taking time to familiarize yourself with all the concepts. You should also set aside 3–4 hours to do the activities suggested. The activities are important to help your understanding and allow you to relate the concepts to reality. You should always be prepared when working through this book by having a pen, a pencil, writing paper and a calculator to hand.

This first unit will also help familiarize you with the approach and style of our workbooks. It has been designed to ensure that you acquire not only the knowledge necessary for examination success but also to develop the skills needed to apply that knowledge to marketing and sales management problems. You will find the boxed panels clearly signposted to help you practise, evaluate and extend your knowledge and these will be used throughout this workbook. The signposts should help you to manage your own learning by carefully planning your study time and the speed at which you want to progress.

Study Tips

Begin as you mean to continue by careful planning and organization of your study materials. It is important to do so from the start. Do not be daunted by the prospect of the work ahead as from small increments to your study you will achieve success. It is far better to do a little each day than to cram three weeks before the examination. A little each day allows time for learning to take place.

- Use file dividers to index broad topic areas in your notes.
- Add any relevant material you come across elsewhere. For example, newspaper and magazine articles relevant to the study of management information and technology.
- Output from your activities.
- Cross reference your file where appropriate since questions may address more than one part of the syllabus and areas are interrelated.
- Incorporate past questions, examiner reports, suggested answers and revision notes when available.
- Edit and summarize your file notes into bullet points for revision purposes.

Introduction

Marketing and sales managers need to find ways of satisfying customer wants and needs but at the same time they need to make a profit in the process and may also need to achieve other organizational objectives. Marketing managers need information on which to base their decisions. For example decisions to forecast changes in demand, to introduce, modify or delete products, to evaluate profitability, to set prices, to undertake promotional activity, to plan budgets and to control costs amongst other things.

Marketing and sales management decisions may be strategic, operational or tactical in nature.

Figure 1.1
Levels of information for decision making

Marketing managers need to access a wide range of information sources in order to support the decisions they take. It is not possible to prescribe the decisions or information sources that may have to be used for all the decisions that marketing managers take. However, it is possible within this introduction to provide the reader with examples of the types of decisions that managers may need to make and the types of information and sources of data that they may need to access in order to make those decisions. Table 1.1 provides details of the types of decision, information required and how it is applied and the sources of data.

Design of information systems

Information systems must be designed following some basic principles but the detailed structuring of any information system needs to recognize fully the context in which it is to be used and the purposes it is to be used for.

Table 1.1 Some examples of data used by marketing managers

Data sources	*Internal*	*External*
Sales records	These are internal records used by sales personnel and created specifically for their purposes. This would be regarded as a primary database for sales managers.	
Budgets for sales and marketing These could include departmental budgets; product groups; responsibility centres, revenue centres, and profit centres within the control of sales and marketing managers.	These are internally prepared financial plans. The sales and marketing budgets will be put together by sales and marketing managers with assistance in some cases from the accountants or financial managers in the organization. Once again they can be regarded as primary data for sales and marketing managers.	
Variance reports prepared by financial managers or by marketing or sales managers.	These reports would be prepared to analyse performance of a particular section, business segment or for product groups. They may have been prepared by marketing or sales managers for their own purposes in which case they are primary data or they may have been prepared as a matter of course (routinely) or for a specific accounting purpose in which case they may be regarded as secondary data used by marketing and sales managers.	
Forecasts	Sales forecasts are the most widely used forecast required by marketing and sales managers. The forecasts are usually prepared by them for their planning purposes but these forecasts will also be used by financial managers, accountants, production managers and others in the organization. For example, budgets that are prepared for the organization will require sales forecasts as their initial starting point. Cash flow forecasts will usually be prepared by financial managers in the organization to ensure that there are sufficient funds coming in at times to meet the organizational obligations, e.g. to pay creditors, to pay fixed interest charges, to pay dividends to shareholders and so on. It may also be necessary for marketing and sales managers to prepare cash forecasts for projects that they wish to implement. For example, a promotional or advertising campaign.	The preparation of sales forecasts will also require external data about the state of the economy, predictions about the future economy, e.g. disposable incomes, demographics, spending habits, interest rates, exchange rates for international trading and so on. An organization may have to prepare forecasts with regard to these issues and how they might impact upon their own plans.

Table 1.1 Continued

Data sources	*Internal*	*External*
Costing data is usually prepared by cost accountants or financial managers in the organization.	This data may also be useful to marketing and sales managers in planning product ranges, taking decisions about pricing or pricing strategies (e.g. full cost or marginal cost pricing; or using standard costs for margin or pricing decisions). Cost data are also useful to plan volumes, determine unit and total profit margins, to decide upon volumes and other planning decisions. Risk assessment and contributions will need to use cost data. Cost data will be necessary and useful for marketing and sales managers when they prepare their own fixed or flexible budgets.	
	Cost data are also used to prepare cost control ratios, e.g. cost of sales/sales as a proportion or percentage; material cost/total cost %, labour cost/total cost %, overheads or specific overhead category/total cost % or overheads or specific overhead category/sales %.	
	Costing projects and investment appraisal decisions.	
Various financial data	May be used in a variety of ways for marketing and sales managers' specific purposes. For example, overhead reports may be investigated to see that they are being attributed in a reasonable manner to their own areas of responsibility or to specific product groupings. The question might be are appropriate overhead absorption rats being used or in an activity-based cost system (ABC) have activities and cost drivers been correctly identified and applied.	
Profit and loss statements; and balance sheets	These statements may be prepared by the financial managers weekly, monthly, quarterly and annually. They will be prepared for the organization in total but they will also be prepared for market segments and for responsibility centres, e.g. product group, departments, factory sites and retail areas. Marketing and sales managers can use the data to analyse performance either using financial ratios that are given in the internal reports or by preparing their own.	

Table 1.1 Continued

Data sources	*Internal*	*External*
Published market research reports		There are a number of market research reports published by research companies such as: Keynote, Mintel, Neilson, Dunn and Bradstreet, Interfirm Comparisons, Economics Intelligence Unit (EIU) and others. This secondary data source is often a starting point for managers investigating a specific market. For example, size, structure and an overview of the current economic conditions in particular countries can and are often stated in specific reports published by these companies.
In-house marketing research	Organizations often produce their own in-house reports either ad hoc or on a continuous basis. Some organizations will also have electronic point of sale data available daily, weekly and monthly. This data when processed and analysed may reveal information for a specific purpose, e.g. effectiveness of promotional offers.	
Commissioned marketing research May generate primary quantitative and qualitative data.		Primary data are often generated by external marketing research companies undertaking work, e.g. consumer surveys, surveys, observation, experimentation (postal, mall intercept interviews, hall tests, store trials, telephone surveys CATI, CAPI, electronic observation techniques, focus groups, etc.).
Electronic data	These are usually internal and primary in nature. The company's own information systems may generate electronic data at point of sale (EPOS) or may have electronic metering devices, e.g. attached to TV sets as BARB or at point of entry to a store or attached to telephones, etc. Data are gathered and processed either by the company itself or on behalf of the company by an external agent. These types of data are usually quantitative in nature. Video cameras can be used to obtain qualitative data, e.g. to record in-store behaviour of customers.	

There are a number of fundamental questions that need to be answered before any information system can be designed which are:

- What is the information to be used for
- What types of data will be needed
- How will the data be gathered
- How will the data be stored
- Who will be allowed to access the data
- How will data be accessed
- How much will it cost
- What are the main benefits of having this information
- What alternatives are there if the system is not designed as planned
- What are the cost of the alternatives
- What limitations would the alternatives identified impose upon the benefits previously identified

In developing any management information system a number of key steps need to be followed in order to address the types of question listed. The steps are commonly known by an acronymn SREDIM.

- Select
- Record
- Examine
- Develop
- Implement
- Maintain

Selection

Selection is dependent upon purpose (what is the information going to be used for?). Selection involves a number of different choices that will need to be made involving hardware, software, data sources and configurations for all these.

Recording

Appropriate devices, tools and systems need to be in place to ensure that processes are recorded. Flowcharts are often used to record the system itself. Sources of data to input into the system for use immediately or at a later date also need to be recorded.

Examination

This step involves an examination or analysis of the ways in which the processes making up the system can be configured to provide the most efficient means of achieving the aims.

Development

Once the system has been examined and alternatives have been examined it is necessary to develop the 'best' system. This involves designing appropriate processes and adapting them as problems are identified until you are satisfied that the system will work and in the most efficient manner to achieve the purpose.

Implementation

Having completed all the other steps and being satisfied with the system developed it is time to implement the new or reworked system. This usually involves running any existing system in parallel with the new system. The purpose of this is to ensure that if any problems or system failures occur with the new system you still have a back-up while the old system is working in tandem.

Maintenance

The final step is to continuously maintain the system. For example if changes in any processes occur then the system or sub-systems may need to be redesigned or adapted to take account of changes. It is very important that systems are kept up-to-date in this way.

Levels of decision and information to inform decision making

Strategic decisions	*Tactical decisions*	*Operational decisions*
Product/market decisions Product life cycles Product development Entry into new markets Investment decisions Database development Positioning	setting short term prices discounting promotional campaigns advertising distribution product service levels customer service levels packaging planning sales territories short-term agency agreements	pricing including discounting competitor tracking customer research consumer research distribution channels and logistical choices sales and marketing budgets database management

In practice managers will often complain that:

- There is too much information
- They don't receive enough of the right type of information
- The information received is always too late
- Information is not in the right format to be useful

Information needs to have value. Value of information is determined by its usefulness in the context of decisions to be taken. It is important that information is accurate, timely, relevant and in an appropriate form. Marketing management activities are described by Kotler *et al.* as: analysing, planning, implementing, organizing and controlling. In order to carry out these marketing management activities managers require information.

Actvity 1.1

As you read this introductory unit you may like to consider the types of information you use in your job and how it helps you to do any of the management activities listed (i.e. to analyse, to plan, to implement decisions, to organize or to control).

Organizations require information on which they can base their decisions. Data is the raw material that needs to be processed to provide information. Information itself may be regarded as an input to be processed in order to provide intelligence. Raw data has no value but it does have a cost. Data costs money to acquire and to store and retrieve. Processing data also costs money but in turn may provide you with information. Information may be further processed to yield intelligence. Data processing and information handling should be value adding activities. If these activities are not adding value to the decision making process then you need to ask why you are performing them. Information is required to reduce uncertainty. Information is required to reduce risk in the decision making process.

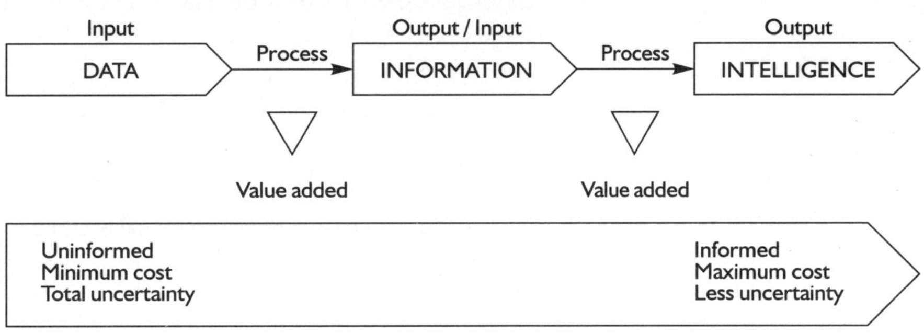

Figure 1.2
Data, information, intelligence (cost and uncertainty)

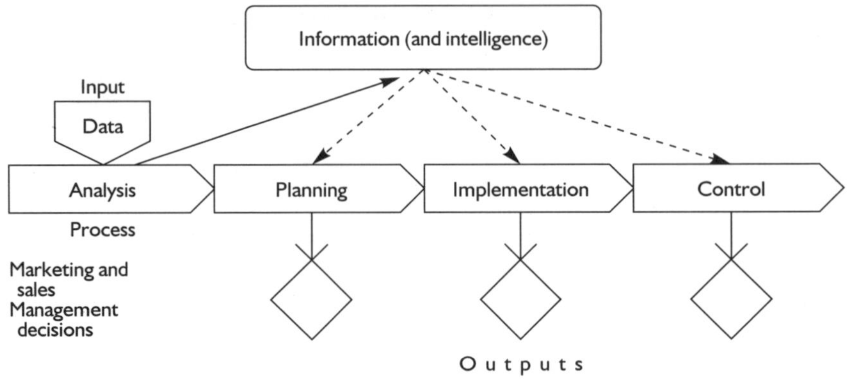

Figure 1.3
Input, process and output of MIS

Data from a variety of sources: internal databases; external databases; and marketing research is an input to marketing information and intelligence systems. The raw data needs to be processed in some way before it provide managers with information. Taking a traditional view of management the information obtained may be used to take decisions about planning, implementing and controlling business activities.

To manage the future requires information which is accurate, timely and relevant. Too much information may be just as much a problem for the busy manager as too little. This is often referred to as information overload. Information overload occurs when managers feel swamped by the amount of information they have to handle and as a consequence they are unable to make an *informed* decision. This is because they are uncertain about the relevance of the information they have and are forced to make selections that may be incorrect. In order to avoid the problems of information overload managers need to:

- Identify their information needs (*relevance*)
- Design appropriate data capture systems (*accuracy/relevance*)
- Store information in a meaningful way (*useful*)
- Retrieve relevant information when required (*timely*).

The value of information lies in its utility to reduce uncertainty and hence risk. The trade-off as far as managers are concerned is in terms of cost and value. Information has a price, it takes time and effort to collect, classify, store, retrieve and analyse.

The purpose of information is to reduce uncertainty and provide a deeper knowledge and understanding of the firm, its markets, its customers and its competitors. The cost of obtaining this information must be balanced against the benefits.

Decision making and information

Selling and marketing management decisions are made usually in advance of the particular time period in which the activity takes place. Decision making, therefore carries risks since outcomes are uncertain as indeed are other factors affecting decision. The benefits of having information should outweigh any costs.

Marketing information cannot eliminate risk, but may reduce it and provide decision makers with greater confidence about decisions they take. Marketing information is needed for strategic decision making, tactical and operational decisions.

Choosing and using appropriate data

Choosing and using appropriate data to achieve your research objectives are the keys to effective use of information. Knowledge of where the data can be located both internally and externally is also a management task. It is not essential that all data is collected and analysed internally. It may be appropriate in many instances to employ external agencies to acquire the data, analyse the data and present you with a report that meets your information needs. In such circumstances it is important to know on what basis these choices should be made.

Forecasting

Data is required for management decisions in sales and marketing for a variety of reasons. Examples could include data for making forecasts. These forecasts could be market forecasts predicting such things as market size or market trends or they could be sales forecasts for specific product lines.

Market forecasts

A market forecast is a forecast for the whole market. The forecast needs to take account of macro environmental factors (political, economic, social and technological). Market research will be undertaken to find information about specific markets and market size on which to base the forecast. It is important to evaluate market demand for the whole market and what proportion of that total demand the firm can expect to achieve. In this evaluation it is important to identify competitor products which are the same or near substitutes.

Table 1.2 Data for forecasting could include the following

		Source
Quantitative data		
Sales	by product line	Internal e.g. EPOS
	by service	Internal e.g. sales records
	by geographic area	Internal e.g. sales/accounting records
	by store	Internal e.g. sales returns
	by division	Internal e.g. accounts
	by value	Internal e.g. accounts
	by volume	Internal e.g. sales/stores/accounts
Market	market size	External published reports
	market trends	External specially commissioned research
		Internal sometimes firms may store their own data in-house
Demographic	by sex	External published sources
	by age	External published sources
	by country	External published sources
	by ethnic group	External published sources
	by social class	External published sources
Economic	National Income	External published sources
	Government statistics	External published sources
	Wealth distribution	External published sources
	Income distribution	External published sources
	Number of households	External published sources
	Characteristics of households	External published sources
	Employment statistics	External published sources
Qualitative data	Expert opinion	External published or primary data usually
	Focus groups	External commissioned research
	Depth interviews	Primary data

Sales forecasts

Sales forecasts estimate sales for a future period and are concerned solely with the firm's products and services. Sales forecasts are expressed in volume, value and profit.

Sales forecast	–	how many, at a given price
Sales forecast	=	100,000 units at £20 = £2,000,000

The sales forecast is essential information required for budgeting purposes. The sales forecast is the starting point for the compilation of sales budgets.

Marketing Information Systems (MKIS)

A marketing information system is that part of the management information system (MIS) concerned with marketing and may be classified as:

- *Planning systems* – which may provide information on sales, costs and competitive activity.
- *Control systems* – which provide monitoring information. Control information will highlight any variance from the plan so as management may take corrective action.
- *Marketing research systems* – which provide management with a means of testing the acceptability of new products or how particular groups of customer may behave.
- *Scanning and external monitoring systems* – will provide managers with information about the wider economic, social, political and technological environment beyond the boundaries of the firm.

Marketing research and market research

Definition 1.1

Marketing research refers to both market research and marketing research which may be more clearly defined as:

1 The American Marketing Association defines marketing research as 'the systematic gathering, recording and analysing of data about problems relating to the marketing of goods and services'. Similarly, the Chartered Institute of Marketing definition is 'objective gathering, recording and analysing of all facts about problems relating to the transfer and sale of goods and services from producer to consumer or user.'

Marketing research is a broadly based concept which includes market research, product research, price, place (distribution) and promotion. Marketing research provides information for managers to make decisions about all aspects of the marketing mix.

2 Market research is that part of marketing research which provides information about the market for a particular product or service.

A summary of marketing research activities

Type	*Application*
Market research	Forecasting demand (new and existing products) Sales forecast by segment Analysis of market shares Market trends Industry trends Acquisition/diversification studies
Product research	Likely acceptance of new products Analysis of substitute products Comparison of competition products Test marketing Product extension Brand name generation and testing Product testing of existing products Packaging design studies
Price research	Competitor prices (analysis) Cost analysis Profit analysis Market potential Sales potential Sales forecast (volume) Customer perception of price Effect of price change on demand (i.e. elasticity of demand) Discounting Credit terms
Sales promotion research	Analysing the effect of campaigns Monitoring/analysing advertising media choice Evaluating sales force performance to decide as appropriate sales territories and make decisions as how to cover the area Copy research Public image studies Competitor advertising studies Studies of premiums, coupons, promotions
Distribution research	Planning channel decisions Design and location of distribution centres In-house versus outsource logistics Export/international studies Channel coverage studies
Buyer behaviour	Brand preferences Brand attitude Product satisfaction Brand awareness studies Segmentation studies Buying intentions Monitor and evaluate buyer behaviour Buying habit/pattern studies

Stages in the marketing research process

1 *Problem definition* – identify what you are trying to find out with the research.
What is the exact purpose of this research?
What information do I expect the research to provide?
What will the value of the research answer be?
How much should we be prepared to spend on the research?

2 *Research design* – once you know what you want to find out you can think of ways to answer the question. Are you planning to use secondary data or primary data? Secondary data is usually lower cost. Primary data is usually collected in one of three ways: survey methods; observation or experimental design.

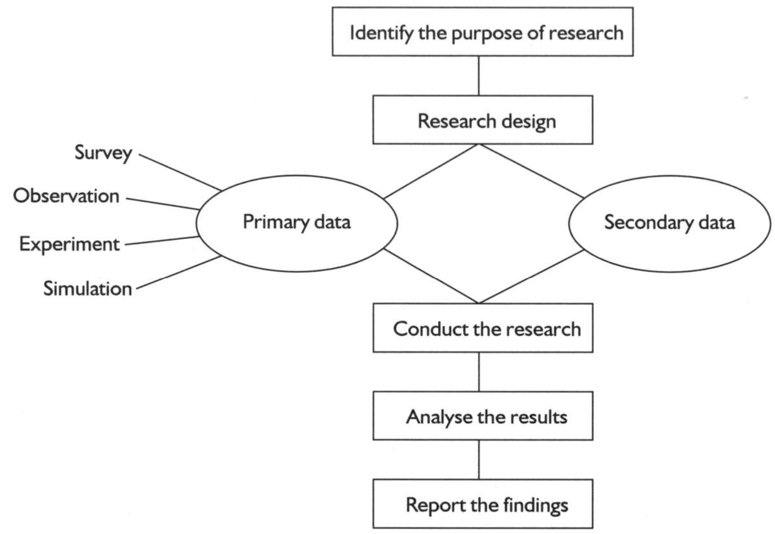

Figure 1.4
Stages in marketing research

It is important to know:

- What type of data to collect.
- How the data will be collected, e.g. postal questionnaire, administered questionnaire, telephone interview, personal interview etc.
- Whether or not you will conduct the research in-house or use an external agency.
- The population from which you wish to select data and the techniques that will be employed, e.g. sample, census.

3 *Data capture* – collect the data using appropriate methods and techniques that maintain the integrity of the data ensuring that the data is both reliable and valid.

4 *Analyse the data* using appropriate quantitative or qualitative methods.

5 *Present a report* with recommendations that lead to a management marketing decision. The decision because it is informed should be of better quality than a decision that would have been taken without information. Uncertainty should be reduced and hence risk should be minimized as a result of information.

Question

List the main steps that are involved in conducting any marketing research study.

(**Answer** See end of chapter.) See above

Sources of data

There are two types of data:

- Primary data
- Secondary data

Primary data is data collected in the field. For this reason it is also called field research. Primary data is data collected for a specific purpose to answer a specific research question. The necessity to collect primary data is a consideration in research design. Primary data usually costs more to collect and is more expensive in terms of processing time.

Field research studies may be undertaken in a number of areas such as customer research, consumer research, product research, promotion research, distribution research, price research, packaging research and advertising research. A number of different research techniques can be employed, for example: experimentation, observation, sampling, questionnaire, consumer panels.

Secondary data is not collected by the use nor specifically for the use to which it will be applied. Secondary data sources may include both internal and external sources. Records inside the firm, collected for another purpose may provide useful information in desk research. For example, cost data collected specifically for accounting purposes may be useful when undertaking competitor analysis looking at firm or product cost/price structures. Customer research may be undertaken using sales records or accounting records which provide data on:

- Percentage of repeat customers – Debtor ledger
  – Sales invoices
- Number of complaints received
- Customer service time – Average order to delivery

Internal data sources

- Financial and management accounting records (cost data, cost analysis and reports, sales data, segment reports, budgets, variance reports, ratios and trends).
- Purchasing and inventory records (stock levels, lead times, suppliers etc).
- Production records and statistics (standard times, efficiencies, costs).
- Sales records (customer names, addresses and contact details, customer buying history, discounts allowed, terms and conditions of business, sales visits, sales budgets, cost of servicing accounts, sales personnel and performance data).
- Customer records if held separately from sales may for example, give background information about the customer, product specifications, returns information, customer complaints and so on.

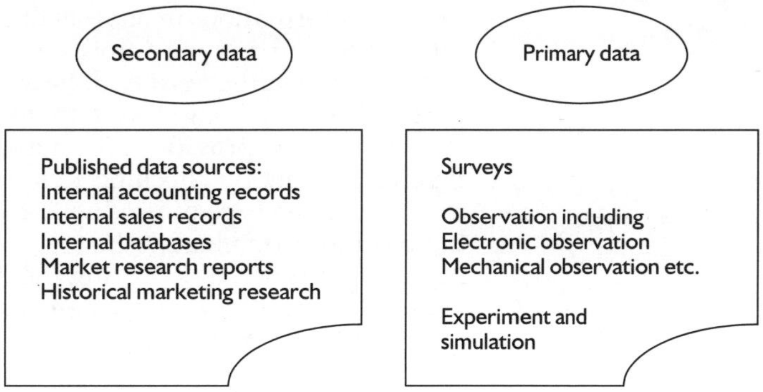

Figure 1.5
Types of data

- Internal market records and marketing reports held by the firm. These reports could have been bought in from outside sources and may be in published hard copy format or on disk or CD ROM formats.
- Other internal databases.

External data sources and published information

- Market research reports, e.g. Keynote, Mintel, Euromonitor, Nielson Index, Target Group Index (TGI).
- Government statistics (CSO and HMSO publications).
- Trade journals.
- Newspapers and magazines.
- Professional journals.
- CD ROM systems, e.g. McCarthy, Extel, British Library, FAME, FT Profile, ABI/Inform, Anbar and various databases sold in this form usually on subscription.
- On-line subscription databases, e.g. Dialogue, British Library, Reuters.
- Data on the Internet (e.g. world-wide web (WWW) 'superhighway'). Many of the on-line database systems are accessible via the internet using GOPHER or WWW. You can only gain access to many databases with a password and there are fees payable to subscribe to many of the more useful databases.
- Company reports (also available through CD ROM subscriptions and various on-line services).
- Year books and directories.
- Trade and professional bodies (often compile membership lists and statistics about the trade or industry).

Activity 1.2

As part of a marketing team responsible for developing new business in an overseas market that your firm is not currently involved in, consider what type of research you think would be necessary in order to identify potential opportunities for your existing products in the new market. What type of research data do you think you would need? List the possible sources of data for your research? What type of research design is needed?

(You should spend about 10–15 minutes on this activity before continuing.)

Databases and technology

Databases may be generated in two ways: either by the business building its own database, or by acquiring the database from an external agency. Mailing databases are swapped and bought and sold by many organizations legitimately for commercial gain. Databases should provide an on-tap source of data which when combined in various ways can be used to provide information on aspects of the business. For example, a mail order catalogue company may store customer data: names, addresses, telephone numbers, when they ordered, how they ordered, how they paid, when they paid, what they bought and so on. A marketing manager may be able to use the data to provide information for specific promotions on a certain type of product by checking to see which customers are most likely to be attracted to the type of product being offered in the promotion by checking the customer purchasing history and targeting those customers likely to buy. Furthermore, by checking the database to see if there is any significant time of the month or year when customers are likely to buy, the marketing manager could time the promotion to coincide with the *customer's most likely to buy period*. Preferred payment methods could be identified and used in the promotion to make it attractive.

Databases have always been available to managers in organizations, in paper form in files, and in card indexes but it is technology that has transformed the way in which we view and value databases. Computers have enabled managers to store vast amounts of data and to combine it in ways which were previously only dreamt about, since it would have taken too long to collate the data and retrieve it in the required format. Today it is possible to store, retrieve and combine data sources quickly to provide managers with vast amounts of information.

The development of computer databases has however, presented problems of security with associated problems of control and access. There are horror stories and apochryphal stories about hackers breaking into high security databases using the worldwide web (the internet). Some of these stories are greatly exaggerated by the press, but do demonstrate the sensitive nature of information. For example, you would not want your marketing information system exposed to competitors. There is therefore the need to protect the data held in the organization. Simple protections include access codes and security passwords together with physical controls of locking away sensitive data. Just like you might lock away your paper files in a filing cabinet you need to provide your electronic data with similar levels of security.

The law relating to computer security is in an embryonic stage and will become more fully developed as the legal profession and managers come to terms with the nature of the problems or potential problems that may exist. The Data Protection Act 1984 requires all organizations holding data about people and organizations to register with the Data Protection Agency. Nevertheless, there is evidence to suggest that there are probably still many computer database users who are not familiar with their legal obligations under the act. The proliferation of cheaper computers and the wider use in small firms and at a personal level have contributed to this ignorance of the law.

The Computer Misuse Act 1990 is designed to limit unlawful access to computer systems. This is in effect a law to deal with hackers.

Types of data

Data are either said to be quantitative (i.e. numerical) or qualitative (i.e. mainly descriptive). Quantitative data is collected from secondary data souces where it is available, or from primary sources (surveys, experiments, observation and simulation studies). Qualitative data may be obtained from descriptive secondary sources or from primary data collected through open questions (maybe in surveys, more usually in interviews – depth, group).

Hard or soft data

Data are often said to be hard if they are data collected for a specific purpose in an organized way or in a scientific manner. Soft data are acquired by managers often in the course of conversation with suppliers, customers and colleagues in an unstructured and unplanned manner. Such data are not necessarily collected for any specific purpose. Soft data are stored informally usually within the brain of the managers concerned and retrieved when a specific occasion triggers thought processes. Mintzberg and many management commentators stress the importance of this 'soft data' over and above 'hard data'. Soft data often contain a high degree of qualitative information.

For example, a sales manager on a visit to a customer may find out in the course of conversation that the customer buys from two other suppliers who specialize in providing a particular type of service. On returning to base the sales manager could use this 'soft data' to investigate the possibility of supplying the same or a better type of service and thereby competing more effectively with the other two suppliers if this is appropriate. This soft data may not be collected in any management information system planned by the firm.

Furthermore, supposing a member of the sales team speaking on the telephone with a long standing customer acquires information about a third party who also happens to be a customer and the difficulties they are experiencing in obtaining supplies or in paying their bills. This information could be used in the first case to match the demand by supplying relevant goods or services. Or, in the case of the cash flow difficulties that come to light in the discussion, this information could be passed on internally to the accounts department for them to check the customer's account and to evaluate possible risks.

Question 1.2

Name the main types of data sources available to marketing and sales managers?

Financial analysis and tools

Most firms have a great deal of internal financial data about various aspects of their own business, and managers need to know and understand what is available internally so that they can use this source of readily available data to inform their own decision making. Access to such data may sometimes be a problem. Often financial accounting departments may restrict access to other managers in the organization. Sometimes this restriction may be legitimate. It could emanate from concern about security of the data. At other times one needs to understand that accountants have been trained in a particular way with control rather than service in mind. This is not meant to be insulting to accountants but to explain why they might not readily be willing to share data. It is pleasing to report that in many organizations accounting departments work alongside managers in other departments with a view to establishing accessible data.

Managers wanting to use financial data often need to acquire other skills and understand the tools available to help with application and interpretation of financial data to provide information that may help deal with specific problems. The toolkit may comprise:

- Marginal costing for pricing, output and profit planning.
- Budgeting techniques – fixed and flexible budgeting, responsibility accounting, standard costing, variance analysis, control ratios.
- Financial decision making techniques: cash flow, profitability and risk.
- Knowledge and understanding of how to read and interpret financial statements such as profit and loss accounts and balance sheets.
- Financial ratios that can help explain the figures in these and other financial statements.

Data contained within the internal financial information system can prove invaluable in forecasting sales for particular product lines or departments. This data is also useful for analysing performance for specific time periods. Financial analysis may be undertaken using a variety of segmental data that could provide marketing and sales managers with useful, timely and relatively cheap information about specific product performance or store performance or area performance and so on. Internally available financial data could also be useful when planning promotional campaigns, for pricing decisions, for distribution channel decisions, for product/service costing and for costing and pricing decisions related to short or long term projects.

Financial data is used to analyse, plan, implement and control activities. Marketing and sales managers armed with the necessary financial tools and skilled in the language of financial managers are better equipped to take advantage of the many situations that require financial skills. These managers are better able to deal with their counterparts in a financial managerial role and in an age when all managers are expected to have financial acumen those who do not possess such skills are severely handicapped.

In a recent survey of job advertisements for senior marketing jobs in the Sunday broadsheets more than 70 per cent of the jobs specifically requested some financial knowledge and skills (source: Hines, T. 1995). Below are listed a selection of jobs requesting marketing professionals to apply and this will give you some indication of the importance of having financial skills.

Job title	*Skills listed*	*Source*	*Salary*
Market development manager	Analytical Interpersonal IT literate Language	*Sunday Times*	£40,000
CEO	Managing resources at corporate level Excellent communication Flair and vision	*Sunday Times*	£70,000
Area manager retail	Numerate Interpersonal	*Sunday Times*	£30,000
Channel marketing manager	Return on investment	*Sunday Times*	£40,000
Marketing manager	Budget preparation Market planning Market analysis and research	*Sunday Times*	£40,000
Managing director	P&L responsibility	*Sunday Times*	£50,000
Marketing manager	Forecasting Budgeting Marketing planning Market research	*Sunday Times*	£35,000

Accounting as an internal information source

Accounting systems hold vast amounts of data which may provide a useful source of information for marketing and sales management. The aim of management accounting information is to provide management with information which may assist planning, control and decision making. More specifically management accounting information may help managers to:

- Plan and achieve goals.
- Formulate policy (pricing, discounting, credit terms etc.).
- Monitor and assess performance (variance analysis, financial performance measures).
- Appreciate the financial implications of changes in the external environment.
- Appreciate the financial implications of changes in the internal environment (e.g. changes in structure, organization and processes).
- Compare and decide upon alternative courses of action.
- Manage more effectively and efficiently scarce resources at their disposal.
- Control operations on a daily basis.
- Focus attention on specific issues which really need attention.
- Solve specific problems.
- Make investment decisions or decisions about projects, products and markets.

Activity 1.3

List the possible data held internally in financial accounting departments and explain how you may possibly use such data as a marketing and sales manager in your own organization?

(You should take 10–15 minutes to consider this issue.)

The cost of information

Information has a cost. The cost may be divided into acquisition costs, storage costs, retrieval costs and processing costs. Data have to be collected from a variety of sources: internal or external; published sources; secondary or primary. Primary data will nearly always cost you more than secondary data so you need to make sure that the cost is an investment and not merely an unnecessary expense that you could have avoided. You should plan to collect, classify and process only that data that is needed to meet your specific objectives. For example, if it is sufficient to acquire data from three sources to satisfy a specific research objective you should not bother to explore additional data sources, since the cost could not be justified. However, if the additional data sources would provide additional information that is likely to lead to more confidence about the research findings then maybe you would do so. The important decision for all managers to evaluate is whether or not the additional cost incurred will yield better information. In other words, there is a trade-off between cost and value.

The value of information

Information must provide the user with value which should be greater than the cost of collection, storage and retrieval. Higher costs are usually associated with acquiring more accurate information. In reality managers will trade-off accuracy with cost to achieve a satisfactory rather than an optimum solution to a specific research problem. Reliability and validity of the data are often key issues for market researchers. Data is said to be reliable if managers interpret the data in a similar way and achieve the same result on any reassessment. Data is valid if the accuracy of measurement applied to the process or event you want to measure, is indeed properly measured.

Extending Activity 1.1

Supposing you had to undertake market research into the possibility of introducing a new product for a specific market segment, how could you justify this in terms of costs and benefits?

You will need to do some research consulting appropriate library resources to address this problem.

Hints: look at the following terms: marketing projects, project justification and cost/benefit.

(You should take 45 minutes to consider this issue.)

Summary

This unit has introduced you to the main areas of study that you will be looking at throughout the rest of this book. It is important to keep in mind that you are concerned with information that is gathered, stored, processed and applied to marketing and sales decisions. Marketing and sales managers need to draw data from a wide variety of sources. Data may be readily available within the firm i.e. in an internal database (e.g. sales database, customer database, accounting database, production database and so on), or they may be available from external sources (e.g. published market trends for the industry, specific product reports, specific market reports etc.). If secondary data are not available or are insufficient to satisfy the information needs of managers then primary data may need to be collected. Primary data may be collected from within the organization or from external sources.

Managers will always need to evaluate their information needs and balance them against cost and value provided by the information. Let us take an example: if a manager makes decisions that are 60 per cent accurate on average without information, and each decision is valued to make a return of £1,000 then without cost the equation would be as follows for 100 decisions taken:

Accurate decisions = 60 × £1,000 = £60,000
Inaccurate decisions = 40 × £1,000 = £40,000 lost contributions
Net benefit without information = £20,000

Supposing the accuracy of decision making could be improved to 70 per cent by having additional information at a cost of £100 per decision then the equation would be as follows:

Accurate decisions = 70 × £1,000 = £70,000
Inaccurate decisions = 30 × £1,000 = £30,000
Net benefit from information = £40,000
Less Information cost = 100 × £100 = £10,000
Net benefit overall = £30,000

This is rather an unsophisticated and crude example of the analysis, but it nevertheless provides you with an outline of the thinking that should be present when deciding how far the search for information should be taken.

Ten questions to test your knowledge

1 Define the following terms:
   (a) Marketing research
   (b) Market research.
2 Define the following terms: data, information, and intelligence?
3 Identify and list as many marketing research applications as you can?
4 There are two main types of data used in research – name the two types and briefly define each source?
5 List the published sources of data that a marketing researcher may want to access in a column and then alongside your list in a second column list the possible applications?
6 What is the purpose of information?
7 What is the difference between a sales forecast and a market forecast?
8 Explain what you understand by the terms 'hard data' and 'soft data'?
9 What sources of accounting data could be used to help marketing and sales managers?
10 Explain what is meant by desk research and field research?

Answer 1.1

Identify the purpose of the research, design the study, choose secondary and/or primary data, conduct the research, analyse the results, present the findings.

Answer 1.2

Secondary or primary
Quantitative or qualitative
Hard or soft

Unit 2 Forecasting in marketing decisions

Objectives

By the end of this unit you should:

- ❑ Know what types of forecasting is done by organizations.
- ❑ Know why forecasts are necessary and what they are used for.
- ❑ Understand how forecasts are prepared.
- ❑ Understand the importance of having accurate forecasts.
- ❑ Be aware of the major tools and techniques used for forecasting.

Study Guide

This unit introduces you to a definition of forecasting and a number of quantitative and qualitative forecasting techniques that may be used by marketing and sales managers in different circumstances.

The wider aspects of forecasting are discussed in addition to sales forecasting. You should work through the unit carefully and you may want to refer back later when you have worked through some of the financial units, in particular the budgeting unit to see how forecasting is linked.

Exam Hints

Questions about forecasting are more likely to refer to concepts and techniques in the context of a given situation related to marketing and sales information. You will not be expected to apply any specific statistical techniques.

Definition 2.1

Forecasting
Forecasts are predictions about the future. More precisely forecasts identify factors which may be quantified and qualified to determine their effect on the organization and its specific markets.

Forecasts are used as a basis for planning. Forecasts take place at the macroenvironment level and predict change in the political, social, technological and economic environments external to the organization. The purpose of forecasting the changes in the external environment is to determine how such changes may affect the firm in the future. It is also necessary to predict market size and market trends to identify how the firm may take advantage of any opportunities that may present themselves or to minimize the effects of any threats posed.

Definition 2.2

Rolling forecast

A rolling forecast is a continuously updated forecast. Every time actual results are reported a further forecast period is added and existing time periods are updated in the light of the new information.

Budgets

A forecast is not a budget. A budget is a financial plan for a specific time period which is quantified and expressed in monetary terms. Budgets may also be expressed in volume terms (i.e. quantities of output – number of units). Forecasts are used as data to *input* into the budget.

The need for forecasting

All businesses and organizations must plan for the future. It is necessary to have some knowledge and understanding of what is going to happen in future so as to make plans today. Forecasting has an array of techniques that are designed to help predict the future. The techniques fall into two main types: quantitative techniques employing statistical and mathematical models and qualitative techniques based on informed opinion.

Forecasts are undertaken at two levels that economists refer to as the macro level or the micro level. Macro forecasting is concerned with looking at the total picture for an economy or for a market. Micro forecasting is concerned with forecasting at the firm level or within the firm forecasting particular product line sales. The following examples will serve to illustrate these types more clearly.

A firm may want to forecast the size of the total market for fridge/freezers over the next five years. This is a macro level forecast. At the same time the firm may also want to forecast the sales of its own product lines in fridge/freezers for the same period. This is a micro level forecast.

Taking these examples if the firm is wanting to predict its own sales a sensible starting point might be to predict the growth of the total market size over the time period. This is because presumably if the total market is growing this will have an impact on the sales of the firm's product range.

A departmental store buyer may want to predict sales quantities for certain clothing lines for the next three months. In making such a forecast the buyer may use past experience or what statisticians call time series data. Time series data assumes that the future is a continuous reflection of the past. In some circumstances this is reasonable. However, if the future is discontinuous and does not relate to the past in any meaningful way then time series data is not appropriate. Time series models are useful to determine trends.

Supposing we have the following data:

	Sales
January	£100,000
February	£120,000
March	£130,000
April	£140,000
May	£150,000
June	£160,000
July	£150,000
August	£140,000
September	£130,000
October	£140,000
November	
December	

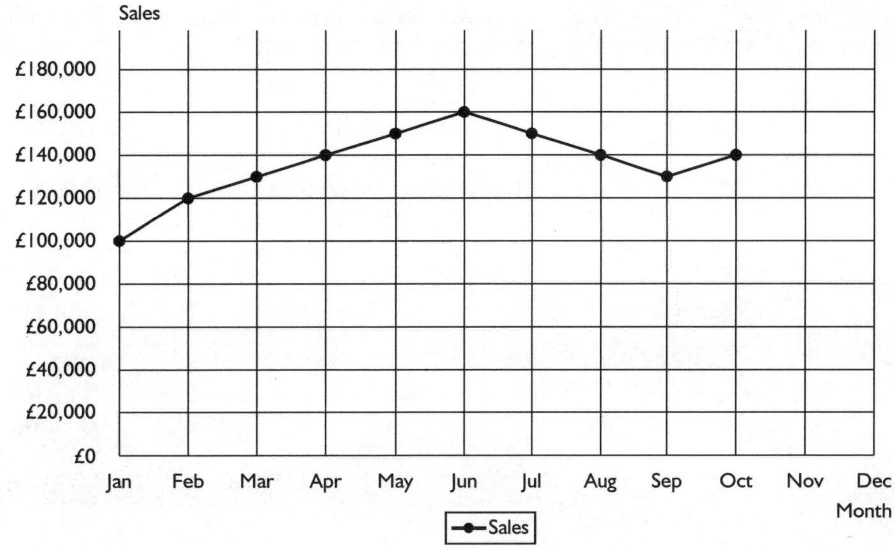

Figure 2.1
Sales by month (1)

If we wanted to predict the next two months sales using the data available for the previous ten months we may predict sales of £150,000 and £160,000 since the trend is now upwards. This forecast may be very inaccurate since November and December in retailing are the months when many stores can sell more than in the rest of the year put together. However, without this additional piece of data your forecast of £150,000 and £160,000 using the trend depicted in the chart would seem reasonable.

This chart shows the trend line drawn in for November and December.

Figure 2.2
Sales by month (2)

Time series models can take account of secular trends (*Tt*), Cyclical movements (*Ct*), Seasonal fluctuation (*St*) and Irregular variations (*It*). The classical time series model takes the form:

$$Yt = Tt \times Ct \times St \times It$$

This equation states that the dependent variable *Yt* (i.e. the forecast) is influenced by secular trends multiplied by the cyclical movements multiplied by the seasonal fluctuation multiplied by the irregular variations.

Time series data covering a small number of years may be fitted by a straight line using least squares. The regression equation for such a line takes the form:

$$Y = a + bx$$

Supposing we want to predict the total cost (Y) when we know the fixed cost (a); the unit variable cost (b) and the quantity produced (x) substituting the following data we could forecast total cost as follows:

Y = ?
when:
a = £25,000
b = £10 per unit
x = 3,000 units

£25,000 + £10 × 3,000 units = £55,000

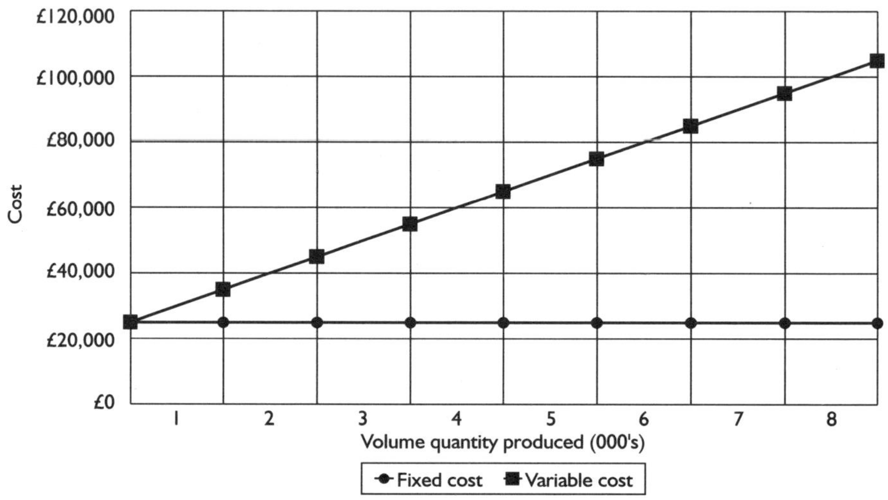

Figure 2.3
Total cost

Forecasting time frames

Forecasts may be prepared for the short term, the medium term or the longer term. Short term forecasting would be for days, weeks and months ahead. The medium term would be one or two years hence and the longer term three, five or ten years into the future.

Short term forecasts

Forecasts in the short term are focused on the microenvironment. For example organizations need to predict the near future to know potential capacity loading. The marketing department may be able to provide forecasts of demand based upon seasonal and cyclical trends or forecast demand based upon current promotional activities or on other specific factors influencing demand. For example the sales team may be able to provide forecast demand based upon actual orders obtained and the likelihood of further orders being obtained within the forecast period. These forecasts are essential in planning loadings and scheduling production within a factory or in planning staff resources to provide a service. *Capacity planning* is an important output from this type of forecast.

Communicating the forecast

Short term forecasts are often about the transmission of data stored from the sales team or the marketing team who are aware of what they expect to happen within the time-frame to others inside the organization who are concerned with producing a product or service to satisfy forecast demand. Only when the data is retrieved and communicated will it provide useful information.

Control

Short term forecasts are also a means of controlling the activities of the organization. For example, if the sales team forecast demand lower than originally expected for the time of the year they are actually providing an early warning message for marketing and sales management to act upon. Adjustments to capacity loadings, schedules, predicted (forecast) cash flows, promotional activities and tactical marketing could all be appropriate responses.

Market demand

One of the main purposes of forecasting is to predict the market demand for particular goods and services supplied by the organization. This assumes that one is able easily to identify the particular discrete market for the goods or services supplied. This is not always easy particularly in growing or newly established markets. Imagine estimating the market demand for motor cars in 1900; aircraft in 1930; photocopiers in 1950; video recorders in 1960; fax machines in 1970; personal computers in 1975; personal telephones in 1985 and so on. The establishment, development and nature of market demand are constantly changing. Research into market demand needs to be continuously undertaken for this reason. The market demand for the Betamax format video-recorder and complementary products such as Betamax recording tape has changed substantially from 1980 to the present day. Market demand for large cubic capacity British motorcycles declined throughout the 1960s as smaller cubic capacity Japanese motorcycles entered the market. There are many such examples of the changing nature of market demand. It is not always easy to identify the causes of the change clearly. Firms that constantly scan their environment are more likely to pick up on some of the factors causing change, and develop an ability to respond positively to the changes.

Let us take as an example a long established and more easily defined market, the market for clothes in the UK. The clothing market at retail prices in 1991 was estimated to be some £32 billion in the UK. This market demand was satisfied by a large number of firms not all of whom were in the UK. In other words overseas suppliers satisfied some of that market demand. Furthermore, the market for clothes may be subdivided into various categories as defined by Standard Industrial Classification Codes (SICs):

SIC Division 4
Class 45
Group 453 Clothing, hats and gloves
Description

4531	Weatherproof outerwear
4532	Men's and boys' tailored outerwear
4533	Women's and girls' tailored outerwear
4534	Work clothing and men's and boys' jeans
4535	Men's and boys' shirts, underwear and nightwear
4536	Women's and girls' light outerwear, lingerie and infants' wear
4537	Hats, caps and millinery
4538	Gloves
4539	Other dress industries (swimwear and foundation garments, umbrellas)

If you wanted to forecast the market demand for men's suits as a starting point you would need to extract the actual sales figures for Code 4532 and then establish how much of the demand was due to men's suits. Boys' tailored outerwear and other men's tailored outerwear would need to be excluded from the calculation. The next step in the process would be to prepare a market forecast.

Definition 2.3

Kotler (1994, p.247) defines market demand as follows:

> Market demand for a product is the total volume that would be bought by a defined customer group in a defined geographical area in a defined time period in a defined marketing environment under a defined marketing programme.

Market forecast
This is a forecast of expected market demand.

Market potential
A market forecast gives the expected market demand. It does not predict the maximum market demand. Maximum market demand is a function of market potential.

Company forecast
The company forecast is the expected level of sales for the company based on a chosen marketing plan and an assumed marketing environment (Kotler, 1994, p.249). This is the share of the market demand the company expects to realize. The forecast must be based on certain assumptions about the marketing environment in which the firm will operate during the forecast time-frame.

Sales budgets
These are usually based on company forecasts for sales, but may be adjusted to take a prudent/conservative view of the expected volume and value of sales. The sales budget is then used to budget for all other costs during the period and to make expenditure decisions. Capital expenditure, purchasing, production and other revenue expenses may be based upon the sales budget as will cash flow decisions.

The importance of accuracy

Accurate forecasting processes can lead to better planning decisions. Shorter control periods and continuous updating of forecasts also enable more accuracy in planning including budgeting. Accurate forecasts are important in determining resource allocations in the budgeting process. Control is therefore an important aspect of both forecasting and budgeting. As new data is obtained it is input to the forecast so it yields information which may reduce the uncertainty and improve the accuracy of the forecast.

Consider the analogy of a weather forecast. Each day a forecast of the weather for the next twenty-four hours is given, together with a forecast for the next few days. They may also occasionally provide a longer term outlook for the month ahead. Weather forecasts are updated daily in the light of new data (changes in weather conditions: wind flows, cloud formations, rainfall, sunshine and so on). In terms of accuracy forecasts for the day ahead are usually good. In probability terms they may be 95 per cent accurate. However, the forecast for the next few days ahead is probably slightly less accurate, perhaps only having a probability of 90 per cent. That means that only nine times out of ten is it accurate or alternatively there is a one in ten chance of the forecast being inaccurate. The further into the future the forecast prediction is, the more uncertain it will be and the less accurate in terms of actual result. People relying on such forecasts would be taking less of a risk if they rely and act upon the next twenty-four hour forecast than if they rely on a forecast for the week ahead. The uncertainty attached to weather forecasts for the month ahead would be much greater and the risks associated with individuals relying on forecasts would be much greater.

Forecasts are often the basis of planning. Taking our analogy further, supposing that you were planning a holiday and you wanted to have good weather you may listen to the forecast and if it was good for the next week you may decide to go on your holiday. Control periods (each day) would provide you with a new forecast of the weather ahead and you may decide to adjust your route or you may decide to reduce or increase the time spent on your holiday. Planning has implications for resource allocation. In this case your personal resources (time and money) are being reallocated in view of the forecast information you are receiving. Forecasts are used in exactly this way in business.

Forecasting and marketing decisions

Market information is by nature imperfect. It is often incomplete. Furthermore, because we often make estimates about a future that has not yet arrived it is uncertain. Decisions in business often need to be made using imperfect information, which may be incomplete and about which we may feel uncertain. A forecast is such a decision. Forecasts may be formal or informal in nature. An informal forecast is often similar to our best guess.

There are a number of formal statistical forecasting techniques which may be employed to provide forecasts. It is important to keep in mind the cost and value relationship of information when deciding whether or not to employ formal statistical techniques. Formal statistical forecasting models would include: time series decomposition, exponential smoothing, correlation models and econometric models. A high degree of forecasting accuracy usually means incurring higher costs (in data collection and processing). It is often not worth pursuing a high degree of accuracy since the benefits the additional accuracy of the information yields are not greater than the cost.

Marketing and sales managers are often asked for forecasts of sales, profits, costs and market shares. Forecasts are sometimes made to identify possible problems and then to take appropriate action. For example, a sales forecast may be required for a particular market segment. This sales forecast may be used as the basis of a budget for regional sales areas. It will help identify problems by measuring the actual sales per period against the budget and the variance acts as a control to re-inform the planning process. Sales forecasts are also used to set standards of performance. Standards provide performance measures by which personnel and departments may be judged. If sales standards are not then achieved the performance measurement has identified a problem that may require attention and corrective action.

A sales and profit forecast for a range of products may assist with the allocation of promotional budgets. For example, supposing a firm has three products A, B and C each selling for £7 and that it has forecast sales for a period in total amounting to 25,000 units, made up of 12,000 units of A; 8,000 units of B; and 5,000 units of C. The firm may decide to allocate an advertising budget for the product grouping on the basis of sales quantities or sales values. In this case let us assume an advertising budget in total of £100,000 and that it is apportioned on the basis of quantities since they are of equal value then Product A would receive £48,000; Product B £32,000 and Product C £20,000. You should note that it may be more appropriate to allocate the advertising budget in other ways, for example using a profit forecast so that the more profitable products are rewarded. It may seem more equitable to support those products which will achieve higher profitability for the firm.

Forecasts are also important when attempting to evaluate alternative courses of action. For example, supposing we have the option to invest in developing only one of three alternative products X, Y and Z. It would be important to try to forecast likely revenues and likely costs over the lifetime. Let us suppose that we prepare forecasts of sales and forecasts of costs over a two-year time period for our three products.

	Product X	Product Y	Product Z
Forecast quantity in units	35,000	30,000	34,000
Forecast selling prices per unit	£6.00	£5.20	£4.10
Forecast variable cost per unit	£5.00	£4.00	£3.00
Unit level contribution	£1.00	£1.20	£1.10
Forecast sales	£210,000.00	£156,000.00	£139,400.00
Forecast product costs	£175,000.00	£120,000.00	£102,000.00
Forecast contribution	£35,000.00	£36,000.00	£37,400.00

You can see from the table that based on our forecasts product Z appears to be the best choice since it makes the largest total contribution to profit over the two-year period. However, supposing our forecast for product Z is inaccurate by –2,000 units. How would this affect our decision?

	Product X	Product Y	Product Z
Forecast quantity in units	35,000	30,000	32,000
Forecast selling prices per unit	£6.00	£5.20	£4.10
Forecast variable cost per unit	£5.00	£4.00	£3.00
Unit level contribution	£1.00	£1.20	£1.10
Forecast sales	£210,000.00	£156,000.00	£131,200.00
Forecast product costs	£175,000.00	£120,000.00	£96,000.00
Forecast contribution	£35,000.00	£36,000.00	£35,200.00

If you look at the revised table with the forecast for product Z revised by 2,000 units downwards (a percentage change of –5.88 per cent on 34,000 units) you will see it will alter our decision and product Y now makes the best total contribution. Accurate forecasts are therefore important since future decisions will be affected by the quality of the forecast. This decison is, therefore, very sensitive to a small change in the sales forecast.

Activity 2.1

Using the original forecast data: forecast quantity in units X = 35,000 units; Y = 30,000 and Z = 34,000, calculate the effect of understating the forecast sales for each product X, Y and Z by 10 per cent and see if this would alter the decision in any way if we had to choose only one of the products.

Sensitivity analysis and forecasting

Sensitivity analysis is a technique used to evaluate how sensitive the plan is to changes in key variables which affect the plan. The aim is to assess how critically affected the outcome is. The activity you have just completed is a type of sensitivity analysis. You were investigating the sensitivity of the plan for products X, Y and Z to the change in the forecast. Sensitivity analysis may be conducted to see how sensitive a sales budget or a production budget is to changes in the level of forecast sales. It may also be applied to an analysis of the costs and expenditures in the budget as required to evaluate which costs will be affected by the change in sales volumes forecast and to estimate by how much each cost will be affected.

Long term planning and resource implications

Firms need to plan for the longer term as well as the short term. Long term planning is also referred to as *strategic planning* since it is usually involved with making strategic decisions. In other words *how* to meet the long term goals specified by the organization. In this context long term forecasts are necessary in order to plan future resourcing. If a long term forecast is made which predicts growth in particular product markets presenting particular opportunities for the organization in the five to ten year time-frame then the firm may want to plan for investing in new plant. Research and development may need to be undertaken to meet the needs and take advantages of the opportunities identified in the long term forecast. Training for existing employees to meet the new challenges may be required and it may be necessary to recruit people with different knowledge and skills.

Macroenvironmental forecasting methods

Long term planning usually involves making some sense of the organization's external environment and forecasting how changes over the next five- to ten-year period may impact upon the organization and its market opportunities. Organizational survival and growth are dependent upon the firm's ability to adapt its strategies to this changing environment. This process is dependent upon the ability of managers to anticipate and predict future events accurately. For example, a company may anticipate a particular marketing environment in which the firm expects to have rising sales levels. In such an environment the firm's budgets would be constructed to accommodate this expected increased demand for the firm's products. The firm's other budgeting plans are all dependent on the level of expected sales. Supposing, however, that the firm made incorrect assumptions about the macroenvironment and that as a result the company forecast was inaccurate this would lead to lost sales and loss of market share against competitors. Larger firms have their own in-house planning departments which forecast the macroenvironment. Smaller firms can buy in forecasts from the numerous suppliers of marketing research firms and specialist research firms.

Long term forecasting methods

A number of methodologies may be employed by macroeconomic forecasters which include:

- Expert opinion.
- Trend extrapolation.
- Trend correlation.
- Econometric modelling.
- Cross-impact analysis.
- Multiple scenarios.
- Demand/hazard forecasting.

Expert opinion

Expert opinion is a qualitative method of forecasting. Sometimes qualitative data may be quantified by assigning probabilities to possible outcomes. Data are obtained when key knowledgeable people or industry players are selected and interviewed with a view to identifying issues and trends. It is possible to ask the experts to assign probabilities to possible future outcomes. Sometimes expert panels are constructed with the aim of meeting regularly to comment upon specific factors shaping the industry. The most refined version of this is known as the DELPHI method, which puts an expert through several rounds of such interviews and keeps refining their assumptions until a final decision is reached. Usually a group of experts are consulted independently of each other so that there is no group bias in decisions reached. Expert opinion may use in-house expertise in the marketing and sales team as well as customers and industry experts.

This method of forecasting the possible impact of specific factors identified in the external environment is becoming more popular with researchers and forecasters using computer technology to assist the process. For example a panel of experts could be constructed drawn from the various industry players shaping the particular industry. Each player could use a personal computer to communicate with a panel chair who can allow each individual to identify key issues as well as asking for information about 'what if ....?' At the end of each round of discussion the panel chair could collate the different views to build a view of the future. Choosing and using expert opinion requires great skill if bias is to be eliminated.

Trend extrapolation

This is where the researcher fits a line of best fit to the past time series and uses the data to extrapolate into the future. The least squares technique is such a method of extrapolation. Growth curves may be linear, quadratic or S shaped. The method can be very unreliable since new developments in the macroenvironment could completely change the direction of any extrapolation. Trends assume that historically predicted patterns will exist into the future. This may be all right if the conditions applying to the specific situation are stable. Computer statistical packages such as STATGRAPHICS or SPSS may be used to process the data. These computer packages will take your data and process them using appropriate forecasting techniques to produce statistics and graphical representations.

Trend correlation

Trend correlation is a technique used by statisticians to correlate various time series in the hope of identifying leading and lagging indicators that they can use to predict trends. It is useful when there are a number of time series that relate to each other and that can be used to make predictions about the future. Some national economic forecasts are produced using this technique.

Econometric modelling

Econometricians build mathematical causal models to explain economic behaviour. These are sets of equations which fit statistically to the behaviour observed. Many economic forecasts are built using mathematical models to explain key variables. For example, a macro-economic forecast may identify that the Gross National Product (GNP) is dependent upon: inflation, unemployment and growth. Each of the variables would then be said to have a causal effect upon the GNP. Forecasting GNP would be explained by expected changes to the variables identified in the model. The accuracy of such models is variable. Economic forecasts are published by various economic forecasting groups e.g. Henley Forecasting, London Business School, Liverpool University and various private economic forecasting firms. The *Financial Times* publishes from time to time a table of forecasting groups ranked by the accuracy of their predictions about the UK economy. Forecasting firms travel up and down the table from year to year suggesting that their econometric models are sometimes more accurate than at other times and leading to the conclusion that there is no best model that describes the workings of the economy perfectly. This is not to say that these models are not useful. The models do at least seek to explain and predict macroeconomic behaviour and in doing so help forecasters and economists better understand some of the relationships causing change.

Cross-impact analysis

A number of key trends are identified as those having high importance or high probability of occurring. The question is then asked, 'If event A occurs, what will the impact be on each of the other trends identified ?' The results are used to build sets of domino chains with one event triggering other events. In other words cross impacts are taken into account. For example, supposing the following key trends are identified:

- A rise in the disposable income of high income earners as a result of changes to the tax system.
- A fall in the disposable incomes of lower income earners as a result of reductions in tax allowances.
- A higher percentage of lower income groups' disposable income being taken up by basic necessities: housing, heating and food.
- Increasing indirect taxation (e.g. Value Added Tax).
- Increasing interest rates.
- Increasing trend towards more tailor-made holidays rather than cheaper packages in the middle and higher income groups.
- An increase in low price discount holidays.

Each of the trends identified may have a cross impact effect. For example, a rise in the disposable income of high income earners may be responsible for the growing interest in tailor-made holidays. Changes to the tax system affecting this group may increase the growth in tailor-made holidays or reduce demand for them. Similarly, the falling incomes of the lower income groups may be responsible for the growth in low cost cheap holidays. Increases in the disposable incomes of low earners may lead to a switching of expenditure from low cost to higher cost holidays. Increases in indirect taxation such as VAT may be partly responsible for the higher percentages of disposable income for lower income groups being consumed by housing, heat and food. It should be noted that although some food products are zero rated some are not and in any case increases in VAT or extensions to the coverage drive up cost for suppliers who in turn increase their prices to customers some of whom are on low incomes. The proportion of disposable income spent by high income earners on food, heating and housing may be lower than for those people on very low incomes. Increases in interest rates may also have an impact on housing cost. Higher interest rates may induce higher income earners to save more of their disposable income. You can see from this simple example that in simply identifying a small number of trends they may have a cross impact effect.

Understanding the cross impact effect of changing trends may be very useful for marketing and sales managers as they plan the future.

Multiple scenarios

Scenario building involves the senior management team in describing alternative futures, each one of which is internally consistent with the other and has a certain probability of occurring. The major purpose of building alternative futures in this way is to stimulate management thought and to plan for contingencies.

Demand/hazard forecasting

Researchers identify major events taking place in the environment which could impact upon the firm. Each event is rated for its convergence with several major trends taking place in society and for its appeal to major publics in society. The higher the event's convergence and appeal, the higher the probability of its taking place. The critical events identified in this way are then researched further.

Qualitative methods

Expert opinion, the Delphi Technique, jury methods, technological forecasting, scenario planning (multiple scenarios and demand/hazard forecasting) are mainly the methods of forecasting described as 'Qualitative' meaning that they describe what will happen using words but with some numbers to give an indication of the scale of the impact the events will have. Qualitative methods are an array of interpretive techniques which seek to describe, decode, translate and otherwise come to terms with the meaning, not the frequency, of certain phenomena in the social world (Van Maanen, 1983, p.9).

Jury method

Most of the more sophisticated methods of long-term forecasting still rely upon individual judgement – but try to average out individual bias by taking an 'average' of a number of experts. The jury method is the most obvious approach to this. It simply asks the question of a number of experts gathered together in a group. Like the jury in a trial this method seems, despite the obvious limitations, to come up with sensible, workable forecasts. On the other hand, at least in theory, the jury could tend to reinforce one another's prejudices (or be swayed by an influential individual).

Extending Activity 2.1

See if you can find out what types of forecasting your own organization does and who does it. Ask them what techniques are used and what is the main purposes of the forecasting that is done. This should provide you with a better contextual understanding of forecasting and approaches to forecasting.

Ask the people preparing the forecasts how accurate they are and if they consider accuracy to be important and if they do why they do.

(Do not confuse budget preparation with forecasting.)

Decision trees

Tree structures may help qualitative methods of forecasting by plotting decision points using a branching technique. The main value of the technique is that it attempts to consider all the possible alternatives. However, in attempting to consider all alternatives this may also be a drawback since there may be a very large number of such alternatives.

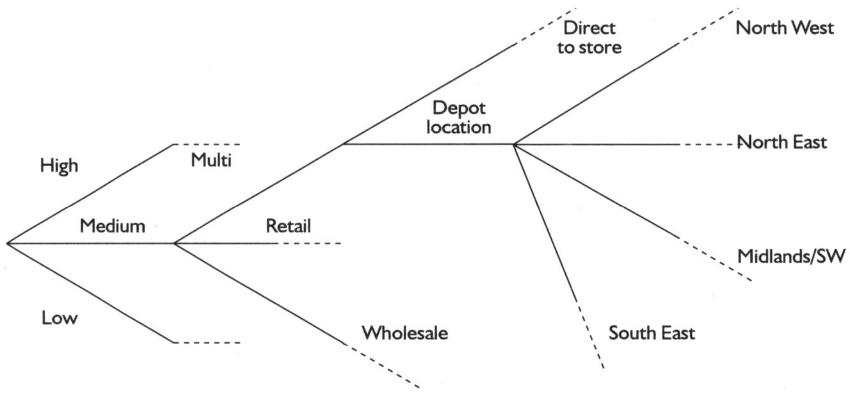

Figure 2.4
Decision tree (1)

The decision tree in Figure 2.4 shows some possible decisions about pricing and channel choice. There are three possible pricing positioning decisions – *high, medium, low;* then there is the choice of channel for each price possibility. The tree diagram shows further choices if the multiple chainstore option is chosen and were supply to be direct to a single delivery point or to various central depot locations in the regions shown.

3 price decisions × 3 channel choices × 2 delivery choices ×4 regional choices = 72

If we assume that the decisions are similar for each option represented by the dotted line the possible choices on each route would be 72.

Activity 2.2

Supposing you were about to purchase a new computer system and you have done some preliminary research and decided to limit yourself to the following options:

5 possible processors
3 possible video display screens
2 possible mouse devices
10 possible keyboard choices
4 possible modems
3 possible sound cards

Draw a decision tree similar to the one in the text showing only one possible system choice with other branches represented by a dotted line at each decision point. If you do not follow these instructions carefully you will need a lot of paper. The full tree could be over 300 feet tall!

Calculate the total number of possible systems that you could buy.

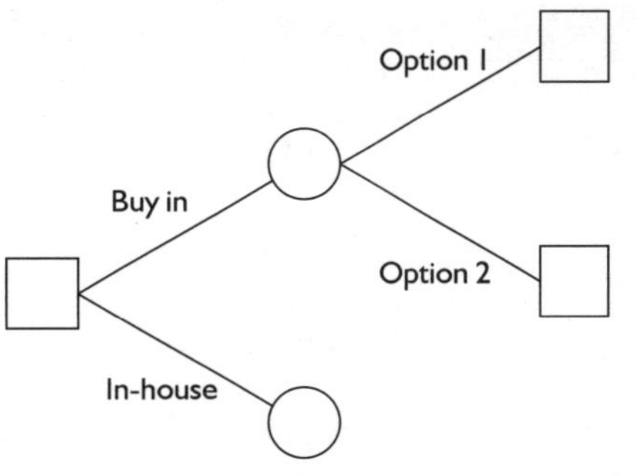

Figure 2.5
Decision tree (2)

Decision trees are useful in assisting managers with both qualitative and quantitative decisions. In the tree diagram above consider a manager with two distinct options to consider when choosing marketing research. The firm could buy in the necessary research from an external marketing research agency, or it could choose to conduct the marketing research in-house. If the firm chooses to buy in the research a further decision point is reached whereby the firm can choose option 1 which is to accept syndicated research or option 2 which is to carry out some tailor-made research unique to the firm. Values may be assigned to each decision point if we wish. For example, in our example, we may forecast the costs for each alternative as follows:

In-house research = £36,000 *or*

Buy in research = £25,000 basic research

Option 1 = an additional cost £7,000 syndicated research report

Option 2 = an additional cost £14,000 tailor-made research option.

If we ignore any qualitative factors and make a rational decision based on a forecast of the research costs, a manager may choose option 1 as the lowest cost option. A decision tree helps think the problem through. The tree will help identify decision points. Decision trees can be further refined to take account of uncertainty and risk in decision making by assigning probabilities to each of the possible decisions. Supposing for example a manager forecasts that the buy in decision has an 80 per cent chance of answering the research problem and the in-house option has an 90 per cent chance. Let us look at the costs and expected revenues streams.

Decision point 1

1.1 Buy in research = £25,000 basic research (80 per cent chance of success). A successful outcome is expected to create an additional £35,000 to revenue.

1.2 In-house research = £36,000 (90 per cent chance of success). A successful outcome is expected to add £40,000 to revenue.

Decision point 2

2.1 Option 1 = an additional cost £7,000 syndicated research report (50 per cent chance of success). A successful outcome is expected to create an additional £10,000 to revenue.

2.2 Option 2 = an additional cost £14,000 'tailor-made' option (50 per cent chance of success). A successful outcome is expected to add £15,000 to revenue.

Each decision point may now be considered. Given the forecast cost and revenue for each decision point you will see that if the firm chose to buy in the research and reject both options 2.1 and 2.2, a gain of £10,000 is forecast assuming that the forecast revenue is 100 per cent correct (in other words if there were no uncertainty attached to the option). If the firm decides to pursue decision point 1.2 and carry out research in-house the revenue forecast is lower at £4,000. If option 2.1 is chosen the expected outcome at 100 per cent probability is £3,000 and option 2.2 will result in an additional £1,000 revenue.

Decision	*Revenue*	*Cost*	*Expected outcome*
1.1 Buy in	£35,000	£25,000	£10,000
1.2 In-house	£40,000	£36,000	£4,000
2.1 Option 1	£10,000	£7,000	£3,000
2.2 Option 2	£15,000	£14,000	£1,000

Now let us consider how each decision point is affected by the probabilities we have attached to the outcomes:

Decision	*Probability*	*Revenue*	*Cost*	*Expected outcome*
1.1 Buy in	80% × £35,000	£28,000	£25,000	£3,000
1.2 In-house	90% × £40,000	£36,000	£36,000	£0
2.1 Option 1	50% × £10,000	£5,000	£7,000	–£2,000
2.2 Option 2	50% × £15,000	£7,500	£14,000	–£6,500

You can see now that the only decision worth pursuing is to buy in basic research but go no further. The forecast revenues together with the expected probabilities show that all other possibilities are likely to result in additional costs without benefit. More importantly the decision to do any research is now becoming a more marginal issue since the gains are low given the risks. The risks in our example are the cost of carrying out the research and the uncertainty attached to the probabilities we have assigned to the revenue forecast. It is important to recognize that in our example the costs are assumed to be fixed. It is not always the case that costs are fixed, and costs too may require some judgement to be made about their certainty. Where this is the case, costs will need to be assigned probabilities also.

In practice decision trees can be very complex and can deal with many decision points covering all the possible options. Having to consider a large number of options may be time consuming and costly. The time and cost involved in considering all the options may be excessive. However, it is a useful technique for considering a reasonable number of options. Like many statistical techniques that appear to be objective it can suffer from the qualitative judgements required to assign probability values to outcomes. Although the technique itself may be objective, the subjective inputs to the model may make the results from the model subjective.

Network planning and forecasting

A network plan may be produced to provide a forecast for the total time it will take to complete a number of related activities forming parts of a project. Some events may only be completed sequentially whilst others can be planned to be done at the same time or in parallel. Network analysis is also known as Critical Path Analysis or Project Evaluation and Review Techniques (PERT). Inputs to a network model are a set of technological or economic factors forming the project. These activities together with estimates of the time it takes to complete each activity are used to forecast the total time for completing the project and to identify a critical path of activities that need to be carefully controlled if the project is to be completed on time. An approach to deal with uncertainty in time estimation is to use optimistic and pessimistic completion times in the network.

Supposing you were in charge of a promotional campaign you might prepare a network forecast as follows based on forecast times for the activities detailed. The critical path is the heavy black line in the network. The path is critical because if any of the estimated activities along that line take longer than forecast the total project time will increase and there will be a delay.

Activities	*Estimated time in weeks*	*Event numbers*
Explore possible promotions options	7	1
Evaluate options	3	2
Develop promotional materials	5	3
Plan and brief sales team	1	3
Obtain further market research	4	4
Plan promotional activity	3	5
Final negotiations with retailers	2	6
New packaging design	5	7
In-store support material	3	8
Campaign launch	0	9

In this example you can see that events 1, 2 and 3 are sequential. This means that event 2 can only take place after event 1 has finished and event 3 after event 2 has been completed. Events 4, 5 and 6 are sequential events but they may be completed in parallel with events 7 and 8 which are sequential to each other. If you follow the bottom path it will take only 19 weeks to complete those activities. However, if you follow the top path you will see that it will take 24 weeks in total to complete the route. The non-critical path has 5 weeks slack in it. This means that any single activity could slip 5 weeks, providing all the other activities were completed on time or that each activity could slip, providing the total time of the activities on the non-critical path did not slip more than a total of 5 weeks without affecting the project. This top path shown with the heavy black line in the diagram represents the critical path. There can be no slippage on this critical path if the promotional campaign is to happen on time.

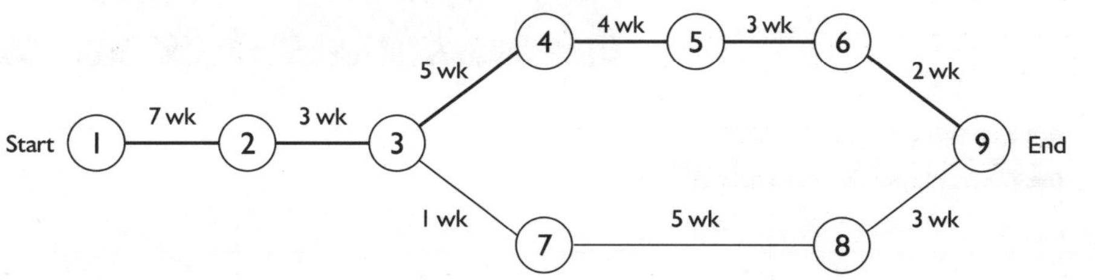

Figure 2.6
Critical path analysis

Summary

Forecasting is about being able to make sense of the future. Marketing and sales managers need to be able to plan on the basis of forecasts: forecasting sales, forecasting market trends and forecasting how various marketing mix factors may change in future. Forecasts are prepared for short term, medium term and long term. Short and medium term forecasts tend to be focused on sales and market trends for particular products or market segments. Longer term forecasts tend to be used for strategic planning. Long term forecasts inform decision makers about the opportunities and threats posed by the external environment and tend to focus on changes in the macro-environment: changes to the political, economic, social and technological environments in which the firm operates. Forecasting has an array of techniques that are designed to help predict the future. Some of the most widely used techniques have been explained briefly in this unit. The techniques fall into two main types: quantitative techniques employing statistical and mathematical models, and qualitative techniques based on informed opinion.

Exam Tip

Make sure you understand why forecasts are needed in the marketing and sales environment and how they are used. It is important to know and understand why accurate forecasts are needed. It is important to recognize how sales forecasts are used in financial planning and how changes to forecasts could affect the plans.

Question 2.1

(*Examination Type Part B*)

A marketing manager planning a promotional campaign has received sales forecasts for three products that are being considered for a special promotion during the next financial period.

Product A forecast is for 9,000 units to be sold without promotion.
Product A forecast is for 11,000 units to be sold with promotion.
Product B forecast is for 10,000 units to be sold without promotion.
Product B forecast is for 14,000 units to be sold with promotion.
Product C forecast is for 7,000 units to be sold without promotion.
Product C forecast is for 13,000 units to be sold with promotion.

The manager is 95 per cent confident about the sales forecasts for all products without promotion. The forecast for all three products with promotion, the manager has only 90 per cent confidence in being accurate. The promotional budget for the period is £12,000. The cost of the promotion for each product is estimated at £6,000 for product A; £6,000 for product B and £8,000 for product C. The costs are not forecasts but are based on quotations. Product A makes a contribution to profit of £6 per unit; product B = £5 per unit and product C = £4 per unit.

(a) Outline the options available in the form of a decision tree.
(b) Calculate the expected outcomes.
(c) Give your recommendations in a brief report to the sales manager.

Answers

Answer 2.1

(a)

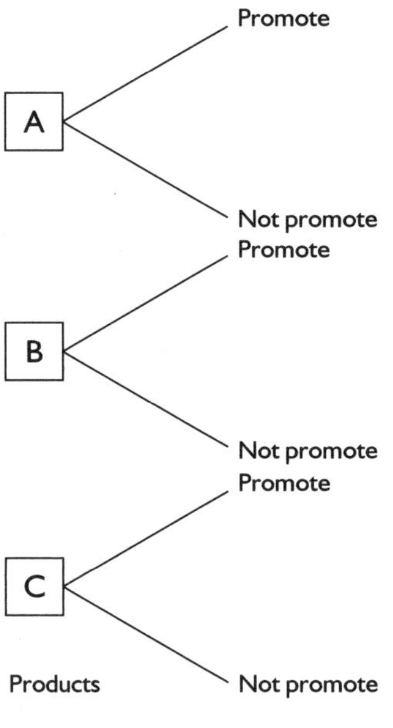

Figure 2.7
A decision tree

(b)

	Product A	*Product B*	*Product C*	*Total*
Before promotion				
Quantity sold	9,000	10,000	7,000	
Contribution per unit	£6	£5	£4	
Total contribution	£54,000	£50,000	£28,000	
95% certain	95%	95%	95%	
Expected outcome	£51,300	£47,500	£26,600	£125,400

	Product A	Product B	Product C	Total
After promotion				
Quantity sold	11,000	14,000	13,000	
Contribution per unit	£6	£5	£4	
Total contribution	£66,000	£70,000	£52,000	
90% confident	90%	90%	90%	
Expected reveune	£59,400	£63,000	£46,800	
Less promotion cost	£6,000	£6,000	£8,000	
Expected outcome	£53,400	£57,000	£38,800	£149,200
Net promotional gain	£2,100	£9,500	£12,200	£23,800

(c)

To: The Sales Manager
From: Promotional Manager
Date: xx/xx/xx

Promotional budget and forecast sales

I have prepared some preliminary calculations attached and you can see that if we use the budget of £12,000 to promote products A and B this would achieve a net gain from the promotional spend amounting to £11,600. If we choose to spend only £6,000 promoting product A you will see that this only provides a gain amounting to £2,100 whereas the £6,000 spent on promoting product B returns £9,500. The £6,000 spent on product A would be better used on promoting product B to achieve a better return. Alternatively, it has been costed at £8,000 to promote product C as shown and this promotion is expected to yield a total return of £12,200.

Options

If we decided to promote both B and C we could expect a return amounting to £21,700 in total for an outlay of £14,000. I realize that this is £2,000 above the budget we have been allowed but it would seem to make sense to increase this budget with the expected gains that could accrue. Alternatively maybe we could use the remaining £4,000 budget to scale down the promotion on product B or use £6,000 on promoting product B and scale down the promotion on product C.

To summarize, below I have provided a table that clearly shows the expected return for each of the products for each £ promotional spend.

	Product A	Product B	Product C
Spend	£6,000	£6,000	£8,000
Gain	£2,100	£9,500	£12,200
Expected gain per £ spent	£0.35	£1.58	£1.53

This table clearly demonstrates that for each £ spent, the promotion of product B provides a superior return to any other promotion. It may be that we should concentrate our efforts on a larger spend of promoting this product if our main objective is to achieve superior profit from the promotion.

I suggest we meet to discuss the options further and to clearly identify our objectives for this promotion before proceeding further. We are 90 per cent confident about our forecasts for the promotional sales but you may like to consider how sensitive a 5 per cent change in confidence either way may affect the outcomes expected. Please let me know your thoughts on the matter.

Activity Debrief 2.1

In calculating the effect of the forecast being understated by 10 per cent, for each product the result would be:

Product X loses 3,500 sales (10% x 35,000)
Product Y loses 3,000 sales (10% x 30,000)
Product Z loses 3,400 sales (10% x 34,000)

Therefore

X	= 3,500 × £1	= £3,500	Contribution	= £35,000 – £3,500	= £31,500
Y	= 3,000 × £1.20	= £3,600	Contribution	= £36,000 – £3,600	= £32,400
Z	= 3,400 × £1.10	= £3,740	Contribution	= £37,400 – £3,740	= £33,660

Product Z therefore remains the best choice.

Unit 3 The role of management accounting in the marketing information system

Objectives

After studying this unit you should:

- ❑ Be aware of the nature and sources of financial information.
- ❑ Understand the importance of financial information in planning and control.
- ❑ Know the main financial statements and their use to managers.
- ❑ Know the objectives of cost accounting.
- ❑ Know the differences between financial and cost and management accounting.
- ❑ Be able to explain how cost data is collected, classified and recorded.
- ❑ Understand and explain the differences between fixed and variable costs.

Study Guide

This unit introduces the role of management accounting and its application to marketing and sales information systems. It is an important unit and is the basis for the next three units of study. It is essential that you understand all the concepts introduced in this unit before you move on to the next unit which builds on some of these issues.

You should have a calculator to hand and a pencil to make notes.

The marketing information system

The marketing information system is essentially a number of independent systems that may be combined to provide marketing information and marketing intelligence. Data are stored in a variety of places within an organization. When managers recognize a use for data held for another specific purpose they are beginning to think systematically about their own data needs. Identifying what information you require to manage in your own organization is a starting point for designing an appropriate information system. Data sources may be represented as in the diagram below.

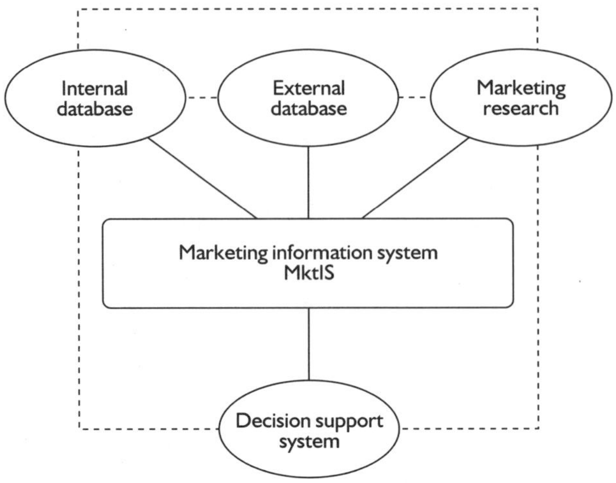

Figure 3.1
The marketing information system

Data are held internally or externally. Data may be supplemented by gathering data for a specific marketing need using marketing research techniques. In this unit we are concerned with using a ready-made source of data collected for the purpose of accounting. Accounting data is collected for financial reporting that is required by law and for internal management to help inform their decision making. Accounting data are held internally and may form part of our internal database.

Sources of financial information

Financial data comes from transaction data such as sales invoices and purchase invoices. Financial data are also obtained from forecasts and budgets. Product or service cost data come from estimates of resource utilization in terms of *materials, labour and overheads* which are referred to by accountants as the *elements of cost*.

Financial information comes from a variety of sources. The types of information most commonly required by sales and marketing managers take the form of:

- Sales turnover figure which may be total or by product or product segment (e.g. a product segment may be a group of products or a specific area of operation).
- Profitability figures by product or market segment.
- Customer account information (history, payments, outstanding debt etc.).
- Cost data.
- Pricing policy and price information (discounts allowed, payment terms etc.).
- Budgets (sales budgets, product profitability budgets, market segment budgets, departmental budgets, company budget).

Definition 3.1

Accounting is the process of identifying, measuring and communicating economic information to permit informed judgements and decisions by users of the information.

Source: American Accounting Association 1966 reported in Hines, T. (1990, p.14).

Accounting information may be used by people and organizations externally (financial accounting) or by internal parties inside the organization (management accounting).

Financial accounting

Financial accounting is concerned with stewardship, that is looking after the assets of the business on behalf of the owners. Financial accounts are reported to external users with an audit report. They are required by law.

This is the score-keeping and is essentially concerned with historic data collected to record what happened in the past. This financial data are then used to prepare the financial statements mainly for external use by the following groups:

- Shareholders – potential and existing.
- Employees and employee organizations (e.g. unions).
- Government departments (e.g. Inland Revenue).
- Competition.
- Business analysts.
- Public at large.
- Other interested parties – creditors.

The published financial statements include:

- The trading and profit and loss account.
- The balance sheet.
- A cash flow statement (historic).

A business which is organized as a private or public limited company is required to produce the above financial statements by law (The Companies Act 1985). The financial statements would require an audit opinion from an independent firm of chartered or certified accountants.

Activity 3.1

You may like to obtain the *published financial statements* for your company to familiarize yourself with the three major financial statements that are published for external reporting purposes.

Financial statements may also be produced for internal use but would not be subject to audit for this purpose. Also the financial statements for internal use are far more likely to contain more detailed information about the firm's performance in terms of segmented reports by geographical area (territories) or by product or service, in other words the type of information that you may wish to access as a marketing and sales manager. Trading and profit and loss statements will be produced probably monthly to provide managers with information on how they are doing against budget. Variances between budget and actual figures will require analysis. The purpose being to identify the causes of the variances identified. Control will be exercised by managers taking decisions to ensure the original plan is achieved or by revising the plan to take account of changes identified.

Cost and management accounting

Cost and management accounting is concerned with planning, control and decision making. It is essentially forward looking, that is concerned with future costs although it may use past cost data in the provision of information. It is a management tool.

Definition 3.2

Cost accounting is the application of accounting and costing principles, methods and techniques in the ascertainment of costs and the analysis of savings and/or excesses as compared with previous experience or with standards. Management accounting is the preparation and presentation of accounting information in such a way as to assist management in the formulation of policies and in the planning and control of the activities of the undertaking.

The purpose of costing is to work out how much a particular product, job, contract, batch, process or department costs. Such costs could be actual past costs or budgeted future costs. Furthermore, to classify and control costs are essential functions of a costing system. Cost information should be presented in such a way that it enables management to plan, control and make decisions.

Cost information can come from a variety of sources and the same cost data can be used for a variety of applications.

Activity 3.2

What sources of cost data are available in your own organization and what is it used for? Do managers in marketing and sales have access to such data and do they make use of it? How do you think you may be able to use the data sources you have identified in your job?

Benefits a costing system may provide

There are a number of benefits a costing system can give which may include:

1. Identifying profitable and unprofitable products, services, centres etc.
2. Identifying waste and inefficiency.
3. Help in setting prices.
4. Accurate stock valuations.
5. Analysing profit change – cost, volume, profit.
6. Planning, control and decision making (budgets, pricing, output, etc.).
7. Evaluation of the effectiveness of decisions.

The justification for a costing system must be that such benefits outweigh the cost of the system.

You can see that many of the purposes a costing system is required for are similar to the types of financial data that you may want as a marketing and sales manager. It is doubtful that the published financial statements of your firm would be much use. However, you may want to get hold of copies of the published financial statements of firms you deal with or those of competitors. These statements will only be of use to you if you are able to apply the financial tools to analyse the statements. Financial reporting is like a foreign language. You have to learn it if you want to understand it.

In the previous unit you began to work with some financial data related to forecasting. In this unit you will be introduced formally to the major financial statements that you will become familiar with in the next four units. You will be able to recognize the purpose of each type of financial statement and learn some of the important tools necessary for working with financial information.

Let us begin by looking at how financial data are collected and aggregated to provide the published financial statements mentioned earlier.

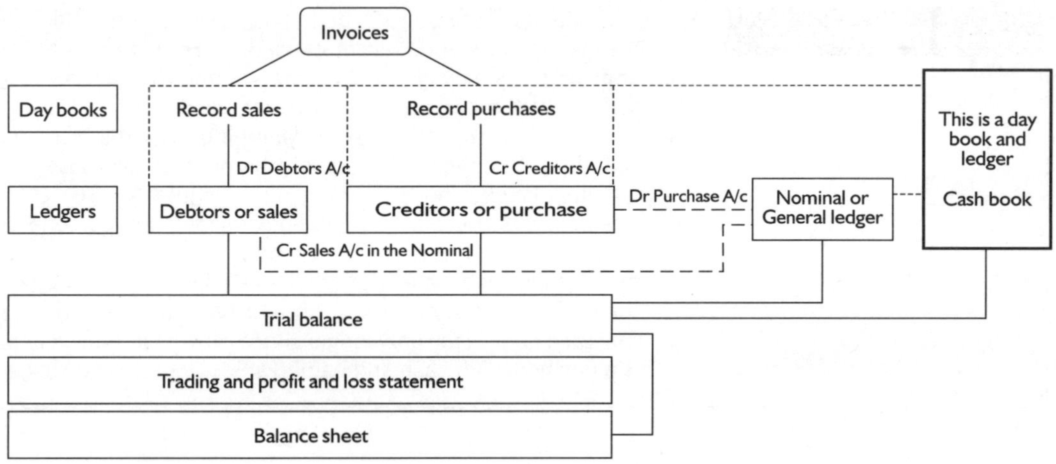

Figure 3.2
Source documents

The major transactions made by most organizations are sales and purchases. Purchases when used by accountants means stock bought for resale. Other expenses are recorded like purchases but referred to as expenses or overheads. Transactions are first recorded from the invoice and entered into a daily record of sales invoices and purchase or expense invoices. These daily records are still referred to as day books. Even modern computer systems refer to day books. The listings from the day books are then recorded using double entry system (debit and credits) into the appropriate ledgers. For example, a sales invoice will be listed initially in the day book and then it will enter the double entry system being recorded as a *debit* in the debtor/sales ledger and recorded as a *credit* in the sales account in the nominal or general ledger. At the end of an accounting period, each of the ledgers is balanced and the balancing figures from each ledger are taken to a listing called the trial balance. The sum total of all listings in this trial balance should agree. The total of debit balances taken from the ledgers should be the same as the total of all the credit balances. This is in effect a control mechanism designed to ensure that the data taken to the final financial statements has been recorded correctly. The trial balance is then used to construct the trading and profit and loss account and the balance sheet.

Exam Hints

You do not need to know which accounts are debited and credited and the examiner will not be testing your knowledge of double entry book-keeping. In describing the financial accounting system it is necessary to inform you about double entry since the whole system is based around it and some understanding may help you understand finance better. In the examination you will be concerned with knowledge, application of the knowledge to specific information needs and for financial solutions to specific marketing and sales problems. Choosing and using appropriate financial tools for analysis and evaluation are important.

Definition 3.3

- *Day books* record the daily transactions of sales, purchases, expenses and cash.

  Ledger: The ledger system is split into four. Each of the four ledgers are explained below:

- *The debtors or sales ledger* holds all the personal accounts for customers. Customer accounts should only be set up after making appropriate credit checks. Control accounts and credit control procedures will need to use this ledger. Aged debtor analysis can be undertaken using data in the debtors ledger. All sales invoices are recorded first in the day book and then in the ledger.

A sale needs to be recorded twice hence the term double entry. Firstly, the customer personal account needs to record the debt (account debited) and the sales account held in the nominal or general ledger records the sales values for the period (account credited).

- *The creditors or purchase ledger* holds all the personal accounts for suppliers. Supplier accounts will be opened for those organizations and individuals who the firm trades with regularly.
- *The nominal or general ledger* holds all the non-personal accounts for the organization. That is why it is called a general ledger. All the remaining profit and loss accounts and balance sheet accounts by name apart from the debtors, creditors and cash and bank are recorded in this ledger.
- *The cash book* is the only ledger that also acts as a book of prime entry, that is a day book. All cash and bank transactions pass through this ledger.

Each of the ledgers may record one entry for a transaction. For example, an invoiced sale to a customer will be recorded in the customer's personal account in the debtor ledger and recorded as a sale in the sales account in the general ledger. When this customer pays by cheque the customer's personal account in the debtor ledger will be credited to clear the debt and the cash book will record a receipt in the bank column as a debit. Note: The terms debit and credit simply mean left and right and refer to the side of the account in which they are recorded.

Ledger accounts or double entry accounts are sometimes referred to as 'T' accounts because they are shaped like the letter T.

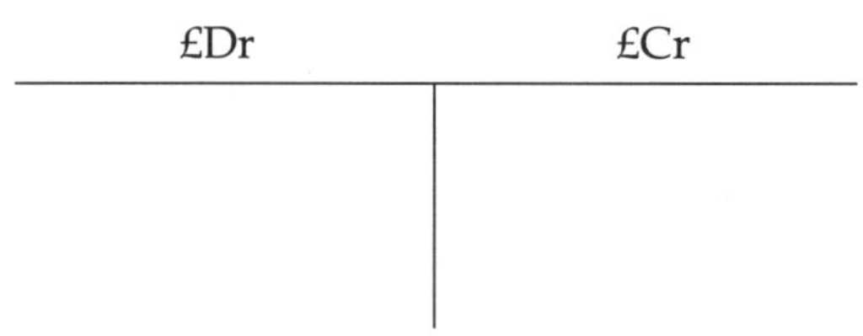

If you would like to find out more about how financial accounting systems work you should consult a text such as *Foundation Accounting* by Tony Hines or *Basic Accounting* by Glautier and Underdown.

The trading and profit and loss account

This is one of the most important financial accounting statements. This type of account is also prepared for management. Trading and profit and loss accounts are flows of income and cost and expenditures for a specific period of time. For example, they are for the week ending or the month ending or the year ending..... Trading and profit and loss accounts may be prepared for the whole company, a division or part of a company, for specific market segments, for particular product lines, for particular geographic areas and so on.

X Ltd Profit and loss summary

for the year ended 31.12		*1994*		*1995*
1 Sales		£500,000		£600,000
2 Less cost of sales		£255,000		£270,000
3 Gross profit		£245,000		£330,000
4 *Less expenses*				
Administration	£120,000		£120,000	
Sales and marketing	£80,000		£90,000	
Distribution	£40,000		£54,000	
Finance overheads	£25,000		£30,000	
		£265,000		£294,000
5 Net profit/(loss)		(£20,000)		£36,000

Above is an example of a simple trading and profit and loss account. In the statement shown there are two years presented side by side for comparison 1994 and 1995. Statements are sometimes provided like this to make comparisons for two financial periods or sometimes only a single period is shown. If you look at the number key in the first column a brief description to explain each important term is given below:

1 This is the sales turnover for the period. It sounds obvious to say sales turnover is the number of items sold times the selling price for each item sold. Nevertheless, this is important to understand. This sales turnover figure could be actual sales based on invoiced and cash sales made in a financial period. It could also be based on a forecast figure for a budgeted trading and profit and loss statement.

Sales made on credit terms are sold to debtors who owe money to the supplier for the goods or services provided. Sales are recorded as sales in a profit and loss statement regardless of whether cash has been received at the statement date. This is because financial statements are constructed using basic guiding principles or generally accepted accounting principles (GAAPS). The principle referred to here is known as the accruals concept or the matching principle. This states that sales are matched to the financial period in which they occur.

Definition 3.4

There are four basic principles you should keep in mind which are: accruals or matching principle; prudence or conservatism; going concern and consistency. Each of these principles is briefly explained as follows:

- *Accruals:* matching sales and costs with the financial period in which the transactions take place (it has nothing to do with when cash is paid or received).
- *Prudence:* states that you should be prudent when constructing a financial statement and include any expected costs or expenses that are known to exist even if you have not yet received an invoice or demand.
- *Going concern:* all financial statements are constructed assuming that the enterprise will continue to exist in the future.
- *Consistency:* is concerned with ensuring that financial statements are prepared in a consistent manner from one period to the next.

2 Cost of sales is the sales quantities at cost price. Cost of goods sold in practice may be arrived at in a variety of ways. Cost of goods sold in a period will include not only the material costs but also labour costs in production and production overheads attributable to the products sold.

3 Gross profit is the sales less the cost of goods sold. It does not include any expenses or non-production overheads.

4 Expenses in a profit and loss account are matched to the particular time period. Expenses are called time based costs or period costs. Sometimes expenses not related to production are referred to as overheads.

5 Net profit is arrived at by deducting the expenses from the gross profit. Sometimes expense will exceed the gross profit and in this case a loss will arise.

Question 3.1

Can you recall what a person or firm who buys goods or services using credit is called?

(**Answer** See end of chapter.)

The balance sheet

A balance sheet is a statement of assets and liabilities held by an organization at a specific date. The values are stated at historic cost. In other words the values shown in a balance sheet represent the entry value, usually an invoiced cost. In the case of fixed assets these are shown at historic cost less a charge representing the fall in value due to use of the asset or ageing referred to as depreciation.

Definition 3.5

Assets: Assets are objects that an organization owns and uses in the business. Assets wear out over time and will need replacing. In accounting terms depreciation is the charge for usage or ageing of an asset. Assets may be fixed which means they are meant to last longer than a single financial period (one year). Or assets are said to be current which means they will change form in less than one financial period (one year). In other words stock will be sold and may become a debtor or cash; debtors turn into cash after the credit period has elapsed.

Liabilities are amounts owed by the organization to people or other organizations. Liabilities may be long term, that is greater than one year (e.g. 2-year loan or 5-year loan). Current liabilities are amounts falling due within one year.

	X Ltd Balance sheet as at 31 December			*19XX*
1	*Fixed assets*			
	Land and buildings	£100,000		
	less depreciation	£30,000	£70,000	
	Plant and machinery	£30,000		
	less depreciation	£9,000	£21,000	
	Motor vehicles	£20,000		
	less depreciation	£4,000	£16,000	
				£107,000
2	*Current assets*			
	Stock	£20,000		
	Debtors	£5,500		
	Bank and cash	£1,500		
			£27,000	
3	*Current liabilities*			
	Trade creditors	£6,000		
	Other creditors	£1,000		
			£7,000	
	Net current assets			£20,000
				£127,000
4	*Financed by*			
5	*Equity capital*			
	Ordinary share			
	Capital		£60,000	
	Reserves		£37,000	
6	*Loan capital*			
	5% Debentures		£30,000	
7	*Capital employed*			£127,000

1 *Fixed assets* are such things as land, buildings, plant, machinery, motor vehicles and intangible items. An intangible is something you cannot touch or necessarily see but nevertheless it exists like goodwill or property rights (e.g. leases).

Extending Activity 3.1

Obtain a dictionary or a financial dictionary and look up the term 'goodwill' unless you are already familiar with the term.

2 *Current assets* are: stock in trade; debtors (people who owe money for goods and services that have been invoiced); any amounts paid in advance e.g. rent in advance of the period in which it is due, and cash in hand or at the bank. They are current assets because they will change form within the year as previously explained.

3 *Current liabilities* are amounts owed that need to be paid within a year. Trade creditors are a current liability. A trade creditor is a supplier of stock in trade who supplies you with goods allowing you credit by invoicing rather than demanding immediate cash payment. Other current liabilities may include amounts owed to non-trade creditors such as: wages and salaries owed to employees; amounts owed for services such as light and heat; rent and rates; PAYE, National Insurance charges on behalf of employees and dividend payments due to shareholders that have not yet been paid. Amounts that you owe to creditors who have not yet invoiced you are called *accruals. Remember the accrual concept explained earlier. This is what an accrual is*. You are matching a known cost in this case before being invoiced.

Definition 3.6

Working capital

Current assets less current liabilities are referred to as net current assets. This is the working capital of an organization. A firm should aim to have as little as possible tied up in its working capital.

4 There are basically two parts to a balance sheet. Balances on accounts are either on the left (debit) or on the right (credit) in the ledgers from where the trial balance and hence the balance sheet data are extracted. *Asset and expense accounts* usually have debit balances and *capital and liability and revenue accounts* have credit balances. This is known as the balance sheet equation.

Definition 3.7

The balance sheet equation

£DR Balances			£CR Balances		
BS	PL		BS	BS	PL
Assets	Expenses	=	Capital	Liabilities	Revenue

Note expenses and revenue represent the profit and loss account (PL). Assets, capital and liability represent the balance sheet (BS). The equation shows more completely the relationship between the two financial statements.

The first part that we have just looked at lists the assets and the liabilities and the next part tells you how those assets and liabilities have in effect been funded, hence the term 'financed by'.

5 *Equity finance* is what the owners have put into the business from their own funds. Equity is increased by adding profit to the original funds once the business is trading profitably. Equity can be reduced if losses occur. In the balance sheet for X Ltd reserves are the amounts of undistributed profit. Retained profits are usually added to a reserve account such as the profit and loss reserve. The term reserve does not mean what reserve means in every day language. Reserves are simply amounts set aside out of profit and may include profit itself that is not distributed or applied in any other way.

6 *Debt funding or loan funding* is borrowed from a lender (an individual or institution prepared to lend in return for interest). In this balance sheet we have 5 per cent debentures which are a form of loan instrument paying the lender a fixed rate of 5 per cent per annum.

7 The final figure in the balance sheet is called the *capital employed*. Capital employed represents the total sum that has been invested in the business from all sources to fund the assets and liabilities listed.

Extending Activity 3.2

Obtain a profit and loss account and a balance sheet for your own or any organization and see how it differs from the statements shown above. Investigate why it is different.

The trading and profit and loss account and the balance sheet are related statements. Transactions affecting the trading and profit and loss account may have an effect on the balance sheet.

Question 3.2

What is a balance sheet?

Transaction effects

The table below gives you some idea of the interrelationship between the trading and profit and loss account and the balance sheet. An increase in invoiced sales will increase the balance sheet figure for debtors. An increase in cash sales would simply increase cash on the balance sheet. An increase in cost of sales means a reduction in stock value. An increase in invoiced expenses will increase the creditors shown on the balance sheet. An increase in cash expenses will reduce the amount of cash.

Profit and loss		*Balance sheet*	
Invoiced sales	Increase	Debtors	Increase
Cost of goods sold	Increase	Stock	Reduces
Invoiced expenses	Increase	Creditors	Increase
Cash expenses	Increase	Cash	Reduces

Question 3.3

If a firm receives an invoice from an advertising agency for services, how would this be reflected in both the profit and loss account and the balance sheet?

Exam Hints

You need to learn the financial terms listed in the profit and loss account and the balance sheet. Unless you know and understand what each of the terms means you will not be able to interpret the financial statements. The examiner will expect you to know these terms and to be able to read, interpret and use financial data.

Key terms: P&L a/c: sales revenue, cost of sales, gross profit, expenses/overheads, net profit. Balance sheet: fixed assets, current assets (stock, debtors, prepayments, bank and cash); current liabilities (trade creditors, creditors, accruals); net current assets or working capital; equity; long term liabilities (i.e. long term loans) and capital employed.

Table 3.1 The table provides you with a balance sheet structure and demonstrates how marketing variables affect the balance sheet.

Balance sheet	*Marketing variables*	*Specific examples*
Fixed assets	• Decisions to outsource marketing services • Decisions to establish in-house marketing services • Decisions to develop new products • Decisions to delete products from the range • Decisions to enter new markets • Decisions to retreat from markets	• Buy in marketing research rather than establish your own department. Effect would be not to increase fixed assets in this case • Investment in new plant and equipment to produce a new product or investment in new warehousing and distribution facilities. Effect would be to increase fixed assets • Investment in new retail stores (increase) or the disposal of retail stores, warehousing and distribution centres (reduce)
Current assets: • Inventories • Debtors • Cash	• New products • Promotional decisions • Extended credit allowed to customers • Customer service level decisions • Pricing and payment policies • Order cycle and order completion times • Returns policies • Efficiency in the handling of customer complaints	• Introduction of new products would increase stock-holding costs or the build-up of inventories for a promotion would do the same • Extending credit as part of a promotional decision could increase accounts receivable (debtors). It may also reduce your cash inflows • If you take a decision to increase customer service levels this might lead to higher stock levels being held
Current liabilities: • Trade creditors	• Purchasing policies • Marketing and selling decisions	• Sourcing of materials/merchandise • Decisions taken on what to sell and where to sell it may affect trade creditors (supplier accounts)
Financed by: • Equity • Debt	Company-wide decisions regarding the best way to finance new market development or new product development	Entering new markets overseas could involve the establishment of new sites (offices, warehousing, retail selling space, etc.). The company has a choice on how to finance this type of expansion either through increasing its debt (loan financing) or through issuing new shares (equity capital).

Why profit is important to managers

Managers need to know what the profit is for the firm or for a product group in a specific financial period. Profit is a measure of performance. All profit organizations use profitability measures to judge their performance. Even non-profit organizations will have some activities that use profit or a surrogate for profit as a measure of performance.

Profit is the future. If firms are profitable or products are profitable the financial future is secured. If firms are unprofitable they can only exist through support of a parent company or other such subsidy in the short term. In the long term subsidies dry up. Profit funds the growth of the organization. It is usually the cheapest source of finance but it is not always available.

Profit is not cash

Profit should not be confused with cash. It is not the same thing. We have seen that sales are made on credit to debtors, and goods and services are purchased from creditors on credit. Cash transactions may take place after the end of the financial reporting period. Let us consider the simplest example of this difference which is important to understand. Supposing you buy ten chocolate bars to sell at a profit. The bars cost 10 pence each and you promise to pay your supplier next week in cash. In the meantime you sell 5 bars at 20 pence each and are paid in cash. What would your profit and loss account and balance sheet look like after the first week's transactions before you pay your supplier?

Trading and profit and loss account for the week

Sales	5 bars at 20 pence each	£1.00
Cost of sales	5 bars at 10 pence each	£0.50
Gross profit		£0.50
Cash outlay		£0.00
Cash inflow		£1.00

Balance sheet at the end of the first week

Assets	
Stock of chocolate bars	£0.50
Cash	£1.00
	£1.50
Liabilities	
Creditor supplier of chocolate bars	£1.00
Capital	
Profit	£0.50
	£1.50

The gross profit in this example is also the net profit since there are no other expenses incurred. We have received cash £1 and made a profit of £0.50. Note we have only matched the stock sold with sales and this is shown in the cost of sales 5 bars at 50 pence in total. We still have an asset of unsold stocks of chocolate bars 5 x 10 pence = £0.50. Our assets at the end of the first week are cash from the sales £1 and stock at £0.50 = £1.50. This has been funded by a creditor we owe £1 to and 50 pence we have earned in profit. We started this venture without any capital and the profit we earn increases capital so we now have 50 pence.

What happens next?

We pay the creditor next week £1. What does our balance sheet look like now?

Balance sheet at the end of the first week

Assets	
Stock of chocolate bars	£0.50
Cash	£0.00
	£0.50
Liabilities	
Creditor supplier of chocolate bars	£0.00
Capital	
Profit	£0.50
	£0.50

We reduce cash by £1 to pay for the supply of the 10 chocolate bars at 10 pence each and we discharge the creditor so we no longer have a liability.

Activity 3.3

Now you try to work through the following transactions to produce a profit and loss statement and a balance sheet for an imaginary trader who has just started to trade.

Jane has £5,000 to invest in her own business. During the first month she completes the following transactions:

Buys 100 units of stock for cash £1,000
Pays rent in cash £250
Pays wages in cash £100
Sells some of the stock 50 units at £20 per unit for cash
Sells 10 units at £25 allowing credit to the customer who will pay next month in cash

Cost and management accounting reports

All organizations need to keep control of costs. Costs need to be identified, classified, recorded and analysed to make sense of the organization's cost structure, cost of products and marketing, distribution and selling amongst other things. Cost data may be obtained from financial accounting sources if it is an actual cost for a past event or from budgets, forecasts, estimates and quotations if it is a future cost.

Some costing and management accounting reports will be presented using financial accounting reporting conventions and some will simply use the relevant data to present simple calculations to support recommendations. The inputs to the reports are shown as the sources of cost data and the outputs are shown in the diagram as the reports. Processing the cost data may require particular financial tools that are explained in the following units. For example: marginal costing, absorption costing, activity based costing and various decision making tools.

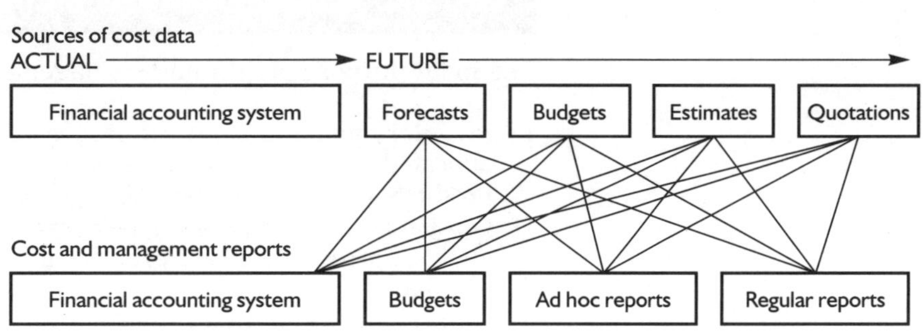

Figure 3.3
Sources of cost data

Marketing and sales managers may want to use the tools to analyse performance of particular product lines, sales force or channel performance, evaluation of advertising and promotion campaigns, pricing decisions and investment decisions including new product development. In addition it is necessary to measure profit performance for various market segments. Marketing and sales management activities can have the greatest effect upon the organization's profit and cash flows.

Summary of differences between financial and management accounting

Financial accounting		*Management accounting*
Statutory requirement	v	No legal requirement
Based on actual transactions	v	May use forecasts, budget data Future cost/revenue data
For the whole organization P&L, balance sheet, cash flow	v	Reports on parts of the business segments, products/market reports (P&L)
Prepared in accordance with the law, SSAPs and GAAPs	v	No specific requirement but usually follow GAAPs
Historical report past events	v	Estimates of future cost/revenue
Published annually	v	Reports produced more frequently

SSAPs are Statements of Standard Accounting Practice issued by the Accounting Standards Board in the UK.

Extending Activity 3.3

Using the published financial report you obtained earlier see if you can identify any references to the SSAPs. Do you know how many SSAPs there are in total? Why are SSAPs necessary? There has been much debate about external financial reporting standards in the press. You may like to keep up-to-date by scanning the broadsheets.

The focus for the rest of your study in this area will be based upon management accounting tools and analysis. It is management accounting that most managers need to understand and gain experience in. Management accounting departments are nevertheless run by accountants who speak the language of finance and financial accounting. Many management accounting tools have financial accounting concepts underpinning them and this is why it is necessary for you to be introduced to the financial concepts in this unit.

Cost and management accounting systems

The main purpose of cost and management systems is to provide:

1 Inventory valuation and profit measurement. To do so costs need to be allocated or apportioned between products sold, partly completed products (work-in-process) and finished stocks that remain unsold.
2 Guidance for decision makers by producing segment profitability analysis, product prices, product mix, channel mix and make or buy evaluations.
3 Control and performance measures.

Cost data may be combined in different ways to achieve the cost and management system objectives.

Cost elements for any product or service may be classified into materials, labour and overheads.

Summary

This unit has introduced you to the main financial statements and some of the important concepts that underpin their construction. The profit and loss account which shows the profit made by a firm over a specific period of time includes non-cash items such as depreciation and stocks sold. The difference between cash and profit is explained. The balance sheet is a statement of financial assets and liabilities on a specific date.

The differences between financial and management accounting have also been explained. Sources of financial data and how financial information fits into the marketing information system are discussed.

Answers

Answer 3.1

Debtor.

Answer 3.2

A statement of financial assets and liabilities at a point in time.

Answer 3.3

Increase expenses for advertising in the profit and loss account and increase creditors on the balance sheet.

Activity Debrief 3.3

Jane's trading and profit and loss account for the month

Sales turnover		£1,250
Credit sale	£250	
Cash sales	£1,000	
Cost of sales		£600
Gross profit		£650
Expenses		
Wages	£100	
Rent	£250	
		£350
Net profit		£300

Remember: Sales turnover = Quantity sold × Selling price
Cost of sales = Quantity sold at cost price
Rent and wages are expenses
Goods sold allowing credit to a customer are counted as sales and the money owed to the firm is shown as an asset (debtors).
All other transactions are made in cash.

Jane's balance sheet at the end of the first month

Fixed assets		None	
Current assets			
Stock 40 units remain @ £10		£400	
Debtors 10 units sold @ £25		£250	
Cash at bank		£4,650	
			£5,300
Current liabilities			
Trade creditors for stock	none		
Other creditors	none		
Net current assets			£5,300
Financed by			
Capital		£5,000	
Add net profit retained		£300	
Capital employed			£5,300

Unit 4 Management accounting decisions

Objectives

After reading this unit and completing the activities you should be able to:

- Recognize the important contribution that management accounting decision tools can make in achieving marketing and sales objectives:
  - (a) Know and understand typical types of cost behaviour.
  - (b) Understand the different types of cost and how they affect total and unit cost.
  - (c) Describe product costing and overhead treatment.
  - (d) calculate overhead recovery rates and comment upon absorption costing and the appropriateness of using particular types of basis and rates.
- Describe activity based costing (ABC) techniques and discuss their appropriateness as an alternative to traditional absorption costing.
- Know and understand how to analyse the effects of *cost, profit and volume.*
- Identify the main sources of data for *planning for profit.*
- Understand the financial information needs of marketing and sales managers.
- Calculate and evaluate *pricing and output* decisions using management accounting decision making techniques.
- Understand time values for money and the concepts of payback and discounted cash flows.

Study Guide

This unit should take between 4 to 6 hours to read and work through. It is a very long unit with some difficult concepts to grasp. You should take it slowly making sure you understand the concepts presented. It is important that you already have a thorough grasp of the earlier unit related to profitability. If you are in any doubt you should quickly revise the previous unit before proceeding. Each of the financial units requires a build-up of knowledge and skills in applying the knowledge from the previous units.

This unit begins by looking at the effects of volume on cost and profit. Product costing is then given a thorough treatment applying *absorption based costing.* This is followed by a brief discussion on a relatively new technique *activity based costing.* The rest of the unit is devoted to two major decision making techniques: *marginal costing* which is most useful for short term decisions, and *discounted cash flow techniques* that are mainly applied to long term decisions. It is very important to follow each stage of the unit carefully so that you build up your knowledge and skill. Marginal costing is at the heart of cost, volume and profit decisions and the contribution concept is a central theme.

Exam Hints

One or more of these techniques is almost certain to be on your exam paper either as part of a mini case or as a part B question.

Study Tips

You should make notes of key words and anything you do not understand. As you read through the unit the concepts and questions you initially noted may become clearer to you. This unit requires your careful concentration. Make sure you have a complete block of time without distractions to concentrate on the work ahead. Complete the activities in order and do not move on until you understand what you have done in each activity.

You should be sure to have to hand:

- A pencil
- A rubber
- A calculator

Introduction

The management process is often said to be one of:

Planning
Controlling
Organizing
Communicating
Motivating

Management accounting can be placed in this process context as follows:

- *Planning* To help formulate plans for different activities and co-ordinating plans to prepare a budget for the whole organization.
- *Controlling* To produce reports that compare performance of actual outcomes against the planned performance. These reports are sometimes presented as variance reports.
- *Organizing* To ensure that the accounting reporting and information system is closely aligned to the organizational structure and organizational goals.
- *Communicating* To ensure plans are communicated and that appropriate feedback mechanisms are in place in the system.
- *Motivating* To motivate employees to meet performance objectives through the budgeting process.

Cost classification

Traditional cost accounting systems classify costs into categories such as cost elements.

Product costing requires that you identify variable or direct costs that will change as a result of changes in output and fixed costs or overhead costs that are related to time rather than volume. Direct material costs plus direct labour cost plus any direct expenses will provide the prime cost of production. This is in effect the marginal cost of production. It does not take any account of any time based costs. Time based costs need to be included in the product cost to arrive at a full cost of production. The way in which this can be done is through a cost accounting technique known as absorption costing. The production overhead is added to the prime cost of production to give a cost of production. The total cost is obtained by adding other non-production overhead costs. To the total cost must be added the profit margin. Remember Total Cost + Profit Margin = Selling Price.

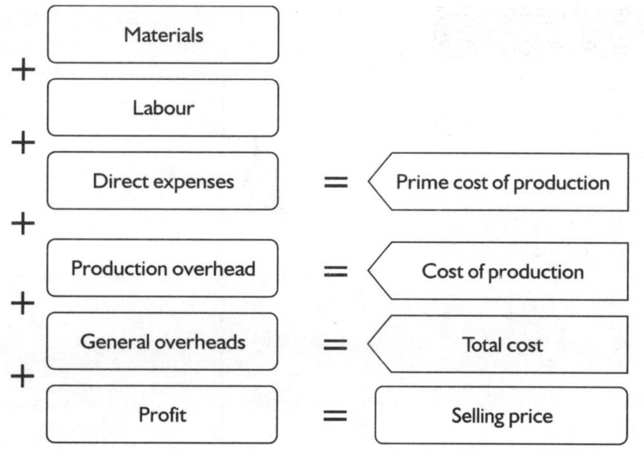

Figure 4.1
Cost accounting systems

Question 4.1

You were introduced to the elements of cost in the previous unit. Can you recall what they are?

Answer See end of chapter. labour, materials, overheads

Cost objective

A cost objective is any activity for which a separate measurement of cost is required. For example, the cost of making a specific product or the cost of providing a specific service.

Costing systems usually account for costs in two stages:

1. Cost classification: labour, material and overheads
2. Tracing the cost to the cost objective: absorption costing and activity based costing techniques may be appropriate.

Types of cost

Definition 4.1

Variable costs change as a result of changes in output (volume). These costs are also referred to as direct costs and marginal costs.

Fixed costs do not change with output but remain fixed. For example, if a firm pays rent for premises this cost remains the same if the firm produces nothing or thousands of units of output.

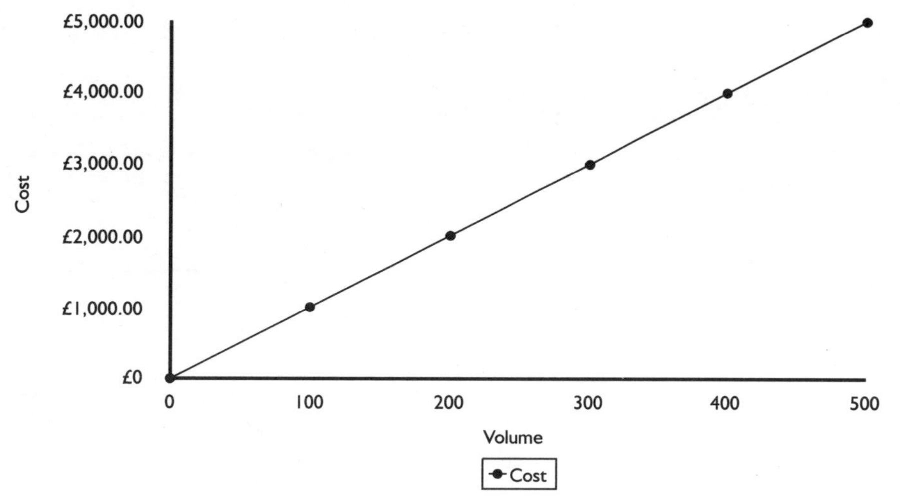

Figure 4.2
Variable cost (linear relationship)

Fixed cost would be represented graphically as follows:

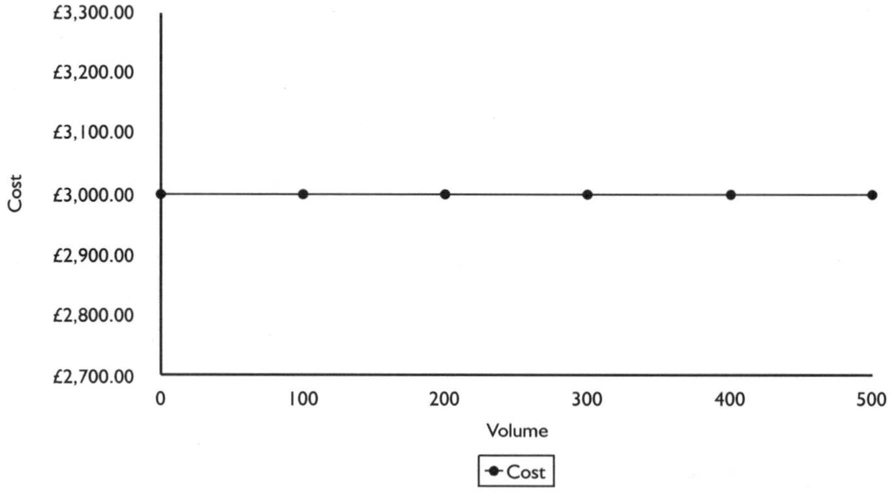

Figure 4.3
Fixed costs

Step variable costs

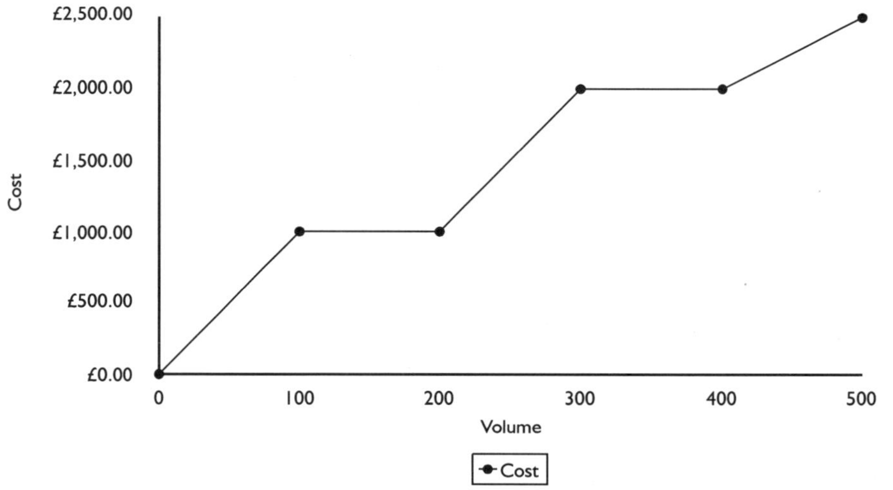

Figure 4.4
Semi-variable/semi-fixed costs

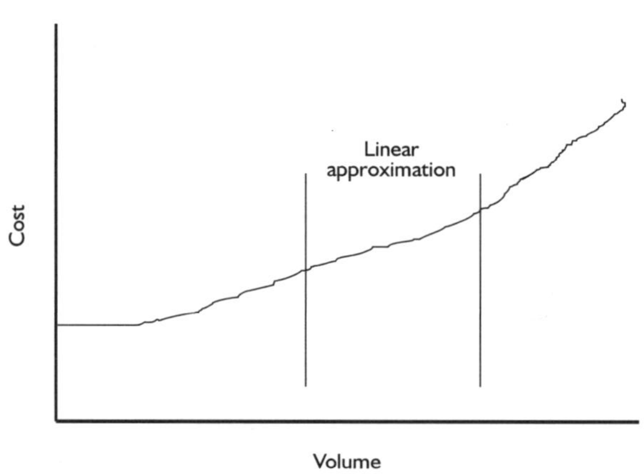

Figure 4.5
Linear approximation

Costs may also have non-linear relationships. However, even when costs do not have a complete linear relationship it may be possible to approximate the cost by focusing on a small portion of a curve to provide a linear approximation.

Cost

We have already looked at cost and how it may be divided into elements of cost: *material, labour and overheads*. We have also seen how cost may mean product cost, period cost and total cost. Remember product costs are the direct costs. However, direct costs alone are insufficient to recognize when calculating product profitability since there may be shared or common costs that we call overheads. These overhead costs need to be related to the product and the way in which we do that is by absorbing the production overheads into the product cost using one of the absorption costing bases discussed elsewhere (e.g. on the basis of £ per direct labour hour). To arrive at a total cost we need to take account of non-production overhead costs also.

Let us look at a brief example just to make sure you understand what we mean. Supposing we decide to make a single unit of a particular product then we may have the following cost data:

Direct material cost is £2.00 per kilo.

Direct labour cost is £5.00 per hour.

The cost units are kilograms in the case of material and labour hours.

In addition we are told that production overheads are recovered on the basis of direct labour hours. Therefore, we need to know the *overhead recovery rate* which has been calculated at £4.00 per direct labour hour. Remember this will have been calculated as follows:

$$\frac{\text{Budgeted production overheads for the period}}{\text{Activity (no. of direct labour hours available in the period)}}$$

We are also told that non-production overheads for such things as administration, selling and marketing and finance are estimated to be recovered at 10 per cent of the production cost. Each product requires 100 units of material and takes 3 direct labour hours. Our product cost sheet may look as follows:

Product costing sheet

	Cost per unit	*Quantity required*	*Total cost*
Direct costs	£	*Number of units*	£
Material	£2.00	100	200.00
Labour	£5.00	3	15.00
Prime cost	£7.00		215.00
Overheads			
Production	£4.00	3	12.00
Production cost			227.00
Non-production	Add 10% to the production cost		22.70
Total cost			249.70

Activity 4.1

Now you try to complete a product costing sheet based upon the following data:

Direct labour cost is £6 per hour.
Direct material cost is £7 per metre.
There is a direct expense of £2 per unit of product.
Production overheads are recovered as a percentage of direct labour at a rate of 20 per cent.
Non-production overheads are recovered on the basis of 20 per cent being added to the total production cost.

Product costing

Product costing can be a tricky problem because of the nature of the costs involved. For example, direct costs are those costs that are traceable to the specific cost object. Supposing we were producing tins, the direct costs could be identified as tinplate (materials) and assembly labour (direct labour). However, this is not the end of the cost since there are costs called overhead costs which are common costs or shared costs. The difficulty in product costing is twofold: firstly how much overhead cost should be included in the product cost and secondly overhead costs are only ever known with accuracy at the end of a financial period. How can these problems be addressed?

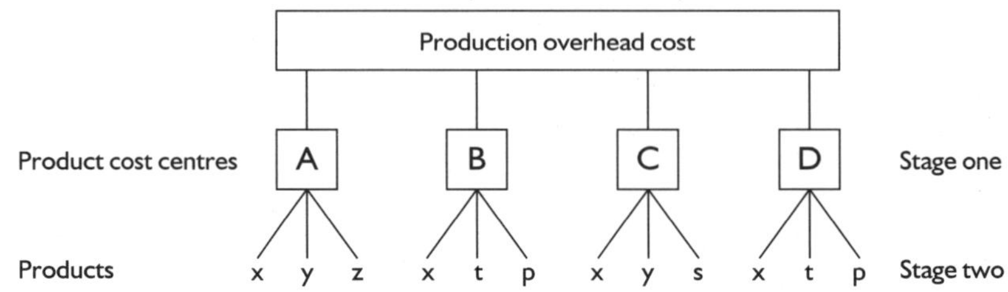

Figure 4.6 Product costing

Traditionally accountants have attributed overheads to products in an arbitrary manner. Firstly, the overhead cost is allocated to a cost centre or apportioned across several cost centres using some equitable basis of apportionment. For example, if three product cost centres used production overheads in equal amounts then it would be reasonable to apportion the cost by splitting it three ways. On the other hand, if three products shared the overhead cost for rent of a factory, one may choose to divide the cost among the three product cost centres in proportion to the amount of floor space taken up by each product. The second step is to move the cost into the cost unit. For example, if you want to share £50,000 overheads amongst several products you first need to decide how much is attributable to each product, and then at the second step, how much of the overhead cost needs to be carried by each unit of production.

Stage one

Requires that the overhead costs are apportioned to cost centres applying an equitable basis of apportioning the cost. The basis of apportionment will be dependent on the type of overhead cost.

Examples of basis of apportionment

1 Floor area – for the cost of rent, rates, heat, light, storage, repairs and maintenance, depreciation on buildings.
2 Number of employees – for the cost of personnel department, accounts department etc; canteen, general supervision.
3 Volume, weight or quantity of materials – cost of stores personnel, warehousing costs, transport.
4 Book values or cost of fixed assets and equipment – depreciation, insurance of equipment, etc.
5 Technical estimates (or export estimates) – occupancy costs, service centre costs.
6 Number of machines – depreciation, insurance of equipment, maintenance costs, supervision.
7 Number of radiators – heating cost.
8 Number of lights etc. – lighting cost.
9 Any other reasonable basis.

Sources of information

Making decisions to apportion overhead costs requires information. Typical sources of useful information include the following:

- Statistics relating to the factory: e.g. occupancy details, who occupies what spaces, and floor areas used by particular production cost centres.
- Personnel statistics: number of employees, total departmental breakdown, personnel establishment versus in post.
- Statistics regarding production, plant, machinery and equipment. These statistics may be available from work study engineers, e.g. capacity, average output, output over a period from machinery or by department or cost centre.
- Accounting records. The plant register, the property register, the patent register. Original documents such as: purchases invoice, stores requisitions, payroll analysis etc.

Stage two

This involves absorbing the overhead cost apportioned to each cost centre into specific products. There are a number of traditional methods of absorbing cost that include:

- Units of product = Overhead rate per unit.
- Direct labour hours = Overhead rate per direct labour hour.
- Direct machine hours = Overhead rate per machine hour.
- Direct material cost of production = Overhead rate percentage of direct material.
- Direct labour cost of production = Overhead rate percentage of direct labour cost.
- Prime cost of production = Overhead rate percentage of prime cost.
- Standard hours = Overhead rate per standard hour.

Definition 4.2

Absorption costing

The CIMA define it as 'a principle whereby fixed as well as variable costs are allotted to unit costs and total overheads are absorbed according to activity level. The term may be applied where:

a) production costs only, or
b) costs of all functions are so allotted'.

A share of fixed overhead costs are added to the marginal cost of the product (i.e. direct costs).

Usefulness of absorption costing (or full costing as it is sometimes called)

It is necessary to attribute overhead costs to the products so as to establish a product cost that can be used for: stock valuation; pricing and to determine profitability at the product level. If common costs (i.e. overheads) were not included in the product cost the basis on which stock values, pricing and profitability decisions were arrived at would only take into account the marginal costs of production (i.e. the direct costs).

1 *Stock valuation* – Stock and work-in-progress should comprise those costs which have been incurred in the normal course of business in bringing the product (or service) to its present location and condition.

Such costs will include all related production overheads. Stocks are therefore valued at full factory cost, providing of course this is lower than net realizable value (selling prices). This definition is given in *Statement of Standard Accounting Practice No.9*.

2 *Pricing* – Although price setting is ultimately a matter of marketing policy with consideration being given to the market, it is essential for a business to make certain it does at least cover the full cost of production. Full cost is only known if an appropriate proportion of overheads are charged to the product. Full cost = marginal cost of production + overheads.

3 *Profitability* – can be measured by product. However, for profitability to be measured at the product level it is important to know the unit cost of production. The unit cost of production will comprise direct costs for material and labour plus an appropriate proportion of overhead costs. Full cost = MC + O

Choice of absorption method

Overheads may be recovered by using different methods of absorption. The method chosen should take account of:

- The accuracy in applying overhead rates to units of output, so as to recover the overhead equitably.
- It should be simple to understand and easy to calculate.
- If the business is organized departmentally, then it is better to apply departmental rates of recovery rather than factory-wide rates.
- Since many indirect costs are period costs, account needs to be taken of time as well as the level of activity.

Example of product costing

Let us suppose that we want to establish the product cost for two different products produced in the same factory using similar resource inputs. We first need to know what the direct costs of production are. This may be established by estimating the quantities of direct material (remember direct material is the material that will vary directly with the volume of production) and the quantity of direct labour used in the manufacturing process. Having established the prime cost of production we need then to estimate how much of the overhead cost is attributable to each unit produced.

In our example, we have the following data:

	Product A	*Product B*
Direct material	3 kg at £2 per kg	2 kg at £2 per kg
Direct labour	2 hours at £4 per hour	1.5 hours at £4 per hour

Production overheads are budgeted for the year ahead at £21,000. Note that production overheads are referred to as *Time based costs* or *Period costs*. The direct costs are referred to as *Product costs*. The perennial overhead problem is to turn the time based cost into a product cost. It is also important to recognize that overhead costs are usually budgeted costs for costing purposes since actual overhead costs are only known after the period.

If we assume that the production overhead costs are to be shared between the two products manufactured we need to estimate how much is attributable to each product. One way in which this could be done is to estimate how much time will be used producing each product and then to apportion the overhead on the basis of time. For example, supposing we estimate that there are 6,000 production hours in total available in the period (i.e. one year) and that product A plans to use 4,000 hours and product B plans to use 2,000 hours then it would be appropriate to apportion the overhead cost as follows:

Product A = 4,000/6,000 hours × £21,000
Product B = 2,000/6,000 hours × £21,000

Product A would therefore, need to carry £14,000 of the production overhead and product B would carry £7,000. The next stage is to determine how much of the overhead each unit of product needs to carry. The traditional absorption costing methods mentioned earlier could be used to establish this cost.

Units of product = Overhead rate per unit
We may have prepared a budget based on forecast sales quantities for the year ahead.

Budgeted Sales Quantity	Product A = 40,000 units
	Product B = 20,000 units.

Using the unit cost basis of absorption, each unit that is produced would need to recover production overhead costs as follows:

$$\frac{\text{£14,000 budgeted production overhead cost attributable to product A}}{\text{40,000 units budgeted production of A}}$$

= £0.35 per unit

Similarly, for product B we have:

$$\frac{\text{£7,000 budgeted production overhead cost attributable to product B}}{\text{20,000 units budgeted production of B}}$$

= £0.35 per unit

In preparing a cost estimate for a single unit of product A we would have the following costs:

Product A (B)	*Units*	*Cost per unit*	*£ Cost*
Direct costs			
Materials kgs	3 (2)	£2.00 (2)	£6.00 (4.00)
Labour hours	2 (1.5)	£4.00 (4)	£8.00 (6.00)
Prime cost			£14.00 (10.00)
Production overheads absorbed			£0.35 (0.35)
Production cost per unit			£14.35 (10.35)

You should make sure you understand exactly what we have done. We have worked out the production overhead cost based upon budgeted figures and we have budgeted to produce 40,000 units of product A. Providing 40,000 units are produced and sold in the next year our overheads will be recovered in full. In other words 40,000 × £0.35 = £14,000 the sum that we apportioned to the manufacture of product A.

Activity 4.2

Now you produce a cost estimate in the same way for product B.

Direct labour hours = Overhead rate per direct labour hour
Another widely used method for recovering overhead costs is to base the recovery on the direct labour hours used in production.

Supposing we establish the following data about factory production:

There are twenty people who are classified as direct labour in the factory and the same people are used to make either product A or B. These people work for 40 hours per week for 45 weeks allowing for statutory and other holidays.

People	*Hours*	*Weeks*	*Total direct labour hours*
20	40	45	36,000

Since we have established that there are 36,000 direct labour hours in total we could work out the direct labour hour absorption rate by simply dividing the direct labour hours total into the production overhead cost to establish an hourly rate.

$$\frac{\text{Budgeted production overhead cost £21,000}}{\text{Budgeted direct labour hours 36,000}}$$

$$= \text{£0.5833 per hour}$$

In preparing costings for each of the products, we could use the overhead absorption rate we have just calculated to determine how much production overhead cost we need to recover. You should note that in this example we did not apportion the production overhead between the two products before calculating the absorption rate. We simply took the total overhead cost and divided the total direct labour hours into the cost to arrive at an absorption rate. It was possible to do this since we have assumed the utilization of exactly the same types of direct labour for both products. It is the overhead cost per direct labour hour that is important. In any costings for the two products, production overhead costs need to be added to direct costs by multiplying the number of direct labour hours by the overhead recovery rate £0.5833.

Activity 4.3

Prepare a cost estimate for each of the products A and B applying the appropriate overhead recovery rate based upon direct labour hours.

There are a number of other possible ways to recover the overheads that have been listed previously: £ per machine hours; percentage prime cost; percentage direct labour cost; percentage direct material cost; standard cost etc.

Comparison of the different methods of overhead absorption

The choice of an appropriate method for recovering overheads depends upon a number of things. Firstly, do not lose sight of the fact that you are trying to turn a period (time-based cost) into a product cost. It is time that gives rise to the overhead cost. For example, factory rent and rates are a charge based upon a period of time such as rent for the quarter. In trying to recover the charge you may need to try and work out what the production is likely to be in that quarter and then charge an appropriate portion of overhead to each unit.

The suitability for each basis of recovery is summarized below:

- *£ per unit of output basis of overhead recovery* It is easy to calculate and easy to understand. It is only really suitable for a single product firm. In a multi-product firm the recovery basis could cause an inequitable allocation of overheads. It ignores the relative weightings of cost in the products.
- *£ per direct labour hour or percentage of direct wages* This is suitable when labour is the major resource consumed. It is simple to calculate and it is easy to understand. Furthermore, it does take account of time and is

therefore useful in apportioning time based overhead costs. Accurate labour records must be maintained if products are to be apportioned with the correct amount of overhead. Most work is measured in units of time and this method of recovery is suitable when production is not uniform.

It is best suited to large companies employing the same or similar grades of labour and the payment rates are standard. It is most appropriate where labour costs form a large proportion of total product cost. This method is not so useful if the business has many different grades of labour on different pay structures, e.g. if low paid grades of labour are used on a particular job, overhead absorptions would be unfairly charged at the same rate, as if higher paid grades of labour were used. In such circumstances this would cause an inequitable distribution of overheads.

- *£ per machine hours* This is a suitable method when machine hours are the major resource input. It has the advantage of being related to time. There could be a problem in cases where production does not utilize any machine hours, since they would not be charged any overhead. Hence machine production would unfairly absorb all overheads.
- *Percentage of direct materials* It is easy to calculate and simple to understand. It is really only suitable where the input cost of materials for each unit that a firm produces is the same. Otherwise it suffers from the same problems as percentage of direct wages (i.e. in this case, different grades of materials having different costs). Time is not taken into account, which is probably the most important factor in choosing an overhead absorption rate.
- *Percentage of prime cost* It is simple to understand and easy to calculate. The main problem is that it ignores time. However, it does take account of weightings for the cost of materials and labour.

Activity based costing (ABC)

Before we move on to marginal costing, it is worth drawing attention to a more recent development in full product costing.

ABC is a technique that recognizes that many overhead costs are caused by activities that the firm has to perform. It therefore tries to compute product costs by identifying activities associated with the product and adding these costs to the direct costs using cost drivers rather than absorption rates. Because ABC is concerned with identifying activities that cause cost it is able to deal more easily with non-volume related overhead costs.

Traditional absorption costing techniques identify overheads, apportion or allocate them to a cost centre and then charge a proportion of the appropriate cost centre cost to each product that uses the resource based on volume (i.e. some measure of volume e.g. percentage direct materials consumed in the product, percentage labour number of machine hours

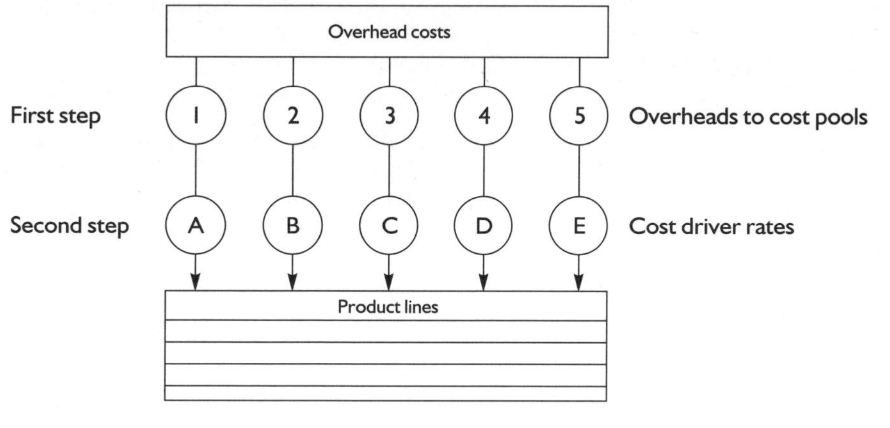

Figure 4.7
Activity based costing

used etc). ABC recognizes that many of the costs in modern business are not necessarily related to volume but to the support activities that a firm needs to provide. For example, the number of sales visits, set-up times for machines, the time it takes to provide customer service and support, time taken to procure materials, quality and conformance costs, and the cost of information systems to support the operations.

ABC recognizes the complexity of costing by (1) pooling costs according to activities that cause them, and (2) applying cost driver rates to derive product costs.

Cost drivers in this case may be:

- A set-up times in minutes – non-volume related cost.
- B number of batches produced – volume related.
- C quality conformance time – non-volume related cost.
- D materials movement times – non-volume but could also be volume related.
- E production information system time – non-volume related cost.

From a marketing and sales decision making point of view, ABC systems may provide more information than simple product costs. Other information provided from an ABC system could include product and customer account profitability and market segment profitability analysis. An example is shown in Figure 4.8

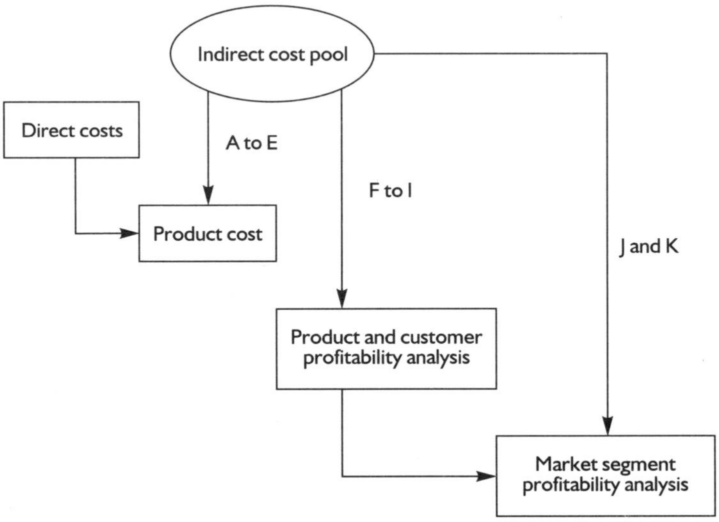

Figure 4.8
ABC systems – other information provided

Product related costs from the cost pool would be apportioned to the relevant products using appropriate cost drivers. For example, the costs from the previous example A to E are product related costs and they would be added to the direct costs to arrive at a product cost. Other costs, i.e. non-production overhead costs for support activities such as marketing and sales would still be apportioned to make up the total cost using appropriate cost drivers.

For example:

- F Number of sales visits.
- G Time spent providing customer support.
- H Time spent on providing quotes for customers.
- I Number of supporting promotions to customers.

These indirect costs (i.e. non-production overhead costs) make up the total cost and are apportioned using the appropriate cost drivers to provide product and customer account profitability and for market segment profitability. Cost drivers J and K might be marketing research time and marketing information systems time.

Advocates for ABC systems claim that product costing achieves greater accuracy and is more relevant to managers in their decision making. Some commentators have argued that ABC is really just a more sophisticated system of absorption based costing (Bromwich and Bhimani; Davies and Hines). It is doubtful that the technique leads to better decision making. It is not really a decision making model, it is an analytical model. Marginal costing may still be a superior decision model.

What we have looked at so far then is absorption costing. We have absorbed overhead costs (time based costs) into the product cost using absorption costing techniques. ABC is a more refined version of this. Now let us turn our attention to marginal costing (i.e. direct costing).

Activity based costing and activity based management

Cost systems are designed to perform three primary functions according to Kaplan and Cooper (1998:2):

1 Valuation of inventories and the measurement of cost of sales.
2 Estimation of the costs of activities, products, services and customers.
3 To provide managers with feedback on their performance and operatives about process efficiency.

ABC systems emerged during the 1980s as a response for more accurate information about the cost of resource demands with an emphasis upon products, services, customers and channels. ABC systems support decision making by presenting a clearer picture of costs. Indirect or support costs are driven first to activities and processes, and secondly to products, services, customers and channels.

The clearer picture obtained from ABC led to the development of activity based management (ABM). Figure 4.9 divides ABM into operational and strategic issues which an organization manages. Operational ABM is about doing things right focusing upon efficiency, cost reduction and asset utilization. Resources are released by changing business processes, by eliminating activities that do not yield value in excess of their cost or by increasing the efficient use of assets. Cost reduction programmes may provide better use of existing resources and therefore obviate the need for further capital investment.

Strategic ABM focuses upon doing the right things and in so doing attempts to lower the demand for resources. For example by designing products or services better it may be possible to lower resource requirements. It is estimated that 80 per cent or more of manufacturing costs are determined during product design and development (Blanchard, B.S. (1978), *Design and Manage to Life-Cycle Cost*, Portland (USA): M/A

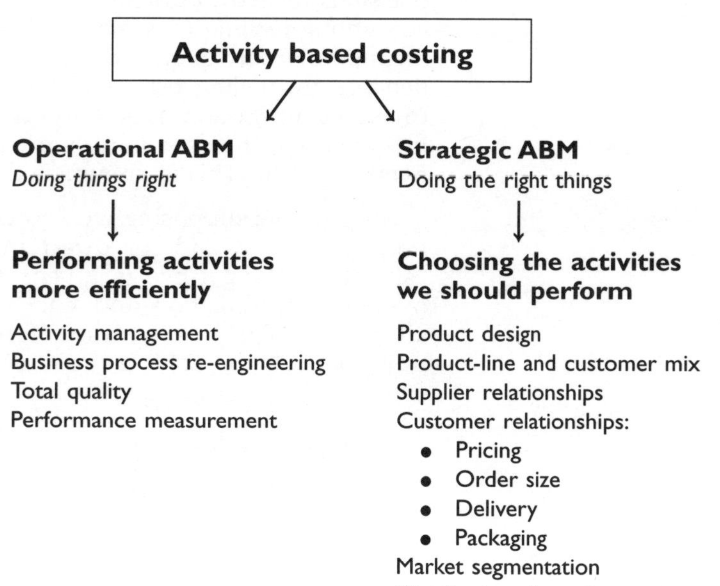

Figure 4.9
How activity based costing turns into activity based management

Press, and J.E. Michaels and W.P. Wood (1989), *Design to Cost*, New York: John Wiley & Sons). Unprofitable activities can be identified and eliminated. Effective suppliers and profitable customers can be developed and the inneffective and unprofitable ones can be removed. Information can be used by marketing managers to explore ways of increasing incremental revenues and reducing incremental costs by identifying highly profitable products, services, customers or channels. Similarly low cost rather than low price suppliers may be expanded.

Table 4.1 and Table 4.2 demonstrate the shift in focus away from expense categories towards activity analysis. In the example, four expense categories are re-analysed to yield an activity based costing.

Table 4.1 From traditional to activity based costing

Traditional costing by function	
Salaries	£250,000.00
Occupancy	£100,000.00
Technology	£150,000.00
Materials	£50,000.00
Total	£550,000.00

Table 4.2 Activity based cost analysis

Activity	*Salaries*	*Occupancy*	*Technology*	*Materials*	*Total*
Process customer orders	£50,000.00	£12,000.00	£30,000.00	£500.00	**£92,500.00**
Purchase materials	£37,500.00	£15,000.00	£22,500.00	£600.00	**£75,600.00**
Schedule production	£45,000.00	£22,000.00	£27,000.00	£250.00	**£94,250.00**
Move materials	£17,500.00	£5,000.00	£10,500.00	£8,500.00	**£41,500.00**
Set-up machines	£25,000.00	£4,000.00	£15,000.00	£2,500.00	**£46,500.00**
Introduce new products	£50,000.00	£41,000.00	£30,000.00	£35,000.00	**£156,000.00**
Resolve quality problems	£25,000.00	£1,000.00	£15,000.00	£2,650.00	**£43,650.00**
	£250,000.00	**£100,000.00**	**£150,000.00**	**£50,000.00**	**£550,000.00**

Marginal costing

When our cost objective is related to profit and volume or for short term decisions related to pricing and output then an appropriate management accounting technique is marginal costing. In marginal costing we do not attempt to absorb overhead cost but rather we find out what the difference between the selling price and the direct costs of the product are. This is called a contribution. It is not profit since the overhead cost has not been included. We then see how many contributions it will take to cover the overhead cost. (This is known as the break-even quantity.)

For example supposing we know direct costs for labour are to be £2 per unit of product and for direct materials £3 per unit of product. The estimated selling price is given at £10 per unit of product, and total overheads (production and non-production) are budgeted for the year ahead at £100,000. How can marginal costing help us decide how many units need to be sold (a) to break even and (b) to make a profit of £50,000?

Selling price per unit	£10.00
Less Direct cost per unit	
Labour	£2.00
Material	£3.00
Contribution	£5.00

Definition 4.3

- Contribution per unit = selling price per unit – direct costs per unit
- Total contribution = sales revenue – total direct cost

To answer part (a) How many units we need to sell to break even, we need to calculate the number of contributions it will take to cover the overhead costs as follows:

- Break-even quantity $= \dfrac{\text{Total overhead costs}}{\text{Contribution per unit}}$
- Break-even quantity $= \dfrac{£100{,}000}{£5}$

$= 20{,}000$ units

Therefore we can see that 20,000 units is the break-even point.

The table below provides a fuller breakdown of volume, revenue, cost, contribution and profit:

Sales quantity	*Revenue*	*TV cost*	*T contribution*	*Fixed cost*	*Profit/(loss)*
0	£0	£0	£0	£100,000	–£100,000
5,000	£50,000	£25,000	£25,000	£100,000	–£75,000
10,000	£100,000	£50,000	£50,000	£100,000	–£50,000
15,000	£150,000	£75,000	£75,000	£100,000	–£25,000
20,000	£200,000	£100,000	£100,000	£100,000	£0
25,000	£250,000	£125,000	£125,000	£100,000	£25,000
30,000	£300,000	£150,000	£150,000	£100,000	£50,000
35,000	£350,000	£175,000	£175,000	£100,000	£75,000

TV = Total variable; T = Total

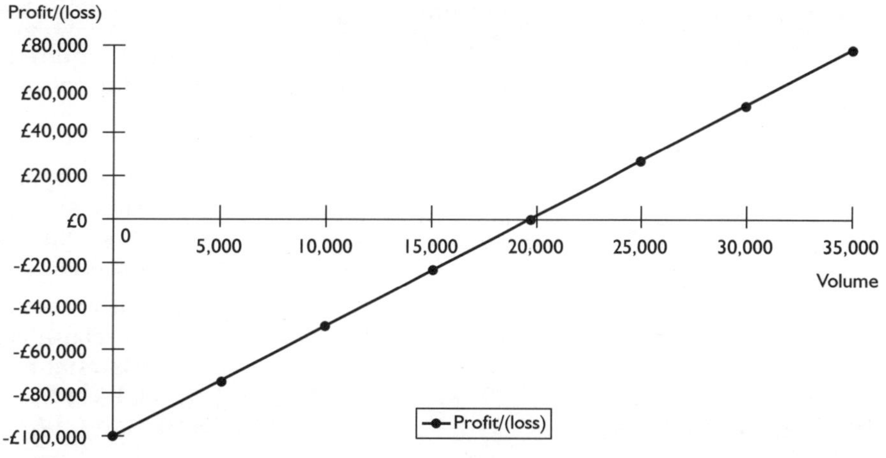

Figure 4.10
Profit/volume chart

The profit/volume chart shows the profit or loss plotted against the sales quantities. The break-even point is where there is neither profit or loss. In this case you can see that break-even is at 20,000 units of sale. Below the horizontal line represents loss, and above is profit.

The break-even chart shows the sales revenue, total cost and fixed cost lines across sales quantities. The break-even point indicated may be read as £200,000 sales value (being break-even this is also the total cost figure) or as 20,000 units of sale. The distance between the revenue and total cost line represents profit to the right of the break-even point, and loss to the left of the break-even point. The distance between the total cost line and the fixed cost line represents the variable cost. Break-even charts are useful to provide a visual picture of the key variables.

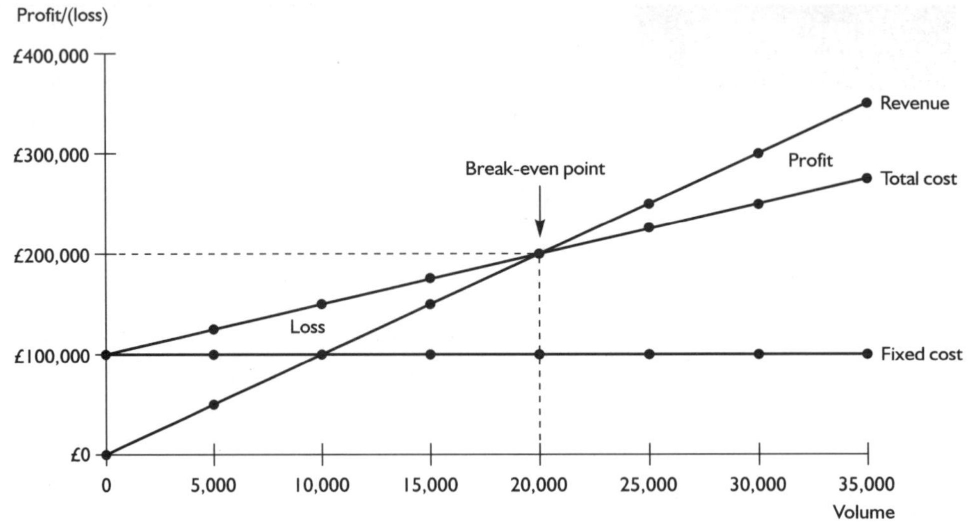

Figure 4.11
Break-even chart

Planning for profit

Supposing we want to make the £50,000 profit as per part (b) then all we need do is calculate how many contributions are necessary to cover the overheads and cover the required profit as follows:

$$\text{Number of units} = \frac{\text{Total overhead + profit required}}{\text{Contribution per unit}}$$

$$= \frac{£100{,}000 + £50{,}000}{£5 \text{ per unit}}$$

$$= 30{,}000 \text{ units}$$

You can refer to the profit/volume chart and the break-even chart and read the position on the chart at 30,000 units of sale and you will see that £50,000 is the profit figure. Alternatively, you can read it from the table of costs and revenues.

Below is a list of information required and possible data sources that may be accessed to yield the information on cost, volume and profit.

Information required	*Possible data sources*
Cost	*Direct labour records* Time sheets Wage payment records e.g. wage rates Job sheets/cards etc.
	Direct material records Purchase invoices Material usage sheets/cards Job cards
	Overheads Expense invoices Budgets Costing records Overhead recovery rates (cost manual) Calculations
Volume	*Production records* *Sales records* *Budgets* *Forward orders* *Forecasts*
Profit	*Budgets* *Historic profit from job cards/records etc.* *Job/contract/batch estimates* *Computations you make*

Extending Activity 4.1

See if you can find out how product or service costing is carried out in your organization and see if you can compile a similar list.

A clear understanding of marginal costing and how it is different to absorption and activity based costing are important for non-financial managers to understand, since discussion and argument revolving around profit and cost form the basis of most financial decisions. Marketing and sales managers need to acquire the knowledge and skills to be able to talk to financial managers about the issues from a position of equal understanding. A failure to understand the concepts could lead to an abdication of decision making to those who are financially literate in relation to cost, volume and profit decisions.

Exam Hint

This is a particularly fruitful area for examiners to test your knowledge and understanding of management accounting tools and concepts.

Activity 4.4

Below is an examination style question for part B of the Chartered Institute of Marketing, Management Information for Marketing and Sales paper which you are now in a position to have a go at. Why don't you try to do this without referring to the answer guide and see how you do?

Question 4.2

Existing retail price for a can of beer is £1.25 and the product is sold in cased packs of 24 cans. The average retail margin is 20 per cent, which means that the manufacturers achieve a gross selling price of £1.00 per can or £24.00 per pack. It has been suggested that a reduction of 10 pence per can retail will increase overall sales. Promotion costs are to be absorbed by the manufacturer and the retailer's margin will be maintained at 25 pence per can.

Cost structure manufacturer

Selling price per cased pack	£24.00
Direct costs	£12.00
Contribution per case	£12.00

Sales forecast '000 cases

Week	*1*	*2*	*3*	*4*	*5*	*6*
Without promotion	20	20	20	20	20	20
With promotion	21	21	30	33	24	21
Gain/(loss)	1	1	10	13	4	1

The promotion is forecast to result in an additional 30,000 cases of the product being sold over a six-week period. On the face of it this appears to be extremely good.

(a) As a marketing manager responsible for evaluating the possible effect of the promotion you are requested to write a brief report to the sales and marketing director which evaluates and explains the possible financial gains and losses and your recommendation as to whether or not the promotion should go ahead, with supporting reasons and appropriate calculations.

15 marks

(b) Explain the importance of having accurate sales forecasts with particular reference to this example.

10 marks

Planning for profit

If you wanted to plan for a certain level of profitability in a given period then if you know what the fixed costs are and what the total variable costs are and you have a target profit figure in mind then you can calculate either:

(a) A selling price to achieve the required profit at a given volume, or

(b) A sales volume/quantity to achieve at a given selling price

$$\text{Selling price per unit} = \frac{\text{Fixed cost + Total variable cost + Profit}}{\text{Volume of output (i.e. number of units)}}$$

or

$$\text{Volume} = \frac{\text{Fixed cost + Total variable cost + Profit}}{\text{Selling price per unit}}$$

Supposing we sell 100,000 units and total variable cost is £40,000 and the fixed cost is £20,000, and let us also suppose that we wanted to achieve profit £15,000. We need to know what selling price we should charge in order to achieve this profit level.

$$\text{Selling price?} = \frac{\text{£20,000 FC + £40,000 TVC + £15,000 P}}{\text{100,000 units}}$$

$$\text{the selling price} = \text{75 pence per unit}$$

Although cost-volume and profit are important factors in setting prices, so too are market factors including positioning and management pricing policy.

Consider the position if we could not alter the price owing to market factors and policy. Let us assume that the price is 50 pence per unit and let us assume that required profit is still £15,000 and fixed costs remain at £20,000. How many units would the firm need to sell in order to achieve the target profit level?

$$\text{Volume?} = \frac{\text{£20,000 FC + Q (0.40) + £15,000}}{\text{0.50 SP}}$$

Note quantity Q is not known but the variable cost per unit has been derived by dividing the total variable cost £40,000 by the 100,000 units.

We do not know the total variable cost in this case. It is easier therefore to use the *contribution* concept to solve the problem as follows:

Selling price	£0.50
Variable cost	£0.40
Contribution	£0.10

$$\text{Volume} = \frac{\text{£20,000 FC + £15,000 P}}{\text{Contribution}}$$

$$\text{Volume} = \frac{\text{£20,000 FC + £15,000 P}}{\text{£0.10 C}}$$

$$= \text{350,000 units}$$

So at a fixed price of 50 pence per unit we would need to sell 350,000 units to achieve our target profit of £15,000.

Note how easily the concept of contribution resolved the unknown total variable cost problem. This is because SP – VC = Contribution. The contribution is a *contribution to fixed cost* until it is covered and then it becomes a *contribution to profit.*

To break even we only need to know how many contributions it will take to cover the fixed cost. In other words since each unit sold makes a contribution how many units need to be sold.

$$\text{Break-even quantity} = \frac{\text{Fixed cost}}{\text{Contribution per unit}}$$

$$= \frac{£20{,}000 \text{ FC}}{£0.10 \text{ C}}$$

$$= 200{,}000 \text{ units}$$

Budgeted profit and loss account for the year to ....

	£
Sales (200,000 × 50p)	100,000
Less direct costs	(80,000)
Contribution to fixed cost	20,000
Less fixed overheads	(20,000)
Profit/(Loss)	NIL

Question 4.3

Given a fixed price of 60 pence and the same cost structure as in the example, i.e. fixed costs £20,000 and variable cost per unit 40 pence, how many units would need to be sold to achieve a target profit figure of £25,000 in the period?

Pricing decisions

Pricing is a matter of policy. Cost data can inform pricing decisions but it must not determine the price. Setting prices is a marketing decision and will be linked to the marketing objectives of the organization. For example, if you want to set a price to enter a market you may decide to set it low hoping to attract large numbers of new customers. On the other hand you may decide to set a high price so as to position your product alongside your competitors hoping that potential customers perceive your product in the same category as the particular competitors you have selected. Setting appropriate prices is a difficult topic and marketing texts devote many pages to the relative merits of setting prices. The main purpose within this section is to illustrate how cost data can assist marketing managers in their decision making.

The price is the value a customer is prepared to pay to obtain the goods or services required. Price is determined in a market. Economists refer to the laws of supply and demand in price setting and those of you who studied economics will know that where the supply curve crosses the demand curve is where the market sets the price. Organizations do not have perfect information about supply and demand. They have partial information that may relate to how existing products are performing by examining sales data. In the case of new products they may only have forecast data based upon market research. Once a price is set the organization will need to monitor performance and make adjustments to price as necessary. This is often easier said than done.

Transfer prices

We know that markets set transfer prices, i.e. prices at which buyers and sellers are agreeable to exchange goods and services. However, what happens when there is no direct market how are prices then set? Well, the concept of a transfer price will be applied but in a slightly different way. For example, take the case of a company that has two distinct operational divisions – a manufacturing division and a retailing division. This vertically integrated organization may purchase finished goods from its own manufacturing division. In so doing the organization will need to decide a price at which the goods will be exchanged between the two divisions. The company may decide to transfer the goods at cost or it may decide to transfer the goods at a price that yields a profit for the manufacturing division. In setting a price that yields a profit for the manufacturing division the organization may decide to operate a standard mark-up to achieve a standard margin or it may decide to try and establish a surrogate market price for the goods. The second pricing strategy is probably the more sensible given that there is a retail market price for the goods produced. Choosing a standard mark-up might distribute profit shares between the two divisions unfairly. Often, where divisions both buy from their own manufacturing division and also from outside suppliers the company may decide to set a price equivalent to that of an alternative external supplier. Once again such pricing decisions are not simple but they are extremely important in determining internal profitability.

The concept of transfer prices is also related to the notion of cost centres and profit centres. If in the example given the manufacturing division is simply a cost centre meaning that it is responsible only for cost then it will be appropriate for the exchange of goods between the two divisions to take place at cost. In such a case all the attributable profit accrues to the retailing division when the goods are sold. However, where the organization has two divisions, both of which are designated profit centres, then it is important that the transfer price contains some element of profit. It is for the organization to set an appropriate transfer price that rewards both divisions appropriately and according to their efforts.

Many public services do not have market prices and are therefore reliant on setting appropriate transfer prices.

Pricing and mark-up and margin

Two very useful simple and related ratios are the *margin* and the *mark-up*. When accountants refer to the margin they could be referring to either a gross margin (the *gross profit margin*) or to the *net margin* (i.e. the *net profit margin*). For the purpose of pricing the margin nearly always refers to the *gross margin*. The gross profit margin may be expressed as follows:

$$\frac{\text{Gross profit}}{\text{Sales turnover}}$$

This ratio may be expressed either as a ratio or as a percentage. For example, if the gross profit is £2,000 on sales turnover of £8,000 as a ratio the margin is 1:4 and as a percentage it is 25 per cent.

Supposing as a marketing or sales manager you know that a particular product line has a margin of 25 per cent or 1:4. If you were given a sales forecast for the month ahead amounting to £20,000 of sales turnover you could immediately assess the forecast profit situation. You would know that your gross profit margin should be £5,000.

The *mark-up* is the addition to the cost of goods to produce a selling price and is often expressed as a percentage. It may be defined as follows:

$$\frac{\text{Gross profit}}{\text{Cost of sales}}$$

Direct product profitability (DPP)

This is a concept that has been extensively used in retailing environments. The logic behind the concept is that in many transactions the customer incurs costs other than the agreed purchase price of the goods from a supplier. These hidden costs can be substantial and can in some cases eliminate profit on a particular product line.

DPP		£
Sales		100
Less cost of goods sold		25
Gross profit margin		75
Add allowances and discounts		10
Adjusted gross margin		85
Less warehousing costs		
Labour costs	6	
Occupancy cost	5	
Inventory cost	4	
		15
Less transportation costs		5
Less retail costs		
Stocking labour	3	
Occupancy cost	2	
Inventory cost	4	
		9
Direct product profitability		56

From the above you can see that the selling price for a particular item is fixed at £100 and that the invoiced cost of the item from a supplier is £25. The gross margin before any adjustment is 75 per cent. Suppliers may give the retailer a discount for early settlement or an allowance as part of a promotion from the supplier or an allowance in respect of the quantities the retailer is prepared to take or for some other reasons. These allowances or discounts have an effect upon the gross margin the retailer is able to achieve. So in this case we have an adjusted gross margin as a result of the allowances given by the supplier. However, the retailer incurs other costs in relation to warehousing, transportation and the very business of retailing itself. These additional costs have been grouped together and are then deducted from the adjusted gross margin to provide the retailer with direct product profitability (DPP). This information will then be used to compare similar products across a particular range or category. The buyers, buying teams or decision making units (DMUs) will take decisions regarding which products to stock. These decisions are not purely financial decisions they are in reality marketing decisions. Marketing managers must be involved in this process. It would be foolish to base the decision regarding which products to stock simply on the basis of this financial information. Nevertheless, it is important to be informed about which products achieve higher profits after all the costs of ownership are taken into account.

Question 4.4

You are told that a particular item retails for £25 and that the supplier's invoiced price to you is £5. The supplier has agreed further discounts amounting to 20 per cent off their price if you agree to take a minimum quantity. Warehousing costs based upon average inventories that you expect to hold, the space the items will occupy in the warehouse and labour handling costs are estimated to add a further £4 per item. Additional transport costs moving goods from the regional distribution centre (RDC) to the stores are expected to add a further £2 cost per item and retail costs will add a further £3 per item. You are asked to compute the direct product profitability for this item assuming you will take the minimum order quantity and hence the additional discount.

Exam Hints

You could be asked further to comment on the profitability for the product, product group or category using the gross margin and the net margin for the DPP figures. You may be given information for the question in a different way. For example, you could have been told that the gross margin before adjustment is 80 per cent and you would have had to work out the cost of the goods sold.

Always try and think around the question as to what the implications are for the decision makers. A further alternative way to present the question might have been to state the selling price and then simply to give you expected percentages for the costs. You could also be faced with a mark-up to margin conversion in such a question. Let us now try a further question presenting you with information in precisely this way.

Question 4.5

A particular line item sells for £10 per unit. The retailer's standard mark-up is 50 per cent. Other costs are estimated as follows – warehousing and distribution at 7 per cent of the selling price, retailing costs at 5 per cent of the selling price. The supplier also gives the retailer a discount for prompt settlement, which the retailer always takes, at 5 per cent of the invoiced price from the supplier. Prepare a direct product profitability statement for this line.

Relationship between margin and mark-up

$$\text{Margin} = \frac{\text{Gross profit}}{\text{Sales turnover}} \text{ per cent} \qquad \text{Mark-up} = \frac{\text{Gross profit}}{\text{Cost of sales}} \text{ per cent}$$

You should remember from earlier in the unit that the selling price is comprised of the cost of the goods sold and profit.

$$\text{Selling price} = \text{Cost of goods} + \text{Profit}$$

$$\text{Selling price 100 per cent} = \text{Cost of goods per cent} + \text{Profit per cent}$$

Supposing we know our usual required margin is 25 per cent and we buy in a new product line for £3 at cost per unit – how much should we be selling it for ?

We know the margin = GP/S per cent = 25 per cent. We now need to use this data to convert it to the required mark-up information as follows:

$$\text{Mark-up} = \frac{\text{Gross profit per cent}}{\text{Cost of sales}}$$

Cost of sales = Sales less gross profit

Cost of sales = 100 per cent – 25 per cent

Cost of sales = 75 per cent

The mark-up therefore must be: $\frac{\text{25 per cent}}{\text{75 per cent}}$

which is 33.33 per cent.

This means that we should be marking-up the cost of the goods bought by 1/3 or 33.33 per cent to achieve our required profit margin.

Let us now look at the cost structure to see if this calculation is correct:

$$\text{Selling price} = \text{Gross profit margin} + \text{Cost of goods}$$

$$\text{100 per cent} = \text{25 per cent} + \text{75 per cent}$$

If the cost of the goods is £3 and we mark the goods up by 33.33 per cent on cost, i.e. £1 the selling price will be £4.

Cost structure

Selling price	=	£4	100 per cent
Cost price	=	£3	75 per cent
Gross profit	=	£1	25 per cent

Risk and uncertainty

Risk may be treated in a variety of ways. We may decide to produce cost and revenue figures at various levels of ouput: for example, best position, expected or average position and worst position. Supposing we had a sales forecast for a particular period: 100,000 units to be sold at a price of £15 per unit. Direct costs for labour, £3; for materials, £4; and the fixed overheads for the period budgeted at £500,000. However, supposing we also wanted to see the effect of a 10 per cent change either above or below the forecast level then we would need to prepare a budget at 90 per cent of the sales forecast and at 110 per cent as follows:

Flexible budget

Activity level	90 per cent	100 per cent	110 per cent
	£	£	£
Sales	1,350,000	1,500,000	1,650,000
Direct costs			
Materials	360,000	400,000	440,000
Labour	270,000	300,000	330,000
Contribution	720,000	800,000	880,000
Fixed overheads	500,000	500,000	500,000
Net profit	220,000	300,000	380,000

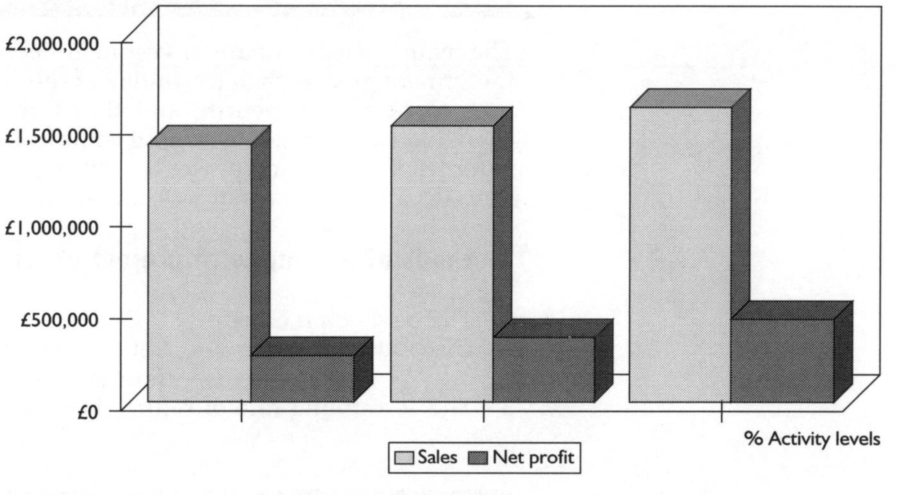

Figure 4.12
Sales and net profit 90 per cent, 100 per cent and 110 per cent

This flexible budget provides the decision maker with an understanding of the sensitivity of the profit position. In this case a 10 per cent rise or fall in volumes will cause an £80,000 change in the profit position up or down. In other words a 10 per cent shift in volumes will cause a 26.66 per cent shift in the profit position.

Cash flow and profit

It is important for marketing and sales managers to understand the difference between cash and profit. Many people mistakenly assume that if you make a profit you can spend it. This is not true because, as you are about to find out, profit is not cash. Let us take a simple example where we buy 10 items for £5 each and we sell 5 for £10 each. The cash and the profit positions are shown as follows:

	£		£
Sales	50	Cash received	50
Cost of sales	25	Cash spent	50
Gross profit	25	Cash in hand	0

Although we have made £25 in profit we have no cash. This is because in calculating the profit we have only charged the cost of making the 5 sales at £5 whereas in cash outlay we have bought 10 units at £5. The profit is not in cash but in the form of another asset i.e. stock. We have stock valued at cost 5 units @ £5 per unit = £25.

Investment, cash flows and opportunity cost

The cost of following one course of action may well be the lost value of the opportunity foregone. Economists refer to this as opportunity cost. For example, given that an organization has limited resources and competing projects such as: (a) to develop a new product, or (b) to undertake further marketing research before developing any further products; then if it chooses project (a) the opportunity cost (i.e. the alternative foregone) would be project (b). This is an example of projects which accountants refer to as 'mutually exclusive'. On the other hand there may be projects which because of the method of funding or because of the nature of the projects are independent of one another, but this is unusual, if resources are scarce. Again in this section we are concerned with projects which are 'mutually exclusive'.

Purpose

The main objective of any investment decision is to obtain a return on the investment greater than the outlay at the start. Of course it may take some time to obtain the return, and therefore account must be taken of the changing value of money. Pound coins in 1990 will not have the same value in terms of purchasing power as, say, pound coins in 1996. Discounted cash flow (DCF) techniques of investment appraisal may take account of this.

Methods of dealing with project costs:

1 The payback method
2 Discounted cash flow – Net present value
– Internal rate of return
3 The accounting rate of return (book rate)

The payback method

The criterion for investment using this method is how quickly the investment cost will be returned. For example, if we have two investment alternatives both costing £10,000 initially and returns as follows, which alternative should we choose?

	A	*B*
	£	£
Year 0 initial outlay	–10,000	–10,000
Year 1 cash receipts at year ends	+ 3,000	+ 1,000
Year 2	+ 2,000	+ 3,000
Year 3	+ 5,000	+ 3,000
Year 4	+ 2,000	+ 3,000

Investment opportunity A repays the initial outflow of cash by the end of the third year, whereas B is not repaid until the end of the fourth year. Using our criterion for the payback method we would choose A.

Supposing the two investment opportunities had cash flow streams as follows:

	A	*B*
	£	£
Year 0 initial outlay	−10,000	−10,000
Year 1 cash receipts at year ends	+5,000	+1,000
Year 2	+4,000	+3,000
Year 3	+1,000	+6,000

Now which alternative investment opportunity should we choose? Using our payback method criterion, i.e. how quickly the initial outlay is repaid, we cannot differentiate between A and B. Both investments look equally attractive. This is because the payback method takes no account of the time value of money. As we stated earlier, pound coins in year 1 may not be worth the same as pound coins at the end of year 3 owing to rising price levels (inflation).

Question 4.6

On the basis of payback, if your firm was considering a promotion campaign over a period of six months from January to June and the choice was between (a) point of sale displays and competitions, and (b) a promotional discount to the retailer to take more stock given, the cash flows listed which project would you choose?

(a)	Net cash flows +/	(b)	Net cash flows +/–
Jan.	−£20,000	Jan.	−£15,000
Feb.	−£10,000	Feb.	−£15,000
Mar.	+ £5,000	Mar.	+ £10,000
Apr.	+ £10,000	Apr.	+ £10,000
May	+ £15,000	May	+ £10,000
June	+ £5,000	June	+ £10,000

Definition 4.4

Discounted cash flow (DCF)

The value of future expected cash receipts and expenditures at a common date which is calculated using *net present value* (NPV) or *internal rate of return* (IRR).

Application: *capital investment appraisal* – *securities investment*

- *Payback* Finds the period of time projects have to run before their original investment (cash outlay) is returned.
- *Internal rate of return (discounted cash flow)* Finds the average return on investment earned through the life of the investment. It determines the discount rate that equates the present value of future cash flows to the cost of the investment.
- *Net present value (discounted cash flow)* Applies a rate of discount (interest rate) based on the marginal cost of capital to future cash flows to bring them back to the present.
- *Accounting rate of return (or book rate of return)* Measures profit on the project each year by the projects total investment cost to give a rate of return. This is not a discounted cash flow method of appraisal.

Time value of money

The net present value techniques are a way of dealing with time values of money and can be used to account for risk and uncertainty associated with decisions over time periods usually longer than a year. They are commonly described as investment appraisal techniques. NPV techniques can of course be applied to any financial decision where the time value of money is important to the decision.

Net present value (NPV)

The formula for *compound interest* is:

$$A = P(1 + r)^n$$

where A is the amount
P is the principal (or present value)
r is the rate of interest
n is the time period

Example

If we invest £100 at 10 per cent per annum what will the compound accumulated interest be in 5 years?

For the present value, we need to transpose the formula as follows:

$$P = \frac{A}{(1 + r)^n}$$

therefore

$$A = P(1 + r)^n$$

$$= 100(1 + 0.10)^5$$

$$= £161.05$$

Using the above example, what would £161.05 at the end of year 5 be worth in present value terms today (i.e. time 0), given an annual rate of interest of 10 per cent?

Working back we can prove this:

$$P = \frac{£161.05}{(1.10)^5}$$

$$= £100$$

Formula for net present value:

$$\sum_{0}^{n} = \frac{1}{(1 + r)^n}$$

where: $\sum$ = Sum of from time *zero* to time *n* (end of project)
n = number of periods
1 = sum invested
r = rate of interest per period

The present value of a future stream of cash flows will be the sum of those discounted cash flows from the present period to the end of the project period.

Supposing a firm could invest its funds at 10 per cent per annum for the next 5 years in a bank, or it could develop a new product to sell. The estimated cash flow for the 5-year period being as follows:

Year end	*1*	*2*	*3*	*4*	*5*
Amount £	−10,000	+2,000	+2,500	+3,000	+4,000

Would the investment in the project be worthwhile?

To find out if the project is worthwhile we will discount the returns at 10 per cent per annum (i.e. the alternative rate at which we could invest capital to see if it is a better investment). Thus we need to know the discount rate for each year:

Year	*1*		*2*		*3*		*4*		*5*
	$\frac{1}{(1.10)^1}$	+	$\frac{1}{(1.10)^2}$	+	$\frac{1}{(1.10)^3}$	+	$\frac{1}{(1.10)^4}$	+	$\frac{1}{(1.10)^5}$

The discount factor is:

0.909	0.826	0.751	0.683	0.621

We then need to multiply the outflows and inflows by the discount rate.

	Cash flow		*Discount rate*		*NPV £*
End of year 1	−10,000	×	0.909	=	−9,090
2	+2,000	×	0.826	=	+1,652
3	+2,500	×	0.751	=	+1,878
4	+3,000	×	0.683	=	+2,049
5	+4,000	×	0.621	=	+2,484
			Net present value		−1,027

The project is not worth investing in since it yields a negative NPV. If, however, the NPV was positive, we would accept it.

Let us suppose that the cost of the funds, that is, the *cost of capital* was only 5 per cent, given the same cash flows, would the project be worthwhile?

Let us make a similar appraisal on this basis.

	Cash flow		*Discount rate*		*NPV £*
End of year 1	−10,000	×	0.952	=	−9,520
2	+2,000	×	0.907	=	+1,814
3	+2,500	×	0.864	=	+2,160
4	+3,000	×	0.823	=	+2,469
5	+4,000	×	0.784	=	+3,136
			Net present value		+59

Yes, the project is worth accepting since it yields a positive net present value.

Problems in practice

- Cash flows are subject to uncertainty and risk.
- Interest rates are also uncertain, and therefore the cost of capital is not known with any certainty unless fixed interest rates for the period of a loan can be agreed but this is only applicable to debt finance. Equity funds will still be subject to uncertainty

Advantages of the NPV rule

- The method does take account of the 'time value' of money.
- It is relatively easy to calculate.

The internal rate of return (IRR)

Definition 4.5

Internal rate of return (discounted cash flow). Finds the average return on investment earned through the life of the investment. It determines the discount rate that equates the present value of future cash flows to the cost of the investment.

Taking the following example:

			Project A £	*Project B £*
Year	0	Initial outlay	−10,000	−10,000
	1		+5,000	+1,000
	2		+4,000	+3,000
	3		+1,000	+6,000
	4		+2,000	+3,000

We need to choose a discount rate that equates the inflows in each of the years 1 to 4 with the cash outflow at the start.

Let us try 10 per cent:

$$= -\ 10{,}000 + 5{,}000\ (0.909) + 4{,}000\ (0.826) + 1{,}000\ (0.751) + 2{,}000\ (0.683)$$
$$= -\ 10{,}000 + 9{,}966$$
$$= \underline{-\ 34}$$

10 per cent p.a. is just a little too high, we need therefore to try a lower rate. Let us try 8 per cent.

$$= -\ 10{,}000 + 5{,}000\ (0.926) + 4{,}000\ (0.857) + 1{,}000\ (0.794) + 2{,}000\ (0.735)$$
$$= -\ 10{,}000 + 10{,}322$$
$$= \underline{+\ 322}$$

We know that the IRR lies somewhere between 8 and 10 per cent p.a. If we take the lower rate (8) and add the difference between the highest rate we chose (10) and the lower rate (8), which is 2, multiplied by the difference we obtained at the lower rate, +322, divided by the total difference between the two rates, we will obtain the IRR. That is: [(+322 − −34) = 356]

$$8 + \frac{(2 \times 322)}{356} = 9.81$$

Check that this is correct:

$$9.81 \text{ per cent} = -\ 10{,}000 + 5{,}000\ (0.911) + 4{,}000\ (0.829) + 1{,}000\ (0.755) + 2{,}000\ (0.687)$$
$$= -10{,}000 + 10{,}000$$
$$= \underline{0}$$

The internal rate of return on this project is therefore 9.81 per cent. You can now attempt to evaluate the project B in exactly the same way. What is the significance of the IRR? Well, if the firm can borrow capital at a lower rate than 9.81 per cent p.a. it will find the project worthwhile. A cash stream equivalent to that in project A could be obtained if the firm could invest £10,000 today at a return of 9.81 per cent p.a. for four years.

The IRR differs from other discounting methods for the following reasons:

- It does not obtain a cash figure to determine whether or not an investment should be undertaken, but rather seeks to find a discount rate at which the NPV is zero.
- It takes no account of the absolute size of a project investment cost, nor its total cash returns. It is a measure expressing the net returns as a percentage of investment cost.
- The criterion for acceptance or rejection of a project is that the IRR must be greater than some other rate. For example, if we had two projects, A and B, and A had an internal rate of return of 9.81 per cent and B had an internal rate of return of 8.00 per cent, project B would be preferred but neither would be acceptable if a higher rate of return than 9.81 per cent was required as a cut-off when retaining available capital finance.

The accounting rate of return or book rate of return

This is:

$$\frac{\text{Average annual net profit after tax}}{\text{Average investment}}$$

Thus, if we know that the average net profits after tax for each of three years were as follows, and that also the book value of the investment, i.e. capital employed is also as follows, we can calculate the accounting rate of return.

Year	*Average net profit*	*Capital employed*
1	£1,000	£12,500
2	£1,000	£11,000
3	£1,000	£10,000

Year 1 2 3

$$\frac{1{,}000}{12{,}500} = 8 \text{ per cent} \qquad \frac{1{,}000}{11{,}000} = 9 \text{ per cent} \qquad \frac{1{,}000}{10{,}000} = 10 \text{ per cent}$$

Over a three-year period the accounting rate of return would be:

$$\frac{(1{,}000 + 1{,}000 + 1{,}000)}{3} = £1{,}000$$

$$\frac{(12{,}500 + 11{,}000 + 10{,}000)}{3} = £11{,}166.67$$

$$= \frac{1{,}000}{11{,}166.67} \times \frac{100}{1}$$

$= \underline{8.95 \text{ per cent}}$

Problems

The measure deals with book values for capital employed. Therefore, rate of return on investment may be inaccurate and is subject to variations because:

- Net book values are based on historic cost and take no account of changing price levels.
- Profits include allocations such as depreciation and other provisions which may distort the decision.
- From the point of view of an investment decision it is better to consider cash flows which do not suffer from the drawbacks mentioned in (a) and (b) above.

Question 4.7

Using payback and NPV with a discount rate at 10 per cent per period, consider an investment decision in a new product that has expected cash flows as follows:

Start of year 1 −£50,000, end of year 1 +£10,000, end of year 2 +£40,000 and the end of year 3 +£10,000

Credit control and cash flows

As discussed, cash flow is particularly important for firms to control since it is cash that pays the bills and not profit. No matter how profitable a business is, it requires cash to discharge its liabilities as they fall due. It is important for managers to recognize the effects of decisions they take in respect of profit impact and cash effect.

For instance supposing a sales manager accepts a profitable order from a firm to supply engineered components over a six-month period. The customer agrees to call off 10,000 units a month at a price of £5 per unit. The cost of making one unit is £2 at marginal cost. The customer wants extended credit because they will not be paid by their customer until the job is completed. The sales manager agrees to allow 90 day credit terms i.e. 3 months after delivery to the customer. Material and labour costs have to be paid monthly by the selling firm.

The profit and loss summary is as follows:

Profit and loss summary

Months	*1*	*2*	*3*	*4*	*5*	*6*	*Total*
Sales	50,000	50,000	50,000	50,000	50,000	50,000	300,000
Cost of sale	20,000	20,000	20,000	20,000	20,000	20,000	120,000
Contribution	30,000	30,000	30,000	30,000	30,000	30,000	180,000

Assuming that the firm started the project without any cash in hand, you can see that it would have to lay out £60,000 before the first receipt from the sale is received. This assumes payment is received at the beginning of month 4. It is not until the sixth month that the firm would achieve a positive cash flow from this project. Assuming that there is a time value to money this firm is losing money as a result of the credit allowed by the sales manager.

Cash flows

Months	*1*	*2*	*3*	*4*	*5*	*6*	*Total*
Receipts							
Cash in hand b/f	0	−20,000	−40,000	−60,000	−30,000	0	
Debtors (Sales)				50,000	50,000	50,000	150,000
Payments							
Material and labour	20,000	20,000	20,000	20,000	20,000	20,000	120,000
Cash balance c/f	−20,000	−40,000	−60,000	−30,000	0	30,000	30,000

Bad debt risk

If customers do not pay their sales invoices by the due date they become a bad debt risk. This is to say that there is the possibility that they may not pay at all. Sometimes firms will make a provison in their financial accounts for a doubtful debt. If the doubtful debt becomes a 100 per cent certainty then it is a bad debt and will, therefore, need to be written off the debtors, and profit is reduced by the amount of the debt written off.

Assessing risk

There are two main sources of data that could be used to assess the level of bad debts that may be incurred by the business which are:

- Internal data from customer account records could be used to provide an estimate of the normal bad debt level for the firm expressed as a percentage of total sales. Financial accounts for the last five years may provide a reasonable indication of the ratio within the firm. An average figure could be used as an estimate for the current level providing conditions have not substantially changed, e.g. external market conditions, customer base.
- External data sources may include industry averaged ratios of bad debts to sales supplied by credit rating agencies such as Dunn & Bradstreet, Extel, McCarthy or there may be an industry trade body that collects the relevant data.

Supposing a firm has the option of either offering customers interest free credit or a 10 per cent discount off the price how should it decide which is the best option on financial grounds?

Well the first piece of data required is an estimate of the expected level of sales as a result of each option. In other words the starting point is a sales forecast. Let us assume that the effect of the interest free credit would lead to increased sales volumes of 2,000 units and the discounted price leads to an increase of 1,500 units. The current selling price of the items is £10 per unit. The usual profit mark-up is 100 per cent on cost. Interest free credit is expected to double the bad debts from 5 per cent to 10 per cent.

Evaluation of the sales strategy alternatives

The following calculations provide details of the effects for each of the suggested strategies: (1) Interest free and (2) 10 per cent discount.

(1) Interest free credit and increased bad debt risk:

	Units	*Price/CPU*	*£ Total*	*Effect of increasing bad debts to 10 per cent*
Sales increase	2000	£10	20,000	
Cost of sales	2000	£5	10,000	
Extra contributions			10,000	10,000
Less usual bad debts			1,000	2,000
Extra contribution after bad debts			9,000	8,000

Note the cost price per unit was derived as follows: selling price £10 represents 100 per cent on cost, therefore cost must be 1/2 of the selling price and 50 per cent of the selling price is £5.

(2) Effect of 10 per cent discount on selling prices

New position after 10 per cent discount

	Units	*Price/CPU*	*£ Total*
Sales turnover	1,500	£9	13,500
Cost of sales	1,500	£5	7,500
Contribution			6,000

Recommendation

From the data provided and on the basis of the calculations provided here it is recommended that option (1) is favoured and would lead to a higher contribution to profit assuming that the forecast sales provided from market research are accurate.

Contribution and limiting factors

It may be that a business is not able to increase its contribution indefinitely owing to a constraint (limiting factor). Limiting factors could be:

- Limited production capacity.
- Limited demand for the product.
- Limited available labour hours.
- Limited available materials.

In such a case it is sometimes useful to work out a contribution to the limiting factor, e.g. contribution per production hour, contribution per unit, contribution per direct labour hour or contribution per unit of direct material.

- *International exchange rates* and their effects on costs and revenues. When marketing and sales managers are dealing with customers from overseas, special considerations are required, related to the risk and uncertainty involved in trading in foreign currencies.
- *Costs* Where a business is trading in the international marketplace, it is at risk from the volatility of sharp changes in the exchange rate particularly between the date a deal is struck and the date the goods are paid for. For example, supposing a UK business agrees to buy goods from the US when the exchange rate is $1.80 to the £ sterling, but when the payment is made it has fallen to $1.50 to the £ sterling and the contract was agreed at a total cost of $100,000. If the price had been paid when the rate was $1.80 it would have cost the business £55,555 excluding any transaction costs incurred for changing the currency. If it was paid when the rate had fallen to $1.50 it would have cost the company £66,667, an increase on the agreed cost of 20 per cent. Of course, the company could make gains on currency fluctuations if the reverse situation had occurred and the value of sterling had risen against the dollar between the contract date and the payment date. It is important for marketing and sales managers to be aware of the effect of such changes in global markets. Some larger companies attempt to minimize the risks through corporate treasury functions, who hedge against risks by buying and selling currencies forward, but this is speculative.
- *Sales* If sales are made to overseas companies and agreed prices are made in foreign currency, say dollars, then a fall in the dollar exchange rate from $1.50 to $1.80 to the £ sterling would mean that the dollar would be worth less when it was converted to £ sterling. Supposing a sales was contracted at $20 million for one aeroplane and between the date of contract and the payment date the exchange rate moved from $1.50 to $1.80 to £ sterling, the resultant loss for a British supplier excluding transaction costs would be:

		£ sterling
Original rate of exchange $1.50	=	13,333,333
Revised rate of exchange $1.80	=	11,111,111
Loss on exchange	=	2,222,222

Activity 4.5

Look up the current rate of exchange between £ sterling and US $ in an old newspaper, say three months ago and look at the rate of exchange today. Assume that you had sold goods and invoiced them in dollars at the older rate of exchange, the £ sales value being £100,000. Compare the value of the dollars received when converted to sterling at the current rate of exchange and work out a profit or loss on exchange.

Question 4.8

Plastic Toys Ltd produce 10,000 units per annum. Budgeted costs are as follows:

Direct labour	£20,000
Direct materials	£10,000
Direct expenses	£1,000
Factory overheads	£20,000
Production cost	£51,000
Administrative overheads	£5,000
Selling and marketing overheads	£5,000
Finance overheads	£2,000
Total cost	£63,000

All the overheads are fixed costs. Each toy sells at £12 from the factory. The factory is currently budgeted for 50 per cent capacity. The sales director has been on an export sales drive to France with the aim of developing new markets for the existing product. A French company has shown interest in buying an additional 10,000 units but only if a 50 per cent discount is given from the normal factory selling price.

The sales director has sent you a memo to ask what you think the firm should do in the circumstances.

1 Reply to the sales director in a memo with a summarized profit and loss statement attached that clearly shows what would happen if:
   (a) The French order is not accepted.
   (b) The French order is accepted.

You are specifically asked to comment on:
(i) profitability.
(ii) the effect of discounting on normal sales.
(iii) long term effect of doing business on a marginal cost basis.
(35 marks)

2 If the French order became more than just a 'one-off' explain what share of the overheads you think it would need to carry and why?
(15 marks)

Answers

Answer 4.1

The elements of cost are: labour, material and overheads.

Activity Debrief 4.1

Direct labour	£6.00
Direct material	£7.00
Direct expenses	£2.00
Prime cost	£15.00
Add	
Production overhead (20% × £6)	£1.20
Total production cost	£16.20
Add	
Non-production overhead (20% × £16.20)	£3.24
Total cost	£19.44

Note: This costing assumes that:
(a) It takes one hour to make one unit and hence direct labour is charged at £6.
(b) It takes one metre of material to make one unit.

Answer 4.2

(a) Report to the sales and marketing director

Subject: Evaluation of proposed promotion

Preliminary calculations on the financial effects of the proposed promotion are detailed below:

Cost structure manufacture	*With promotion*	
Selling price per cased pack	£24.00	
Direct costs	£12.00	
Promotional allowance	£2.40	i.e. 10p per can × 24 cans per case
Contribution per case	£9.60	

The usual contribution per case is £12.00 (Selling price less Direct costs) if we introduce the proposed promotion the direct costs will be increased by £2.40 per case. This is because we have decided to maintain the retailer's margin and absorb the full cost of the promotion ourselves. The effect is to reduce the contribution we receive by £2.40 per case. This may be worthwhile if we are able to increase sales volumes through the promotional period.

Below I have presented a table showing the total gains and losses for the period of the promotion.

Week	*1*	*2*	*3*	*4*	*5*	*6*	*Totals*
Without promotion	240,000	240,000	240,000	240,000	240,000	240,000	£1,440,000
With promotion	201,600	201,600	288,000	316,800	230,400	201,600	£1,440,000
Gain/(loss)	−38,400	−38,400	48,000	76,800	−9,600	−38,400	£0

Using the sales forecasts we have been given for the six-week period and using the contributions calculated above you can see the effect of the promotion week by week and in total for the six-week period.

The effect of the promotion overall is zero. It has not achieved any additional contribution to profit. It will condense the sales into a two-week period in weeks 3 and 4 when volumes increase substantially to 30,000 and 33,000 units. In these two weeks there are high positive contributions. However, balanced against this in the earlier weeks 1 and 2 the increase in sales volumes is not sufficient to earn a positive contribution, given that there are higher costs incurred in respect of the promotion. Similarly in weeks 5 and 6 volumes are not high enough to outweigh the promotional costs. It may be that we need to rethink the promotion in terms of the discount structure to consumers and retailers to make it work. If we go ahead with the promotion as it stands we would need to ensure that we were achieving other objectives (e.g. sales maximization) apart from increased sales contributions. If increasing the contribution on the product line is our only objective then it is clearly not worthwhile.

Recommendation

It is my recommendation not to proceed with the promotion in its present form for the reasons stated in my analysis above.

It is further recommended that:

1. Clear promotional objectives are stated. These objectives need to consider non-financial as well as financial objectives.
2. Sales forecasts are checked for accuracy and revised as appropriate. We need to be as accurate as possible in our estimate of the effects of the promotion proposed.
3. We review the possibility of sharing costs with those who may benefit from any increased sales the promotion may achieve. The promotion in its current form is unable to demonstrate any tangible benefit to retailers in sharing costs.

4 Alternative methods of promotion be considered and possibly a combination of promotional methods used to achieve our stated objectives. The promotion in its present form only appears to be shifting sales contributions across time periods but not increasing total sales contribution over the promotional period. This provides little benefit to either ourselves or the retailers we supply.

(b) The importance of accurate sales forecasts

In determining the impact of any sales promotion it is important to have accurate sales forecasts. The sales forecast is all-important to the decision. It can be seen from the above example that it is the sales forecast for the promotional period that we have used to calculate our costs and revenues. Accuracy of sales forecasts in making evaluative judgements of this nature are of paramount importance.

Evaluations made based upon less than accurate sales forecasts may lead to incorrect decisions and may as a result lead to unnecessary costs being incurred. Alternatively we may take decisions that overestimate profit contributions for the same reasons. This is why I have stated in my further recommendations that these forecasts are checked for accuracy.

To summarize, accurate sales forecasts should lead to accurate decisions about the effects of promotional activity. It is recognized that predicting future events is risky and uncertain but that we want to minimize risk as far as we can by forecasting as accurately as we can. Overstated sales forecasts will result in decisions that may incur extra costs without any increase in profitability. Understated sales forecasts may lead to a decision that rejects a promotion and which may have proved to be profitable.

Pricing and output decisions

Pricing policy is extremely difficult and there are no easy answers or easy formulae that can be used to decide on a price. Price is dependent on:

- Volume, i.e. sales/output quantity
- Cost structure
- Profit required
- What the market will bear, i.e. market price
- Policy, i.e. management decision
- Market positioning – a management decision related to policy

Cost, profitability and volume may lead us towards a particular pricing decision but market positioning and the longer term strategic pricing objectives also need to be considered. Marketing and selling decisions particularly in the short-term will often revolve round cost–volume–profit decisions. Decisions need to be made with consideration to the available alternatives and questions such as:

- Is the profit level reasonable?
- Can costs be reduced?
- Can volume be increased perhaps through more effective selling or through better planning and more effective promotional activity?
- Is the sales forecast accurate?
- Is the price right, or could volumes be increased at a lower price? In other words how sensitive is demand to price changes?

Answer 4.3

$$\frac{\text{£20,000} + \text{£25,000}}{\text{20 pence contribution per unit}} = \text{225,000 units}$$

Answer 4.4

DPP	£
Sales	25
Less cost of goods sold	5
Gross profit margin	20
Add allowances and discounts	1
Adjusted gross margin	21
Less warehousing costs	4
Less transportation costs	2
Less retail costs	3
Direct product profitability	12

Answer 4.5

The first thing to work out is the margin to establish the cost of the goods sold. You are given the mark-up, which is the profit/cost relationship. The margin is the profit/sales figure. Profit on cost is given at 50/100 to convert this to a margin. The selling price of £10 consists of two elements (cost + profit margin), i.e. 100 + 50 = 150. Therefore, your margin becomes $P/C + P$, i.e. 50/150 = 1/3 or 33.33 per cent.

DPP1	£	*Percentages*
Sales	10.00	100.00
Less cost of goods sold	6.67	66.70
Gross profit margin	3.33	33.30
Add allowances and discounts	0.50	5.00
Adjusted gross margin	3.83	38.30
Less warehousing and Distribution costs	0.70	7.00
Less retail costs	0.50	5.00
Direct product profitability	2.63	26.30

Answer 4.6

On the basis of payback there is no difference between the two promotions; both payback in the fifth month, May. However, from a cash flow point of view promotion (b) would appear to be the one to choose since net cash flows are even at –£15,000 in Jan. and Feb. and positive thereafter at a rate of +£10,000 per month.

Answer 4.7

The project will payback at the end of the second year but this takes no account of the time value of money.

Using a DCF technique such as NPV the cash inflows and outflows are as follows:

Time	*Date*	*£*	*Discount rate*	*£ NPV*
Year 1	Start	–50,000	1.000	–50,000
	End	10,000	0.909	9,090
Year 2	End	40,000	0.826	33,040
Year 3	End	10,000	0.751	7,510
				–360

On the basis of the net present value which is negative at –£360 the decision would be not to go ahead.

Adjusting cash flows for uncertainty

Supposing we were only 95 per cent certain about our forecast cash flows? In such a case we can take account of the uncertainty by adjusting the expected values to 95 per cent of the full value.

Time	*Date*	*£*	*Discount rate*	*£ NPV*	*95 per cent confident*
Year 1	Start	−50,000	1.000	−50,000	−47,500.00
	End	10,000	0.909	9,090	8,635.50
Year 2	End	40,000	0.826	33,040	31,388.00
Year 3	End	10,000	0.751	7,510	7,134.50
				−360	−342

Answer 4.8

Plastic Toy Co. Ltd

Budgeted profit and loss summary for the year ending . . . .

Activity level	*10,000 units Normal production*		*10,000 units French order*		*20,000 units Total*	
	£	£	£	£	£	£
Sales		120,000		60,000		180,000
Less direct costs						
Direct labour	20,000		20,000		40,000	
Direct material	10,000		10,000		20,000	
Direct expenses	1,000		1,000		2,000	
Prime cost		31,000		31,000		62,000
Contribution		89,000		29,000		118,000
Production overheads	20,000	20,000	0	0	20,000	20,000
Production cost	51,000		31,000		82,000	
Gross profit		69,000		29,000		98,000
Less overheads						
Administration	£5,000		0		5,000	
Sales and marketing	£5,000		0		5,000	
Finance overheads	£2,000		0		2,000	
Total overheads		12,000		0		12,000
Net profit		57,000		29,000		86,000

	Before	*After*	*Combined*
Contribution/sales ratio	74%	48%	66%
Gross profit/sales	58%	48%	54%
Net profit/sales	48%	48%	48%

To: Sales director

From: Sales and marketing manager

Date: xx/xx/xxxx

Subject: viability of the proposed French order

(a) You will see from the profit and loss summary attached that if we do not accept the French order we would make a profit for the year of £57,000 based on our budgeted 50 per cent capacity.

(b) If we accept the French order, you will note that the annual profit is increased by £29,000 to bring the annual budgeted profit to £86,000 overall. This is because we do not incur any additional fixed costs on the export order. The only additional costs are the marginal cost of producing an additional 10,000 units. The fixed overheads are fixed whether we make only 5,000 units or 20,000 units. The French order should be accepted since it will make a positive contribution to profit.

(i) If we analyse the profit margins for the position before the order and the position after the order we get the following:

	Before	*After*	*Combined*
Contribution/sales ratio	74%	48%	66%
Gross profit/sales	58%	48%	54%
Net profit/sales	48%	48%	48%

Although the contribution to sales ratio and the gross profit to sales ratio will fall substantially from the normal (budgeted) position i.e. 74 per cent to 48 per cent this is not important to our decision. You will see that net profit margins have been maintained at 48 per cent. It is the 50 per cent discount on the overseas order that has led to the gross margin decline. Furthermore, total profitability will increase by £29,000 if we accept the order.

(ii) The only concern about accepting the French order would be the effect that it may have on our existing customers should they discover that we have discounted a 'one off' order when they are buying regularly at full price. It is important that confidentiality is maintained.

(iii) Whilst I am recommending that we accept this order based on marginal cost it is important to recognize the dangers of judging all orders on this basis since we could end up with substantially reduced profit margins. Marginal costing is suitable for considering 'one-offs' or special orders but if we applied marginal costing to all decisions in the long term we could end up not covering overhead costs. For instance, consider a situation where a firm has ten production lines all costed to recover the firm's total overheads. If we were happy that full recovery of all overheads could be achieved by running eight of the lines at full cost, this would allow flexibility for the two of the lines to charge only marginal costs. Any contribution made by the two lines would make a contribution to profit. If however we decided to expand this to further production lines, you can see that we would not cover our overheads in full. It is important to recognize that pricing on the basis of marginal costs may be dangerous in the longer term.

2 Supposing the order from the French firm became a regular order rather than a 'one-off' then it should carry a proportion of overhead costs. If we take the current position where the factory is essentially producing an identical product for the home market and the export market with the same direct cost structure, it would be necessary to apportion overheads on some reasonable basis. If we did not charge overheads to the French orders we would be effectively subsidizing the French production costs from the home produced plastic toys. This is not equitable. Since all

production would be using resources in equal amounts it would seem reasonable for each unit of product to carry its fair share of overhead costs. Therefore, on the basis of the financial data we have, I would suggest overheads could be recovered on a unit cost basis. This would mean, for example, in the case of production overheads which are currently £20,000 we would need to recover £1 for each toy produced (£20,000/20,000 plastic toys). It is also important to recognize that the production of 20,000 plastic toys represents 100 per cent. This means that there is now no room for any margin of error in production. Any down time and the production would be lost. If the firm is able to secure additional production capacity through efficiency gains then any overheads charged against that production would in fact be an over-recovery of the total overheads which in effect is additional contribution (and in this case would increase profit by the same amount of over-recovery).

Unit 5 Budgeting

Objectives

After studying this unit you should be able to:

- ❑ Define budgeting and recognize the part that budgets play in providing managers with financial information on which to plan and control activities.
- ❑ Know what is meant by the terms fixed, flexible and zero based budgets.
- ❑ Know the various sub budgets and how they link with the master budgets.
- ❑ Recognize the importance of cash budgeting.
- ❑ Know and understand the importance of standard costing and variance analysis in providing managers with information on which to plan and control.

Study Guide

This is a very important unit. It is also a very long unit. A number of concepts underlying budgeting and budgetary control systems are explained within the unit. It is also probably one of the major concerns for marketing and sales managers as they develop in their careers. It is essential that budgets are understood thoroughly. Budgets are operational plans that need to be controlled by managers who have responsibility for them. You may need to budget for people, resources, sales, costs and overhead expenses. Departmental budgets are often the responsibility of a department manager. Product and brands may have their own budgets and the product manager or brand manager will have responsibility for costs and revenues associated with them.

You will probably need to concentrate hard when working through this unit. There may be a number of new terms that you need to learn and understand. In addition you will need to learn how to prepare budgets and interpret them.

It is important to recognize that costing systems may use forecasts, actual costs or standard costs on which budgets may be based.

Exam Hints

Exam questions in this area may require you to prepare summarized budgets from data given. The question will nearly always have a part related to the underlying principles. It is the information that budgets provide for marketing and sales managers that is important and it is insufficient merely to develop proficiency in computational skills.

Budgeting questions could investigate: master budgets for the whole firm (P&L, balance sheet and cash flow statements) or for specific products or departments e.g. a promotional budget, a marketing budget, a budget for product X etc.

Introduction

Budgets are needed to plan, control and implement decisions based upon the plan or in the light of a control variance i.e. a difference between the plan and the actual result. A budget is a financial plan. Budgets are statements that show expected income and expected costs and expenses for a specific time period. Budgets are prepared annually but they may have weekly or monthly control periods. In profit organizations the budgeting process will begin with a sales forecast. The sales forecast is needed to work out what other costs and expenses will be necessary to support that level of sales. The sales forecast itself is not a budget. It is a forecast. Sales forecasts will be estimated based upon forecast demand for each product or service provided by the firm. The sales budget will then be produced, based on the sales forecast quantities at the forecast selling prices by product, and for the budget period. Once the sales budget has been agreed, it is necessary to work out the cost of the products or services sold. This is calculated by taking the sales budget at cost prices. For example, if you sell 100 items at £20 each it may only have cost £10 to produce the item and therefore, the cost of making the sale is £10 × 100 = £1,000. The sales income will be £20 × 100 = £2,000 and gross profit is £1,000.

Activity 5.1

You have been given a sales forecast quantity of 1,000 units for the month of April. The forecast selling price is £15. The forecast selling price is usually cost plus 100 per cent. Prepare a brief budget for this particular product line that shows: sales budget, cost of sales budget and gross profit budget. (**Answer** See end of chapter.)

Definition 5.1

A budget is a plan in financial and/or quantitative terms. It may show volumes as well as values. It is normally for a specific period of time, e.g. most organizations will prepare an annual budget which will normally be split up into smaller control periods – say one month. Budgets are prepared for the various activities undertaken by the firm or they may be for products, locations (sites or strategic business units) and functions (e.g. production, sales, marketing, administration etc.)

Fixed and flexible budgets

Budgets may be either fixed, meaning that the budget is fixed at the start of a period and is not adjusted to take account of any changes to volumes sold or prices; or a budget is flexible, meaning that it can be changed during the budget period to reflect changing quantities sold or prices.

Definition 5.2

A *fixed budget* is set at the start of the budget period and is unable to be adapted to changes in volume or price. A *flexible budget* is adjusted for changes in volumes and prices when necessary.

Zero based budgeting (ZBB)

A zero based budget means exactly what it implies – you commence the budgeting process from a zero base. The firm will begin its estimations for each category of expense assuming that we begin from scratch a zero base, unlike ordinary budgets which usually start their estimate from a previous year's actual expenditure and increase it by a set percentage. The major advantage of this method of setting a budget is that managers need to analyse their resource requirements for the present budget period without referring back to previous budgets. The major disadvantage of zero based budgets is the time needed to prepare them.

Definition 5.3

Zero based budgeting is the preparation of a budget for the current period based upon the current period sales forecasts and management forecasts of costs and expenditures that are likely to happen as a result of that sales activity. There is no need to refer to historical budgets or actual results.

Extending Activity 5.1

See if you can identify what type of budgeting is undertaken by your own organization. Do they use fixed budgets, flexible budgeting or zero based budgeting?

The chart shows the relationship between the various parts of a budgetary control system. There may be limiting factors or budgetary constraints. For example, the demand for the firm's products may be limited in some way, or the firm's capacity to satisfy the demand is limited or there is a shortage of available materials to produce the goods required. Any sales forecast produced by the firm will need to take account of these limiting factors. Once the sales forecast is complete for each activity and a sales budget is agreed the next step is to produce the production budget. Production will be dependent upon the stocks available and the materials that may be purchased in the period. Material purchases do not merely depend upon availability of materials but will depend upon the working capital policy i.e. will enough cash be generated from sales and will it be collected from customers (debtors) in time to pay suppliers (creditors) as their accounts become payable? The firm's policy towards working capital is important. Remember working capital consists of stocks, debtors and prepayments, bank and cash, less any sums owed (current liabilities) to suppliers.

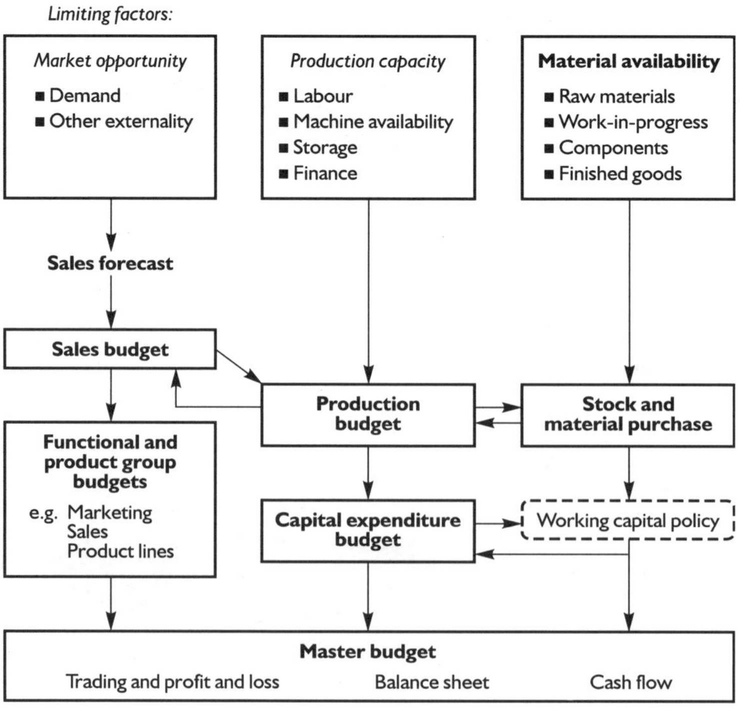

Figure 5.1
The budgeting process

Definition 5.4

Current assets less current liabilities is the working capital.

Working capital policy is laid down by the managers and will cover such things as the amounts of stock that should be held at any point in time, how much credit to extend to customers and how quickly creditor accounts will be settled. You can see that this policy will affect the firm's cash flows. For example, if you decide not to limit the amounts of stock held and you decide to extend credit to customers for 90 days and creditors demand that their accounts are settled promptly within 30 days of the purchase, your cash flow will be slow and may at times be insufficient to meet current liabilities as they fall due. Let us further consider the example with some numbers attached. We find that we need to produce 12,000 units in a year: materials cost £10 per unit and have to be paid for within 30 days; on average it takes 30 days in store before production commences on 1,000 units, and 30 days more to produce the finished article and sell them; customers agree to pay 90 days after they receive delivery. The selling price per unit is £20.

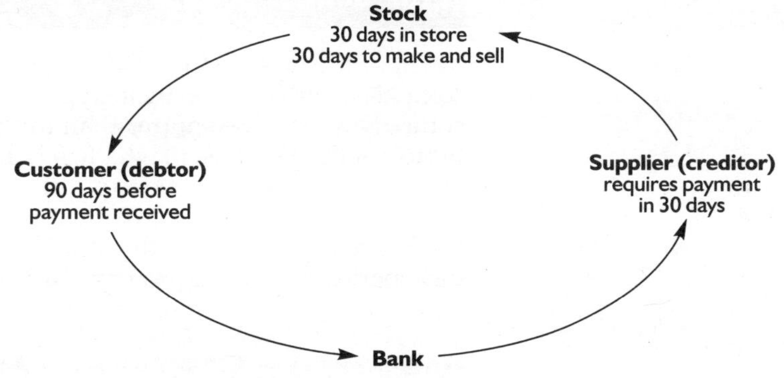

Figure 5.2
Working capital cycle and policy (1)

You can see if we just follow through one monthly cycle that the supplier will need to be paid in 30 days time from delivery of the materials and that the firm will not be paid by the customer until 150 days have elapsed (i.e. 30 days in store + 30 days to make and sell + 90 days credit allowed). The supplier will want 1,000 × £10 = £10,000 in thirty days and the firm would have to meet this liability from other sources of capital (e.g. money already in the bank or an overdraft facility). In 150 days time the firm will receive in cash 1,000 × £20 = £20,000 thus earning a gross profit on the sale of £10,000. However, if the firm had to use an overdraft at 12 per cent per annum it would be costing 150/365 × 12 per cent × £10,000 = £493.15. The introduction of a policy towards working capital could significantly reduce this cost. Let us consider that the firm is able to renegotiate with suppliers to extend their credit to 60 days; a just-in-time policy towards stock on hand is introduced so that stock arrives only on the day required for production to commence; goods are sold in advance of ordering any stock and customer credit is reduced to 60 days. The cycle now looks like this:

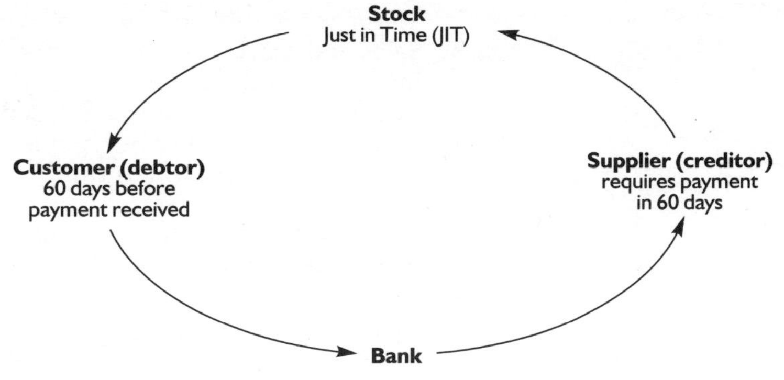

Figure 5.3
Working capital cycle and policy (2)

You can see that the money will arrive from the customer at the same time the supplier is paid. Assuming no transaction times (e.g. cheque clearing the bank) the cash will be available when required to settle the liability. This is why a working capital policy is needed. Cash budgets (and cash flow forecasts) will be based upon this working capital policy.

Once the production and material budgets are complete, functional and expense budgets can be completed for all the relevant overhead accounts such as marketing, selling and promotional costs, distribution, administration and so on. Also the production budget may identify capacity problems that can only be rectified by capital expenditure on fixed assets: plant, equipment, machinery, vehicles etc. Working capital policy may affect the funding decision related to capital expenditures. For example, sufficiently healthy cash flows might mean that capital expenditure is financed through sales revenue rather than fresh capital or a loan.

Once all the sub budgets are completed, the master budget for the whole company is produced in terms of a trading and profit and loss account for the period, a balance sheet and a cash budget.

The budget period

In most businesses the budget period is for one year, and it normally coincides with the financial year of the business. Control periods will certainly need to be shorter than one year. A critical factor is that a specific period of time is chosen, which is most suitable to the business in question. As previously mentioned control periods are usually weeks, months or quarters. Budgets that are drawn up for a period longer than one year may tend to lose impact and deviate from their original objective, because the time period is too long to estimate activities with accuracy.

Budgetary control and variances

To be effective in achieving any plan you need to control the plan and it is the same for budgets. A budget needs to be controlled. One way this is achieved is to break down the budget into smaller control periods, and to measure variances between the actual results and the plan (budget). Action will need to be taken as appropriate either to adjust the budget or to adjust the actual activities to keep to the plan. Variances may occur for the following reasons:

Internal factors

- The organization may change in terms of structure and therefore the planned expenditures are not appropriate within the budget headings originally assigned. For example, if previously when a budget was set and agreed, sales and marketing were a single departmental function but during the budget period they were reorganized into two separate departments, one for sales and one for marketing then the budgets would need to be adjusted in some way to reflect the change.
- Productive capacity may change, owing to the purchase of new plant and machinery or methods of working.
- Sales and marketing policy may become more effective, thus penetrating new markets or by increasing market share. Opening up new markets may mean that a revised sales budget is needed.
- Other personnel may become more or less effective in their roles, and this may be identified through efficiency variances actual against budget.
- Constraints originally imposed when the budget was set may have been removed, e.g. shortage of capital for expansion.
- The firm may develop new products and services that require a switch in the way resources were originally allocated. Alternatively, existing products or services may be deleted.

Summary	£ Actual	£ Budgeted	£ Over Budget	£ Under Budget
Total income	131,000.00	138,400.00		–7,400.00
Total expenses	99,620.00	101,300.00		–1,680.00
Income less expenses:	31,380.00	37,100.00		–5,720.00

Income details	Actual	Budgeted	Over Budget	Under Budget	Notes
Sales	120,000.00	130,000.00		–10,000.00	
Interest earned	5,000.00	4,500.00	500.00		
Fees	2,000.00	500.00	1,500.00		
Commissions	1,000.00	200.00	800.00		
Rent	0.00	0.00			
Royalties	3,000.00	3,200.00		–200.00	
Other	0.00	0.00			
Total Income:	131,000.00	138,400.00		–7,400.00	

Expense details	Actual	Budgeted	Over Budget	Under Budget	Notes
Marketing and selling					
Salaries and wages	35,000.00	34,000.00	1,000.00		
Sales Commissions	3,500.00	3,400.00	100.00		
Promotion	7,500.00	9,000.00		–1,500.00	
Advertising	15,000.00	17,500.00		–2,500.00	
Delivery	1,000.00	500.00	500.00		
Shipping	500.00	150.00	350.00		
Travel	2,000.00	2,500.00		–500.00	
Other	0.00	0.00			
Total sales expenses:	64,500.00	67,050.00		–2,550.00	
Percent of total:	64.75%	66.19%			
Administrative					
Salaries and wages	25,000.00	26,500.00		1,500.00	
Employee benefits	3,000.00	3,400.00		–400.00	
Payroll taxes	2,000.00	2,300.00		–300.00	
Insurance	1,000.00	1,200.00		–200.00	
Loan interest	150.00	150.00			
Office supplies	200.00	100.00	100.00		
Travel and entertainment	220.00	250.00		–30.00	
Postage	300.00	350.00		–50.00	
Other		0.00			
Total admin. expenses:	31,870.00	34,250.00		–2,380.00	
Percent of total:	31.99%	33.81%			
Service and equipment					
Accounting	1,000.00	750.00	250.00		
Legal	500.00	300.00	200.00		
Utilities	300.00	240.00	60.00		
Telephone	200.00	190.00	10.00		
Rent and maintenance	1,250.00	1,250.00			
Other	0.00				
Total S&E expenses:	3,250.00	2,730.00	520.00		
Percent of total:	3.26%	2.69%			

Figure 5.4
Business budget – 05/96

External factors

- Market conditions may change causing a shift in demand.
- Government policy with regard to the industry or the particular type of business may also change, e.g. increased or reduced taxation, legislation and general attitude.
- Inflation may increase costs and revenues. In monetary terms variances may occur but in volume terms the budget may be achieved.
- Exchange rate fluctuations may affect imports and exports.
- Changes in the demand for and supply of labour and other resources may give rise to price changes and wage rates.

These lists are not exhaustive, but rather they give some measure of the considerations to be made when budgets are formulated, and furthermore show why longer periods than one year are difficult to plan for. Nevertheless most businesses of medium or large size will tend to plan for a period of five years. This is often referred to as the corporate plan. The annual budget will be only one component in that plan.

The corporate plan is designed to focus attention on the longer term. It may therefore be regarded as a policy document or as an executive plan, rather than an operational plan which is what the budget is. A typical budget report for a service company is given for the month of May.

Variances are identified in terms of budgeted and actual out-turns. Rather than a single column showing variances, this particular budget report highlights the important variances as under budget or over budget and shows them in a different column for ease of reading. The report also highlights the main overhead cost centres as a proportion of total cost. For instance, total service and equipment costs are shown at 3.26 per cent for actual and 2.69 per cent budget. This is in fact being used as a control ratio to measure the actual performance against the budget.

Control ratios and budgeting

Budgets may be provided showing control ratios that indicate how well you are or are not doing against the budget. Control ratios may be expressed as percentages of the total spend or as percentages of sales turnover. In our budgeting example we had some control ratios provided in terms of a percentage of the total spend.

Ratios can be provided for gross profit to sales or contribution to sales; net profit to sales and for each cost or expense category to sales. Ratios may also be prepared for the budgeted balance sheet as a control against the actual balance sheet. The purpose of the ratios when acting as a control measure is for managers to act upon the information revealed from actual out-turns against the budget so as to keep the budget on course for the next financial period. (**See** Ratios and their interpretation.)

Extending Activity 5.2

Try to obtain a copy of your firm's budget reports and see how that is laid out. Note there are many ways to report variances. The usual way is to show some kind of profit and loss summary, showing a budget an actual and a variance. Are any control ratios shown?

Flexible budgeting – an example

A flexible budget is designed to recognize the difference in behaviour between fixed and variable costs in relation to changes to output or turnover. The budget will therefore be amended in each control period in line with the level of current activity.

Given the data supplied below, your sales manager has asked you to prepare a flexible budget at the 80 per cent level of activity for two product lines P and Q.

Sales at 100 per cent of budget are expected to be £312,500 for P and £375,000 for Q.
Direct labour cost is 10 per cent of the sales value for P and 12 per cent for Q.
Direct material cost is 30 per cent of the sales value for P and 35 per cent for Q.
Variable overheads are 20 per cent of sales value for both P and Q.
Fixed overheads are budgeted at £15,000.

Flexible budget for product lines P and Q for the year to 31 December – activity level 80 per cent

	P	*Q*
	£	£
Sales	250,000	300,000
Direct costs:		
Labour	25,000	36,000
Materials	75,000	105,000
Variable overheads	50,000	60,000
Contribution	100,000	99,000
Fixed overheads	15,000	15,000
Net profit	85,000	84,000

Cash budgeting

Cash budgets are essential forecasts to keep the business alive. Cash flow is the life blood of the business – without cash, no matter how profitable a business is, it cannot survive. Sufficient cash needs to be generated from operations to oil the working capital cycle.

Cash is necessary to pay suppliers (trade creditors), and expenses as they fall due. It is important therefore to ensure liquidity. The business will have to make sure that enough cash is available to meet its liabilities when payments fall due. This demands cash planning (or cash budgeting). Cash planning and control will also involve managing the working capital of the business as discussed elsewhere.

If the firm's liquidity is reduced and there is a shortage of cash a number of options are possible, some of which are listed below:

- The firm may have sufficient cash from other sources to pay the creditor but of course the firm should recognize that there is an *opportunity cost* in doing so. For example, had the firm not used its own cash it may have invested that cash and earned interest.
- The firm could try to renegotiate the credit period being allowed by the supplier. Alternatively, the firm could extend the credit period without asking the supplier but at the risk of not being supplied in future or at being charged higher future prices by the supplier or receiving a reduced credit facility.
- The firm could choose to borrow funds as a short term basis to tide it over the short term cash crisis. For example, negotiate a bank overdraft.
- The growing business, finding itself in a liquidity crisis, could be the victim of its own success and be experiencing a position known as *overtrading*. This is when a firm is successfully increasing business turnover quickly and, because of this expansion of sales, debtors are increasing, stock levels increase and creditors grow to supply the extra stock needed to supply customers. In such cases, the firm is really under capitalized for the level of activity it is now undertaking. The firm should consider the introduction of fresh capital to reduce the risks of a liquidity crises that may damage the growth.

Profit is not cash

Profit will be different from the cash position owing to: matching period costs such as depreciation, other non-cash provision and expenses and owing to adjustments for stock, debtors and creditors. The cash flow statement will also include opening cash balances, capital or borrowed funds introduced, other cash receipts which do not affect profit and cash payments to creditors which do not affect profit and to purchase capital items not affecting profit immediately but charged as depreciation in the appropriate period.

Cash budget example

Eric Nixon decides to set up a business with £10,000 in capital on 1 January and completes the following transactions:

Buys fixtures for a shop paying £4,000 by cash on 1 January.
Agrees to rent a shop at a cost of £8,000 per annum payable quarterly on the first day of January, April, July and October.
Stock is purchased on credit terms payment to be made one month after the month of purchase. £6,000 is purchased in January, March and May.
Monthly expenses paid in cash are: wages £500 and promotion £600.
Business rates are payable £1,920 per annum. The full amount is payable by 30 June.

(**Note**: Fixtures will be depreciated at 20 per cent per annum on cost.)

Sales for each of the first six months to 30 June have been forecast and the sales budgeted are as follows: January, £6,000; February, £4,000; March, £8,000; April, £7,000; May, £10,000 and June, £8,000.

Payment is expected from customers in the month following the month of sale. Nixon intends to achieve a gross profit margin of 50 per cent. Let us now take a look at the cash budget for this business for the first six months:

Eric Nixon – Cash budget for six months to 30 June

	Jan	*Feb*	*Mar*	*Apr*	*May*	*Jun*
Cash balance start	10,000	2,900	1,800	4,700	3,600	9,500
Receipts						
Debtors (customers)	0	6,000	4,000	8,000	7,000	10,000
Other						
Total receipts	10,000	8,900	5,800	12,700	10,600	19,500
Payments						
Creditors (stock)	0	6,000	0	6,000	0	6,000
Rent	2,000			2,000		
Rates						1,920
Promotions	600	600	600	600	600	600
Wages	500	500	500	500	500	500
Capital expenditure (fixtures)	4,000					
Total payments	7,100	7,100	1,100	9,100	1,100	9,020
Cash balance end	2,900	1,800	4,700	3,600	9,500	10,480

Let us now take a look at the trading and profit and loss account for the first six months of this business and confirm that cash is not the same as profit.

Eric Nixon – Budgeted trading and profit and loss account for six months to 30 June

	£	£	
Sales turnover		43,000	
Less cost of sales	21,500		
Gross profit		21,500	50 per cent margin
Less expenses			
Rent	4,000		
Rates	960		
Promotion	3,600		
Wages	3,000		
Depreciation*	400		
Total expenses		11,960	
Net profit/(loss)		9,540	

Note: Depreciation is a non cash expense not included therefore in the cash flow statement but it does affect profit (calculated 20 per cent × £4,000 cost × ½ year).

Important points to note are:

- Gross profit is:

  = 50 per cent (margin) × £43,000 (sales)

  = £21,500

  Cost of sales = sales £43,000 – Gross profit £21,500

  Cost of sales = £21,500 *in this case* COS is also 50 per cent.
- Only cash payments and receipts appear in the cash flow statement and they appear in the period (month) in which they are paid or received in cash.
- Non-cash items such as provision for depreciation and doubtful debts do not have a place in the cash flow forecast. Such items are profit and loss account allocations. They do affect profit, but are not cash receipts or payments.
- Profit is not the same as cash. For example, in the example the cash available to Nixon at 30 June is £10,480. Profit for the 6 months to 30 June is £9,540. The difference between cash and profit may be explained as follows:

  Differences between cash and profit

  Reconciliation statement

		£
Closing cash balance		10,480
Net profit per P&L a/c		9,540
Difference		940
Explained by:		
Debtors		8,000
Prepayment (rates)		960
Less:		
Creditor (stock bought)		–3,500
Non cash exp. depreciation		–400
		5060
Change in cash due to cap. exp.		
Opening cash balance	10,000	
Capital expenditure	–4,000	
		6,000
Difference between cash and profit		940

The cash position is £940 less than profit because:

- Sales income for June is still outstanding as 'Debtors £8,000'.
- Stock purchased for £3,500 is included in the cost of sales figure and has been budgeted for in the trade creditors figure shown on the budgeted balance sheet. Note we were originally told that Nixon planned to buy 3 × £6,000 lots of stock in the period, but when we calculated the cost of sales at 50 per cent of the sales revenue this came to £21,500 which would mean that he would not have enough stock to sell, i.e. a shortfall of £3,500. We therefore adjusted the plan (budget) by allowing for an extra stock purchase of £3,500.
- Only the expenses for the period (following the matching principles) are charged against the profit and loss account, whereas all cash paid for expenses regardless of the period for which they are incurred have been paid in cash. There is a prepayment of rates £960 for ½ year.
- Capital expenditure has been paid in cash, whereas in the profit and loss account only the estimated proportion of capital cost deemed to have reduced the value of the asset through usage (i.e. depreciation) is charged against the profit and loss account for the period, once again following the matching principle.
- The final difference between cash and profit comprises the change in the opening cash balance.

To summarize, profit will differ from cash owing to: matching period costs such as depreciation, other non-cash provision and expenses, and owing to adjustments for stock, debtors and creditors. The cash flow statement will also include opening cash balances, capital or borrowed funds introduced, other cash receipts which do not affect profit, and cash payments to creditors which do not affect profit. Buying any capital items does not affect profit but will affect the cash position if payment is made. *Capital expenditure* will add to the firm's *fixed assets* and a charge for their use will later affect profit as *depreciation* is charged in the appropriate period.

For completeness Nixon's budgeted balance sheet is given below:

Eric Nixon's balance sheet as at 31 December

	£	£	£
Fixed assets	*Cost*	*Depreciation*	*Net Book value*
Fixtures	4,000	400	3,600
Current assets			
Stocks and WIP	0		
Debtors	8,000		
Prepayment (rates)	960		
Bank and cash	10,480		
		19,440	
Less current liabilities			
Trade creditors (stock sold)		3,500	
Net current assets + working capital			15,940
			19,540
Financed by			
Capital	10,000		
Add retained net profit	9,540		
Capital employed			19,540

You should note that a trade creditor has been included for stock budgeted to be sold in the period that was not indicated in the original plan. This is because we worked out that a 50 per cent margin would mean that 50 per cent of the sales value represents the cost of the goods sold. Since Nixon only plans to buy 3 lots at £6,000 each time, he will be £3,500 short of stock to sell at the planned level of sales, i.e. £21,500.

Question 5.1

From the following transactions prepare a cash budget and a budgeted profit and loss for the three months to May:

Sales are £3,000 each month paid by the customer one month after the sale is invoiced.

Purchases of stock £4,000 in March and £2,000 in May payable one month after purchase.

Other cash expenses include:

Wages paid each month £250.
Telephone payable in May for March, April and May £300.
For the profit and loss account you will need to charge depreciation for existing fixed assets at 25 per cent per annum of their cost £10,000.
The opening cash balance at the bank on 1 March is £2,000.
Debtors due to pay in March are £2,000.
The gross profit margin is 40 per cent.

Responsibility accounting and budgeting

A budget is a plan. Plans need to be controlled. For a plan to have effective control someone needs to accept responsibility for the plan. Usually departmental heads will be responsible for a department. Brand managers or product managers will have responsibility for the brands or products within their domain.

Definition 5.5

Responsibility centre A unit or function of an organization headed by a manager who has direct responsibility for its performance. For example a marketing manager may head the responsibility centre for marketing. This will mean having full responsibility for all revenue and costs attributable to the centre. The manager will be involved in setting and agreeing budgets and for controlling them.

Other types of accountability and responsibility may be agreed with a manager in terms of a budget. For example the manager may be given responsibility for profit. A *profit centre* is a division of an organization to which both expenditure and revenue are attributable and in respect of which profitability can be assessed (CIMA terminology). Alternatively managers may be given responsibility for costs only. In other words they are not responsible for any revenue.

You are presented with the planning process in diagramatic form in Figure 5.5. Planning begins with a forecast of conditions and expectations. For example, forecast sales for a future period. The forecast needs to take into account all the external factors in the environment. The forecast will impact upon objectives, strategies and tactics. Another factor impacting upon the objectives will be recent experiences of the organization in terms of capability and achievements. Once the plans are agreed, standards will be set that are capable of measuring the performance with a view to controlling them. One such standard is a budget. Having set budget standards somebody needs to be assigned responsibility for achieving them. For example, the sales director or a sales manager will be responsible for all sales. Performance will be measured by comparing the actual results against the budget and appropriate corrective action will be taken by the people responsible for achieving the plan.

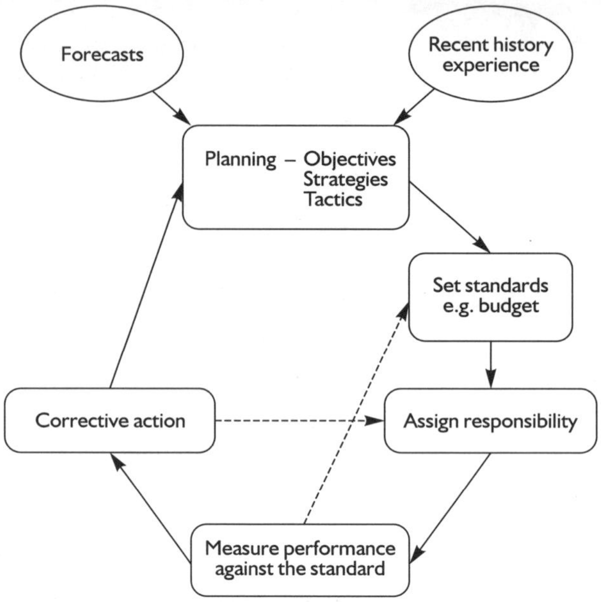

Figure 5.5
The planning process

Standard costs and variances

Many organizations operate a standard costing system. Their budgets will be prepared using standard costing. A standard cost is a pre-determined estimate which may be compared with actual costs as they are incurred. The difference between the two is described as a *variance. A favourable variance* occurs when the actual cost is lower than the standard cost, an *unfavourable variance* (also referred to as an adverse variance) is when the actual cost exceeds the standard. Standard costs are useful to control the activities of the firm. Actual costs may be compared against a predetermined standard cost to see how well the department or firm is doing against the standard. It is important that the standards being used are up to date if they are to act as a control in the way explained. In practice one of the many problems with standard costing systems is that they are not kept up to date, and therefore their relevance may be lost as a means of control. A firm may be trying to control against a standard that is out of date. For example, if organizational structures change or methods of production are changed then standards need to reflect the changes.

Exam Hints

You should make sure that you understand the nature and purpose of standard costing in relation to budgeting and budgetary control. An examination question could ask you to calculate a simple variance from data provided to reveal information about sales or costs. The calculation itself will never form the whole question, and it is the underlying principles that are important from an information viewpoint. In other words what does the variance tell us?

(The examples shown in this section on standard costing are provided with permission from *Foundation Accounting* written by me.)

Material price variance

Price variance = (Standard price – actual price) × actual quantity (SP – AP) × AQ

Material usage variance

Usage variance = (Standard quantity – actual quantity) × standard price (SQ – AQ) × SP

Direct wage rate variance

= (Standard rate per hour – actual rate) × no. of hours worked (SR – AR) × AH

Direct wage efficiency variance

= (Standard no. of hours – actual no. of hours) × standard rate per hour (SH – AH) × SR

Example

The standard cost information for the production of one unit of product X is as follows:

Direct materials 5 kilograms of material Y at 60p per kilogram.

During a certain cost period, 4,000 units of X were manufactured and the material used in production was 20,200 kilograms of Y at a total cost of £11,716. Calculate the material cost variance and separate the results into a price and usage variance.

		£
STD direct materials (4,000 × £3)		12,000
Actual cost		11,716
	Favourable variance	284 F

The question now arises – was it a price or material usage variance?

Price variance

= (SP – AP) × AQ

= (£0.60 – £0.58) × 20,200

= £404 (favourable price variance)

Price variance £404 F

Material usage variance

(SQ – AQ) × SP

(20,000–20,200) × £0.60 = £120 (adverse material variance)

Material variance (£120) A

Taking the two constituent variances together we have a net favourable material cost volume of £284 F.

Reasons for material price variance

- Efficient or inefficient buying of materials.
- A reduction in production may mean smaller amounts purchased, therefore a loss of quantity discount. The reverse may also be true i.e. an

increase in the amounts of material bought leading to increasing discounts.

- The need to acquire emergency supplies may lead to higher prices. For example, when your *just-in-time* system of stock replenishment fails.
- Changing quality of the material purchased.
- The loss of a source of supply which was inexpensive.
- External factors, e.g. if you buy from abroad, exchange rates. Other factors – inflation.

Reasons for usage variance

- Inefficiency by an operator using the material (if not watching a machine and a fault occurs, e.g. in printing – operative may fail to turn off machine in time to minimize quantity of paper spoilt).
- Spoilages – due to insufficient maintenance of machinery.
- Substitution of poor quality material resulting in lost production.
- Change in the methods of production which makes the standard being used obsolete.
- Inadequate storage, causing damage.
- If the actual mix of materials in the product changes, then the usage variance would change also.

Direct wage cost variances

Using the same example, direct wage costs at standard for product X are 3 hours at £2 per hour.

4,000 units were produced in 11,750 hours, at a labour cost of £24,675. Thus the actual hourly rate paid was £2.10.

		£
STD direct wages (4,000 units at £6 p.u.)		24,000
Actual cost		24,675
	Adverse variance	(675) A

This may be further analysed to reveal the following information:

		£
Direct wage rate variance		
(SR – AR) × AH		
= (2 – 2.10) × 11,750	=	(1,175) A
Direct wage efficiency variance		
(SH – AH) × SR		
= (12,000 – 11,750) × 2	=	500 F
		(675) A

Here it is wage rates that are the cause of the adverse variance overall. For example, a pay rise may have been agreed at some time during the year after the standards had been agreed. There is also an efficiency variance that means the employees have produced the goods at less than the standard time allowed.

Reasons for wage rate variances

- Pay rises which have not been budgeted for.
- Using different grades of labour whose rates differ from those specified in the standard cost of the product.

Reasons for labour efficiency variances

- The efficiency or inefficiency of the labour employed on production. This may arise from using different grades of labour from those who normally do the job, for example, trainees.
- A change in production methods.
- Machine breakdowns.
- Correction of spoiled work.
- Bad production planning, e.g. machines not available when required or material stockouts.
- The purchase of new or more efficient machinery leading to better labour utilization.

Variable production overhead variance

This is the difference between the standard variable production overhead absorbed in the actual production and the actual variable production overhead. There can be no quantity variance, this is because the standard and the actual are measured using the same level of output, e.g. the budgeted variable production overhead for the month of June is £15,000 for a budgeted production of 12,000 units. The actual figures were £14,600 variable overhead expenditure for an actual production of 12,500 units.

Variable overhead production variance

	£
Standard cost of actual production	
$£15{,}000 \times \dfrac{12{,}500}{12{,}000}$	15,625
Actual cost	14,600
	1,025 F

Fixed production overhead variance

This is defined in the CIMA terminology as 'The difference between the standard cost of fixed overheads absorbed in the production achieved whether completed or not and the fixed overhead attributed and charged to that period'. It consists of two elements: a volume variance and an expenditure variance.

Volume variance

= (Actual hours – budgeted hours) × budgeted absorption rate

Expenditure variance

= (Budgeted fixed overhead – actual fixed overhead)

Example

The budgeted fixed overhead for May was £12,000.

The budget output in terms of standard hours was 5,000 hours. The actual fixed overhead was £12,300, and the actual production expressed in standard hours 5,500.

$5{,}500 \times \dfrac{£12{,}000}{5{,}000 \text{ hrs}}$	i.e £2.40	13,200
Actual fixed overhead		12,300
		900 F

Volume variance

= (Actual hours – budgeted hours) × budgeted absorption rate

		£
=	(5,500 – 5,000) × 2.40	
=	500 × 2.40	1,200 F

Expenditure variance

=	12,000 – 12,300	(300) A
		900 F

Sales variances

Operating profit variance due to sale

Sales price variance	*Sales volume variance*
(ACT SP – STD SP) × ACT Q	(ACT Q – budgeted Q) × STD unit operating profit

Example

A business manufactures a single product. The budget for May gives the following information relating to sales:

Quantity	10,000 units
Selling price	£20 p.u.
Standard cost	£14 p.u.

During the month 9,600 units were sold and the invoiced value of sales £196,800 = £20.50 per unit.

Let us now calculate:

- The operating profit variance due to sales.
- The sales price variance.
- The sales volume variance.

Reasons for a sales price variance

- Offering a discount.
- Changing selling price.

Operating profit variance

			£
a)	Budgeted operating profit 10,000 units × £20 p.u. – £14 p.u.		60,000
b)	Actual sales	196,800	
c)	Standard cost of actual sales 9,600 (actual sales) × £14 (standard cost)	134,400	
d)	Margin between actual sales and standard cost of sales (b) – (c)		62,400
	Operating profit variance due to sales (60,000 – 62,400)		2,400 F

	£
Sales price variance (ACT SP – STD SP) × ACT Q (20.5–20) × 9,600 0.50 × 9,600 = 4,800 F	4,800 F
Sales volume variance (ACT Q – budgeted Q) × STD unit operating profit (9,600 – 10,000) × £6 –400 × 6 = (2,400) A	(2,400) A
	2,400 F

Reasons for volume variance

The budget sales figure is not achieved for various reasons. For example:

- More fierce competition in the marketplace hence a loss of markets to competitors.
- New products introduced causing a change in buying preferences, hence lost sales (makes the product obsolete).
- Production hold-ups which prevent the achievement of target delivery dates.

This list is not exhaustive and you might like to consider other reasons, drawing on your own experiences.

Question 5.2

Section B type

Given the data supplied below, your sales manager has asked you to prepare a flexible budget for two product lines X and Y. It is company policy to apportion overhead costs to the products using direct labour i.e. £ per direct labour hour or percentage direct labour method.

(a) Prepare a flexible budget at the 70 per cent activity level and at the 90 per cent activity level from the budget data supplied below.

(b) Comment upon the suitability of using overhead absorption rates based upon direct labour hours and offer advice on possible alternative methods that may be more appropriate stating why that is the case.

Flexible budget for product lines X and Y for the year to 31 December
Activity level 80 per cent

	X £	Y £
Sales	160,000	200,000
Direct costs:		
Labour	16,000	24,000
Material	64,000	70,000
Variable overheads	24,000	30,000
Contribution	56,000	76,000
Fixed overheads	10,000	10,000
Net profit	46,000	66,000

Question 5.3

Control ratios
Explain how control ratios may be used in budgeting.

Question 5.4

Standard costing and variances
Some firms use standard costing systems and the budgets they use will be produced using predetermined standard costs. Variances may be calculated between the actual and budgeted standard cost. What benefits, if any, do you consider a standard costing system might provide?

Question 5.5

The following details of product B are provided:

Standard cost	£
Direct material – 2 lb. at £2 per lb	4.00
Direct wages – 1 hour of work	1.00
	5.00
Standard selling price	10.00

The budgeted product and sales are 1,000 units for each of the 13 reporting periods in the year. In the 7th reporting period the actual results were as follows:

		£
Sales	980 units sold for	10,200
Material purchases (all used)	2,000 lb. costing	5,000
Labour	800 hours paid and worked	1,000

Required:

a) Prepare a report of performance for the period in a form suitable for presentation to management. Your report should briefly provide possible explanations for the results.

(17 marks)

b) Explain what you understand by the terms 'forecast' and 'budget', distinguishing carefully between them.

(8 marks)

Answers

Activity Debrief 5.1

A budgeted trading account for this product for April would show:

	Quantity	*Unit price/cost*	*£ Total*
Sales	1000	15.00	15,000.00
Cost of sales	1000	7.50	7,500.00
Gross profit		7.50	7,500.00

Answer 5.1

Cash budget for three months to May

	£ Mar	*£ Apr*	*£ May*
Balance b/f	2,000	3,750	2,500
Receipts			
Debtors	2,000	3,000	3,000
Total receipts	4,000	6,750	5,500
*Payments or disbursements*tb	Creditors		4,000
Wages	250	250	250
Telephone			300
Total payments	250	4,250	550
Balance c/f	3,750	2,500	4,950

Trading and profit and loss account for the three months to May

		£	%
Sales turnover		9000	100.00
Cost of goods sold		5400	60.00
Gross profit		3600	40.00
Less overheads			
Wages	750		
Telephone	300		
Depreciation	625		
Total overhead costs		1675	
Net profit/(loss)		1925	21.39

Difference between cash and profit	£
Closing cash balance	4,950
Net profit P&L a/c	1,925
Difference	3,025
Explained by	
Add debtors outstanding	3,000
add back non cash expense	
Depreciation of fixed assets	625
Less:	
Change in stock between P&L	
and CB (6000-5400)	600
	3,025

Answer 5.2

(a) *Flexible budget for product lines A and B for the year to 31 December*

Activity level	*70%*	*80%*	*90%*	*70%*	*80%*	*90%*
	X	*X*	*X*	*Y*	*Y*	*Y*
	£	*£*	*£*	*£*	*£*	*£*
Sales	140,000	160,000	180,000	175,000	200,000	225,000
Direct costs:						
Labour	14,000	16,000	18,000	21,000	24,000	27,000
Material	56,000	64,000	72,000	61,250	70,000	78,750
Variable overheads	21,000	24,000	27,000	26,250	30,000	33,750
Contribution	49,000	56,000	63,000	66,500	76,000	85,500
Fixed overheads	10,000	10,000	10,000	10,000	10,000	10,000
Net profit	39,000	46,000	53,000	56,500	66,000	75,500

(b) The company policy of apportioning overheads on the basis of direct labour hours would seem inappropriate for the two products X and Y shown here. Direct labour represents only a very low proportion of the total cost. It would be more appropriate to apportion any overhead cost to these two products using a different basis. For example, materials form by far the highest proportion of direct cost and could be used (percentage direct materials). Alternatively, percentage of prime cost could be used (prime cost = direct material + direct labour). The number of units produced and the machine hour rate do not seem applicable here since there are no machine hours and the unit basis of recovering overheads is really only suitable for a firm producing a small number and similar range of products.

Activity based costing may be appropriate and may provide a more accurate apportionment of any overheads. ABC involves identification of the cause of the overhead cost (i.e. activities that cause cost). For example, it may be that in the case of products X and Y a major overhead cost activity is marketing communication. The first stage is to collect marketing communication costs to cost pools and the second stage is to allocate or apportion the costs from the cost pools to each of the products using appropriate *cost drivers*. In this case they are likely to be transaction based cost drivers which could include: number of advertisements, number of sales visits, number of special promotions and so on. If ABC was to be used it would need to be introduced across the firm so it is a major change that needs to be looked at carefully before changing the whole system.

In conclusion the one thing that is definitely clear is that apportionment on the basis of direct labour which forms such a low proportion of total cost for both products X and Y does not seem sensible and may distort product profitability. Maybe we need to talk with our management accountant about this?

Answer 5.3

Control ratios are an important element of monitoring the budget. The ratios may be used to compare similar periods of time. For example, January against December to see how things are changing monthly; or quarter by quarter or year on year. The ratios may be used to compare the same month this year with the same month last year or for several years to determine any cyclical trends. Control ratios may also be used to analyse changes in volumes. For example, the budget may have been prepared assuming particular sales volumes based on forecasts which turn out to be inaccurate and therefore expenses and costs as a percentage of the budgeted sales may turn out to be higher proportions when control ratios are calculated. It is important that control ratios when analysed are able to throw light on cause and effect.

Answer 5.4

A standard costing system is useful for the following reasons:

1 Variances against standard may be quickly analysed (*comparing actual costs with standard costs*), causes can be identified (*where the variance occurred, why it happened and who is responsible*) and appropriate corrective action applied.
2 Product costs can be quickly computed using predetermined standard costs for material, labour and overheads.
3 Standard costing systems can lead to effective budgetary control since variances are continuously analysed and investigated. Standard costing is helpful to the budgetary planning process since the standard costs act as a basis for control; information revealed by the variance analysis guides control and appropriate action can be taken to achieve the plan.

In order for standard costing systems to be effective they must be continuously reviewed and the standards set need to be meaningful.

Answer 5.5

(a)

		£ Budget	£ Actual	£ Variance
Sales at standard price,	1,000 units @ £10 p.u.	10,000	10,200	200 F
Direct material	1,000 units @ £4 p.u.	4,000	5,000	1,000 A
Direct wages	1,000 hours @ £1 p.h.	1,000	1,000	Nil
Profit		5,000	4,200	(800) A

The variances can be further analysed into quantity and price elements. In the case of sales variances these are referred to as volume and price. For materials they are usage and price and for wage rates they are called efficiency and rate.

(1)
Sales variance
Standard 1,000 units × £10
Actual 980 units × £10.408 (i.e. £10,200/980)

Sales volume variance 20 units lower at £10 per unit = (£200) A
Sales price variance 980 units at a higher unit price £0.408 per unit = £400 F
Total sales variance = £200 F

(2)
Direct material variance
Standard 1,000 units × £4 p.u. = £4,000
Actual 980 units × £5.102 = £5,000

Direct material usage variance 20 units × £4 = £80 F
Direct material price variance 980 units × £1.102 = (1,080) A
Total direct material variance = (£1,000) A

(3)
Direct wage variance
Standard 1,000 hours @ £1 per hour = £1,000
Actual 800 hours @ £1.25 per hour = £1,000

Efficience variance 200 hours @ £1 = £200 F
Rate variance 800 hours @ £0.25 = (£200) A
Total direct wage variance = Nil

Taking the total variances and summing them we get back to the profit variance

£200 F + (£1,000) A + Nil = (£800) A

Notes on the calculations

The sales variance £200 F may be explained in two parts as follows:

(i) 20 units less than budgeted sales gives a loss in sales at £10 standard price amounting to £200.
(ii) The budgeted loss due to the fall in sales volume is more than offset by an increase in price over the budgeted figure by 40.8 pence per unit (i.e. £10,200/980 = £10.408 as the actual selling price). The actual units sold 980 × the increase in price of 40.8 pence per unit gives rise to a favourable price variance £400.

The direct material variance £1,000 A may be explained as follows:

(i) 20 units less of material × £4 per unit at standard cost gives the favourable variance £80.
(ii) A material price variance (actual price £5.102 less standard price £4) means that £1.102 more was paid for each 2lb of materials, i.e. 55p per lb. 980 units produced × £1.102 additional material price gives an adverse variance £1,080.

The direct wage variance may be explained in terms of (i) efficiency and (ii) a rate variance as follows:

(i) 200 hours of labour budgeted has not been used and results in a saving of 200 hours at the budgeted wage rate £1 per hour = £200 F efficiency gain.
(ii) The efficiency gain is offset by the actual hourly rate for labour increasing by 25 pence per hour more than that budgeted. This results in a rate variance being calculated at 800 hours actual × 25 pence = £200 A.

(b)
A forecast is an estimate often expressed in quantitative terms about a future event. For example, organizations will give a prediction of expected future sales in quantitative terms (values and volumes). The forecast will take into account external factors and uncertainties that may affect it like changes in disposable income, changing tastes, trends and other political, economic, social or technological changes that may impact on the forecast. Forecasts will also take into account internal factors such as technical efficiencies or capacity of the organization to meet the forecast. Forecasts may also be qualitative.

A budget is a plan expressed in quantitative terms (values and volumes) for a specific period of time. The plan is what the organization expects to achieve in the specified future period. Budgets are usually prepared for a year at a time. Forecasts are used to inform the budgeting process. However, whereas a forecast is a prediction a budget is a plan. It is important to control the plan by monitoring variations from the plan and making any necessary adjustments to get the plan back on course.

Unit 6 Interpretations of financial statements

Objectives

After studying this unit you should be able to:

- ❑ Know the usefulness of having key performance indicators for:
  - Profitability
  - Liquidity
  - Use of assets
  - Return on investment
  - Gearing/leverage
- ❑ Calculate all the major ratios in the unit and be able to comment analytically on them.
- ❑ Apply appropriate ratio analysis to specific situations/problems

Study Guide

This unit is long and involves many calculations. You should have a pencil and a calculator to hand as you work your way through the unit.

Study Tips

You should try to work through this unit very carefully. Keep in mind how the key ratios break down into: profitability, liquidity, use of assets (efficiency), return on investment, and gearing. Take a section at a time and master the ratios in that section. Do not tackle the end of unit question until you have fully learned all the ratios.

Exam Hints

Ratio analysis in various forms may be called for in parts of a question or in the mini case in Section A of the paper. They are very important to your understanding and interpretation of financial data. Make sure you learn them well. A thorough understanding of this unit may earn you easy marks in an examination.

Financial data may be analysed using specific accounting ratios in order to provide managers with information about their financial performance during specific time periods. Ratios are also useful in order to monitor actual performance against planned performance. The results of such analysis should provide managers with information which may be used to plan, control and take decisions. For example, if a manager analyses a product cost structure over two financial periods and realizes that particular costs are increasing, this may be a cause for concern and the manager may decide to focus on control activities that realign a particular cost.

Product cost	*Period 1* £ *per unit*	*Period 2* £ *per unit*	*Variance*	
Direct labour cost	£10.00	£10.00	None	
Direct material cost	£15.00	£15.00	None	
Overhead costs attributed	£20.00	£25.00	£5.00	
Total cost	£45.00	£50.00	£5.00	Adverse

In this example managers may think that since the product cost has increased by £5 per unit, it may be worth investigating further what has caused the cost to increase. Maybe a particular overhead cost has increased, or the way in which overheads have been attributed to product costs, have changed (e.g. a change in the basis of apportionment). In our example, actual costs have been given but we could equally have used percentages rather than £ costs to provide us with similar types of control information.

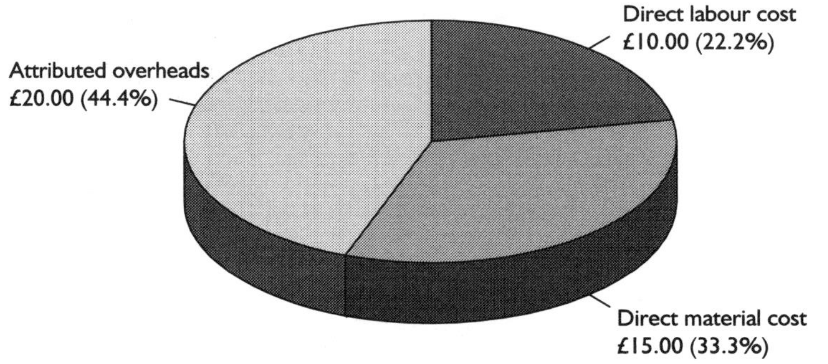

Figure 6.1
Product cost structure – Period 1

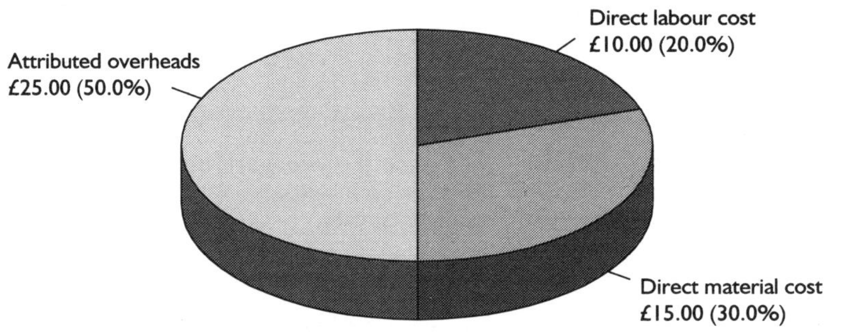

Figure 6.2
Product cost structure – Period 2

You can see from the two pie charts above both the actual values of the cost elements for the product and their relative percentages. In percentage terms overhead costs have increased by 5.6 per cent while the other two elements for direct labour and direct materials have reduced as a percentage of the total cost. Financial ratios are often expressed as a ratio 2:1 or 5:1 or as a percentage value 200 per cent or 500 per cent.

Supposing we have a cost structure which expressed in percentage terms is as follows:

Product cost	*% of cost*
Direct labour cost	20%
Direct material cost	30%
Overhead costs attributed	50%
Total cost	100%

Direct labour costs represent 20 per cent of the total cost of the product or, expressed as a ratio direct labour accounts for 1:5 of the total cost. That is one part in five or £1 in every £5 of total cost. If we knew this ratio to be true and it held good over time or over a certain output quantity then if we knew the total cost of a product to be £50, we could estimate the direct labour content to be 1:5 (20 per cent) = £10. Similarly the direct material content could be estimated at 30 per cent = £15 and so on.

Question 6.1

The estimated direct material cost is £3 per unit; direct labour cost is £2 per unit and the usual required profit margin is 50 per cent. What is the cost structure for this product?
(**Answer** See end of chapter.)

Purpose

Accounting ratios are used so that comparisons can be made quickly between different time periods for the same business or between different businesses in the same time periods. We need to be careful when making comparisons to ensure that they are meaningful by comparing like with like. For example, it would not be useful to make a direct comparison between pounds and dollars from 1975 with pounds or dollars in 1995 since they are not the same thing (the purchasing power is totally different). Although we refer to accounting ratios, they may be expressed as fractions or percentages as well as ratios in order to achieve our specific objective.

Problems with making comparisons

1. When we compare the closing financial statements of a current period with a previous period, even if only twelve months earlier, we need to remember and be aware of the fact that what we are measuring cannot possibly be exactly the same thing. For example, distortion may have taken place owing to rising price levels (inflation).
2. Sometimes the accounting policies applied by the organization will have changed, thereby making comparison between periods difficult, for example, a change in depreciation policy. If we are making comparisons between companies for the same periods of time, we would need to take account of the different accounting policies in order to make the comparisons meaningful. This is not always possible as we are limited by the amount of disclosure in the published financial statements. Therefore accuracy may be sacrificed and meaningful comparison limited.
3. When comparing different businesses the financial periods do not always coincide so direct comparison cannot be made. Nevertheless, intelligent estimates can often prove useful.
4. The nature and type of business may vary between accounting periods. Therefore, when making comparisons, we need to understand and take account of such changes in order to obtain meaningful results.
5. It should be remembered that ratios are records of past events. They are historical measures. Therefore, if we use ratios to obtain a trend we should remember their limitations in predicting future events. They will only be useful indicators of future events if there are no changes in the business structure, products sold, markets engaged in and the economic environment. Remember, it cannot be stressed enough that they are measuring historic events, their predictive powers are limited and they should not be taken in isolation. They may, of course, be used as part of a financial forecast providing factors which affect their accuracy as predictors are also considered.

Types of accounting ratio

We may classify the main accounting ratios as follows:

1 Profitability ratios.
2 Liquidity ratios and activity ratios.
3 Capital structure (gearing measures).
4 Asset turnover.
5 Investment and market based ratios.

Profit margin ratios

The simplest form of profitability ratio is the *margin*. This may take the form of a gross profit to sales turnover ratio or a net profit to sales turnover ratio.

Trading and profit and loss account for the period ending 31 December

	£ '000	£ '000	Margins	
Sales turnover		200,000		
Cost of sales		80,000		
Gross profit/(loss)		120,000	60.00%	Gross profit/sales %
Overheads				
Administration	25,000			
Marketing and sales	38,000			
Distribution	16,000			
Finance costs	2,000			
Total overheads		81,000		
Net profit/(loss)		39,000	19.50%	Net profit/sales %

These two margin ratios are the most important profitability ratios that you need to learn and understand to make sense of product, service, department or firm profitability.

Sometimes it is important to measure the proportions of expense categories against sales turnover. This could be done in a similar way by taking the trading and profit and loss account and measuring each of the expense categories as a percentage of sales as follows:

Trading and profit and loss account for the period ending 31 December

	£ '000	£ '000	Ratios	
Sales turnover		200,000	100.00%	
Cost of sales		80,000	40.00%	
Gross profit/(loss)		120,000	60.00%	Gross profit/sales %
Overheads				
Administration	25,000		12.50%	
Marketing and sales	38,000		19.00%	
Distribution	16,000		8.0%	
Finance costs	2,000		1.0%	
Total overheads		81,000	40.50%	
Net profit/(loss)		39,000	19.50%	Net profit/sales %

Now you can see for instance that administration overheads represent 12.50 per cent of the sales turnover. If this particular overhead could be reduced by 1 per cent it would have the effect of increasing the net profit earned by the firm to 20.50 per cent of sales. Similarly if an investigation of the particular marketing and sales overheads led to a reduction of overhead cost by say, 5 per cent this would lead to a corresponding increase in the net profit earned. These two reductions in overheads combined would mean that the overall net profit would be increased to 6 per cent.

In monetary terms: $0.06 \times £200{,}000{,}000 = £12{,}000{,}000$

To summarize, there are a number of profitability ratios and the most popular measures are listed below:

Profitability	Gross profit margin	$\frac{\text{Gross profit}}{\text{Sales}}$
	Net profit margin	$\frac{\text{Net profit}}{\text{Sales}}$
	Return on investment	$\frac{\text{Net profit}}{\text{Capital employed}}$
	Return on equity	$\frac{\text{Net profit}}{\text{Equity}}$

Before we move on to discuss liquidity measures it is important to understand exactly what is meant by the term liquidity.

Definition 6.1

Liquidity is the ability of a firm to meet its liabilities as they fall due. Sufficient cash must be generated from sales and other sources of revenue or capital injections to meet both current and long term liabilities. This ability to meet liabilities out of revenue is dependent on the working capital cycle.

Working capital

The working capital of any organization consists of current assets (stock, debtors, bank and cash) less current liabilities (creditors less than one year). It can be seen from the diagram that the cycle begins when stock is purchased on credit from a supplier known as a *creditor*. The *stock* is then sold to a customer maybe allowing credit (a customer who is allowed credit is called a *debtor*). Debtors will pay by cheque or in cash to discharge their debt. The firm will bank the cash which consists of the *sales revenue*. Sales revenue consists of *cost* and *profit*. The cost element is paid to the *creditor* to discharge the firm's debt. It is the speed with which this cycle turns which is important.

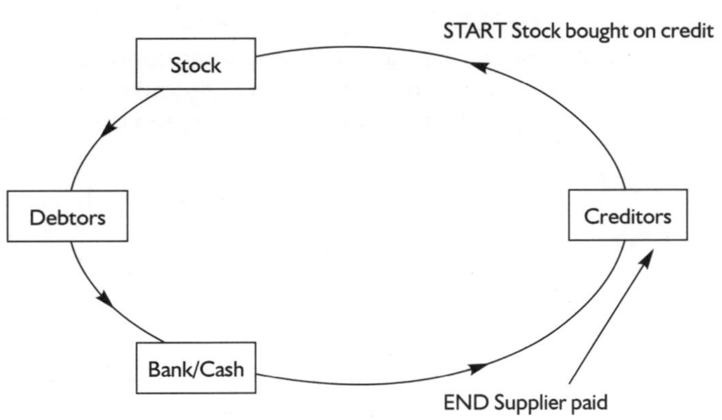

Figure 6.3
Working capital cycle

For example, supposing stock is bought on 30 days credit and stock is sold within 30 days for cash, then there is no problem since the cash received may be used to discharge the creditor. However, supposing the sale of stock takes 30 days and customers (*debtors*) take another 30 days credit before settling their account, this would mean that the firm would need to fund the position for 30 days while it waits for the customer to pay. This means that the firm would need cash resources of its own to draw on to meet its own obligation to pay the *creditor*. Alternatively, the firm would need to arrange some short term finance such as a bank overdraft to cover the position.

Question 6.2

What is the working capital for any firm?

Liquidity

It is the working capital position that determines the liquidity position of the firm. Liquidity means having enough cash to meet creditors' claims as they fall due. It is essential to ensure that the firm has enough cash flowing in to the business. Marketing and sales managers have a responsibility to ensure that any sales they make are made to people and organizations who are not only likely to pay but are likely to pay at the agreed settlement dates. Customers who settle their bills by the due dates are highly valued customers. It is not these customers who may cause cash flow problems (*liquidity* problems).

Balance sheet as at 31 December

Fixed assets	*£ Cost*	*£ Depreciation*	*£ Written down value*
Plant and machinery	100,000	20,000	80,000
Fixtures	20,000	5,000	15,000
Motor vehicles	25,000	15,000	10,000
	145,000	40,000	105,000
Current assets			
Stock	60,000		
Debtors	20,000		
Bank/cash	10,000		
		90,000	
Current liabilities			
Creditors	25,000	25,000	
Net current assets			65,000
Net worth			170,000
Financed by			
Capital	100,000		
Profit	70,000		
Equity			170,000
Capital employed			170,000

Note in this case the equity and the capital employed figures are exactly the same. This is because this firm has no long term debt funding (i.e. long term liabilities). Written down values are sometimes referred to as net book values.

Looking at the balance sheet above we can see that the working capital of the organization is the same as the net current asset position. If you are in any doubt about this look back to the definition given earlier. From a liquidity point of view it is important for the firm to measure how quickly stock is turning over (i.e. stock to sales); how quickly debtors are paying their bills and the capacity of the firm to meet its responsibilities by having the ability to pay creditors as they fall due. Liquidity ratios are the measures that provide us with some information on these matters.

Question 6.3

Stock is £10,000; debtors £5,000; trade creditors £3,000; bank and cash £1,000. What is the firm's working capital or net current asset position?

Stock turnover

It is important to know how quickly the firm is turning its stock into sales. However, before we can measure this we need to know what the sales are for the period we are looking at. Supposing in our example the sales turnover is £500,000 for the period. However, remember that we are trying to obtain a measure of stock turnover. It is not sales turnover that is important but rather the cost of sales turnover since stock is valued at cost price. If we knew the gross margin to be 40 per cent, in other words the cost of the goods sold is £300,000, we can determine the stock turn as follows:

$$\text{Stock-turnover ratio} = \frac{\text{Cost of goods sold}}{\text{Stock at cost on balance sheet}}$$

$$\frac{£300{,}000}{£60{,}000}$$

$$= 5 \text{ times in the period}$$

If the period in question is one year this would indicate that stock is turning over at the rate of five times in a year or 365 days/5 times = 73 days.

Question 6.4

If the stock turnover has been calculated at six times per annum and the average stock held shown on the balance sheet is £100,000, how much stock does the company turn over in a year?

Question 6.5

Using the same data
How many months' stock does the firm hold at any one time?

Activity 6.1

Get hold of a set of your firm's management accounts or a published report and see how quickly stock is turned over in your own firm. If you have no stock then obtain a published report for another company (Plc).

Question 6.6

Cost of goods sold in the year is £500,000 and the average stock shown on the balance sheet is £50,000. How many times a year does stock turn over?

Question 6.7

Supposing you know the annual sales figure but are not able to find out cost of sales but you deduce that the firm on average achieves a gross profit margin of 25 per cent, what is the stock turnover if the average stock shown on a published balance sheet is £1,000,000 and sales are shown at £4,000,000 in the profit and loss account?

Debtor turnover

A similar calculation may be made to determine the debtor position. Let us assume the same sales turnover £500,000 and take the value of debtors from the balance sheet at £20,000.

$$\frac{\text{Sales Turnover}}{\text{Debtors}}$$

$$\frac{£500{,}000}{£20{,}000}$$

$$= 25 \text{ times}$$

This indicates that debtors are turning over 25 times in a year. In other words it is taking approximately ½ a month to turn the debtor sale into cash at the bank. Dividing 365 days by 25 times would give you the number of days it is taking for debtors to pay on average. You should get an answer of 14.6 days.

If you add the number of days it is taking for stock to become a sale and for debtors to pay in cash you will arrive at a time it takes on average from the purchasing of stock to turn a profit on the sale. It is approximately 73 days plus 14.6 days = 87.6 days.

Question 6.8

Debtors given on the balance sheet are £60,000 and sales in the year are given in the profit and loss account as £600,000. How many days on average is it taking for debtors to pay?

Creditor turnover

We can measure how quickly creditors are being paid by taking the balance sheet value for stock creditors and dividing it into the cost of goods sold for the period. Notice the term stock creditors. This is mentioned because sometimes the balance sheet value for creditors comprises both stock creditors and other creditors for such things as wages and salaries, dividends and expense creditors (such things as light and heat, rent etc.). A more correct term for a stock creditor is *trade creditor.*

In our example let us assume that all creditors on the balance sheet are trade creditors. Remember the cost of goods sold in the period was £300,000.

$$= \frac{\text{Cost of goods sold}}{\text{Trade creditors from balance sheet}}$$

$$\frac{£300{,}000}{£25{,}000}$$

$$= 12 \text{ times in the period}$$

It would appear that trade creditors are being paid once a month since the creditor turnover is 12 times a year.

Question 6.9

Trade creditors given on a balance sheet are £60,000 and the cost of goods sold in the period are given in the profit and loss account at £720,000. What is the average payment period for creditors in this case?

Liquidity	Current ratio	$\frac{\text{Current assets}}{\text{Current liabilities}}$
	Quick ratio (acid test)	$\frac{\text{Current assets} - \text{stock}}{\text{Current liabilities}}$
Activity	Average collection period	$\frac{\text{Debtors}}{\text{Credit sales}} \times 365$
	Inventory turnover	$\frac{\text{Cost of sales}}{\text{Average stock}}$
	Average payment period	$\frac{\text{Creditors}}{\text{Purchases on credit}} \times 365$
	Fixed asset turnover	$\frac{\text{Sales}}{\text{Fixed assets}}$
	Total asset turnover	$\frac{\text{Sales}}{\text{Total assets}}$

Capital structure

Ratios to interpret and analyse the capital structure of the firm are:

Financial leverage or gearing

Debt ratio	$\frac{\text{Total debt}}{\text{Total assets}}$
Debt-to-equity	$\frac{\text{Total debt}}{\text{Total equity}}$
Times interest earned	$\frac{\text{Earnings before interest and tax (EBIT)}}{\text{Interest charges}}$
Times fixed charges earned	$\frac{\text{EBIT} + \text{Lease payments}}{\text{Interest} + \text{fixed interest charges} + \text{dividends gross}}$

The debt ratio provides a percentage measure of total debt to total assets, i.e. all liabilities as a proportion of assets. It is in effect a measure of financial gearing. There are a variety of ways that gearing can be measured. Debt to equity is another such measure. Gearing measures are important in assessing the risk for further borrowing. The measure is also useful to evaluate alternative funding sources. For example, if the total funding from debt and equity is 100 per cent and the proportions are 20 per cent total debt and 80 per cent equity it may not be too risky to increase the proportion of debt finance. However, the measure on its own does not tell us enough. We would need further information about interest rates versus dividend payments (this provides us with some indication of the different costs of capital available to the firm), together with some information about the timing of repayment (interest and capital) and information on the cash generating abilities of the business.

Investment or market based ratios

Investment ratios are important to potential and existing investors in the firm to help them make choices about which stocks they should be investing in. These ratios are also performance measures by which external analysts and the financial market place judge the firm.

Market based

Price to earnings ratio	$\frac{\text{Market price per share}}{\text{Earnings per share}}$
Market to book ratio	$\frac{\text{Market price per share}}{\text{Book value per share}}$
Earnings per share	$\frac{\text{Net profit after tax less preference dividend}}{\text{Number of ordinary shares issued}}$
Earnings yield	$\frac{\text{Earnings per share}}{\text{Market price per share}}$

Extending Activity 6.1

Get hold of a copy of your firm's published financial statements and see if you are able to analyse profitability, liquidity and gearing.

We are now going to look at a full example using most of the important ratios with explanations given below the calculations:

Zed Ltd. Balance sheet as at 31 December

			1994			*1995*
Fixed assets						
Land and buildings	£100,000			£90,000		
less depreciation	£50,000	£50,000		£55,000	£35,000	
Plant and machinery	£30,000			£30,000		
less depreciation	£9,000	£21,000		£12,000	£18,000	
Motor vehicles	£20,000			£20,000		
less depreciation	£4,000	£16,000		£8,000	£12,000	
			£87,000			£65,000
Current assets						
Stock	£20,000			£25,000		
Debtors	£5,500			£10,000		
Bank and cash	£1,500			£4,000		
		£27,000				£39,000
Current liabilities						
Trade creditors	£6,000			£15,000		
Other creditors	£1,000			£2,000		
		£7,000			£17,000	
Net current assets			£20,000			£22,000
			£107,000			£87,000
Financed by equity capital						
Ordinary share Capital		£60,000			£60,000	
Reserves		£27,000			£7,000	
Loan capital						
5% Debentures		£20,000			£20,000	
Capital employed			£107,000			£87,000

Zed Ltd. Profit and loss summary for the year ended 31 December

		1994		*1995*
Sales		£250,000		£202,380
Less cost of sales		£112,500		£91,071
Gross profit		£137,500		£111,309
Less expenses				
Administration	£25,000		£40,476	
Sales and marketing	£37,500		£62,500	
Distribution	£17,500		£18,214	
Finance overheads	£12,500		£10,119	
		£92,500		£131,309
Net profit or (loss) from operations		£45,000		–£20,000

Ratios	*1994*		*1995*	
Profitability				
Cost of sales/sales %	45.00%		45.00%	
Gross profit/sales %	55.00%		55.00%	
Net profit/sales %	18.00%		–9.88%	
Admin/sales %	10.00%		20.00%	
Sales and marketing/sales %	15.00%		30.88%	
Distribution/sales %	7.00%		9.00%	
Finance/sales %	5.00%		5.00%	
Balance sheet				
Current assets/current liabilities	3.86	times p.a.	2.29	times p.a.
Current assets – stock/current liabilities i.e. the Acid Test Ratio	1.00	times p.a.	0.82	times p.a.
Stock/cost of sales	64.89	days	100.20	days
Debtors/sales	8.03	days	18.04	days
Trade creditors/purchases*		days		days

*We do not have a figure for stock purchases so we cannot compute the days.

Return on capital employed		
Profit/capital employed	42.06%	–22.99%
Gearing ratios		
Debt/equity	22.99%	29.85%
Debt/capital employed	18.69%	22.99%

Profitability ratios

	1994 %	*1995* %
1 $\frac{\text{Cost of sales}}{\text{Sales}} \times \frac{100}{1}$	45.00	45.00

There has been no change in the percentage cost of sales. If there had been a change it could be due to a reduction or increase in the cost of material. For example, larger discounts or falling prices or material usage in production is more efficient or a less expensive grade of materials has been used.

	1994 %	*1995* %
2 $\frac{\text{Gross profit}}{\text{Sales}} \times \frac{100}{1}$	55.00	55.00

This is the corollary of the cost of sales/sales ratio. Profitability at the gross margin stage has not changed.

3 $\frac{\text{Expense classification as a \%}}{\text{Sales turnover}}$

	1994	*1995*
	%	%
Administration	10.00	20.00
Sales and marketing	15.00	30.88
Distribution	7.00	9.00
Finance	5.00	5.00

4 $\frac{\text{Net operating profit}}{\text{Sales}} \times \frac{100}{1} = \%$

Net profit/sales % *1994* 18.00% *1995* –9.88%

1994

$$\frac{45{,}000}{250{,}000} \times \frac{100}{1} = 18.00\%$$

1995

$$\frac{-£20{,}000}{202{,}380} \times \frac{100}{1} = -9.88\%$$

The operating profit has fallen by 27.88 per cent on a reduced turnover even though gross margins were maintained. The answer to why there is a loss and a dramatic year on year change lies in the fact that sales turnover has reduced whilst the expense categories have increased.

It might be useful to look at the two years in percentages at this stage to see the changes more clearly.

Zed Ltd. Profit and loss summary for the year ended 31.12		*1994*		*1995*	*Year on year change*
Sales		£250,000		£202,380	–24%
Less cost of sales		£112,500		£91,071	
Gross profit		£137,500		£111,309	–24%
Less expenses					
Administration	£25,000		£40,476		38%
Sales and marketing	£37,500		£62,500		40%
Distribution	£17,500		£18,214		4%
Finance overheads	£12,500		£10,119		–24%
		£92,500		£131,309	30%
Net profit from operations		£45,000		–£20,000	–225%

Comparing the two profit statements in this way we can observe the major differences and areas for further investigation and control.

Return on capital employed

There are a number of ways to measure a rate of return on capital employed. For comparability it is essential that the measure used is consistent between different periods and different business organizations.

One way is to measure $\frac{\text{Net profit (after tax)}}{\text{Total assets}}$

Total assets are all fixed assets plus working capital (i.e. current assets less current liabilities). If working capital is negative it should be ignored. There are two problems with using this measure:

1) The net profit after tax is after charging loan interest (debentures, mortgages, loans, overdrafts). The return on capital employed will be distorted by the interest charges if they are material. That is, the return is understated.
2) Total assets will include intangibles such as goodwill. Such assets are liable to fluctuations in value and subjective.

To overcome these problems a better measure is:

$$\frac{\text{Net operating profit}}{\text{Operating assets}}$$

Operating profit ignores such things as interest charges and non-trading income (profits on disposal, investment income etc).

Use of assets – ratios

These ratios assess asset utilization. They show how effective management have been in using the assets at their disposal; they are in effect efficiency ratios. An external analyst could use a simple ratio of asset to sales.

		1994 Ratios
Fixed assets:sales	87,000:250,000	1:2.8735
Stock in trade:sales	20,000:250,000	1:12.5
Debtors:sales	5,500:250,000	1:45.45
Cash at bank:sales	1,500:250,000	1:166.66
Current assets:sales	27,000:250,000	1:10.8

If we take the fixed assets to sales ratio what we are in effect saying is that each £1 of fixed assets has generated £2.8735 in sales.

Furthermore, in making comparisons between different businesses or different time periods, we need to ensure that depreciation policies are consistent. This is difficult if not impossible for an external analyst.

Liquidity

Current assets: current liabilities

This is a simple liquidity measure. It measures whether or not a business has enough current assets to meet its current liabilities.

	1994	*1995*
$\frac{\text{Current assets}}{\text{Current liabilities}} =$	$\frac{27{,}000}{7{,}000} =$	$\frac{39{,}000}{17{,}000} =$
Debtors/sales	3.857:1	2.294:1

Current assets are those which are or will become liquid within 12 months with liabilities due for payment in that time. A creditor will want to make sure that the business has sufficient current assets to meet its obligations. It is often said that as a rule of thumb a ratio of 2:1 is appropriate. However, this can be misleading since it depends on the nature of the business and type of industry. In our example, it would appear that Zed Ltd. has sufficient current assets to meet current liabilities in both periods. For every £1 liability it has £3.85 in current assets in 1994 and £2.29 in 1995.

The acid test or quick ratio

$$\frac{\text{Current assets less stock in trade}}{\text{Current liabilities}}$$

This is a better measure of liquidity since it may take time for stock to become a sale, thus a debtor, and eventually be turned into cash. It is essential for a business to ensure it can meet its obligations in cash at the due dates. A ratio which showed current assets less stock to be lower than the current liabilities may signify that the business is over-trading.

Zed Ltd		*1994*	*1995*
$\frac{\text{Current assets – stock}}{\text{Current liabilities}}$	=	$\frac{27{,}000–20{,}000}{7{,}000}$	$\frac{39{,}000–25{,}000}{17{,}000}$
	=	1:1	0.82:1

In 1994 liquid assets were 1:1, that is for every £1 in liquid assets the business had a current liability of £1. In 1995 this position worsened to 82 pence in current assets (less stock) for every £1 in current liabilities.

These ratios are likely to prove more useful to external analysis since management would be inclined to plan and control their liquidity by preparing cash flow forecasts (cash budgets).

Stock turnover

We could measure this by dividing sales by stock in trade but there is a problem in so far as stock is at cost and sales includes profit. To overcome this we measure sales at cost which is, of course, the cost of goods sold which is then divided by stock. In the measures given above we have used point measures i.e. the balance sheet figures. This stock figure used should be an average for the period. A true averaged stockholding figure which is representative is usually known to management but for external analysts the next best approximation is obtained by averaging opening and closing stocks. In the example we would only be able to calculate an average figure for 1995 since we could use the balance sheet for 1994 as the opening stock figure and the 1995 balance sheet gives the closing stock figure. Using Zed Ltd. an external analyst would obtain an average thus:

$$\frac{20{,}000 + 25{,}000}{2} = 22{,}500$$

and measuring stock turnover for 1995 would get:

$$\frac{\text{Cost of goods sold}}{\text{Stock in trade}} = \frac{91{,}071}{22{,}500} = 4.0476 \text{ times}$$

This can also be measured in terms of the number of days stock on average which is held at the balance sheet date, assuming that production remains at a similar level and other things being equal:

$$\frac{365 \text{ days}}{4.0476 \text{ times}} = 90.1769 = 91 \text{ days}$$

We could have obtained this figure first by using:

$$\frac{\text{Stock}}{\text{Cost of goods sold}} \times \text{Number of days in the period}$$

Supposing as management we thought the closing balance sheet figures for stock were representative of average stockholding during those years, we could compare the two years thus:

Stock turnover	*1994*		*1995*	
No of times	$= \frac{112{,}500}{20{,}000}$	= 5.625	$\frac{91{,}071}{25{,}000}$	= 3.6428
Days	$= \frac{20{,}000}{112{,}500} \times 365$	= 64.88	$\frac{25{,}000}{91{,}071} \times 365$	= 100.196

Comparing the two years, it can be seen that stock turnover has reduced from 5.62 times per annum to 3.64 and that the number of days now being held in stock has increased to 100.196. This is not so good on the face of it since the business is now tying up more money in stocks.

Debtor turnover

It is important to know the collection period for debtors, that is, how long it takes on average for a sale to be turned into cash. We calculated that in 1994 for every £1 sold, £0.02 was owed by debtors and in 1995 it was £1 to £0.049.

In terms of the number of days it takes for an average debtor to pay, we can obtain this for each year as follows: Debtors/Sales × 365 days in the year.

£5,500/£250,000 × 365 = 8.03 days for 1994

£10,000/£202,380 × 365 = 18.04 days for 1995

The collection period has increased by 10 days.

It is the average debtor balance during the period over which sales are made which the analyst should use to obtain a measure. I have assumed the closing balance sheet figures to be a proxy for that average.

An external analyst might obtain an average for 1995 by adding the opening and closing debtor balances from the balance sheet and divide by two. Thus for 1995 the figures used would be:

$$\frac{5{,}500 + 10{,}000}{2} = 7{,}750$$

$$\frac{7{,}750 \times 365}{202{,}380} = 13.98 \text{ days}$$

Creditor turnover

It is important for management and creditors to assess how quickly on average a business pays its suppliers for goods and services.

For trade creditors; those supplying stock in trade this can be measured as follows:

$$\frac{\text{Trade creditors}}{\text{Purchases}} \times \text{Number of days}$$

$$\text{or} \quad \frac{\text{Purchases}}{\text{Trade creditors}} = \text{Number of times in a period}$$

If we were to assume that the cost of sales in our example was made up of purchased stock items for resale, we could estimate the purchases for 1995 as follows:

Opening stock + Purchases – Closing stock = Cost of goods sold

The opening stock is £20,000 of the closing balance sheet for 1994.
Purchases we do not know.
The closing stock on the 1995 balance sheet is £25,000.
And the cost of goods sold is £91,071.

Stock increased by £5,000 over the year and we consumed £91,071 as cost of sales, therefore the purchase figure for 1995 may be obtained as £96,071.

Trade creditors were £6,000 for 1994 and £15,000 for 1995 at the close. We could therefore decide to take an averaged figure for trade creditors as follows:

$$\frac{£6{,}000 + £15{,}000}{2} = £10{,}500$$

$$\text{No. of days} = \frac{\text{Trade creditors}}{\text{Purchases}} \times 365 \text{ days}$$

$$= \frac{£10{,}500}{£96{,}071} \times 365$$

$$= 39.89 \text{ days}$$

Alternatively, you could calculate the number of times in the year that trade creditors turnover which is 9.1496 times (Purchases/trade Creditors).

We do not have any figure for purchases in 1994 in the example so we cannot take a measure.

The same analysis could be done for other creditors. For example, for service creditors the calculation would be:

$$\frac{\text{Creditors}}{\text{Expenses bought in, in the period}} \times \text{Number of days in the period}$$

We do not have sufficient detail of the expenses bought in, in either year.

The working capital ratio

We can obtain a rough measure regarding the number of days it takes for working capital to turnover.

Zed Ltd.	*1994 days*	*1995 days*
Stock	64.88	100.20
Debtors	8.03	18.04
Less trade creditors	?	(39.89)
	?	78.35 days

This would give us the number of days tied up in working capital.

Capital structure

The analysis of the capital structure of a business is of particular interest to creditors, shareholders and competitors. Gearing is a measure of debt finance to equity, or alternatively debt to capital employed. The gearing ratio has been calculated for Zed Ltd using both methods. It is important for management to know the cost of capital for the firm. Looking at Zed Ltd it has a mixture of debt at 5 per cent per annum and equity capital (share capital and reserves). We do not know how much this is costing because we are not given any details of dividend payments. If we knew that dividends were paid equivalent to 7 pence in the pound in the year then we would know that equity capital was costing 7 per cent per annum and debt finance 5 per cent per annum (the cost of debenture interest). We could calculate the proportion of each type of capital, and weight the interest costs to arrive at a weighted average cost of capital (WACC). Debt represents 22.99 per cent of the total capital employed in 1995 and equity represents 77.01 per cent. If you do the calculation you will obtain a WACC 6.54 per cent per annum.

Net worth/total assets

Net worth is ordinary shares and preference shares plus reserves *or* total assets less current and long term liabilities. Total assets are fixed plus current assets.

Zed Ltd. *1994* *1995*

$$\frac{87,000}{114,000} = 1:1.31\ (76.31\%) \qquad \frac{67,000}{104,000} = 1:1.55\ (64.42\%)$$

This means that the shareholders' stake in the business is approximately 76.31 per cent in 1994 and 64.42 per cent in 1995. It has actually deteriorated from 76.31 per cent in 1994 to 64.42 per cent in 1995. This is known as a measure of gearing.

Fixed assets/net worth

This shows the proportion of fixed assets funded by shareholders.

	1994	1995
Zed Ltd.	87,000:87,000 = 1:1	65,000:67,000 = 1:0.97
	or 100 per cent	or 103 per cent

Long and short term debt/total assets

This is also a measure of gearing. The ratio measures the proportion of debts to total assets; it is the 'other side of the coin' to the previous measurement of net worth/total assets. If that ratio for 19–5 showed the shareholders' interest to be 75 per cent then this ratio should be 25 per cent since the sum of the parts must equal 100 per cent (i.e., net worth + debt = total assets).

Zed Ltd *1994* *1995*

$$\frac{27,000}{114,000} = 1:4.22 \text{ or } 23.68 \text{ per cent} \qquad \frac{37,000}{104,000} = 1:2.81 \text{ or } 35.58 \text{ per cent}$$

A company which has a large proportion of debt funding total assets is said to be highly geared. Zed Ltd has low gearing in 1994 which has increased in 1995 as a result of a decline in equity as a proportion of total funding. The fall in the equity value was caused in this case by a hefty decline in profitability resulting in a loss of £20,000 in 1995.

Interest coverage ratio

This measures the extent to which profit may decline before a company is unable to meet its interest repayments on loans etc. Since interest charges are an allowable tax expense, it is profit before tax which is used in the calculation.

$$\frac{\text{Profit before tax + Fixed interest charges}}{\text{Interest charges for the period}}$$

Looking at Zed Ltd the only fixed interest charges the company appears to have is the 5 per cent debenture interest. This charge, we assume, must be included in finance overheads.

Debenture interest 1994 = 5 per cent × 20,000 = 1,000
1995 = 5 per cent × 20,000 = 1,000

There is no tax shown in the statements and the net profits before tax are £45,000 and a loss of £20,000 respectively.

	1994	*1995*
Interest cover =	$\frac{46{,}000}{1{,}000} = 46{:}1$	$\frac{-19{,}000}{1{,}000}$ = no cover

On average, profits could fall 46 times or to 1/46th of the current level and the business would still be able to pay its interest charges in 1994, but the firm is unable to meet the interest payment in 1995 owing to the loss.

Investment ratios

These are of interest to investors, analysts and the financial managers interested in the market price of shares quoted on the stock exchange.

In the case of Zed Ltd, let us assume that:

- There is no liability to income tax for the year.
- The number of ordinary shares issued are 120,000 at a nominal value of 50 pence per share = £60,000. They must have been issued at par since there is no share premium account shown on the balance sheet. If shares are issued at a premium there is a requirement to show a Share Premium Account separately on the balance sheet.
- The current market prices at 31.12.19–4 = £1.00 and at 31.12.19–5 = £1.20

Note: it is only Plcs which are quoted on the Stock Exchange.

$$\text{Earnings per share} = \frac{\text{Profit after tax} - \text{Preference dividend (gross)}}{\text{Number of ordinary shares issued}}$$

Zed Ltd

$$1994 = \frac{45{,}000-0}{120{,}000} = \begin{array}{l}3.75 \text{ pence} \\ \text{or } £0.0375 \text{ per share}\end{array}$$

$$1995 = \frac{-20{,}000-0}{120{,}000} = \begin{array}{l}-16.66 \text{ pence} \\ \text{or } -£0.1666 \text{ per share}\end{array}$$

In 1994 each ordinary share earned 3.75 pence while in 1995 there was a loss on each ordinary share equivalent to 16.66 pence. Earnings per share are not the amount that the shareholder will receive as dividend, since dividend policy is decided by the directors.

Dividend yield measures the real rate of return on the investment in shares since it is based on market prices and not nominal share values.

In the case of Zed Ltd, let us assume that a dividend is declared at 5 per cent of the nominal value of the shares issued for both 1994. Let us assume also that despite the loss in 1995 the directors decide to declare a dividend of 5 per cent of the nominal value.

$$\text{Dividend yield} = \frac{\text{Nominal share value} \times \text{Dividend per cent}}{\text{Market price per share}}$$

Zed Ltd

$$1994 = \frac{£0.50 \times 5 \text{ per cent}}{£1.00} = 2.5 \text{ per cent}$$

$$1995 = \frac{£0.50 \times 5 \text{ per cent}}{£1.20} = 2.08 \text{ per cent}$$

It can be seen that the real rate of return on the investment in Zed Ltd declined in 1995 as a result of the change in market value of the shares.

Dividend cover or payout ratio

This indicates the proportion of profits retained and paid out as dividend by the business in a period.

$$\text{Dividend cover} = \frac{\text{Profit after tax} - \text{Preference dividend gross}}{\text{Gross equity dividend}}$$

For Zed Ltd, using our previous assumptions, the gross equity dividend or the dividend on ordinary shares was: £0.50 × 5 per cent per share, that is $2\frac{1}{2}$ pence per share gross (before tax). There are 120,000 (£0.50) shares; the total dividend paid would be:

$$120{,}000 \times £0.025 = £3{,}000$$

$$\text{The ratio for 1994 is} = \frac{45{,}000 - 0}{3{,}000} = 15 \text{ times}$$

Alternatively, as a payout measure, 6.66 per cent of net profit is paid out as dividend, or put another way, 93.33 per cent was retained in the business in 1994.

Price earnings ratio

This ratio is an indicator to an investor of the value placed upon a share by the market. It is very important if a company is about to make a new share issue, since an investor may decide to invest or not to invest on the basis of what amount is normally earned by each share in relation to its market price. Remember, investors will be comparing this ratio with other possible investments.

$$\text{Price earnings} = \frac{\text{Market price per share}}{\text{Earnings per share}}$$

$$\text{Zed Ltd. 1994} = \frac{£1.00}{£0.0375} = 26.66$$

The lower the price earnings ratio, the more attractive the investment might be not taking into account other things. In 1994 this appears to be a very high P/E ratio.

This ratio would not be considered in isolation and the potential or existing shareholder would be interested in the payout ratio also, to see what proportion of the earnings he could expect to receive. A business with a higher P/E ratio may be more attractive because its dividend policy is more attractive.

Return on capital employed (ROCE)

$$= \frac{\text{Profit}}{\text{Investment}} \times 100 \text{ per cent}$$

$$\frac{\text{Sales}}{\text{Investment}} \times \frac{\text{Profit}}{\text{Sales}} \times 100 \text{ per cent}$$

$$\frac{\text{Operating profit}}{\text{Operating assets}} = \frac{\text{Operating profit}}{\text{Sales}} \times \frac{\text{Sales}}{\text{Operating assets}}$$

Various definitions of capital employed

- Total capital
- Long term capital (i.e. total capital – current liabilities)
- Shareholders' total capital (i.e. share capital + reserves)
- Shareholder's equity (i.e. ordinary shares + reserves)

Note: you may use $\dfrac{\text{average operating profit}}{\text{average operating assets}}$

This is done by using opening and closing balance sheet figures.

Summary – ratio analysis

Ratios are useful to both internal managers and external financial analysts including your competitors. Ratios summarize key relationships and measure performance. You should be careful to choose appropriate data for the ratios you calculate and be extremely careful in making judgements based upon ratios alone. You need to be particularly experienced in the business to interpret some of the findings and a single measure is never enough on which to base important decisions.

Ratios need to be:

- Prepared regularly and in a consistent manner.
- Consistent with other firms in the same industry if inter-firm comparisons are to be made.
- Interpreted accurately. For this reason if they are considered in isolation they will be much less use. Remember they are historic measures, they may therefore lead to fallacious future predictions if used in isolation.

What ratios?

Prepare those ratios most useful to the situation you are trying to analyse. For example a list of other quantitative measures that may be used in a sales or marketing environment are listed in addition to the traditional accounting ratios we have already discussed.

Other quantitative performance measures

Other quantitative measures with a view to measuring performance might include:

Sales

Sales revenue
Sales revenue as a percentage of quota
Sales revenue per order
Sales revenue per call
Sales revenue from new accounts
Sales expenses to sales revenue

Orders

Number of orders taken in a period
Order per call ratio

Average order value
Average contribution per order

Customer accounts

Number of new accounts per period
Number of accounts lost per period
Total number of accounts

Calls

Number of calls per period
Calls on potential new accounts
Profit per call
Cost per call

Question 6.10

Using most important ratios

Extatic Ltd. Balance sheet as at 31 December			*1994*			*1995*
Fixed assets						
Land and buildings	£200,000			£250,000		
less depreciation	£100,000	£100,000		£120,000	£130,000	
Plant and machinery	£40,000			£40,000		
less depreciation	£15,000	£25,000		£19,000	£21,000	
Motor vehicles	£30,000			£30,000		
less depreciation	£7,500	£22,500		£15,000	£15,000	
			£147,500			£166,000
Current assets						
Stock	£30,000			£25,000		
Debtors	£10,000			£15,000		
Bank and cash	£2,000			£1,000		
		£42,000			£41,000	
Current liabilities						
Trade creditors	£10,000			£15,000		
Other creditors	£1,000			£2,000		
		£11,000			£17,000	
Net current assets			£31,000			£24,000
			£178,500			£190,000
Financed by equity capital						
Ordinary share capital		£100,000			£100,000	
Reserves		£58,500			£70,000	
Loan capital						
5% Debentures		£20,000			£20,000	
Capital employed			£178,500			£190,000

Extatic Ltd. Profit and loss summary for the year ended 31.12		*1994*		*1995*
Sales		£240,000		£250,000
Less cost of sales		£108,000		£100,000
Gross profit		£132,000		£150,000
Less expenses				
Administration	£48,000		£40,000	
Sales and marketing	£43,200		£61,500	
Distribution	£16,800		£24,500	
Finance overheads	£12,000		£12,500	
		£120,000		£138,500
Net profit from operations		£12,000		£11,500
Add profit/(loss) on				

From the balance sheet and profit and loss account given for Extatic Ltd you are asked to calculate as many ratios as you can to analyse and determine:

- profitability
- liquidity
- return on investment
- use of assets
- gearing

Answers

Answer 6.1

You need to work out the selling price first from the data provided. 50 per cent margin means a 100 per cent mark-up

i.e. Margin = 1/2 mark-up = 1/(2–1) = 1/1 or 100 per cent.

Cost structure is as follows:

Sales	£10.00	100%
Cost of sales	£ 5.00	50%
Gross profit	£ 5.00	50%

Answer 6.2

Working capital is the net current assets of the firm.

Current Assets – Current Liabilities.

Stock + Debtors + Prepayments + Short Term Investments
+ Bank and Cash – Creditors and accruals.

Answer 6.3

(£16,000 – £3,000) = £13,000

Answer 6.4

£600,000

Answer 6.5

Two months: 12 months/6 times per annum.

Answer 6.6

10 times per annum or 36.5 days.

Answer 6.7

Sales	100 per cent
Cost of sales	?
Gross profit	25 per cent

Cost of sales are 75 per cent × £4,000,000 = £3,000,000

Stock turnover = £3,000,000/£1,000,000 = 3 times per annum or 121.66 days

Answer 6.8

Sales/Debtors.

£600,000/£60,000 = debtors are turning over 10 times per annum.

In days the calculation is:

Debtor/Sales × 365 = 36.5

Answer 6.9

Cost of goods sold/Trade creditors = £720,000/£60,000.

12 times per annum or once a month.

In days the calculation is TC/COGS × 365 = 30.416, i.e. 31 days.

Answer 6.10

Ratios	*1994*	*1995*
Profitability	*%*	*%*
Cost of sales/sales per cent	45.00	40.00
Gross profit/sales per cent	55.00	60.00
Net profit/sales per cent	5.00	4.60
Admin/sales per cent	20.00	16.00
Sales and marketing/sales per cent	18.00	24.60
Distribution/sales per cent	7.00	9.80
Finance/sales per cent	5.00	5.00

Balance sheet *Liquidity*		
Current assets/current liabilities	3.82 times p.a.	2.41 times p.a.
CA – stock/CL	1.09 times p.a.	0.94 times p.a.
Stock/cost of sales	101.39 days	91.25 days
Debtors/sales	15.21 days	21.90 days
Trade creditors/purchases*	33.80 days	57.63 days
Return on capital employed	%	%
Profit/capital employed	6.72	6.05
Gearing ratios		
Debt/equity	12.62	11.76
Debt/capital employed	11.20	10.53

*The exact figures for purchases in each year are not given. However, what we have is cost of sales £108,000 in 1994 and £100,000 in 1995. Assuming cost of sales were all purchased stock items and that stock throughout is reasonably stable, we can estimate creditor turnover. This is done by substituting cost of sales for purchases. You will note that closing stocks given on the balance sheet are as follows: £30,000 in 1994 and £25,000 in 1995. Using these stock figures it is possible to deduce purchases for 1995 as follows:

Opening stock on 1.1.1995	£30,000
Add purchases	?
Less closing stock on 31.12.1995	(£25,000)
Cost of sales	£100,000

Purchases during 1995 must have been £95,000.

$$\frac{\text{Trade creditors at 31.12.1995}}{\text{Trade purchases for 1995}} \qquad \frac{£15{,}000}{£95{,}000} \times 365 = 57.63 \text{ days}$$

Note the 1994 calculation has used the cost of sales figure as the purchase surrogate. This is correct if opening and closing stocks are the same figure. In the circumstances it is the best estimate we can give.

Unit 7

Marketing information and the role of research

Objectives

After studying this unit you should be able to:

- ❑ Recognize the marketing research process.
- ❑ Know the major steps in conducting research.
- ❑ Understand the nature and roles that marketing research plays in the marketing information system.
- ❑ Know and understand the distinction between primary and secondary data and when and why it might be appropriate to use secondary or primary data.
- ❑ Know and understand the need for sampling and statistical techniques in making sense of marketing research data.

Study Guide

This unit is reasonably straightforward to work through, although it does introduce you to some descriptive statistics that are useful in revealing information about the population under study. However, if you take it slowly you will be alright even if numbers are not your strong point. So do not be afraid or be put off by the statistics. There are plenty of words here to help you.

You may like to have a calculator and a pencil to hand to follow through any workings in the text and to complete the questions as you work through.

This unit should take you about 3 hours to work through. For some of you it may be a little shorter and for others a little longer.

Study Tips

Take this unit slowly and make sure you are able to understand the usefulness of sampling and statistical techniques and how they are applied to specific marketing research problems.

Exam Hints

- It is essential to distinguish between secondary and primary data sources and have a thorough grasp of how such data may be used by marketing researchers and marketing and sales managers. You should make certain that you know the advantages and disadvantages of using secondary and primary data.
- Questions in the examination will require an appreciation of the use of sampling and statistical techniques applied to marketing research. Information and patterns in the data can often only be clearly identified using appropriate statistics. You will not be expected to perform any complex statistical calculations, but you are expected to know how statistics can be used to reveal information at the level explained within the unit.

Marketing and research applications

The marketing research process consists of a number of activities: defining the problem or the subject to study; examining secondary data that is available and that has maybe been collected for another reason earlier; generating primary data (i.e. new data) if required; process the data and analyse the information; make recommendations and implement them.

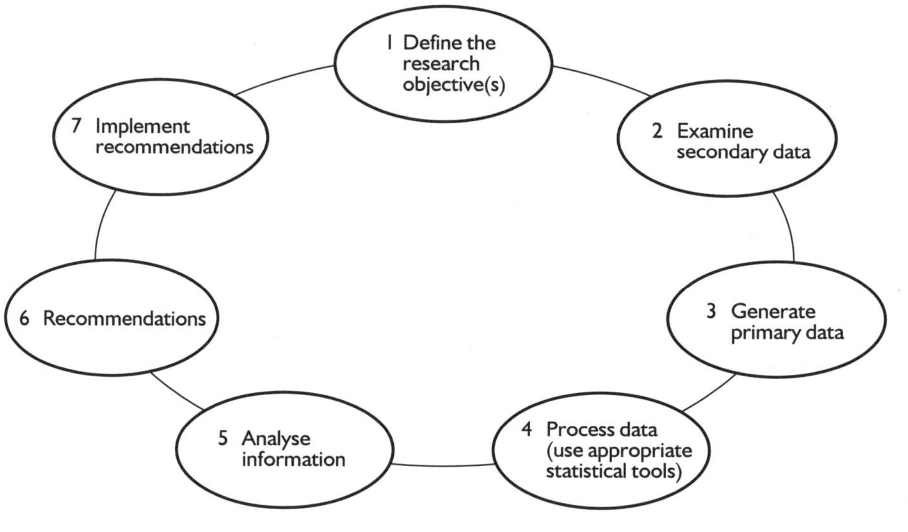

Figure 7.1
Steps in marketing research

There are a number of important steps to follow in conducting marketing research that are detailed in Figure 7.1.

- *Defining the research objectives* is the first important step. This will provide focus for the research project and avoid ambiguity. A practical advantage of having a clear definition of objectives is that it will clearly limit the scope of the research which means you will not waste time collecting unnecessary data which merely adds to cost without providing value.

  When a researcher is unsure about the topic area to investigate it may be appropriate to conduct exploratory research with the sole purpose of gaining a clear focus for later conclusive research.

Vague research area	*Exploratory research*	*Precise topic*	*Conclusive research*
Why have sales fallen?	Discuss issue with sales team and other key staff.	Investigate sales training?	Survey sales personnel.
Effectiveness of promotion campaigns?	Discuss with key staff.	Do people recall our campaign and message?	Survey customers and potential customers to analyse recall.
Could we increase sales through price reductions?	Discuss with key staff.	Would a 5 per cent reduction increase sales?	Test in selected stores. Experimentation
We would like to improve customer service?	Discuss with key staff.	Improve sales team response times by 100 per cent.	Monitor customer response times. Observation.
Would like to improve attitude of customers to the environmental friendliness of products?	Discuss with key staff.	Attitude study towards specific products.	Focus groups with the aim of clarifying the promotional message.

- *Examination of secondary data* Secondary data is data that has been gathered for some other purpose rather than for the purposes of the immediate study to hand. Secondary data can be internal or external to the organization. Secondary data are relatively low cost and readily available. Secondary data may not be sufficient in themselves to satisfy the research objectives depending on the nature of the problem. Nevertheless, it is always worthwhile investigating if secondary data will suffice before proceeding to the expense of generating primary data.

  Secondary data have the following advantages over primary data:

  Advantages
  Usually inexpensive.
  Readily available.
  Often several sources of data to provide different perspectives.
  Sometimes secondary data is of a high quality that would be too expensive for a single organization to obtain, e.g. some government statistics.
  The data are usually highly credible since the source is independent of the firm.
  Useful for carrying out exploratory research.

  Disadvantages
  Available data may not be current or complete.
  The data may be too general.
  Information may be dated or obsolete.
  The research methodology may be unknown (e.g. sample selection, size, date the research was conducted rather than published etc.).
  Related to methodology data reliability and validity may be difficult to prove.
  Conflicting results may exist between sources.
  All the findings from a secondary data source may not have been made public and therefore you are only able to obtain half the picture.

- *Generating primary data* Primary data consist of data collected specifically to meet the research objectives at hand. Primary data are needed if secondary data is not sufficient to prove the case or on which to base recommendations and decisions.

Primary data collection techniques and their application

Technique	*Application*
Survey	Attitudes and motivation research
Observation	Behaviour
Experiment	Cause and effect
Simulation	Identifying and analysing many variables

Advantages
Collected for the purpose of the research investigation.
Therefore data are current.
Methodology is known and can be controlled.
All findings available to the researchers but not available to competitors.
No conflicting data from different sources.
Data are reliable and valid.
Primary data are necessary when there is insufficient secondary data or where data are not available.

Disadvantages
Time consuming.
Expensive to collect and process.
Some types of information cannot be collected, e.g. census data.
The perspective may be limited.
The firm may not be capable of collecting the data required even though it is able to identify the need.

- *Processing data and analysing information*
  Processing data is a research design issue. We need to know:

  Who will process the data (internal or external agency)?
  The population under investigation.
  How we will select the data: sample, survey, observation, experiment, or simulation?
  Quantitative analysis or qualitative analysis?

- *Recommendations*
  Recommendations will be made from the findings and conclusions reached using the information. Recommendations are usually communicated in the form of a report to the person or persons commissioning the research.

- *Implementation*
  The final step is to implement any recommendations made by the research.

Limitations of marketing research

It is important to understand some of the limitations of marketing research. Awareness and understanding of limitations can prevent expensive errors occurring in the research design phase.

Data collection errors may occur either through respondents deliberately misleading the interviewer or more usually through the interviewer incorrectly interpreting and recording a response. For example, a question may be phrased in such a way that it leads the respondent in a biased way to reach a conclusion or the researcher wrongly interprets what is said.

Analytical errors similar to those described in data collection could occur as a result of misinterpreting the data. Furthermore, reporting errors may also take place in the research. For example, findings could be misreported for some reason either through simple error or error due to re-interpretation when writing up the research. In addition, experimental errors could also happen. Uncontrollable events may take place during a marketing research experiment. For example, supposing you decided to test market a new product in a particular geographic area, and simultaneously and coincidentally, a major competitor conducted a similar test for their product in the same area.

Sampling errors could occur whereby the sample is selected from a population which does not fully reflect the target population that you are trying to sample. For example, supposing you wanted to know respondents' attitudes towards your company's promotional offers which are sent by direct mail to a specific target group, say 25- to 30-year-old females, and you decided to approach the group using a telephone survey. A sampling error is built into the design because you would be excluding from your sample frame females in your target group who do not own or are not contactable by telephone.

Non-response errors will also occur and you need to plan how to deal with the non-responses. This is necessary to ensure that your sample remains valid and fully representative of a larger population. The most common way to overcome non-response is to extend the sample size so as to obtain the required degree of accuracy.

The larger the sample drawn from a total population the more chance there is of non-sampling errors. These are errors in data collection and analysis owing to the large volumes of data that need to be handled.

Sampling and marketing research

Selecting individuals who will provide information which is representative of a larger population is the aim of sampling techniques. This sample should provide information about the larger group that has a degree of accuracy about which the researcher can feel confident. Statements such as 'we are 95 per cent confident that all people in our target population will behave in a particular way' are made on the basis of a sample survey. Sampling theory uses probability theory as its basis. This unit is meant to provide a basic understanding of why it is important to sample. We will address a number of key questions which include:

1 What is a sample?
2 Why use a sample?
3 How is a sample taken?
4 What size of sample should be used?

What is a sample?

A sample is a selection of a number of respondents taken from a larger population for testing and analysing data about the sample which is meant to provide information about the total population from which the sample has been extracted. For example, we may want to know how many people from within a particular age group in England earn more than the average national wage.

Why use a sample?

A sample may be drawn from the total population which is intended to provide the answer on behalf of the total population. Samples are obviously cheaper to survey than to survey the whole of the population. Samples are used to make an estimate of what the whole population may think, or the characteristics they possess. If we asked the whole population, this is in effect a census as opposed to a sample. The smaller the sample the less it will cost, the quicker the results may be analysed but we may sacrifice the degree of accuracy. Good quality samples will provide researchers with enough accuracy to make reasonable statements about a total population and are therefore a better means of obtaining results than having to analyse data from the whole population. *Cost, time, use and accuracy* are the important considerations.

Sampling is necessary because either we do not have or we do not wish to devote the resources required to collect data from the whole population. If we decided that we wanted to know the fashion influences affecting 25–30-year-old women, we could design a research project that involved collecting data from every member of the target population. In other words conduct a census of that population. You can see that this would be extremely costly. More importantly, it may not provide us with any better information than would a properly designed sample of that population. Cost, time, accuracy and usefulness are the key criteria by which to judge such decisions. It is worth noting that for industrial marketing research it may be possible to conduct the research by means of a census inquiry rather than a sample. This is because the industry population may be sufficiently small to include the whole population.

How is a sample taken?

The population comprises the whole group which the sample is meant to represent. Data collected from the sample are called statistics and these sample statistics are used to make statements and estimates about the population. There are three main methods for sampling which are random sampling, quota sampling and judgement sampling. Quota and judgement sampling are referred to as non-probability sampling, and random sampling is probability sampling.

Random sampling

Random sampling is based upon statistical probability. Each member of a population must have an equal chance of being selected in the sample. It is possible to calculate a level of confidence and limit of accuracy of the results from such a sample. A level of confidence is a statement about how confident we can be about the results from the sample holding good across the whole population. A 95 per cent level of confidence means that there is only a 5 per cent or 1 in 20 chance that the sample results do not hold good. Confidence levels may be higher than this but to be more accurate and to reduce the uncertainty will be more expensive since you will need to extract a larger sample. The limits of accuracy need to be stated about the population from which a sample is taken. Supposing we use only 100 respondents on which to base a judgement about a population of 10,000 then any calculations made to reach the judgement will be approximate. We may make a statement like the limits of accuracy are + or – 5 per cent.

Deductive reasoning

Deductive reasoning is when you take a general situation and apply the logic of the general situation to a specific situation. For example, from a group of 4 women and 1 man, the chances of choosing the man in a lottery are 4 to 1 against. We may deduce that in 80 per cent of the samples we choose we expect a woman to be chosen.

Inductive reasoning

Inductive reasoning assumes that we know everything about any given population and this knowledge may be used to study the characteristics of any given sample and compare them with the known population. Conclusions are reached by comparing the specific situation with what we already know about the whole population.

It is important to recognize these differences in sampling theory because we need to know how the sample is drawn before we can reach conclusions that generalize from the sample. Deductive and inductive reasoning are complementary tools at our disposal.

Question 7.1

Identify the two types of reasoning that are used by marketing researchers and briefly explain each type.
(**Answers** See end of chapter.)

Samples and the population

A statistical population is a collection of all the possible observations of a specific characteristic that is of interest to study. Populations exist whether or not they can be measured in practice. For example, we know that a population exists for all males in the UK having a shirt collar size of 15. We may not be able to reach the whole population to check how many there are because it is too costly or for some other reason. We may, however, be able to draw a sample from the total population. A sample represents only a portion of the total population. It may be possible to draw a sample at random from the population of males identified and then to make inferences from the statistical methodology employed. Often marketing research analysts have to work with target populations that may exist only in theory and by using appropriate statistical methodology can make some inference about the sample they have drawn from this target population.

It is the observations of characteristics that form the population and not the individuals possessing the characteristics – these are called the elementary units of the population. If we were able to measure a particular characteristic such as shirt collar size for a specific population we may decide to draw our sample from a particular frame we were able to access. For example, for the month of July we may gain access to store purchase data in a particular store in a particular location. From this data we may wish to know how many male shirts with a size 15 collar were purchased. From this specific situation we may wish to make inferences about the total numbers of shirts purchased in all stores in the UK over the same period from this particular store group so as to forecast future requirements. It is important to recognize that it is the shirt collar size 15 that forms our population and not the people who made the purchases. However, we may really need to know who the purchasers of size 15 collars were, and then we would need to redefine the population as people and not shirts.

Definition 7.1

Elementary units	=	the population possessing the characteristics we want to investigate
Sampling frame	=	the source of elementary units
Sample	=	collection of observations

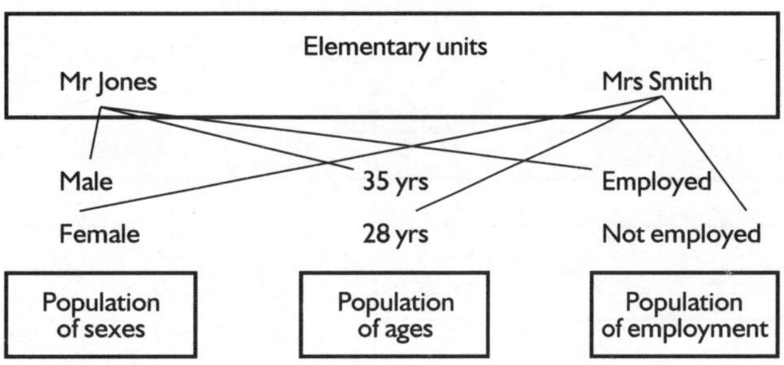

Figure 7.2
Sampling frame: shoppers in a mall on a given day

Quantitative and qualitative populations

Characteristics of populations may be distinguished by two types, either numerical characteristics such as age, values, percentages and so on; or attributes such as male, female. The tables below give some further examples.

Quantitative

Elementary unit	*Characteristic of interest*	*Unit of measurement*
person	age	years
account balance	amount	pounds sterling
firm	size	£ turnover/no. of employees/ £ capitalization
product	weight	lb/ounces
equity shares	dividend	pence in the pound

Qualitative

Elementary unit	*Characteristic of interest*	*Possible attributes*
person	sex	male/female
manager	profession	marketing/sales/finance/engineer
firm	legal form	sole proprietor/partnership/limited/ public limited
product	colour	red/blue/green
shares	type	preference/ordinary

Quantitative data may be of the following types:

- Nominal data is used to give a number to a specific attribute. For example 22 may be a nominal value for accounting research; 33 for marketing research and 51 for engineering research. The numbers themselves do not represent anything else apart from types of research. Nominal data is used for coding questionnaire data. The data types identified are not numerical but we want to classify the data using numbers.
- Ordinal data are used to identify relative importance. Ranking preferences on a scale 1 to 5 is an example of ordinal data. Ordinal scales are used for many different types of data. Likert scales and semantic differential scales are examples of using ordinal data scales.
- Interval data scales provide rankings and arithmetic operations of subtraction and addition are important. The degrees celsius on a thermometer are examples of an interval scale. The same amount of heat energy is required to raise the temperature by 10 degrees at any point on the scale.
- Ratio data may be used to allow basic arithmetic operations. For example, gross profit to sales may be expressed as a ratio of 1:2 when the margin is 50 per cent; or 1:3 when the margin is 33 per cent and 1:4 at 25 per cent and so on. Ratio data are used for business statistics e.g. cost/revenue, earnings per share, price/earnings, working capital.

The role of the analyst

The role of the analyst is to find meaningful patterns in the data. Raw data need to be grouped or classified in some way to establish patterns. Take the following example of ages for 100 respondents which we have entered into the spreadsheet below:

A	B	C	D	E	F	G	H	I	J	K
1	21.9	38.0	16.0	11.6	21.9	38.0	16.0	11.6	16.0	11.6
2	22.8	46.5	15.4	14.9	22.8	46.5	15.4	14.9	15.4	14.9
3	32.0	36.6	56.9	36.6	32.0	36.6	56.9	36.6	56.9	36.6
4	43.0	34.5	38.9	34.5	43.0	34.5	38.9	34.5	38.9	34.5
5	25.6	43.5	39.7	43.5	25.6	43.5	39.7	43.5	39.7	43.5
6	32.8	44.6	53.5	44.6	32.8	44.6	53.5	44.6	53.5	44.6
7	31.4	23.7	64.8	23.7	31.4	23.7	64.8	23.7	64.8	23.7
8	37.0	22.8	72.1	22.8	37.0	22.8	72.1	22.8	72.1	22.8
9	43.2	19.8	22.9	19.8	43.2	19.8	22.9	19.8	22.9	19.8
10	42.6	17.6	12.5	17.6	42.6	17.6	12.5	17.6	12.5	17.6

A convenient way to group data may be to choose class intervals of five or ten years. For example, let us choose a class interval of 10 years. First of all we can look to the tabulated raw data and find the highest and lowest ages. This is called the range. 11.6 is the lowest age in the range, and 72.1 is the highest. We may now decide to group data into ten-year bands such that we count the frequency of observations in each age group as follows:

Age groups	*Frequency*
10 < 20	25
20 < 30	19
30 < 40	26
40 < 50	18
50 < 60	6
60 < 70	3
70 < 80	3
	100

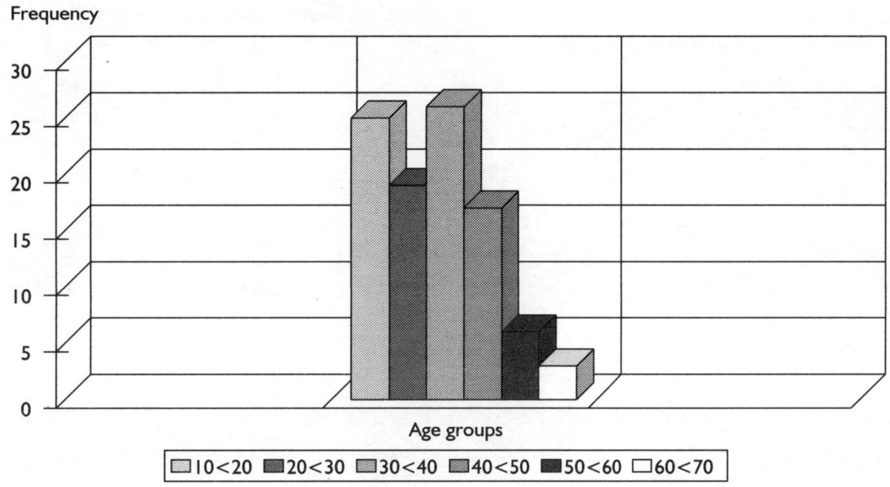

Figure 7.3
Frequency of age by group

We may then want to chart the information we have processed to present a pictorial view that is easy to read and interpret. From the frequency of observations in each age group, we can see that most people are over 30 but under 40. This is the modal group. We could also calculate some simple statistics that describe the age distribution such as those listed below:

33.1	arithmetic mean (average age in years)
15.0	standard deviation for the ages in the sample, in years
100.0	count (the total number of observations)
72.1	maximum age
11.6	minimum age
224.7	variance of ages
3306.7	sum of all ages in the sample

Many computer spreadsheet packages will do these types of statistical calculations for you. Alternatively you may have access to a full statistical package like SPSS in which case descriptive statistics and more advanced procedures can be undertaken to analyse data quickly.

Mean	33.067	S.E. mean	1.507
Standard deviation	15.066	Variance	226.998
Skewness	0.641	S.E. skew	0.241
Range	60.500	Minimum	11.60
Maximum	72.10	Sum	3306.700

Valid observations –100 Missing observations –0

Note: σ^2 = Variance i.e. 15.066 × 15.066 = 226.998

These measures differ slightly from the table above owing to the degree of accuracy provided by SPSS, i.e. 3 decimal places and no rounding up.

We may decide that the age group bandings are too wide and decide to reduce them to 5-year periods as shown in the *histogram* below. A normal curve is superimposed on to the chart to illustrate how we would expect a statistically normal distribution to appear.

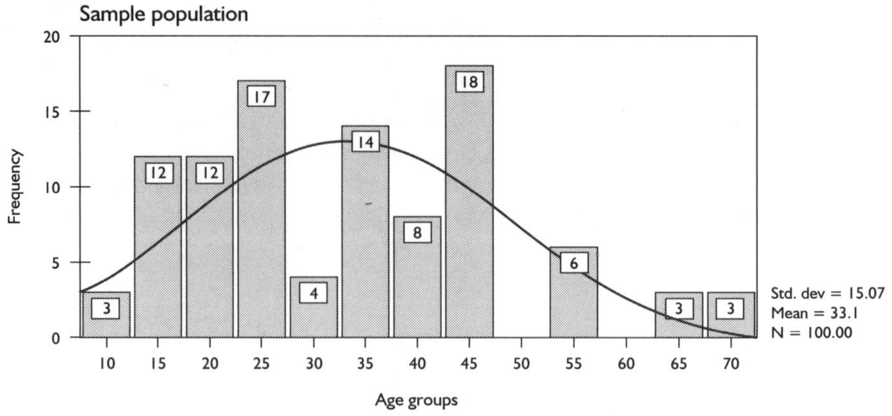

Figure 7.4
Histogram of ages (1)

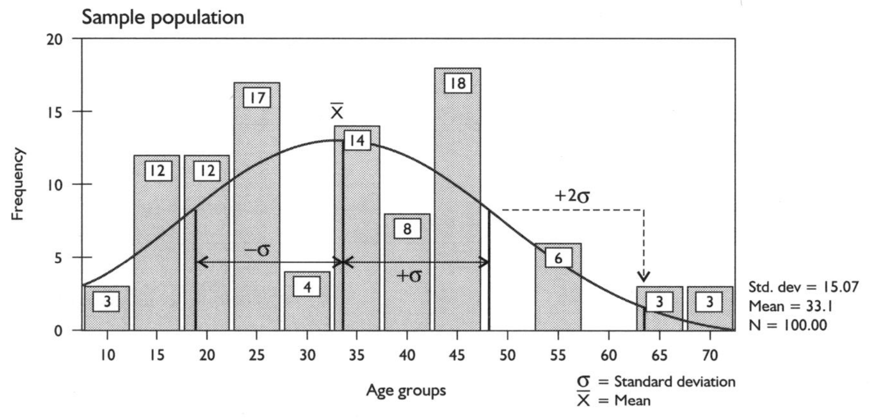

Figure 7.5
Histogram of ages (2)

Definition of symbols:

σ = Standard deviation

$\overline{X}$ = Arithmetic mean of the sample

μ = Arithmetic mean of the population (from which the sample is drawn)

A line showing the arithmetic mean has now been superimposed and you will note it is at the central point of the plateaux of the normal curve. One standard deviation to the right of the mean gives a reading of 48.17 years. Everybody aged over 10 but under 48.17 years will fall under the normal curve within one standard deviation to the right of the mean. In our sample you will see that this represents 88 per cent of the population. 96 per cent of the population fall within two standard deviations from the mean.

The standard deviation σ

The standard deviation is a very useful measure that when combined with other statistical techniques can provide a great deal of useful information. When sample populations have normal distributions we can estimate the percentage of observations falling within one, two or three standard deviations of the mean. If we have a normally distributed sample, then we would expect about 68 per cent of the observations to fall within one standard deviation of the mean and 95.5 per cent within two standard deviations. The data we have are slightly skewed which means they are not normally distributed around the mean, and therefore we have 88 per cent of the sample within + or – one standard deviation but we do have about 95.5 per cent (96 per cent) of all observations within two standard deviations.

Let us look at a further example: supposing we wanted to know the height of women. If we assume that the total population of women is normally distributed and we draw a sample large enough to assume that the sample is also normally distributed then we could describe the characteristics of the total population based on our sample. For example, if we find that the mean height for women in the sample is 5' 6" with a standard deviation of 2" based upon our knowledge of the standard deviation we could say that 68 per cent of all women will be between 5' 4" and 5′ 8″ tall. Furthermore, 95.5 per cent of all women will be between 5' 2" and 5' 10" tall. This along with other information about various measurements could be extremely useful for clothes designers or furniture designers to produce appropriate products.

Question 7.2

Supposing we know the average collar size for a given sample, that we assume is normally distributed, is 15" and that the standard deviation is 1.5" How many people should fall within one standard deviation if we have a sample size of 2,000?

The sampling process

There are three important stages in drawing a sample:

- Identify the target population from which to sample and be clear about the reasons for your choice.
- Choose an appropriate sampling method.
- Calculate the size of the sample required.

A target population is sometimes referred to as the sampling frame. A sampling frame represents that part of the total population that possess the characteristics that are deemed important to the research study. For example characteristics might include: male/female; age group; income bracket; occupation; homeowner and so on. It is important to consider how you can approach your target population. It is no good identifying a target population and then realizing that you cannot gain access to them because there are no listings or databases available. On the other hand you may identify important characteristics and choose to use the characteristics to discriminate between members of the population in a survey, a mall interview, by direct mail and so on by only choosing respondents that fit with your criteria from a larger sample of the whole population.

A sampling frame may be selected in a random or non-random manner. Random sampling involves taking a statistical sample from all groups of the population that have been identified as important to the study. This ensures that there is an equal chance of selection to all sections of that population. A random sample design has a statistical relationship between the sample estimates and the population from which it is drawn. The sample needs to be selected objectively and should avoid any likes and dislikes of the interviewer.

Quota sampling

A non-random sample is also called a quota sample since the researcher is required to interview a set number of people (a quota). Respondents are selected to fit specific criteria which the researcher has identified as important. For example, interview every male wearing a suit who has grey hair aged under 40 years old. A quota (non random) sample requires fewer respondents than a random sample. The results yielded may be just as accurate as a statistical sample if the following criteria are met:

- Up-to-date statistics are available about a particular population.
- Classification questions have been carefully designed to make sure that those selected fit exactly the sampling criteria.
- Interviewers choose the sample carefully following the criteria laid down to avoid any bias.

The larger the sample size the more likely the characteristics will reflect a normal distribution. In our earlier example we had a sample size of N = 100. Maybe had we taken a larger sample it would have been closer to the normal distribution. The standard error statistic gauges how close the sample mean $\bar{X}$ is to the population mean μ. Selecting a random sample from a target population, you would begin by choosing a random number, somehow using tables or a surrogate such as digits from a serialized currency note and then choosing every nth number in the population from which you extract the sample.

$$N = \frac{\text{Population size}}{\text{Sample size}}$$

Multi-stage sampling

Multi-stage sampling may be required to get at the population you want to target. As the name suggests there may be several stages to the sampling process. For example, at the first stage you may need to draw a sample from all the households in a target area. Stage two might require that you identify all married men of a certain age and draw a second stage sample from that population. Single unit or cluster sampling may be performed. This means that rather than selecting single households in an area, you may decide to cluster the sample by using all houses with a particular post code or in a particular road. The sample may be either stratified or unstratified. Stratified samples are necessary when you want to investigate particular characteristics that may be present in an individual sampling unit. A stratum in the population is a segment which has one or more of the common characteristics identified. Stratified samples reduce sampling errors and are usually more representative of the total population than non-stratified samples. As an example, the first stratum may be to identify and sample all those individuals with a particular level of income. The second stratum may be to sample from all those in the population who own a particular type of car. A third stratum may sample from the population on the basis of age. A fourth stratum may relate to employment, and so on.

Cluster samples

Clustering is a way to save costs in sampling from a population. For example, a two-stage design may enable marketing researchers to identify and sample specific clusters that may then be further sampled within the cluster. Using this technique may allow researchers to draw a larger sample at the same cost for a much smaller non-clustered sample.

Examples of clusters that could be used in sampling

Population element	*Possible cluster*
UK adult population	Counties
	Postcodes
	Localities
	Households
	Geographic area
UK telephone households	Exchanges
	Banks of 100 numbers
UK shoppers	Shopping centres
	Day/time
	Supermarkets

Businesses	Locality Plant Store Office
Airline travellers	Airports Flights

Clusters are useful because once you identify a cluster that contains a number of respondents who form part of the target population you can gather data from one centre (a cluster). Carefully designed cluster samples can prove extremely useful as well as cost effective.

Survey and sample costs

Survey costs generally include: fixed overhead costs that do not vary with size of sample; direct costs related to the number of clusters sampled and direct costs related to the number of respondents sampled (e.g. interviewer costs and data processing costs).

Definition 7.2

Survey cost for any marketing research study may be expressed as:

SC = FC + VC

where: SC = survey cost
FC = fixed costs (overheads attributed or allocated to the study)
VC = variable costs or direct costs e.g. interviewers, printing, data processing costs.

Before any survey is undertaken the marketing researchers would need to prepare a detailed budget of cost for the work to be done. It is useful to separate the fixed costs from the variable costs in any budget presented.

The CACI ACORN classification system allows stratification in consumer research. The sampling frame is each sub-group identified in the classification system. Within each of the sub-groups random sampling is used.

Calculating a sample size

The sample size will be dependent on the degree of accuracy required and the marketing research budget available. Using our knowledge of statistics we can estimate the size of the sample required depending on the degree of accuracy we want to achieve. For example, we know that 95.5 per cent of the population should fall within 2 σ of the mean. If 95.5 per cent is the *confidence level* required then we can work out the size of sample needed as follows:

$$\mu = X + \text{or} - \frac{2\sigma}{\sqrt{N}}$$

This means that the true mean for the whole population should be within two standard deviations of the sample mean divided by the square root of the sample size. This is in effect two standard errors of the mean. In our earlier example we had a mean age of 33.067 years with a standard error of 1.51 years. Therefore, the mean for the population $\mu = 33.067 + \text{or} - (2 \times 1.51)$. We are 95.5 per cent confident that the mean age for the population from which we are sampling is somewhere between 30.047 yrs and 36.087 yrs allowing for errors in the sample.

The width of the confidence interval depends on the variability in the data and the size of sample. The confidence interval in this case we have decided is 95.5 per cent but this may change so we will call it W.

$$+ \text{or} - W = \frac{2\sigma}{\sqrt{N}}$$

We would not know the standard deviation σ so we would need to conduct a small survey to get an estimate of σ which we will call s.

$$W^2 = \frac{4s^2}{N}$$

$$N = \frac{4s^2}{W^2}$$

Using the data from our earlier example where we had a sample of 100 ages, the sample standard deviation squared (the variance) was 226.998, and the confidence level required 95.5 per cent say, we would get:

$$N = \frac{4 \times 226.998}{0.912025}$$

$$\underline{N = 995.57797}$$

We would, therefore, need to increase our sample size to 996 people if we wanted to be 95.5 per cent confident about the results of the sample of ages.

Question 7.3

Supposing we wanted to increase the degree of accuracy to 99 per cent confidence, i.e. within + or − 3 σ of the sample mean – what size sample would we require using the same data?

The higher the degree of accuracy required the larger the sample needed and this means a trade off between accuracy and cost is often a problem managers need to resolve. How much are you prepared to pay for the results? This question may also be read as: what degree of accuracy do you require?

Survey data collected using questionnaires may be pre-coded with the aim of analysing data efficiently. Closed questions of the yes/no type are easy to code and analyse. Open questions are more difficult to analyse and will probably require a different approach to interpretion and evaluation.

Data validity and reliability

Data must be valid and, therefore, correspond with the research design. It is also essential that data are collected accurately. Data need to be recorded accurately if results from the analysis are to be reliable. Data analysis comprises a number of key steps which may be described using the following example:

Questionnaire extract		*Coding*	*Total responses*	*Analysis %*
1 Do you eat crisps	Yes	01	470	47.00
	No	02	530	53.00
2 Which of the following types of crisps do you eat?			1000	
	Smiths	03	320	29.36
	Walkers	04	290	26.61
	Sainsbury	05	270	24.77
	Other own brand	06	210	19.27
			1090	

	100%	*47%*	
Proportions of brands	29.36%	13.80%	Smiths
	26.61%	12.50%	Walkers
	24.77%	11.64%	Sainsbury
	19.27%	9.06%	Other own brand
	100.00%	47.00%	

Analysing survey questionnaires

In the example we have coded the questions so that the analysis is easier. Individual questionnaires issued may also be pre-coded to see how many are returned and where they come from. The issue of questionnaires could be controlled in this way if it is important to the research design. Missing respondents in the sample can easily be identified and sent a reminder in an attempt to secure a response. Each of the possible responses may also be coded as in the short questionnaire extract. Question 2 in the extract is a multiple response and so it need not add up to the total of those surveyed since they may eat a variety of brands of crisp at various times. This may be because of availability or they may be indifferent to the brand they eat. Total responses are tabulated on the right hand side. Analysis could take place by referring to proportions. 47 per cent of those surveyed eat crisps while 53 per cent do not. Of the 47 per cent who said they eat crisps, 13.80 per cent said they eat Smiths brand; 12.50 per cent said they eat Walkers crisps; 11.64 per cent said they eat Sainsbury and 9.06 per cent eat another own brand label crisp.

From the analysis conclusions may be reached and recommendations made depending upon the research objectives. It may be necessary to process the data from surveys using particular statistical techniques. Some of the most widely used statistical tools have been listed earlier.

Summary of sampling techniques

Probability sample	Each member of the population has a known (and non-zero) chance of being selected into the sample.
Purposive sample	Selection of sample members is dependent on human judgment.
Stratification	The population is divided into homogeneous groups (strata) whose relative size is known. Strata must be mutually exclusive. A random sample is taken in each stratum.
Proportionate sample	A *uniform sampling fraction* is applied to all the strata, i.e. the proportion of n (the number in the sample) to N (the number in the population) is the same for all strata.
Disproportionate sample	Where there is a marked variation in the sizes of the strata in a population, it is more efficient to use a *variable sampling fraction*. To calculate the sample estimates for the population as a whole, estimates derived from individual strata are weighted according to their relative size.
Quota sample	A method of stratified sampling in which selection of sample members within strata is non-random.
Simple random sample	All the population members are listed and numbered and the sample is drawn in one stage.
Sampling frame	A specification of the population which allows for the identification of individual items. The frame should be complete, up-to-date and without duplication of items.

Systematic frame	The sampling interval is calculated (let $N/n = k$). The first member of the sample is drawn at random from a numbered list. k is added to the number of the randomly selected member. This identifies the second member and the procedure is repeated.
Multi-stage sample	The sample is drawn in more than one stage, usually after stratification by region and type of district. Three stage drawing is quite common: first, constituencies; second, ward or polling districts; third, electors using the Register of Electors as a sampling frame.
PPS	With probability proportionate to size of population/electorate: used in multi-stage drawing and associated with the use of a systematic interval. A range of numbers, equivalent to its population, is attached to each item on the list (e.g. each constituency, each polling district) before the draw is made. A number between one and the total population, divided by the number of sampling points, is drawn at random (or generated by computer). This indicates the starting point; the list of items is then systematically sampled, the probability of selection being proportionate to the size of each item.

Errors avoided by careful research design

The research design should minimize the occurrence of the following errors some or all of which may happen during the research:

- Sampling errors may occur through the selection of a non-representative sample. You should ensure that the sample frame draws from a representative population.
- Non-response errors may happen because those selected in the sample choose not to respond or are no longer located at the address listed. It is important to use up-to-date accurate lists from which to draw samples. It is also important to know what you will do about non-responses in your analysis and reporting.
- Data collection errors may occur because respondents try to please or are badly interviewed. Inexperienced interviewers may record data inefficiently or wrongly select a response. Bias may be introduced by the interviewer at the data collection stage. For example, a structured questionnaire may mislead or the interviewer may wrongly interpret the questions if they are not the designer of the questionnaire but are carrying out the research on behalf of the designer.
- There may be analytical or reporting errors. For example, a particular statistical technique may provide statistics that are misinterpreted by the researcher or worse that the researcher doesn't understand.

It is important to design research with cost in mind. Internal data sources and published secondary data sources are likely to be much lower in cost terms than conducting expensive primary research. You need to trade this off against the potential benefits from conducting primary research which may yield more accurate, more appropriate or more timely information.

Summary

The role of marketing research is to provide information. The information provided will depend upon the purpose. The first step in conducting any marketing research is to set clear objectives that are expected to be achieved by pursuing the research. The marketing researcher must then decide upon a research design. This will depend upon the availability of data, the cost of collection and processing, the time available, the level of detail and accuracy required, relevance and timeliness.

The researcher will usually investigate secondary data sources first either to get some background information or the source may be sufficient to answer the questions and provide the required information. Secondary data is usually less expensive than primary data to collect if it is available. Considerations for the researcher will be how up-to-date the data is, the cost and the relevance for their particular needs.

If primary research is needed then the marketing researcher will need to come up with an appropriate research design to collect, process and analyse the data. This will usually involve the use of some kind of statistical sampling methodology. It is not possible in most circumstances to process all the data from a total population unless that population is particularly small. When the total population is used it is a census rather than a sample.

Answers

Answer 7.1

Deductive and inductive reasoning

Deductive reasoning is applied when you want to generalize to a specific situation from what you already know about a population.

Inductive reasoning assumes that you know everything about a given population and you will test a specific situation against what is known.

Answer 7.2

68% × 2,000 therefore: 1,360.

Answer 7.3

When selecting appropriate sample sizes we noted the relationship between the level of confidence required and the number of standard deviations from the mean. For example, a 68 per cent level of confidence would require a sample to be drawn from + or – one standard deviation. A 95.5 per cent level of confidence requires a sample to be drawn from + or – two standard deviations from the mean. A 99 per cent level of confidence requires a sample to be drawn from + or – three standard deviations. This can be represented diagrammatically as shown in Figure 7.6

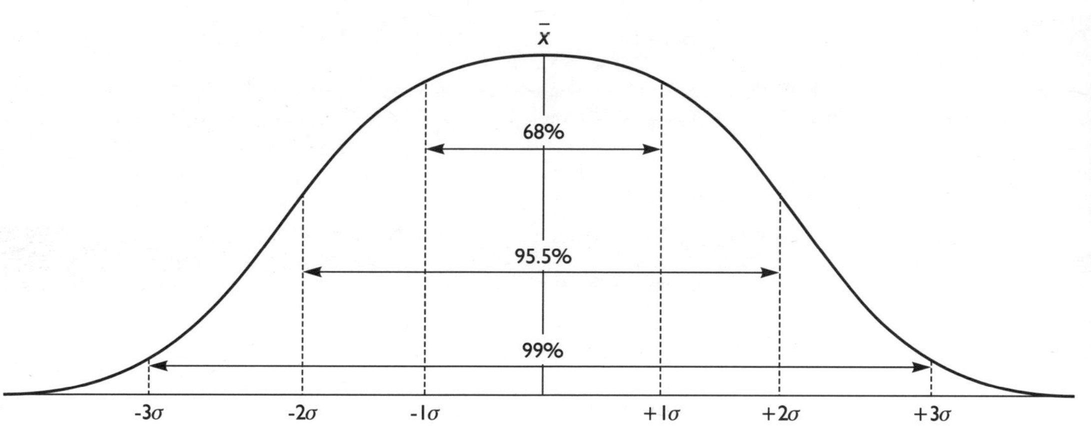

Figure 7.6

You can see from Figure 7.6 that the areas under the curve fall into:

- $\pm \sigma = 68\%$ of total population
- $\pm 2\sigma = 95.5\%$ of total population
- $\pm 3\sigma = 99\%$ of total population

Thus, if we require a sample drawn at 68 per cent level of confidence or covering 68 per cent of the total population we need the formula

$$N = \frac{2s^2}{W^2}$$

where N is sample size, s is an estimate of σ and W is the confidence interval.

The sample required needs to be drawn from the area under the curve falling within one standard deviation to the left and right of the mean ($\bar{X}$).

If we wanted to draw a sample covering 95.5 per cent of the total population then we would need to draw a sample using the formula

$$N = \frac{4s^2}{W^2}$$

Note that 4 is derived from + or –2 estimate standard deviations.

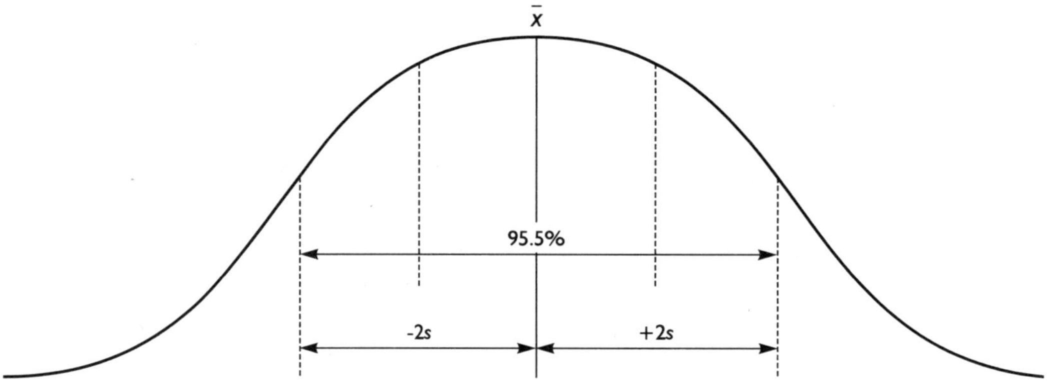

Figure 7.7

The overall area under the curve in Figure 7.7 falls within a total area of 4 standard deviations.

In Question 7.3 we are required to increase accuracy to 99 per cent of the population. Therefore, we need to go 3 standard deviations to the left of the mean i.e. –3s and 3 standard deviations to the right of the mean i.e. +3s. This is a total distance of 6 standard deviations.

$$N = \frac{6s^2}{W^2}$$

$$= \frac{6 \times 226.998}{0.99 \times 0.99}$$

$$= \frac{1361.988}{0.9801}$$

$$= 1389.64$$

You would need to draw a sample of 1390 units in order to be confident in making statements representing 99 per cent of the population from which the sample is drawn, see Figure 7.8.

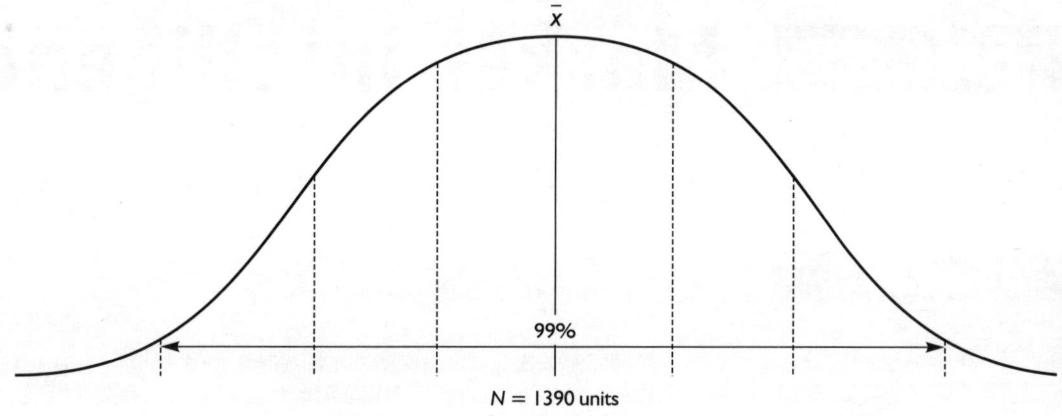

Figure 7.8

Unit 8 Market intelligence

Objectives

After studying this unit you should:

- ❑ Know what a marketing information system is and understand the specific parts of the system and how they link together.
- ❑ Know and understand the marketing research roles within a marketing information system.
- ❑ Know what is meant by the terms customer intelligence and competitor intelligence.
- ❑ Be aware of the importance of understanding industry structure and the forces which shape an industry.
- ❑ Clearly know and understand the types of data that may be gathered to provide information about competitors and customers (although customer/consumer research is more thoroughly treated in Unit 10).

Study Guide

This unit introduces you to the concept of market intelligence. It is important to understand what is meant by the term intelligence and to be able to make the distinction between data, information and intelligence. The unit introduces you to the role of secondary data in providing market intelligence and also to internal and external sources of data.

Marketing research roles are discussed briefly in this unit and are expanded in the next three units. It is important to recognize the need for both competitor and customer intelligence and how this may be achieved. You should keep in mind as you work through the unit how your own organization gathers intelligence about competition and customers. This will help you make sense of the unit.

Exam Hints

The important concepts introduced to you in this chapter could well be applied to specific situations in a mini case or as a part B type question. You should keep in mind as you study how the concepts are or may be applied in practice.

The model shown illustrates the interrelationship between corporate objectives, marketing plans and their implementation and the role played by the marketing information system (MKIS). The dotted line represents a feedback loop. It can be seen that the marketing information system is central to marketing planning and implementation. Corporate objectives inform the marketing planning process which in turn is influenced by the MKIS. Marketing plans are implemented taking account of information. There is feedback at each stage of the model that acts as a control mechanism and may reshape the planning process.

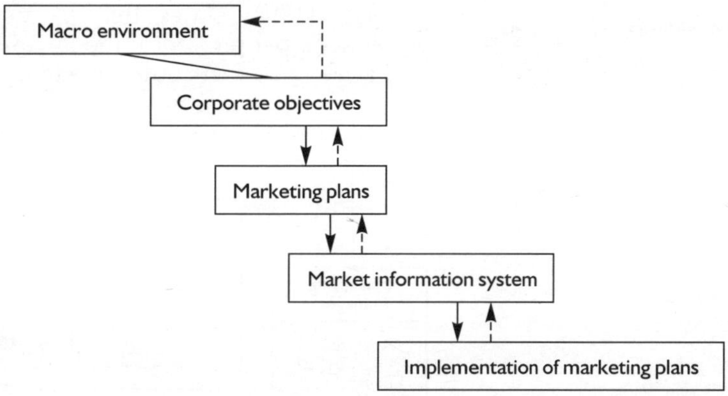

Figure 8.1
Marketing information system

Marketing information systems (MKIS)

Marketing information systems consist of internally collected and stored data from a variety of sources within the organization. MKIS also consist of externally trawled data that is systematically collected for the purpose of providing information to marketing and sales managers. Data collected continuously and in an ad hoc manner can form part of the system as can marketing research that is conducted for specific purposes.

Figure 8.2 shows the main reasons why a firm may want to have marketing and sales information. It is important that the information stored is accurate, timely, relevant and of sufficient quality to provide decision makers with support for their decisions. Managers make better marketing and sales decisions when they have good quality information that informs the decision making process.

Figure 8.2
The value of good information

Definition 8.1

The purpose of a marketing information system A marketing information system should regularly collect, analyse, disseminate and store data relevant to the needs of the organization bearing in mind the cost and the value of the MKIS.

Kotler (1994) states that 'A marketing information system (MKIS) consists of people, equipment, and procedures to gather, sort, analyse, evaluate, and distribute needed, timely and accurate information to marketing decision makers'. Kotler's model of what a marketing information system comprises is adapted in Figure 8.3.

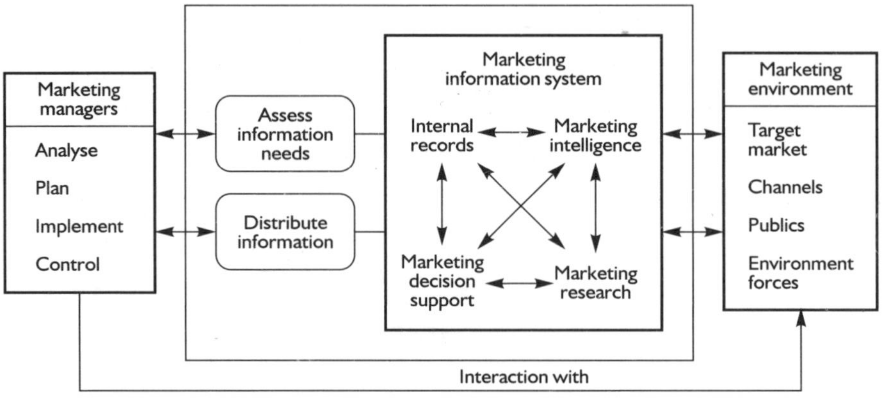

Figure 8.3
A marketing information system (Kotler)

The starting point in designing an information system is to assess what information is required by managers to help them analyse, plan, implement and control marketing and sales activities. Then initiate a search process to find out where this information is available. Does data already exist that may be used to provide appropriate information? If so, is it available within the firm? Or is it published data held by an external source? If data is not available either within the firm's own databases or from external databases (in other words from *secondary data* sources already in existence internally or externally) then the search might entail some *primary data* collection. This may mean conducting our own research or commissioning an external marketing research agency. Once data is available from whatever source it must be processed and analysed to provide information that may be used to support decision making or to further add to and provide market intelligence. The application of the information will of course depend on the original aims of the research and the original need identified as to why information is wanted.

Reduce financial risk

One of the major roles for marketing research is to reduce the financial risks by assessing risk and uncertainty in the marketing and sales environment. For example, supposing a firm is considering investing substantial funds in developing a new product that it will promote heavily then it would want to know:

- Likely consumer acceptance
- Target market segment to communicate with
- Forecast demand at particular price levels
- Possible competitor reactions
- Packaging that will most likely impress the marketplace and provide the right image for the product and so on.

All these factors and some more besides would provide the firm with data that can be processed to inform the marketing and sales managers taking the decisions. Although financial risk cannot be eliminated it can be reduced through having good quality marketing information.

Monitor competitor behaviour

It is important for firms to track and monitor competitor behaviour so as to gain competitive advantage in the marketplace. It is important to know how competitors will respond to particular marketing and sales activities undertaken by the firm. Take the example of the newspaper market in the UK. Firms monitor their competitors and will often respond to their initiatives by doing similar or better promotions that minimize the impact of their competitor's offering and gain an advantage for the firm. For example, if the *Sunday Times* introduce a promotional offer of a price reduction for those who bought *The Times* on a Saturday, then a near competitor who is likely to suffer from this action may decide to make a similar but slightly different offer to try to gain a competitive edge.

Competitive behaviour does of course depend upon many influences not least of which are the market structure and the nature of competition within the marketplace.

Determine customer and consumer attitudes

Marketing information is needed to help understand the attitudes of customers and consumers, so that decisions can be taken that can influence those attitudes to provide a favourable response to the offerings of the firm. Alternatively, attitudes may be neutralized to prevent damage to the firm. Take the case of Perrier Water where the brand had to be removed from supermarket shelves because of contamination. The company reacted quickly to minimize the adverse effects by providing information to customers about the steps they would be taking to safeguard consumers. The damage was limited to the short term, and long term interests were protected by providing consumers with information. It is suggested that this action was possible probably because the company had an MIS that helped them to understand the needs of their customers and consumers enabling them to take appropriate steps quickly and communicate for maximum effect.

Monitor the environment

It is important for firms to be aware of changes taking place in the external environment; they may impact upon decisions being taken internally. A good marketing information system will ensure that regular environmental scanning is conducted with a view to minimizing threats and maximizing opportunities. Political changes, economic conditions, social trends and changes in technology may all combine to affect marketing and selling plans and decisions.

Exam Hints

A useful acronym to remember is PEST (political, economic, social and technological).

Co-ordinate marketing and sales plans

Information is needed so as to be able to co-ordinate marketing and sales activities for maximum effect.

Target promotional activity

Information is required that will enable managers to target promotional activities effectively. An example was given earlier.

Evaluate alternative decisions

Information is always needed for managers to analyse and evaluate marketing and sales decisions in a variety of contexts. Sales opportunities may be maximized and financial risk may be minimized through having relevant, timely, accurate information from appropriate data sources that have used appropriate techniques yielding reliable and valid results.

Measure performance

Benchmarking is the practice of comparing business practices between companies, and it has come of age in the UK. According to a recent survey by Gallup more than three-quarters of the UK's top 1,000 companies claim to use benchmarking to assess and improve their performance. For example, British Rail cut the time taken to clean a train to eight minutes after benchmarking against British Airways. Rank Xerox decided to improve its call handling, and it approached companies with a strong reputation for answering calls quickly such as the RAC and British Gas. As a result they now claim that they have re-engineered call handling. British

Airways also makes benchmarking sound simple. When it wanted to improve the service on its frequent-flier programme, it visited the Oriental Hotel in Bangkok – renowned for pampering its guests – to pick up tips on how to record details of its customers' preferences. When it wanted to improve its passenger handling areas, it analysed its weak points and then studied some of its rivals. Benchmarking against a company which appears to be the best at a particular activity is the most popular option for large, confident companies. (Source: *Financial Times*, August 1994.)

Measuring performance requires information. This may take the form of internal financial and cost data; or internal measures such as the number of sales returns per period or the standard times taken to perform particular tasks. Alternatively, external data sources may be used as in the case of the benchmarking examples given above.

Benchmarking and customer service levels

Benchmarking is a modern term used to measure an organization's products, services, processes and practices against the standards of best competitors and others recognized as leaders in their field. There are often said to be five key stages in undertaking a benchmarking exercise referred to as the service audit. They are:

1 Define the competitive arena.
2 Determine the customer based definitions of service, e.g. using a small sample – a survey, a census may be possible where numbers are low, focus groups – the selection of method to determine this will depend on time, cost and benefits.
3 Use trade-off analysis to identify the key service factors.
4 Benchmark performance against key competitors.
5 Develop service profile and service performance matrix.

Extending Activity 8.1

Investigate the types of information that marketing and sales managers in your own organization use on a regular basis and identify the purpose of such information and the data sources.

Example of using a customer service index measure

Supposing a specific customer decides that a number of the attributes listed in the table are important to them they may decide to allocate a weighting to each measure. Table 8.1 demonstrates how such a service measure may be calculated:

Table 8.1

Service element	*Importance weighting (1)*	*Performance level by a supplier (2)*	*Weighted score (1) × (2)*
On time delivery	50%	90%	45
Order completeness	30%	80%	24
Invoice accuracy	10%	95%	9.5
Returns	10%	90%	9
INDEX			87.5

In making a selection of suppliers the customer may draw up a number of comparisons between competing suppliers. Obviously suppliers who have a higher index of customer satisfaction have a higher chance of being retained by the customer. It is important for suppliers to understand how customers are measuring their performance and take steps to satisfy customers whilst achieving their own objectives.

Many retailing organizations use supplier assessment rating in a similar way to that described.

It is possible to use data generated from a customer service audit (CSA) to compare it with how well an organization is meeting the needs of their customers. A simple way of displaying this is to use a service performance matrix as in Table 8.2. Key service attributes in this example that have been identified from a CSA are:

1 Order cycle time –
2 Completeness of orders –
3 Quality of documentation –
4 Delivery reliability –
5 Technical support –
6 Sales visits –

Table 8.2

		Importance to customer (data from CSA) 1 = unimportant, 5 = very important				
		1	2	3	4	5
Perceived performance 1 = poor 5 = excellent	1				**(1)**	
	2	**(2)**				**(4)**
	3		**(3)**			
	4	**(5)**	**(6)**			
	5					

Interpreting the matrix is relatively easy. In the example given the organization is not meeting customer expectations on attributes 1 (order cycle time) and 4 (delivery reliability) and it is overperforming on 2 (completeness of orders) and 5 (technical support).

Accounting for customers rather than products

Traditionally accounting methods have identified and analysed product costs. However what may be more relevant particularly when considering customer service is a way of measuring customer profitability or customer account profitability (CAP). Activity based costing (ABC) is a way of viewing costs differently. It has often been difficult for marketing managers to obtain the types of financial data that they require to manage more effectively. For example, there has been a general ignorance of the true cost of servicing different customers, different segments and different channels of distribution. This is because costs have focused upon the product and not the market. In other words inputs to the product rather than outputs to the customers. Conventional accounting systems are functionally oriented rather than output focused. They have been designed not as a management tool but as a reporting tool of what happened in the past. Even when accounting systems or parts of the system have tried to look forward they have not focused upon market issues but rather the product has been central to the analysis. This is not to say that it is unimportant to identify product costs but rather to recognize that this is only one perspective for cost management. Furthermore, full costing (absorption costing) is based upon a number of key assumptions relating to the ways in which overheads might be recovered.

Essentially ABC is concerned with the identification of activities that cause cost. Such activities might be the order cycle times required by customers, the availability of stock, frequency of delivery, technical support, order status information and visits to customers by sales personnel. There will of course be many other types of activity. Activity based management involves four key steps:

1 Activity analysis.
2 Cost reduction.
3 Product/service 'offer' profitability.
4 Development of an integrated activity based costing system.

Information and dissemination

User reports must be designed with the following in mind:

- What types of decision are you required to take?
- What information do you need to make them?
- The sources of data available and their cost and quality?
- What information do you currently receive?
- What information do you request from time to time or what would you like to have and in what form?
- Frequency – how often do you require the information?
- What would you like to be kept informed about?
- What hardware or software could help you obtain, analyse or process information better?

Processing data will often involve the use of statistical techniques to simplify and make sense of the data. Some of the techniques are extremely sophisticated and complex and beyond the scope of this syllabus. There are many statistical software packages that are available to apply the tools, and one of the most popular is SPSS (statistical package for social science). Some of the charts in this book have been produced using SPSS. However, a list of definitions of some of the most useful statistical tools is given below:

Definition 8.2

Some useful statistical tools

Multiple regression This is a statistical technique for estimating a *best fitting* equation to explain how the value of a dependent variable varies with changing values of a number of independent variables.

For example, an equation to predict consumer spending, the dependent variable, may be explained by a number of independent variables which may include: disposable incomes, advertising and promotional spend by the brand, marginal rates of tax and the savings ratio. Another example could be: a company can estimate how unit sales are influenced by changes in the level of promotional expenditures, salesforce size, number of sales visits, and price.

Discriminant analysis This is a statistical technique for classifying objects or persons into two or more categories. For example: a retailer may be able to discriminate between store locations of similar products, to see which is providing the optimum sales position.

Factor analysis This is a statistical technique used to determine the few underlying dimensions of a larger set of intercorrelated variables. For example: it may be possible to reduce the number of factors affecting brand choice from say 22 down to three key influencing factors.

Cluster analysis This is a statistical technique for separating objects into a specified number of mutually exclusive groups such that the groups are relatively homogeneous. For example: a marketing researcher might want to classify a miscellaneous set of characteristics about competing products into four clusters (or groups).

Conjoint analysis This is a statistical technique used to rank the preferences of a number of respondents to the different offers which are decomposed, to determine the person's inferred utility function for each attribute and to evaluate the relative importance of each attribute.

For example: a financial services company or an airline can determine the total utility delivered by different combinations of customer services. It may then rank them in order of importance to customers to see which services customers value most.

Multidimensional scaling These are a variety of techniques for representing objects as points in a multidimensional space of attributes where their distance from each other is a measure of dissimilarity.

Multidimensional scaling is most often used in studies related to brand positioning or product positioning. It is a technique that is useful in determining customer or consumer perceptions of the wording used in the survey.

Approaches to marketing research

Primary data may be collected in one of four ways: survey, focus groups, observation and experimentation.

Surveys

Surveys are discussed thoroughly elsewhere. Surveys are useful for descriptive research and are therefore best undertaken to find out about people's knowledge, beliefs, preferences and satisfaction. Surveys usually provide quantitative measures that can describe the various characteristics of the people in the survey (the population). Statistical methods are often applied to survey data so as to make inferences about the particular population being studied.

Focus group research

Focus group research is often a useful exploratory step before designing a large scale survey. It enables the researchers to gain insight into people's perceptions, attitudes, motives, beliefs and satisfaction. Selection to a focus group can be done in a number of ways using various sampling techniques as appropriate. Samples if used will be very small in comparison to the whole population and are usually not random in their selection. As a result any findings from focus group research will have limitations if you try to generalize to the whole population. They are, nevertheless, a very useful means of gaining insight into the issues that you may want to investigate further.

A focus group usually consists of between 6 to 10 people who are asked to take part with a skilled moderator leading the discussion. They last approximately two to three hours and sometimes are recorded using audio or video equipment. It is important that any mechanical or electrical recording devices are unobtrusive, so as not to distract the participants. Surroundings are usually informal, maybe in someone's home or in a comfortable hotel room on neutral ground so as to make group members feel relaxed and open up in discussion. The moderator needs to be skilled in leading and controlling the discussion towards the issues that the research wants to find out about, hence the term *focus* group. Refreshments are often provided to the participants and a small fee may also be paid.

Observation

Observational research is useful in providing data about a variety of situations. Observation takes place in the context of the situation being observed and the matter being the subject of the study. For example, if you want to find out about the important considerations in reaching in a purchasing decision in a car showroom, you might try to observe a number of customers making up their minds and listening to the discussions that take place between the parties concerned. More and more consumer research has been undertaken in this way in the last few years with the emergence of mystery shoppers who are researchers acting as shoppers observing how sales staff deal with them.

Observational research can be used to confirm findings from survey research or to investigate further some of the findings from other research. Observation may also be used to identify issues that can be the subject of further research using other methods such as a survey.

Experimental research

Experimental research is said to be the most scientific type of research. The problem with experimentation in a business or commercial setting is that many of the variables are not controllable in the same way that they would be for scientific study in the physical sciences. People do not always respond in exactly the same way even when confronted with exactly or almost exactly the same situation, whereas an electrical current will always respond in the same way to a given stimuli (e.g. when you throw a switch, a current will pass and a bulb will light or the current will stop and the bulb will not light).

Research instruments

Marketing researchers basically have the following research instruments that they are able to use: *questioning respondents* (questionnaires, interviewing respondents) and *mechanical/electrical instruments* (meters, cameras, audio, EDI systems – EPOS, EFTPOS). The instruments either rely on *questioning* the subjects of the research in some way, assuming that what they tell you is what they do, or *observation* of behaviour using technology in some way.

Questionnaires are by far the most common research instrument in marketing research for collecting data. It is probably the only way at present to collect large survey data. Questionnaires should always be piloted with a small group of people before administering any large scale survey. Questions need to be tested for ambiguity, error (in content or in the way the data could be analysed) and for style, structure, sequence and ease of response. Questions should provide *reliable* and *valid* data.

Interviewers may often use structured or semi-structured questionnaires in their interview.

Sampling in marketing research

Marketing researchers need to decide if they are going to conduct the research using sampling techniques. When the research is small scale or the population under scrutiny is small this may not be necessary. For instance, if a firm had only a small number of customers and it wanted to find out more about better ways to serve them it need not sample, it could use the total population of customers (i.e. a census). This is often the case in industrial marketing research.

When sampling is required it is important to decide:

- The sampling unit – who is to be surveyed? What is the target population from which the sample will be drawn?
- Sample size – how many people will be surveyed? Large samples provide more reliable results than do smaller samples. It is not always necessary to sample the whole target population or even a large proportion of it to achieve reliable results if the sampling procedure is credible. Small samples comprising less than 1 per cent of the population may yield a satisfactory result. Smaller samples are obviously cheaper to conduct and therefore, careful consideration should be given to balance cost, technique and accuracy.
- Sampling procedure – how will the respondents be selected? This is very important. To obtain a representative sample from a target population, a probability sample should be drawn. This will allow for the calculation of confidence limits and sampling error.

Types of sampling used in marketing research

Probability sample	*Non-probability sample*
Simple random sample	Convenience sample
Stratified random sample	Judgement sample
Cluster (area) sample	Quota sample

Sampling is explained further elsewhere.

Activity 8.1

Consider what type of marketing research you might want to undertake if your firm wanted to improve the level of service offered to customers. Prepare a brief summary outlining the steps involved in the investigation. What type of research? What research instruments might be used? Who are the target population? How would you make your selection?

Internal data

- Accounting (cost data, sales data, segment reports, budgets, variance reports, ratios and trends)
- Purchasing records
- Production records and statistics
- Sales records.

External data

- Government statistics (e.g. economic trends, demographics, export and import statistics)
- Published sources (e.g. market reports by Mintel, Keynote, Euromonitor etc.).

Competitor intelligence

Organizations need systematically to collect data that provides information about competitors. Continuous data systematically collected to track competitors may consist of published sources, other secondary data and primary data collected from marketing research (surveys and observation mainly). A firm will also continuously scan its operating environment and note the effects of any changes having an impact. Ad hoc and non-routine intelligence may be added through piecing together a variety of data from different sources e.g. sales personnel in the field may gather competitor data from customers; buyers may gather competitor data from suppliers, accounting personnel may gather data about competitors from their contacts with suppliers and customers and so on. An organization must find a way to gather these data to provide information and intelligence.

For example firms need intelligence that provides them with answers to the following questions:

- Who are our competitors?
- What strategies are they pursuing?
- How effective are those strategies?
- What objectives do they have?
- What are their strengths and weaknesses?
- How do they react to competitive behaviour?

Identifying competitors

On the face of it this seems a relatively easy task. For example, Coca-Cola may identify Pepsi Cola as its major competitor; Du Pont may identify Rhône Poulenc as a major fibre competitor; Unilever may identify Procter and Gamble, Levi and Wrangler for jeans and so on. However, an organization's actual and potential competition may be much greater. For example, Procter and Gamble and Unilever are major players in a global market for soap powders, but also in this market there are many players. The range of competition is much greater than just these two brands. The range and strength of competition will differ in each geographical market segment. The competition may come from other producers of similar products including supermarkets' own brands but may include substitute products such as liquid soap *vis-'a-vis* powders.

Competition may take place based on the degree of product substitution. This will depend upon:

- Brand competition e.g. Miller *v.* Budweiser beers
- Industry competition: all light beers
- Form competition e.g. all alcoholic beer drinks
- Generic competition e.g. all drinks including soft drink products.

Industry structure and competition

People refer to the degree of competition within an industry. An industry may be defined as a group of firms that offer a product or range of products that are close substitutes for each other. Alternative definitions of an industry look at the similarity of markets served or technologies employed. If we accept that an industry serves the needs of customers by offering a number of close substitute products then we are following closely the *Economist's* definition of an industry. This concept assumes that the industry's products have a high cross-elasticity of demand and are in direct competition with each other.

To understand industry competition we need to know the underlying competitive forces within the industry. These conditions give rise to the shape of industry structure which in turn influences industry behaviour in areas like product development, pricing, promotion and logistics. Competitor intelligence systems need to be able to monitor and evaluate such behaviour patterns so as to formulate responses and instigate strategies to offset the threats and to take advantage of the opportunities presented. It is behaviour that determines performance, and analysts may identify this in terms of efficiency measures, profitability measures, growth, return on investment measures, employment, technological developments, innovation and so on.

Porter (1980) refers to five forces which influence the competitive nature of an industry.

1. The number and quality of potential entrants to the industry.
2. The number, quality and availability of close substitute products.
3. The relative bargaining power between suppliers and the industry they serve.
4. The relative bargaining power between the buyers and the industry.
5. The rivalry that exists between the firms comprising the industry.

Marketing analysts wanting to understand the nature of this industry competition and competitive behaviours must understand the forces at work and how they interact. Competitor intelligence systems need to monitor and evaluate the structure of the industry and the behaviours being adopted by the firms in the industry.

Analysing the five dimensions mentioned by Porter may provide the organization with insights into its relationships with key market areas. The threat of new entrants to an industry will be regulated by the barriers to entry that exist. Such barriers may include:

Economies of scale
Economies of scope contained within existing firms in the industry
Product differentiation
Capital requirements
Switching costs
Access to distribution channels
Cost disadvantages other than scale

Government policies
Entry deterring pricing by existing firms
Experiences.

The bargaining power of suppliers may be powerful if there is/are:

Few suppliers
Little or no substitute suppliers
A high degree of differentiation in supplier offerings
A threat of forward integration.

Or finally if the industry is not an important customer group for the supplier, the bargaining power of buyers will be powerful if:

They buy a large percentage of the supplier's sales.
They form a high proportion of the buyer's cost (e.g. bulk discounts negotiated).
The product is not differentiated sufficiently from other competitor products.
There is low buyer switching costs.
There is a threat of backward integration.
The supplier's products are not important to the buyer in terms of final quality of the end product.

Competitor strengths and weaknesses

Competitor intelligence should provide an understanding of the nature of the competition – strengths and weaknesses, attitudes and likely behaviours and responses to your firm's actions or the actions of other firms in the same industry. Competitive strategies will be developed from the information and intelligence gathered by the organization. An indicative list of the types of data and information that may lead to gaining intelligence about competitors is given as follows:

- Sales volumes/values and segments etc.
- Market share
- Cost structures
- Profit levels
- Returns on capital invested
- Cash flow
- Profitability by segment
- Production processes and technologies employed
- Capacity levels and the utilization
- Product quality
- Range of products and any new developments
- Size and structure of the customer base
- Suppliers
- Culture of the organization
- Level of brand loyalty
- Dealer networks and distribution channels
- Core capabilities and competence
- Marketing and selling capability
- Operations and logistics
- Financial structure and capability
- Management capability and attitudes to risk
- Ownership and owner expectations
- Human resource capability
- Response patterns

Building this intelligence is often much more difficult in practice than it may appear in textbooks. The sources of data that provide information and lead to intelligence about competitors will vary from industry to industry, but may typically include:

- Published data sources
- Sales force data
- Trade exhibitions

- Industry experts
- Trade press
- Distributors
- Suppliers
- Customers

Information needs to be collected systematically and recorded systematically. If information is to provide intelligence and bring benefits to the collecting firm, it must be readily accessible to managers to make appropriate marketing and sales decisions and formulate strategy.

Weakness, vulnerability and strategy

Davidson (1987, pp. 139–40) states that knowledge of competitor weaknesses can be used to great effect in formulating marketing strategy. The factors that give rise to weakness and vulnerability include:

- Lack of cash
- Low margins
- Poor growth
- High costs in operation or distribution
- Overdependence on one market
- Strength in falling sectors
- Short term orientation
- People problems
- Lack of focus
- Predictability
- Product or service obsolescence
- High market share
- Low market share
- Premium price positioning
- Slow moving bureaucratic structures
- Fiscal year fixation

This information may be used to attack particular competitors when they are vulnerable by focusing on weaknesses identified.

Competitors may react in a number of ways. Kotler identifies four common response profiles that are described below:

1 *The laid back competitor* – does not respond quickly or strongly to competitor moves.
2 *The selective competitor* – only responds to some moves and not others which it does not perceive to be any major threat
3 *The tiger competitor* – This company acts swiftly to any threats posed.
4 *Stochastic competitors* – unpredictable in nature, they may or may not respond and there is no predictable pattern of behaviour.

Setting up a competitor intelligence system (CIS)

A competitor intelligence system is an essential ingredient of strategy. A CIS system needs to follow the following steps:

- Decide what information you require.
- Design appropriate data capture systems and collect the data.
- Analyse and evaluate the data.
- Communicate the information.
- Incorporate the information and conclusions reached into strategy and feedback results so that the information system may be refined.

Question 8.1

Distinguish between data, information and intelligence.
(**Answer** See end of chapter.)

Customer intelligence

A field sales force or a telephone sales force is often the first point of customer contact. These are the people who acquire information which may be turned into intelligence when pieced together with other systematically collected and ad hoc information. Intelligence may be acquired through environmental scanning, trade exhibitions and trade press. Customer intelligence will help in formulating strategies that serve the customer needs.

Information for competitive advantage

One important effect of information technologies is that firms are becoming increasingly aware of the competitive advantage that may be achieved. Marketing information is an asset. Information systems can affect the way the firm approaches customer service and provide advantages over competitor approaches. Airlines, insurance companies, banks and travel companies are amongst the leading industries that have developed on-line enquiry and information systems to enhance customer service. It is of course only the particular leading firms in each of the industries that are able to achieve advantage and laggards suffer lost orders and falling profits. Customer service can only be achieved by being able to anticipate and satisfy customer needs. In order to meet this objective, information which is up-to-date, accurate, relevant and timely is essential.

Porter (1980) refers to two sources of competitive advantage; to compete on cost, or through differentiation. In a modern society, differentiation may be achieved through the application of information technologies. The better quality data a firm is able to collect, store and retrieve about competitors and customers should enable it to process data and provide information to marketing and sales managers to make better quality decisions. This may allow the firm to adapt its product/service offerings to meet the needs of the marketplace through differentiation. For instance, consider mail order companies that are able to store data about customer buying habits. They are able to exploit such data by using the information they glean to establish patterns of buying behaviour and offer products at likely buying times that are in line with the customer's profile. The information may prove to be a source of competitive advantage.

Databases and information systems

Information systems may alter the way business is done, and may provide organizations with new opportunities. For example, a theatre with the capability to set up a database of theatregoers may increase awareness and desire in potential customers, by establishing regular communications which stimulate the theatregoer to purchase more tickets. Building relationships with existing customers and attracting new customers are the keys to personal selling in the theatre. Consider a theatre in a tourist city wanting to use new technology to build a database. The type of data it may wish to have are as follows:

- Analysis of theatregoers by specific characteristics: age, sex, home address.
- How many performances each theatre customer sees in the year.
- How many days visitors stay in the city and how they choose a day or night at the theatre.
- Types of production customers like to watch.
- Factors important to their decision to visit the theatre, e.g. price, location, play, cast, facilities.
- Where they obtained information on the theatre and its productions: press, hotel, leaflets, mailings etc.
- Other purchases customers make when visiting the theatre.
- Other entertainment theatregoers choose to spend money on.

This data could then be used by the theatre marketing management to build relationships with the customer and to exploit sales and promotional opportunities.

Information as a marketing asset

Information may be viewed as a marketing asset since it impacts on performance as follows:

- Helps improve responsiveness to customer demands.
- Helps identify new customer opportunities and new product/service demands.
- Helps anticipate competitive attacks and threats.

Piercy (1992, p. 176) comments that information relates to the quality of our understanding of the market, and this relates directly to our competitive strength.

Answer

Answer 8.1

Data may be primary, specifically collected for the purpose of the user, or it may be secondary in nature, that is readily available from another source (e.g. published). Although not exactly designed to fit your requirements the data are adaptable to meet your specific information needs. Time, cost, accuracy and value being the major consideration in choosing secondary or primary data sources.

Information is data that has been processed to provide information about a specific item. For example, daily sales records may provide data on sales values, items sold and customers who bought. Until the data is processed you would not know such things as: value by customer, profit margins (sales values less stock sold at cost price), average order values and so on.

Intelligence goes beyond information. It pieces together a number of different information strands and is able to provide a fuller picture that may be acted upon.

Unit 9 Marketing and research applications

Objectives

After reading this unit you should be able to:

- Identify specific types of marketing research.
- Know the application of the various types of marketing research.
- Know and understand why marketing research is necessary and how it may be used to provide appropriate information in specific situations.

Study Guide

This unit will look at some of the main applications for marketing research. It will introduce to you some of the main reasons for conducting marketing research and will give an indication of the types of data that need to be gathered and what sorts of information can be revealed. Specific techniques are mentioned but not discussed in any detail since techniques are the subject of Unit 10. You may like to read Unit 10 at the same time or to refer to that unit for any further information about a technique that would help you understand better the discussion in this unit.

This unit covers 3.3 of your syllabus. It is important that you refer to other books on your reading list if you need to supplement your understanding of any of the important issues in this unit. The broadsheet newspapers and *Marketing* also often report findings from specific marketing research studies that will keep you up to date with current developments in research techniques and application.

Ten good reasons for marketing research

The purpose of marketing research is to produce information that reduces risk and uncertainty in decision making. Research applications may be:

- To find out about a particular market.
- To test products before launch.
- To find out what new products could be introduced to satisfy existing customer requirements that are identified through research.
- To find out how well particular products/services are selling, and who they are selling to.
- To investigate the price of competitor products and to set a price.
- To investigate which channels are the most profitable for existing products.
- To investigate which channels to select.
- To find out what communication messages will work best.
- To investigate media choice/selection.
- To evaluate the effectiveness of promotional/advertising campaigns.

This list is not exhaustive but it does provide you with a clear brief list of reasons why organizations choose to undertake marketing research.

Information is required to anticipate customer needs, to deliver products or services that satisfy those needs, to measure marketing and sales performance, to monitor competitors and competitor products and prices, to formulate marketing strategies, to implement tactics, to manage marketing operations, to identify opportunities and threats. The aim of marketing research is to generate information from a variety of data sources that will reduce uncertainty, minimize risk and enable managers to make effective decisions about marketing operations, tactics and strategy.

Market research

Market research is concerned with finding out about markets. These may be existing markets or potential markets. Information may be required on the following:

- Market size
- Market trends
- Sales forecasts
- Customer information
- Competitor information
- Segmentation studies
- Market characteristics

Market research is required to make decisions about market entry, market withdrawal and to see how existing products are performing in the market. Data will be needed on market size and market structure to address the following issues:

How big is the market?
How profitable is the market?
Is it a growing or declining market?
What are the main products in this market?
Who supplies these products?
How are the products distributed?
What marketing strategies are appropriate to this market?

Studies of market size and market trends are usually relatively easy to research using secondary data carrying out desk research. Sources of data to satisfy these needs may be found from:

Secondary data sources: government statistics; market reports produced by information companies such as Mintel, Keynote, McCarthy, Nielson etc.
Syndicated research may be used i.e. you contact an information provider and pay a subscription to join a syndicate who pay for specific market research on a regular basis. This has the advantage of reducing the cost for any single member of the syndicate and usually provides high quality research. The major disadvantage is probably that all your competitors have access to the same data. There may also be *omnibus surveys* that you could access. These are regular surveys conducted by professional research organizations that are sold on to interested parties.

You may want to investigate market characteristics with a view to identifying specific segments. This data will probably be available from secondary data sources such as:

Market reports previously mentioned (Mintel, Keynote etc.)
Syndicated research services: Target Group Index (TGI), retail audits
Omnibus surveys if the service exists in this particular market.

If you are mainly concerned with finding out how well your products are received or perceived by the market then you need to conduct attitude, motivational or behavioural research. You may want to know the characteristics of your target market. The data required will probably be primary data collected from this target market using appropriate sampling techniques and will make statistical inferences applicable to the total market. You will need to conduct a market segment study either in-house if you have the marketing research expertise or you will need to employ a specialist agency. Geographic, demographic and psychographic data are of most use in this type of research. Characteristics and lifestyle research are needed to address this issue.

Sales forecasts may be supplied by industry analysts or be specifically commissioned from marketing research companies. Customer and consumer information will usually require the collection and analysis of primary data. Competitor information may be gathered in a number of ways from secondary data using industry reports or from other published data (newspapers, trade journals etc.) and it may be obtained from primary sources such as suppliers, customers, sales force and so on.

Segmentation and market research

Market research is necessary to identify profitable segments. The size of the segment is important, and research will be necessary to find out if it is worth devoting limited resources to the segment. The segment must contain buyers and potential buyers who have clearly identifiable characteristics. For example, people in a particular age group who live or work in a particular location and have a hobby in common could form a particular market segment for producers who make equipment for the hobby. The segment identified must be appropriately matched to the product offerings of the firm. Alternatively the firm's product offerings may need to be adjusted to correspond with the needs of the customers in the segment. Access to the segment identified in any research is an important consideration. For example, you may carry out market research and identify a highly profitable segment for products that your firm is capable of producing but you are unable to gain access to the market because of restrictions. These restrictions may take the form of quotas in the case of export markets, e.g. General Agreement on Tariffs and Trade (GATT) restrictions, or quota restrictions in the case of clothing manufacturers under the Multi Fibre Agreement (MFA); exorbitant tariffs; geographical distance and difficulties in transportation; difficulties of control or inexperience in a particular market or channels of distribution.

A typical market research design for segmentation or positioning is detailed in Figure 9.1. The first step is to carry out desk research using secondary data sources which should lead to information about possible market segments. Having identified the possibilities some qualitative research using focus groups may be required with the aim of finding out the important characteristics that could be important to consumers in that segment. This stage of the research could act as a pilot for a much larger quantitative study or may provide sufficient information on which to base a decision. The next stage could be to sample from a larger population of consumers who match the characteristics of those in the segment and measure their attitudes towards the products. This would provide the researchers with quantitative data. The data then needs to be analysed to provide information about consumer perceptions and likely behaviours from the attitudes obtained in the research. A factor analysis using computer programs such as SPSS could be performed to find out which factors in the research are the important ones in determining behaviour. Alternatively, it may be possible to undertake some kind of cluster analysis.

From the research information the managers can then begin to decide which segments they wish to compete in and on what basis. The basis will be backed up from the research findings.

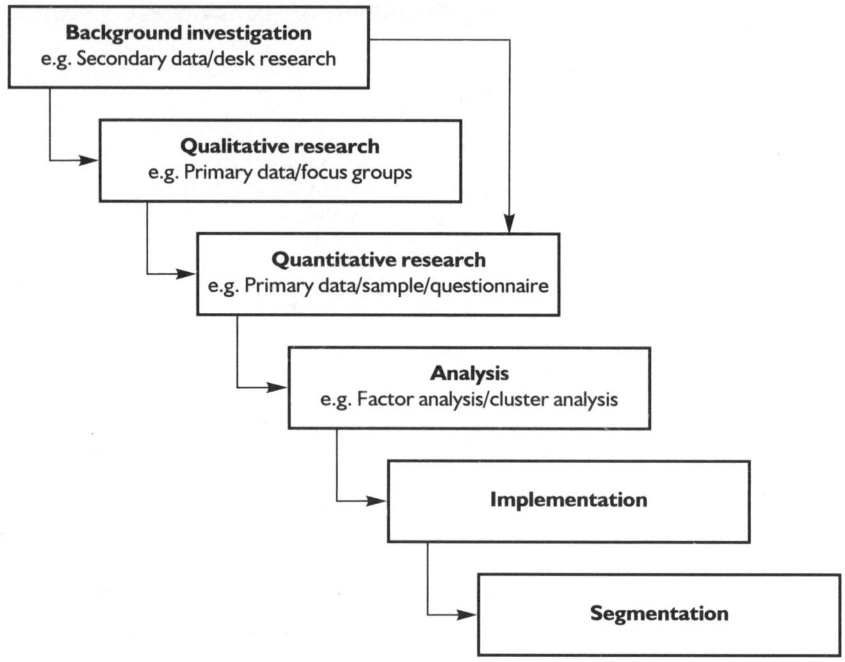

Figure 9.1
Market research is the key to successful market segmentation

Target marketing

Target marketing is developed by gathering data to provide information that will help identify the market segments that are profitable. The second step is to make sure that the firm is able to take advantage of the particular segment identified or at least to choose a segment in which it has some capability and the necessary resources in which to compete. Having identified a segment and chosen a target market there is still the difficulty of positioning the product or brand within that segment. This is why marketing research is necessary.

Question 9.1

Briefly explain the difference between *market research* and *marketing research.* (**Answer** See end of chapter.)

Consumer market research

Consumer market research often tries to identify particular characteristics about respondents based on geographic, demographic or psychographic factors.

Type	*Factors*
Geographic:	Region City/town/county Urban/rural Climate – hot, cold, rainy, sunny
Demographic:	Age Sex – male/female Family life-cycle – young single; young married no children etc. Education – GCSEs; A Levels; NVQs; bachelor degree; masters degree Occupation – professional white collar, skilled worker blue collar

Religion – Protestant, Catholic, Jewish, Islamic, other
Ethnic origin – white, black, oriental
Income

Psychographic: Social class – A,B,C1,C2,D,E

Social grade		*Occupation – head of household*	*% of population*
A	Upper middle class	Senior professional	3
B	Middle class	Managerial	12
C1	Lower middle class	Clerical/junior managerial 'white collar'	23
C2	Skilled working class	Skilled manual workers	33
D	Semi/unskilled working class	Semi-skilled and unskilled	21
E	Lowest level subsistence	OAPs, unemployed, students, casual workers	8
			100

Personality – self confident, ambitious, sociable, extrovert etc.
Lifestyle – Healthy living, conservative

VALS (values and lifestyles) identifies nine categories:

Survivors	Emulators	Experiential
Sustainers	Achievers	Socially conscious
Belongers	I-Am-Me	Integrated

Psychographic factors are useful in determining personality types, lifestyles and social class. Psychographic research is useful for identifying types. It may be useful to adapt the communications message and/or target more accurately those individuals that have lifestyles closely associated with the firm's products. For example, McCann Erickson (advertising agency) studied men in the *Manstudy* (1984). From 1,000 interviews eight clusters were identified of particular types of male:

1 *Passive endurers* Traditional male views about masculinity; intolerant; pessimistic; uninvolved; difficulty in expressing feelings; older and lower social class than average sample.
2 *Sleep walkers* Remote; uninvolved; traditional view of masculinity; contented under-achiever; independent; unsentimental.
3 *Token triers* Try hard but fail; strive to improve; respond to new things; find it difficult to cope with life; under 35 years old.
4 *Self exploiters* Self starters; individualists; success from hard work not luck; confident and manipulative.
5 *Self admirers* Narcissistic; striving; intolerant; innovative; gregarious; like to be well liked.
6 *Chameleons* Followers not leaders; contemporary views on masculinity; followers of trends.
7 *Avant gardians* Optimistic; contemporary views on masculinity; expressive; concerned; younger and higher social class.
8 *Pontificators* Opinionated; contemporary views on masculinity; respond to integrity and discipline. Source: *The Manstudy Report* (1984), McCann-Erickson reported in Oliver (1986, p. 230).

Rogers (1962) identified types in *Diffusions of Innovation:*

Innovators – 2.5 per cent customers who like to be first to try a product
Early adopters – 13.5 per cent customers who like to buy relatively early in the life cycle
Early majority – 34 per cent
Late majority – 34 per cent
Laggards – 16 per cent who come to the product late in the life cycle

The advertising message for particular products was adjusted to reflect the types identified by the research.

Customer profiling – Finding new customer prospects

The best source of prospective purchasers for your products or services is your existing customer base. Marketing researchers want to find out the lifestyles and characteristics of the people already buying goods and services. This information may hold the key to finding other customers who are likely to purchase them in the future.

CACI is a marketing information provider who use customer profiling techniques to provide this type of information. By 'profiling' a sample of your own list of current customers, CACI can build up a picture of these consumer characteristics and tell you which types of people, in which areas, are your best prospects. This list need not necessarily be previous purchasers of your own product or brand, but may include:

- Enquirers who didn't purchase from you.
- Previous respondents to a customer promotion or direct marketing campaign.
- Buyers of your competitors' products or services, perhaps obtained from market research.
- Names and addresses from a purchased list.

Geodemographic targeting

Profiling, using any one or a combination of CACI's powerful geodemographic classification systems such as ACORN, ACORN Lifestyles, MONICA or the Household Classification, will give you the most complete demographic and geographic analysis of your market.

From any given list of names and addresses, CACI can identify who your current customers are, looking at their socio-economic neighbourhood classification and the kind of lifestyle they are likely to have.

By establishing exactly the profile and location of your current customers, you can both position your products precisely and target new prospects with the greatest accuracy.

CACI's detailed customer profiling allows you to:

- Know exactly who your current customers are, and their key characteristics: age, affluence, location, etc.
- Eliminate wastage by identifying the very best new prospects using CACI's ACORN list.
- Select areas with the highest penetration for door-to-door distribution using CACI's ACORN-by-door service.
- Identify and cross sell products to high potential customers on your current database.
- Identify and select those existing customers who are most likely to trade up from their current products.
- Track lifestyle and purchasing pattern changes in your customers.

The profiling process

They require a minimum of 1,000 postcodes for ACORN profiling, and 5,000 names and addresses with postcodes for ACORN Lifestyles profiling. Lists are normally supplied on magnetic tape in fixed field format, although data entry on to tape can be arranged if your list is not on computer. CACI can also add or check postcodes where it is thought to be necessary.

Acorn types

A	Thriving	1	Wealthy achievers, suburban areas
		2	Affluent greys, rural communities
		3	Prosperous pensioners, retirement areas
B	Expanding	4	Affluent executives, family areas
		5	Well-off workers, family areas

C	Rising	6	Affluent urbanites, town and country areas
		7	Prosperous professionals metropolitan areas
		8	Better-off executives, inner city areas
D	Settling	9	Comfortable middle agers, mature home owning areas
		10	Skilled workers, home owning areas
E	Aspiring	11	New home owners, mature communities
		12	White collar workers, better-off multi-ethnic areas
F	Striving	13	Older people, less prosperous areas
		14	Council estate residents, better-off homes
		15	Council estate residents, high unemployment
		16	Council estate residents, great hardship
		17	People in multi-ethnic, low income areas

Question 9.2

Briefly discuss the main types of information that is gathered about consumers.

Product research

Product research is concerned with:

- the generation of new product ideas
- product concept testing
- product tests
- test marketing
- packaging
- core product, actual product, augmented product factors could all be the subject of product research.

Product research is conducted to find new ideas for products and services that are in demand or to select new product ideas that require further consideration and development.

Data are needed to identify new product ideas, gaps in the market to identify unfulfilled customer needs (gap analysis) or data to map brands to identify market opportunity. Data is usually primary in nature developed from synectics, group discussions, depth interviews or surveys of attitudes.

Figure 9.2
New product development and the role of research

Research is also required to decide product attributes and design and to test marketing plans and strategies. Data have to be obtained that can throw light on:

- Consumer attitudes towards attributes
- Data on existing product quality and attributes with the aim of identifying opportunities, attributes and design features for a new product.
- Product testing to measure the performance of existing products against the new product (e.g. using a prototype model to test against)

Data may be gathered from:

- Conducting specialist research to test products
- Test centres, test clinics, in-store testing, mall/hall tests, blind testing, paired testing
- Panel research
- Concept testing

Testing marketing plans before launch

Marketing plans and strategies may be tested using research studies to conduct the testing. For example:

- Geographic testing of a product in particular locations testing for price, packaging, store location, sales pattern, re-purchase, consumer reactions to the control variables etc.
- Testing consumer reaction to promotional offers in selected locations with the aim of adjusting/attuning the promotion to the consumer.
- Paired testing with the aim of conducting experimental research on any element of the marketing mix.

Data may be gathered in a variety of ways using:

- Electronic Point of Sale (EPOS) technology to measure sales performance, re-purchase (maybe), sales patterns.
- Electronic Funds Transfer at Point of Sale (EFTPOS) to test how consumers prefer to pay for goods
- Consumer surveys
- Consumer panels
- Observation

Brand name research may be conducted with the aim of choosing a name that is acceptable and easy to recall. The name may also be easily recognized and have associations with particular lifestyles.

Packaging research

Packaging is a major consideration for most firms in the fast moving consumer goods (fmcg) area. It is usually important for the packaging to be designed to fit with the brand/name. Apart from functionality and convenience, the packaging needs to reinforce brand image and associations. Research may be conducted as follows:

- Test market alternative packaging.
- Focus groups investigating packaging.
- In-home placement testing may be appropriate for functional packaging.
- Consumer surveys to measure: recall, identification and attraction/attractiveness.
- Consumer survey, using rating scales to measure consumer attitudes to the packaging.

Case illustration

Before Ford Motors moved into the small car market in 1976 they carried out large scale marketing research in three phases:

1 Concept testing and selection.
2 Research to determine the specific product proposal: style, size, interior design and space.
3 Research to establish seat design, door panels, exterior styling.

Phase 1 surveyed owners of existing small cars with the aim of identifying strengths and weaknesses in terms of performance, handling, roominess, design and economy. Surveys were also undertaken in two specific market segments: (a) where the small car was a second car and (b) potential first time buyers. Product clinics were held in each of the five main European markets. Models were available with alternative interiors and exteriors and samples of new car buyers were invited to group discussions, to individual unstructured discussions and to fill self-completed questionnaires.

Output from this phase of the research:

1 The main interior design was decided.
2 A direction for styling was established.
3 It provided evidence that an Escort rear wheel drive would be high risk.
4 A range of sales volumes was forecast.

Phase 2 involved 'beauty contest' clinics. Four fibreglass models were built derived from the findings of phase 1 research. A clear winner emerged from these clinics. In phase 3 more clinics were held to refine and design the final detail. During this stage name research, competitor research and advertising research were all done prior to the full scale launch of the car. Product research may be used to find out:

- What market segment is the product addressing? (The type of research we have discussed above for market segmentation may well answer this question.)
- Who are the existing customers? (An analysis of the firm's own customer records could be very revealing about the customer types and their characteristics.)
- Who are prospective customers? (Focus group research may help in identifying possible new customers for the product and the benefits they are seeking from the product.)

New product ideas may be generated from focus group research in trying to establish benefits wanted or needed by customers and those currently being offered. In other words a type of gap analysis is used to identify an opportunity.

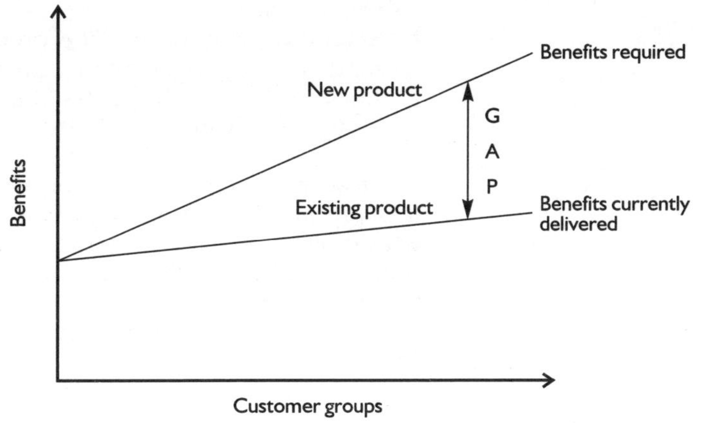

Figure 9.3
Gap analysis

Product development or new product ideas may come from research into customer needs or wants. Specific product research designed to find out those customer benefits which are required may be undertaken with a view to matching customer needs with new product offerings. Product research may be a starting point for a development team to identify key elements that new products must have if they are to stand a chance of acceptance in a particular market segment.

Gap analysis may be further refined to identify:

1. **A usage gap** – market potential and existing usage may be measured to identify a gap, e.g. research may establish that the potential market for a particular shaver is 20,000 units and current usage is only 2,000 units = a gap of 18,000 units.
2. **A distribution gap** – the limits of where and how the product is distributed may be identified.
3. **A product gap** – product positioning and segmentation studies may be useful in identifying this gap.
4. **A competitive gap** – this is the gap left to represent your performance in the marketplace against competition assuming you have closed all the other gaps.

Product research is also important to try to establish where your firm's product might be on the product life cycle.

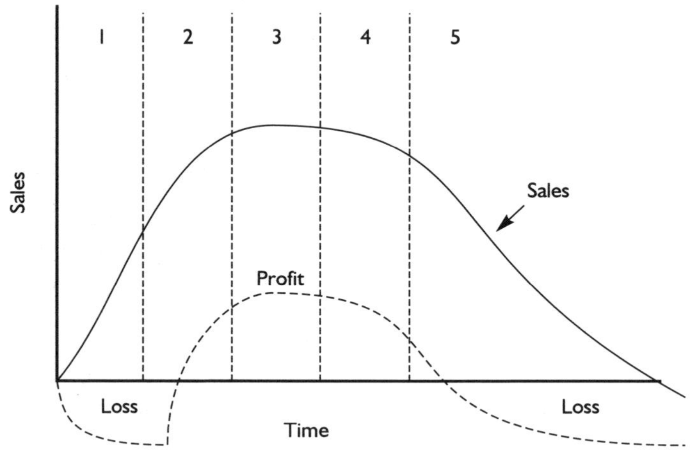

Figure 9.4
Product life cycles

Stages in the life cycle

1. Introduction sales turnover may grow slowly and the product may incur a loss.
2. Growth occurs in sales and the product begins to make a profit
3. Maturity – the product matures, sales and profit margins achieve a steady state.
4. Saturation may occur. The product may not increase its share of the market. Sales are stagnant and profitability peaks.
5. Decline – the product sales begin to fall slowly, and then more rapidly, and profits begin to fall also.

If research could provide you with an indication of where you were on this product life cycle, then you could make decisions about when to withdraw products, when to introduce new products, and when to promote products. These are decisions to support the products. Information from product research may reveal why growth is slowing, e.g. new competitor products matching customer needs and benefits more closely. This would enable managers to develop the existing product to provide extra benefits now required by customers or to consider the introduction of new products in the same or different market segments.

Sales research

Forecasting market sales is an important function of sales research. Test marketing could be conducted in selected stores that are considered representative of the market. EPOS data can track sales and the rate of sale (speed through the store). The sample data could then be grossed up (using an appropriate multiplier) to predict market sales for the product.

Price research

Pricing research is concerned with product pricing and positioning in the marketplace. Choosing value and delivering value to customers are related areas of pricing research. For example does the product or service compete well with competitors' offerings. In the eyes and mind of the customer, does the product or service represent value for money? It may also be concerned with:

- Setting prices
- Discounting
- Credit arrangements
- Margin analysis
- Segment pricing
- Discriminatory pricing
- The effect of prices on demand (elasticity of demand studies).

Distribution research

Distribution research may be concerned with and be applied to:

- Stores and inventory research establishing customer service levels.
- Location studies for distribution and warehousing centres.
- Location of retail stores.
- Logistics and the total distribution concept.

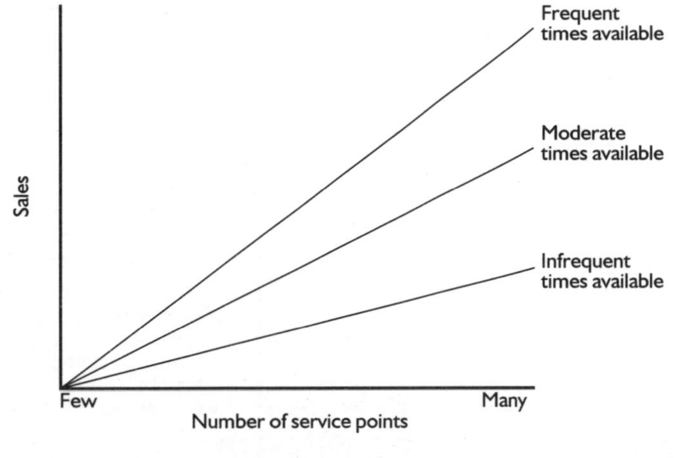

Figure 9.5
Time and place availability

Advertising research

Advertising and communication research is concerned with:

- measuring the effectiveness of marketing and sales communications, e.g. advertising
- media selection studies
- testing copy for promotional activities
- sales force planning and sales messages

The famous and overquoted comment from Lord Leverhulme on advertising is: 'I know that half the money we spend on advertising is wasted but I don't know which half.' Advertising research is, therefore, very important to evaluate how well advertising budgets are spent, and to find out if they do or do not achieve their objectives. Campaign results may be measured as follows:

1 In terms of coverage or reach of the advertisement e.g. 87 per cent of ABC1 males.
2 Awareness and recall studies may provide measures e.g. product/ brand awareness was 45 per cent prior to the campaign and 72 per cent immediately afterwards.
3 Sales volumes increased throughout the campaign period making an additional contribution to profit of £1.5 million over the six-week period.
4 Consumer research to track customer perceptions over the campaign period.

Any research undertaken with the aim of measuring campaign effectiveness must ensure that the measures are related to the advertising objectives. For example, if the objective of the campaign was to raise market share, research would be needed to measure market share before and after the campaign. If the objective was to improve customer attitudes towards the brand, then attitudinal research would be needed to identify attitudes held before and after the campaign. If the objective is to create awareness then you would need to find out the awareness level before and after the campaign, e.g. recall tests.

For media planning it maybe useful to refer to the audience research that is systematically undertaken by the Joint Industry Committee for National Readership Surveys (JICNARS); Joint Industry Committee for Radio Research (JICRAR) and Broadcasters' Audience Research Board (BARB).

Figure 9.6
Specific types of marketing research

Measures are usually in terms of: exposure, reach and frequency. Exposure is the opportunity to see (OTS) an advertisement. Reach is the proportion of an audience exposed to the advertisement at least once. Frequency is a measure of the average number of exposures per individual reached. It is the opportunity to see that is being measured, and not seeing or recalling. The research may, therefore, be limited in its usefulness to the advertiser.

Summary

Marketing research has many applications to specific situations. Figure 9.6. illustrates some of the applications. In other units we have also referred to specific types of research that may be needed to provide information about a specific area of operation.

Exam Hint

It is useful when thinking about marketing research to think – market and then marketing mix (price, promotion, place and product) and finally sales.

Answers

Answer 9.1

Market research is concerned with finding out about the market: its size, demographics, sales forecasts, market trends, segment studies etc.
Marketing research includes market research but it is a much broader concept taking in customer/consumer research, competitor research, product, price, promotion and distribution research etc.

Answer 9.2

A discussion of the main types of data may fall under the following headings:

- Geographic
- Demographic
- Psychographic
- Geodemographic

Consumer profiles are constructed using one or a combination of data collected using the techniques listed.

Unit 10 Specific marketing research techniques

Objectives

After reading this unit you should:

- ❑ Know the major methods for gathering primary marketing data and how the data are used to provide information. Specific marketing research techniques include:
  - Questionnaires
  - Interviews
  - Group discussion/focus groups
  - Motivation and psychological research
  - Hall/shopping mall tests.
- ❑ Understand when it may be appropriate to use specific techniques.
- ❑ Be able to discuss the applications in the context of specific marketing research activities, giving full consideration to the criteria of cost, time and usefulness given the specific research objectives.

Study Guide

This unit is a very long unit and requires your full concentration. Many of the major specific marketing research techniques are explained, and examples of the techniques and the ways in which they are used are provided. It is suggested that you have plenty of time to study this particular unit and to complete the activities. It may be a unit you need to rework because of the many techniques that are covered.

Data collection methods

In this unit we are concerned with a brief discussion of the main methods of primary data collection. So how do we go about the task of collecting data from respondents that will provide us with useful information? Just as in everyday life, if we want to know something, we ask or we observe or we do both. In marketing research we have a number of methods which rely on asking, observing and measuring, that have been formalized into a body of knowledge we refer to as marketing research techniques. We identified earlier the main methods of collecting marketing research data which are:

- Survey techniques
- Observation
- Experimentation
- Simulation

Survey techniques

Most primary research data using survey techniques will require a sample from a larger target population that we want to find particular characteristics about. We may decide to survey the sample by using a questionnaire. Questionnaires may be self completion (usually termed *postal questionnaires*, even though they may actually be handed out to respondents rather than posted), or they may be administered by the researcher, i.e. the researcher asks the respondent the questions and records their answers. *Administered questionnaires* will have a higher response rate than postal questionnaires and are less likely to be corrupted. Remember we draw a sample from the target population because we want to balance time, cost and accuracy.

Interviews

Interview methods are also widely used. Interviews are conducted face to face or over a telephone. To make the most of telephone interviews it is often necessary to have structured questions that can be conducted efficiently and consistently to a number of chosen respondents. This should not only prove effective but efficient, i.e. lower the cost and increase the value of the research. Face to face interviews with respondents are both costly and time consuming. Nevertheless, face to face interviewing may provide the researcher with useful data particularly of a qualitative nature. Furthermore, one is able to see how the respondent reacts to certain questions, not an option available to a researcher using questionnaires or telephone interview methods. Postal research, diary panels, telephone and observation research are lower cost methods of data collection but may provide lower levels of useful information. The key issues that any researcher needs to weigh up are:

- Time
- Cost
- Accuracy of results
- Security of the data

Question 10.1

Name the two major types of data that are used in any marketing research. (**Answer** See end of chapter.)

Types of interview

Interviews are conducted by *personal contact* face to face with the respondent(s) or at a distance *non-personal contact* via a postal questionnaire or the telephone. The main advantage of personal contact methods is that they normally achieve a high response rate and a low likelihood of errors. This is because the interviewer is able to check any ambiguities during the interview with the respondent.

Personal contact methods include:

- Fully structured interviews
- Semi-structured interviews
- Unstructured interviews
- Depth interviews

Fully structured interviews

Questions are formulated in advance of the interview. Questions need to be carefully constructed to avoid any bias or ambiguity. The marketing researcher attempts to ask questions in an orderly fashion and in a systematic way. Fully structured interviews are controlled by the researcher using a structured questionnaire. The interviewer will read the questions to the respondent in an unbiased manner and will need to note their responses exactly as they are given. An interviewer should not provide additional prompts to the respondent. The researcher should not even explain any of the questions since this might prejudice a response and invalidate the data. The researcher will need to have considered all the possible responses thoroughly so as to formulate the questionnaire. The range of possibilities is predetermined by the research design and may not be influenced by the interviewer or the respondent. Respondents are given exactly the same questions and choice of answers that the researcher designed prior to the interview taking place.

This type of research is most useful in providing the researcher with quantitative data such as '65 per cent of the people who buy brand X think that . . .' Fully structured questionnaires require questions that must be easy to ask, and easy to answer. Questions are usually of the 'yes/no' type or 'choose from the following list' or 'rank the following items in order of importance'.

Objectivity is the major argument in favour of the use of questionnaires. Advocates of fully structured interview techniques argue that bias is removed from the research process. This may be true during the interview process since neither the researcher nor the respondent should be able to influence the data. However, bias may be built into the process knowingly or carelessly at the research design stage by the person formulating the questions. The possible responses are often pre-coded for easier analysis of data after all interviews have been conducted.

The major drawback of a fully structured questionnaire is the inflexibility allowed by the structure of the questions. For example, supposing a respondent is asked to tick a number of boxes in answer to a question such as:

What do you regard as the most important factors affecting your choice of hotel?

Cleanliness ☐ Location ☐ Leisure facilities ☐ Price ☐

The respondent may decide to tick all these boxes if a free choice is given. If the researcher wants to know which factor appears to be most important in making a choice a fully structured questionnaire would have to state clearly to the respondent that they may only choose one box, or alternatively the researcher could ask the respondent to rank the items in order of importance. Whichever way, it is the researcher who is choosing what is important. For example, supposing the respondents identified other factors they consider important to the decision, these could not be considered within the structure of the questionnaire since there is no opportunity to respond. A major disadvantage encountered by the researcher is that they may have missed an opportunity to discover more important factors than those already listed. Often researchers will attempt to overcome the problem of limiting questions by adding a catch-all further category question as illustrated:

What do you regard as the most important factors affecting your choice of hotel?

Cleanliness ☐ Location ☐ Leisure facilities ☐ Price ☐ Other ☐

If you ticked 'Other' please give brief details below.

This introduction of category may cause the researcher some problems in terms of analysis and data handling. For example, the 'Other' category may have been identified as necessary, part way through the project, and in such a case how many of the previous respondents already asked the question would have chosen the additional category given that choice being available? A respondent choosing 'Other' may list something that the researcher thinks is similar to one of the predetermined choices. In our example, for instance supposing the 'Other' box is ticked and the respondent goes on to list a golf course the researcher may have thought this was clearly covered under the blanket term leisure facilities. Furthermore, suppose too many alternatives are listed by a large number of respondents, making the analysis difficult or impossible. Respondents may also misinterpret choices given, which may not be corrected by the interviewer. This is because the interviewer does not want to contaminate the data. Data error may occur for these and other reasons in a fully structured interview. It is important for the marketing researcher to be aware of these limitations. It may help in research design if such problems can be considered and eliminated before commencing the research.

Semi-structured interviews

Semi-structured interviews consist of some closed questions that offer predetermined (pre-coded) choices such as those contained within the fully structured interviews, and 'open-ended' questions which give respondents a free choice of response. For example, 'What factors do you consider to be the most important to you when choosing a hotel to stay at?' Open questions give the respondent an opportunity to respond freely without limiting their choices.

Sometimes an interviewer may decide to use probing questions like 'What other factors could there possibly be to the ones you have already listed?' or 'What factors do you think may be considered as important to other people?' Probing questions are useful after a respondent has named a few factors but is finding it difficult to go any further. Probing questions should hopefully trigger further responses, and this will cause the interviewer to feel more confident about the data provided. Probing questions require a high level of skill in application by the interviewer in addition to technical interviewing skills. Semi-structured interviews allow for the collection of both qualitative and quantitative data at the same time. Dealing with the responses is an important consideration when conducting semi-structured interviews. It is often difficult to analyse and interpret the responses given to open ended questions. This problem may be compounded where you have a large number of open ended responses. Furthermore, open ended responses can be lengthy in some cases and it is difficult to extract the important points from the data. Also when free response is allowed, it is important for the interviewer to encourage responses while at the same time limiting or eliminating any irrelevancies from the discussion.

Unstructured interviews

In conducting an unstructured interview neither the interviewer nor the respondent is constrained by the structure of a questionnaire. Interviewers may use a checklist of topics so as to be consistent between different interviews and so as to avoid missing any important issues from the interview. The order of the questions and how they choose to deal with the topic and the questioning are in the control of the interviewer. This provides the respondent with an opportunity to control the flow of data, and for the interviewer to explore more thoroughly particular views of the respondent. The interviewer may want to investigate why particular views are held by the respondent, and an unstructured approach allows for this kind of discussion to take place. Unstructured interviewing is a very useful technique for gathering data that are highly qualitative. Unstructured interviews are also useful in helping the researcher identify other questions which could be asked of a larger group using structured questionnaires or other appropriate techniques. This could provide the researcher with an opportunity to structure particular questions with the aim of obtaining some quantitative data that will help to achieve some of the research aims. Alternatively the quantitative research may support some of the qualitative information already obtained from the interviews.

Depth interviews

Respondents may have underlying motives that determine behaviour. Behaviour itself may be observable, and often we can infer or deduce a motive. Sometimes motives are emotional, subconscious and even irrational to an observer and sometimes motives are conscious and rational. Motivational researchers often use the *psychoanalytic method* of depth interviews to explore these hidden depths. Using this technique allows a pattern of questioning that should assist the respondent to explore deeper levels of thought, since motives and explanations of behaviour often lie well below the surface. Using structured and semi-structured interviewing methods may only scratch the surface. If we require a deeper understanding of the phenomena we may need to conduct depth interviews. Depth interviews are time consuming and they are an expensive method of data collection. Interviews are often taped and transcribed to analyse the data thoroughly. An individual or a small team of people may be used to conduct a series of depth interviews. Depth interviews are usually carried out with a small number of respondents. This is not a technique that you could usefully employ with large samples or groups. This may seem obvious since time and cost of conducting a large number of depth interviews would be prohibitive even if there usefulness could be justified.

Question 10.2

Name the main ways in which marketing researchers collect primary data.

Attitude and behaviour

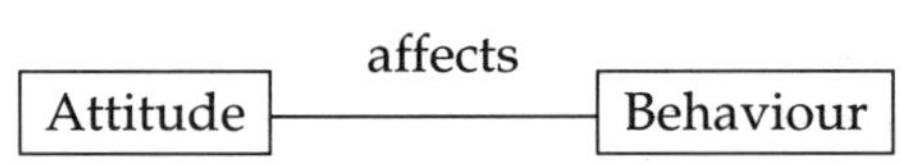

An attitude is a predisposition to behave in a particular way. A knowledge and understanding of attitude is important to allow marketing and sales managers to make predictions about customer or consumer behaviour. It is possible to predict patterns of behaviour based on attitude. You may identify consumer characteristics in a particular market segment or in customer types or in consumer groupings. In making lower level decisions, people often act first and form an attitude later. Impulse decisions are often made without reference to attitude. People taking important decisions will probably make them according to attitudes they have. This is why a study of attitude is important for marketing and sales managers. Information gathered about attitude and behaviour may help managers with a number of marketing and sales decisions.

If a favourable attitude is held by a potential customer towards your company and its products this may lead to a purchase. In reality such a direct causal relationship is very seldom the case and attitudes and behaviours are extremely complex issues. There may be strong personal or social influences preventing an individual from behaving according to their attitudinal beliefs. For example, an individual may hold an attitude that they are capable of drinking and driving, and therefore the individual holds an attitude which predisposes the individual to drink and drive. However, the individual does not actually drive after drinking because of social pressure in the wider community, and pressure from family and friends who hold strong attitudes to the contrary, and who influence the individual because of their relationship and friendship. This is not to mention the legal dissuasion which will affect behaviour despite attitude.

There are three component parts to attitude. They are represented in the diagram as cognitive, affective and conative. The *cognitive* component is what the individual knows or believes about an object or act.

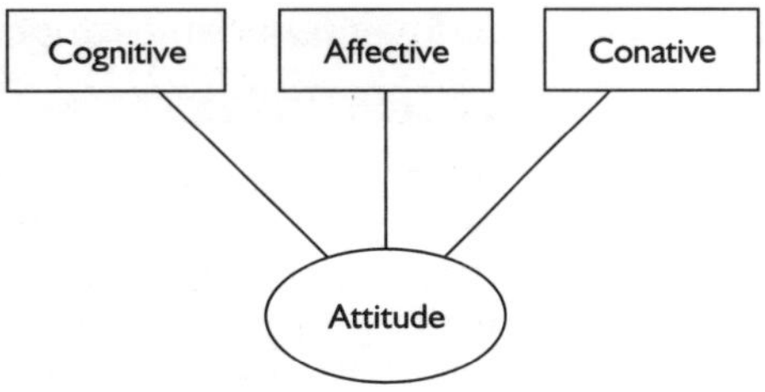

Figure 10.1
Attitude is made of three component parts

The *affective* component is what the individual feels emotionally about an object or act and finally there is conotation. The *conative* component is how the individual is disposed to behave towards an object or act.

One important assumption made about attitude is that it is multidimensional. If you are attempting to measure attitude then any measure must recognize that it is a multidimensional concept. For instance, a number of different attitudes might be present, and affect a particular customer's buying decision.

> I like the colour of that dress, but I feel it is too expensive. It would be useful for that special occasion but the design is a little old fashioned. It is made locally and I could buy one today, but the firm that makes it doesn't have a good reputation. I like the salesperson. She seems to care about how I look and they seem to be extremely positive about the product, but then again the last time I bought something in a hurry I regretted the decision later. Maybe I should think about it a little more. However, it could be sold if I delay too long . . . and so on.

You can see from this example that attitude and behaviour are extremely complex constructs and sooner or later after considering various attitudes to the decision, the purchaser makes a decision to buy or not to buy. It will depend in the end on which attitudes are the most powerful in the particular decision being taken. Sometimes a particular attitude may be present in a person but it will not be important to the buying decision. For example, supposing you hold an attitude which states, 'I do not like any government officials because I do not trust them.' In making a decision to purchase a particular item of clothing you may associate the type, style or design with a particular type of person and initially reject it. However, supposing the message in the advertising campaign says things like, 'It is stylish, trendy, shows you are an important person and the clothes will last for years.' The messages in the communication may counteract your initial attitude which you may then disregard in making the purchasing decision. This does not mean that you have changed your original attitude but that you have modified it for the purpose of making this particular buying decision.

Activity 10.1

Choose a product or service that you have recently purchased and describe your attitude towards the item in terms of:

1. A cognitive component, i.e. what you know about the product or what you believe to be true about the product.
2. Affective component – how do you feel about it, and why do you feel the way you do?
3. Conative component – do you buy such items regularly? How do you treat the item?

Personal construct theory or Kelly grids

It is thought by a number of marketing researchers and academics that there is a need to investigate how consumers interact with the messages they receive, rather than simply to gain knowledge about their attitudes. It may be important to find out how they find out about products and in what settings do they find out, so as to gain a better understanding of the whole process of consumer behaviour. This may be important and useful to marketing and sales managers in designing promotional campaigns, identifying different channels maybe and in forecasting demand.

Kelly (1967), developed a technique for understanding personal constructs known as *'repertory grids' or Kelly grids*. Individuals will try to make sense of things around them or things they come into contact with by relating them to a series of perceptual maps held in store in the brain. These maps have been developed over time through knowledge and experience. Kelly commented that an understanding of these constructs for the individuals concerned can provide insight into personality and behaviour. As individuals gain experience and learn, some constructs will be discarded or modified or completely new constructs will be developed to accommodate the new information.

Respondents are presented with three cards that contain elements for the grid, i.e. items under study. They are asked to comment how any one of the elements differs from the other two. In the case of three people Fred, Tom and Sue the respondent might choose Sue and say that Sue is female whereas Tom and Fred are male. The personal construct by which this respondent has noted a difference is on the basis of sex. The construct being male/female. Tom is small, and Sue and Fred are tall. The construct here is size, tall/small. A list of such bipolar constructs are obtained until the differences for this particular triad have been exhausted. Further, elements are taken in groups of three until all elements have been used and a complete list of personal constructs elicited from the respondent. The grids can be analysed in a number of ways to provide information. Kelly grids could be combined with scaling techniques or indeed attitude scales may be derived from using repertory grid analysis.

Kelly's construct theory has not been widely used in marketing research practice but maybe it deserves more attention. For example, in the field of marketing communication research it could be applied to investigate how individulas respond and interact with the promotional messages. Marketing managers might then decide to adjust the content or focus for their messages, to gain maximum effect.

Scaling techniques for surveys

There are two important scaling techniques that are used by researchers *Likert scales*, and *semantic differential scales*. These scales are used in an attempt to measure attitudes held by respondents. There are other scaling techniques but these two are the most widely used in practice.

Likert scales

A Likert scale is a list of statements with five (or sometimes seven) possible choices such as 'strongly agree', 'agree', 'neither agree nor disagree', 'disagree' and 'strongly disagree'. The scale is used against a battery of questions that are given to respondents. The marketing researcher is then able to measure the attitudes of respondents. Attitude statements to include in the Likert scale questionnaire may be generated from semi-structured depth interviews or from focus group discussions. For example, a firm may decide to invite between 6 and 10 people to a focus group with the aim of finding out some attitudes held by the group. The group would be drawn from the target population so that their attitudes are likely to be valid i.e. consistent with those held by the larger population. The list of attitudes developed in this way is then tested on a sample of respondents drawn from the target population. Each respondent is requested to score each statement using the five point Likert scale. The possible responses take the form:

Strongly agree	Agree	Neither agree nor disagree	Disagree	Strongly disagree
☐	☐	☐	☐	☐

The results from the sample are analysed. Some statements may be removed after analysis leaving only these statements which best discriminate between attitudes about a particular topic under investigation. The scale is then taken to a wider audience of respondents in the form of a questionnaire survey. The responses are scored using a scale of 1 to 5. The overall results from the survey are usually totalled and then averaged to provide a measure of attitude for the sample. For example, if an attitude statement gives the following choices of response:

An attitude statement constructed from some focus group interviews states: 'Spending on glossy magazine advertising increases the prices we pay in the shops.'

Strongly agree	Agree	Neither agree nor disagree	Disagree	Strongly disagree
☐	☐	☐	☐	☐

Attitude statements could be scored in the following way:

Statement	Strongly agree	Agree	Neither agree nor disagree	Disagree	Strongly disagree	
Positive	5	4	3	2	1	*Negative*

A large number of such statements could be constructed so as to determine attitudes held by the group towards a number of items. This list of statements is known as a *battery*. An individual's responses could be compared with the average for all the responses within the group to see if there is any correlation, or to analyse the differences identified further. If we were to ask only 20 questions the maximum score for any one person responding would be 100, i.e. (20 × 5) if they strongly agreed with all the statements. The minimum score would be 20 (20 × 1). Those respondents with high scores could be said to have a positive attitude towards the statements. Those respondents having low scores would hold less positive or negative attitudes to the statements made.

If we presented a group of 2,000 people with just one statement: 'Spending on glossy magazine advertising increases the prices we pay in the shops.'

Strongly agree	Agree	Neither agree nor disagree	Disagree	Strongly disagree
☐	☐	☐	☐	☐

Their responses were as follows:

Statement	Strongly agree	Agree	Neither agree nor disagree	Disagree	Strongly disagree	
Positive	5	4	3	2	1	*Negative*
Response	400	600	200	300	500	

The averaged attitude of the group of respondents could be determined by calculating the weighted average.

Attitude statements could be scored in the following way:

Statement	Strongly agree	Agree	Neither agree nor disagree	Disagree	Strongly disagree	
Scores	5	4	3	2	1	*Totals*
Response	400	600	200	300	500	2,000
Weighting	2,000	2,400	600	600	500	6,100

Weighted average = 6,100 / 2,000 = 3.05

For this group the average attitude 3.05 represents a view that the respondents neither agree or disagree. Or in other words, the opinion held in the group is indifferent to the statement. The *weighted averaged arithmetic mean* does not, therefore, reveal any strong opinion. If we choose the *mode* (i.e. the group showing the highest number of respondents is number 4 (agree) with 600 people out of the 2,000). It is often useful to look at the pattern of responses as well as totals and averages to see if we can determine anything further from the data.

Statistical analysis of multi-dimensional data may help identify groups of responses which have something in common or alternatively highlight significant differences that should be examined further. Data can be analysed using a variety of statistical techniques such as multi-dimensional scaling using statistical computing packages such as *SPSS*. This type of information could be useful when planning a promotional campaign to reinforce any positive images the customers or consumers may have towards the firm or its products. Alternatively you could conduct the research with the aim of finding out people's attitudes so as to try to counteract any negative attitudes.

Activity 10.2

Design a brief questionnaire, no more than ten questions, that could typically use a Likert type scale for any product or service you would like to investigate. This could be personal (e.g. about your favourite food or drink) or something from work. You should be clear about the aims of the questionnaire and how it can be analysed to provide the information you want to know.

Semantic differential scales

Semantic differential scales are designed to measure differences between words. The research is conducted with members of a target population with the aim of generating bipolar constructs. These constructs or dimensions are ways in which people think about products and services. An *attitude battery* consisting of bipolar constructs is developed. The battery may have as many as 20 constructs to the page. The technique was developed by Osgood et al. to measure the connotative meaning of concepts. Words have a more obvious denotative meaning and a more subtle connotative meaning. The semantic differential is used to identify these particular differences in a quantified way. A five or seven point rating scale is often used. For example, the name of a product may appear at the top of the page. Respondents are then asked to rate the product along each of the scales in the battery. For example, a representative sample of respondents could be drawn from the target population and asked to complete the same 'attitude battery'. Computed results could then allow the researcher to produce a product attitude profile. The attitude profile obtained may provide the researcher with information about the particular strengths and weaknesses of the chosen product. A brief example is given below containing a five point rating scale and seven semantics. The bipolar constructs are:

Expensive	Inexpensive
Low quality	High quality
Well known	Unknown
Reliable	Unreliable
Poor value	Good value
Available	Unavailable
Good design	Poor design

Semantic differential scales

In Figure 10.2 you can see an example of a semantic differential scale for a portable radio cassette player. In the example two brands are compared and the results are mapped as illustrated.

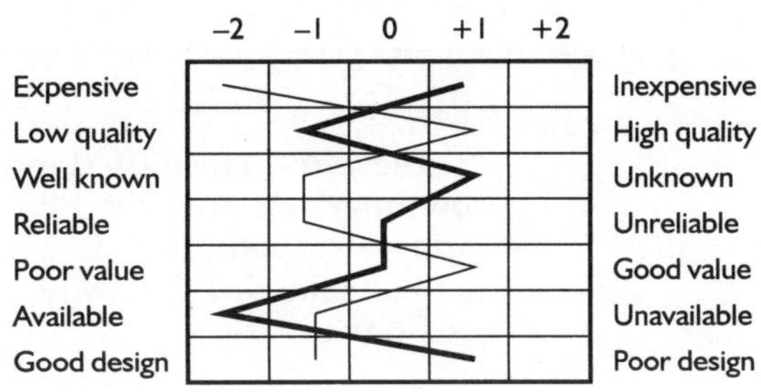

Figure 10.2
Semantic differential scale

Results can be scored:

- Radio Brand A −2 + 1 − 1 − 1 + 1 − 1 − 1 = −4
- Radio Brand B +1 − 1 + 1 0 0 − 2 + 1 = 0

The difficulty for the market researcher is to analyse and interpret this type of data so that meaningful results are obtained. In the example we need to know what –4 or 0 represent.

The data from semantic differential scaling may be plotted as we have done on two dimensions simultaneously to show competing products and how they are related in the mind of the consumer. Multi-dimensional maps may be drawn which demonstrates the consumer's positioning of products. These are called 'perceptual maps'. Perceptual mapping may reveal information about competitor products that have not been identified by a supplier. The perceptual map may also provide the marketing researchers with information about products or services thought to be competitive but which are not perceived as such by the consumer.

Extending Activity 10.1

Obtain a copy of a market research survey, maybe a holiday questionnaire or a questionnaire you have been sent about some consumer product, and see if it contains any questions using either a Likert scale or a semantic differential scale. See if you can identify the aims of the researchers.

Question 10.3

Qualitative and quantitative data may be gathered using survey techniques, but for the data to be qualitative rather than quantitative in nature the questions must be structured in a particular way using specific techniques. Can you name one or more of the techniques that could be used?

Question 10.4

Why might it be important for marketing researchers to measure attitude or motivation?

Projective techniques

Definition 10.1

Projective techniques is a term used to describe a number of different techniques that may be used to find out deeply held attitudes and opinions held by respondents. Respondents are asked to project themselves into a specific situation given by the researcher. The researcher will provide a stimulus such as a picture, cartoon or words depending on which technique is chosen.

The importance of these techniques to the marketing researcher is in investigating how the attitudes and beliefs will affect specific marketing and sales activities. It could for example lead to a refinement or an adjustment in the way marketing ideas are communicated to the customer.

Interview techniques mainly rely on the assumption that you need only ask people and they will tell you what you want to know. However, this is not always the case. People may respond differently to the ways in which they would act. People do not always act the way they say they do or will. Respondents may tell you what they think you want to hear to please you and to minimize their time commitment. Sometimes they will give a different answer because their true answer would reflect badly on them. Research may be of a personal nature and a respondent will not give you a true answer for fear that you will find out something personal about them which they do not want you to know. For example, 'How much do you earn in a year from all sources?' People will sometimes find it difficult to articulate their motives which lie buried deep within the subconscious mind. In order to overcome this type of problem associated with articulating complex or sub-conscious motives, researchers have borrowed techniques developed by psychologists in their studies of mentally disturbed people who have difficulty explaining why they do things. These techniques are known collectively as projective techniques. Attitudes, opinions and motives are established from individual responses to stimuli provided by the researcher.

The techniques employed might be:

Third person
Word association
Sentence completion
Story completion
Thematic apperception
Cartoon completion
Psychodrama
Ink blot tests

Third person or *friendly Martian*, as it is sometimes called, is designed to get the respondent talking about issues that do not really interest them. Therefore, the third person is used, e.g. how do you think most people might respond to . . . ? A researcher asks the respondent to describe what someone else might do (a friendly Martian) in any given situation. For example, supposing your friend wanted to go hang gliding, what would she need to do?

Word association is based on an assumption that if a question is answered quickly, it is spontaneous and as a result sub-conscious thoughts are revealed. This is because the person's conscious mind does not have time to think up an alternative response. This is the oldest and best known technique and you often see examples of its use in psychological thriller movies. Neutral words are often mixed in with test words to overcome any defensive mechanisms and to help reveal the real attitudes and beliefs. Hesitation, usually indicates a blockage or an emotional response to a word. A delay of three seconds or more is regarded as hesitation. Word association tests are often used to select a brand name or for obtaining an evaluation of existing brand names or for finding out attributes of certain products and so on.

You may decide to have a number of words that you consider describe your product or brand and its attributes and test to see that if in the mind of the consumer they make any of the same associations.

Fizzy drinks	=	Coke/Pepsi/7 Up etc.
Red can	=	Coca-Cola
Real thing	=	Coca-Cola
Cola	=	Pepsi/Coca-Cola/Classic Coke/Virgin/Sainsbury

Word association tests could be performed before and after an advertising campaign to test a promotional message. For example, you could have a list of attributes that are reinforced in an advertisement. By asking respondents to make associations if they choose your product or brand in response to some of the words after a campaign which they did not choose before the campaign, you may conclude that the message is getting through.

Free word response is when the respondent simply provides a one word response of their own choice. Controlled responses allow respondents to select a word from a list that they most closely associate with the stimuli word.

Sentence completion is useful way to get people to respond quickly so that underlying attitudes and opinions are revealed.

- Instant tea is not as popular as instant coffee because . . . ?
- Men who drive red cars are . . . ?
- Women who like to play tennis will also like to . . . ?
- People who like to cook are usually . . . ?

Story completion allows the respondent to say what they think happens next and why. This is really an extension of the sentence completion technique. Respondents are presented with a partly completed story (scenario) and then they are asked to complete the story. Again the objective is similar to TAT testing to find out deeply held attitudes, beliefs and motives of the respondent. This is a useful technique for finding out about future directions or vision for the people concerned. For example, if you were to interview a key informant group that represent an industry, you could present the story so far and ask them to complete it over the next few years to reveal how they perceive the future of the industry.

Thematic apperception tests (TAT tests). In TAT tests people are shown a picture and asked to describe what is happening in the picture. Sometimes respondents are asked to say what happened just before or just after the picture they are shown. 'What happened next?' or 'What do you think happened just before this scene?' The purpose of TAT testing is to reveal information about deeply held attitudes, beliefs, motives, and opinions stored in the sub-conscious mind.

Cartoon completion is similar to story completion but this time you are presented with a cartoon and some completed bubbles, maybe, but with other bubbles left blank. Alternatively, all bubbles can be left blank and respondents can be asked to complete the speech bubbles as they wish. They are often used in competitions or in situations where you are trying to identify a key phrase that will reinforce a product/service message.

Psychodrama – Psychodrama as the name suggests could be used to act out a particular situation. These are fantasy situations. Respondents may be asked to imagine that they are a particular product and to describe their feelings about being used. Alternatively, respondents might be asked to imagine themselves as a particular brand and to describe the attributes of the brand or respondents could act out a particular situation in role play. The researcher will observe behaviour and try to interpret that behaviour. The difficulty in this type of testing is the ability to make valid interpretations of what is happening in the psychodrama.

- 'Imagine you are a bar of soap; describe how you think you would feel being used in a shower?'
- 'If you were a Jaguar XJ6 and someone was taking you for a test drive describe how you would feel?'
- 'If you were buying a pair of shoes to wear for a special occasion describe how you might perform the purchase?'
- 'If a Mercedes C class car was a woman how would she be different from a BMW 5 series, what would she be like?'

Rorschach ink blot tests This is another technique that was originally designed for testing personality. Respondents are shown ink blots and asked to say what they see in them. It is claimed that the respondents project their inner thoughts in this way and that it can be useful to guide marketing managers to identify personality types that their products may appeal to. However, there are many sceptics even among the psychology fraternity about the validity of such tests.

A major drawback with projective techniques is that answers given by respondents require considerable and skilled analysis and interpretation. The techniques are most valuable in providing insights rather than answers to specific research questions.

Activity 10.3

There are a number of projective research techniques that try to establish attitudes and opinions held. List all the techniques of which you are aware and then choose two of the techniques and explain how they might be applied to any situation or organization that you have knowledge about. You should state the aim of the research and how the technique could be applied.

Group interviews (including focus groups)

Group interviews and focus group interviews are a useful technique to provide the researcher with qualitative data. Qualitative data often provide marketing researchers with a greater understanding of the processes involved in decision making such as consumer choice and consumer behaviour. Qualitative data allow researchers to gain insight into the decision making process whereas quantitative data measure the outcomes. Qualitative data often require inductive reasoning whereas qualitative data use deductive reasoning to make inferences and reach conclusions. It is often difficult to apply standard statistical methods to qualitative data. However, it is possible to deal with some qualitative issues by assigning numbers to provide quantitative measures, as we have seen with scaling techniques or in ranking qualitative data.

Group discussions usually consist of between 6 and 10 respondents and have an interviewer taking the role of group moderator. Sometimes group discussions may consist of more than 10 respondents but you should be careful not to have groups that are too large and difficult to control and focus. It is also possible to have smaller groups but this may cause concern about limitations in the data. Usually a group moderator introduces topics for discussion and will intervene as necessary to encourage respondents or to direct the discussions if they threaten to wander too far off the point. The moderator will also need to control any powerful personalities so as to prevent them strongly influencing or dominating a group.

A group discussion may be documented or recorded using audio or video tape for later analysis and interpretation. Researchers must be careful not to generalize too much from such small scale qualitative research and need to recognize the limits of such research. A group discussion relies heavily on the skill of the group moderator. They are usually not expensive to conduct and they can be carried out quickly. Group interviews can provide useful, timely, qualitative data at a reasonable cost.

Group discussions are often used at the early stage of research for the researchers to get a feel for the subject matter under discussion and to create possibilities for more structured research. Four to eight groups may be assembled and each group interviewed for one, two or three hours.

Focus group discussions are often used to provide data variables which respondents consider important. Such variables may then provide the researcher with a clearer picture of important issues that may need to be explored further using different research methods. For example, a series of focus group interviews may be conducted by a firm, to find out how people feel about a particular brand. This may help establish attitudes which can be countered, or brand strength which can be exploited. The focus group interviews may provide data on a number of key variables such as:

- Is the brand perceived as strong or weak?
- How it differs from competitor brands?
- Is the brand thought to be exciting or dull?
- Is the brand reasonably priced or not reasonably priced?
- Does the brand represent value for money or poor value for money?

The company may then test findings from the data supplied in the focus group interviews on a wider representative group using sampling techniques and questionnaires developed from the focus group interviews to explore the variables further. The purpose of this type of research would be to establish customer perceptions of the brand.

Sometimes focus group interviews may be the only method employed owing to constraints of time, cost and usefulness. For example, if you wanted to find out information about competitor products and make comparisons with your own company's brands, it may be sufficient to use focus groups as a means of extracting qualitative data. After analysis and interpretation you can extract sufficient information on which to build a new promotional campaign.

Activity 10.4

Explain what you understand by the term focus group. How could focus group research help an organization to achieve increased levels of customer service or customer satisfaction? Describe the steps you might take to set up a focus group for this purpose, and briefly explain what advantages this type of research may have *vis-à-vis* survey techniques.

Synectics and creativity

Synectics is the study of things leading to invention. Synectic discussions are group discussions with the aim of generating creativity rather than measuring attitude. Synectic discussion is used to generate new product ideas, new marketing ideas, new campaigns, and new approaches to the market. Synectic group research may lead to innovations. Synectic groups are usually intensive and often longer than normal group discussions. They may be conducted over a day. Members making up the group are selected for their differences to each other rather than their similarity to each other. Differences may be functional or characteristic in nature.

Originally this type of group was developed for the purpose of working with specialized technical and highly qualified personnel.

Postal research questionnaires

Postal research questionnaires are sent to respondents for self-completion using postal services or other appropriate means of distribution. A major limitation of this type of postal research is the low response rate. Often anything higher than 10 per cent is considered a reasonably good rate of return. You can increase the response rates by using free post, return envelopes and a carefully selected target audience who may have more interest in the subject matter under investigation than would a random sample. After the questionnaires have been issued you can increase the response by follow-up reminders by post and/or telephone reminders. Response rate ranges can and do vary greatly and it is sometimes difficult to identify why this is the case. It is important to try to carefully target postal questionnaires so as to increase response rates and avoid unnecessary cost.

Postal questionnaires that respondents are asked to complete themselves need to have clearly structured and unambiguously worded questions. A combination of closed questions (yes/no), limited choice (tick box, circle, rank) and open questions (what do you think about . . . ?) may be used. Questionnaires are often precoded to make analysis of the data easier to process. Circle, tick box, delete as appropriate and other clear instructions are necessary if respondents are remote from the researcher. Clear instructions will also encourage a response. The easier the questionnaire is for respondents to complete, the more chance you have of a return. Clear instructions and clearly worded questions should lead to a higher return rate. It is important, however, that you do not sacrifice quality for simplicity. The clearer the questionnaire the less prone it will be to error. A good clear layout with lots of white space and not too many words on the page is more attractive to a respondent. The more attractive the questionnaire the better the chances of completion. Questionnaires that have a covering letter explaining the purpose of the survey and the benefits to the respondent also have more chance of completion, with the opportunity for the respondent to obtain some results from the research as an encouragement for them to participate. Confidentiality is also a concern for some respondents since they do not want to be identified. It may be appropriate for the covering letter to put the respondent at ease by informing them that they will not be identified in the report. Alternatively, you may wish to obtain their agreement to being identified. It may be important to qualify your letter so as to make it clear that you will only disclose information about them by agreement or that your results will be aggregated in some way so that competitors and others may not identify them.

Types of question

Closed questions

Type	*Description*
Dichotomous	Only two possible answers
Multiple choice	Three or more possible answers
Likert scale	Testing relative agreement/disagreement
Semantic differential	Relative opinion of bipolar words
Importance scale	A scale showing importance
Rating scale	A scale rating an attribute in some way
Intention to buy scale	Rating intention to buy
Ranking	Rank order of importance

Open questions can be completely unstructured, e.g. what do you think about customer service offered by . . . ? The respondent has a free choice of answer in a completely unstructured open question. You can ask open questions but make the response selection limited in some way for example by *word association*. *Sentence completion, story completion and picture completion* all involve a degree of open questioning that allow a free response which is limited only by the sentence, story and picture. *Thematic apperception tests* involve an open question presented to a respondent along with appropriate stimuli. These are explained further earlier in this unit.

The following steps will improve response rates to mailed questionnaires:

Accurate sampling lists
Accurate addresses
Correctly addressed and stamped envelopes
Showing any organizational affiliation that may encourage a response, e.g. professional body, CIM
Personalizing addresses and named people in letters etc.
Paper quality used
Cover page to explain the purpose and benefits
Well written questions
Questions appropriate to the audience
Freephone or freepost response numbers/addresses
Reminders by post
Provide a second questionnaire
Telephone reminders
Make sure the questionnaire fits in the envelope easily

Question 10.5

Define and distinguish between open and closed questions used in postal questionnaires.

Telephone research

Telephone research is a relatively fast and inexpensive means of gathering data compared to personal interviews. It is most useful when only a small amount of data is needed. It has benefits to the respondent in terms of the short amount of time taken by the interviewer to obtain their responses. It has been particularly useful in terms of industrial research. The telephone research technique has also been widely used for consumer research with the growth in home telecommunications. We may all have fallen prey unsuspectingly to that evening call from a desperate double glazing salesperson posing as a researcher or a financial services company really selling pension products or mortgages. The Market Research Society provides some clear guidelines for using telephone research methods that all researchers would do well to read before proceeding. Ethical as well as economic considerations are important in conducting legitimate telephone research. CATI – computer assisted telephone interviewing – has been successfully used by insurance services and banks as well as consumer research organizations. The telephone interviewer calls up a questionnaire on screen, and reads questions to the respondent. Answers are then recorded instantly by the telephone researcher on the computer. CATI is a useful technique for dealing with complex questions with question routing. For example, if the answer to question 2 is yes proceed to question 7, if the answer is no go straight to question 12 and so on.

Research in the US into telephone research has revealed the following:

Results of first dialling

Result	% Probability
No answer	35
No eligible person	29
Out of service	20
At home	10
On business	4
Too busy	2
Total	100

Source: Kerin and Peterson (1983)

Mail, telephone and focus group methods compared

	Mail	*Telephone*	*Focus Group*
Population	Good chance of locating respondents Reasonable response rate if good, clean, accurate list used	Good chance of locating respondent Co-operation rate reasonable Contact a wide band	High level client involvement Control over respondents in group
Biased response	Avoids interviewer distortion Time to give considered response	Unknown bias from refusal avoided Contamination from others avoided	Quick feedback Generally unbiased
Item construction	Carefully developed questions	Open ended questions carefully structured rotation, control and screening all possible	Open questions screening, control
Costs	Low cost per response can be achieved Low personnel cost	More costly than mail Large number of call backs Personnel cost higher than mail	Can be much less expensive than mail or telephone Depends on videotaping costs transcription fees
Speed	Up to 10 weeks if high response required	Daily CATI could be used	1 to 3 weeks can be done very quickly. Depends on panel selection

Adapted from: Lockhart and Russo 1994, in Bagozzi pp. 127–8.

In summary, mail is usually cheaper but may be less effective than face to face or telephone surveying but this depends very much on the context of the survey and whether or not it is national or local in nature. Face to face will nearly always be more expensive than the telephone.

Question 10.6

Explain the term CATI?

Extending Activity

Obtain a copy of a questionnaire that has been used in any marketing research survey and look at the style and structure of the questions. See if you are able to identify any specific techniques used or particular question types that we have referred to in this unit.

Research on the Internet

Recently I have observed a number of organizations issuing questionnaires or requesting specific data on the Internet. This is in embryonic form but there is certainly plenty of junk mail on the net.

Mall intercept interviews/shopping mall surveys

Shopping surveys or shopping mall interviews are more correctly referred to as *Mall Intercept Interviews*. These interviews take the form of a survey questionnaire administered by an interviewer. You may have experienced such a survey as a respondent when you have been shopping. These personal surveys are often efficiently conducted in stores, shopping centres or in shopping malls. From a research point of view the heavier the traffic the better, since it will offer the researcher more choice in selecting appropriate people to match with the research criteria. Furthermore, the respondents are all located within one place. There is no need to visit door to door. A shopping mall is usually busy with people and there will be a large variety of consumers who will be browsing or shopping and who may be willing to spend time answering questions. The response will be higher if free gifts or vouchers are being given as a reward. These people present the market researcher with a ready made opportunity to gather information about attitudes, past purchases and consumer characteristics. Furthermore, if an individual matching your research criteria refuses to take part there is always another on the way. Shopping malls are ideal places to gather large amounts of consumer research data quickly and comparatively cheaply when compared against postal surveys.

Advantages

It is a personal survey conducted by the researcher in the field face to face with the respondent. It is flexible. The researcher may be given or encourage lengthy replies. The interviewer is also able to reduce ambiguity and clarify responses.

Disadvantages

This type of survey can be expensive if it is not clearly targeted. You may end up collecting a lot of useless data. Consumers may tell you anything just to get away more quickly. It is possible that interviewers interfere with objectivity by unwittingly introducing bias or by creating a particular mood when conducting the interview. For example, if the interviewer is too light hearted or too familiar in their approach it may mean that the respondent treats the survey in a light hearted way and data collected is not meaningful as a result.

Methods of selection

There are two main methods used in selecting consumers for the survey. The first is to draw a *probability sample*, that is a *random sample*. In a random sample, as previously mentioned, every member of the designated population has an equal or known probability of being chosen for analysis.

More sophisticated random samples may identify particular characteristics that consumers need to possess before they enter the count. For example, select every twentieth person passing the survey point from amongst those who fit a particular description or age group. Characteristics such as age may be confirmed before commencing the interview.

An alternative way to sample is to draw a *non-probability* sample. Members of the population are chosen by the researcher on the basis of convenience or judgement. *Quota samples* are sometimes obtained. Each researcher is given a quota – a specific number of respondents that should be interviewed in that place on that day. Either way, for surveys to provide relatively accurate results, large samples or quotas are required which involve time and cost to collect and process the data. Random samples are more accurate in making predictions about behaviour for a larger population than a convenience sample would be. Random samples usually cost more to administer.

The critical question for the researcher is to identify exactly what is required from the research and this should help in selecting an appropriate sampling frame. For example, if you require qualitative insights rather than quantitative accuracy then a non-random, convenience sample will be sufficient. On the other hand if you want to make a statement such as '95 per cent of the consumers who visit shopping malls carry an average of £60 in cash to spend at any time' then it would be necessary to conduct a random sample so as to be certain that the sample results are representative of the population. In statistical terms you will want to be confident or 95 per cent certain that your sample is representative of the total population who visit shopping malls. Confidence limits can be established using statistical sampling methods (see pages 140–3).

Such retail surveys are a convenient way of collecting large amounts of data since shoppers come to the researcher rather than a researcher conducting door to door interviews on a housing estate or several housing estates. As with all research the specific objectives need to be clear and the likely benefits must be balanced against cost, timeliness and usefulness of the research.

Question 10.7

Explain the term mall intercept interview or hall interview.
What are the major advantages of conducting a survey in this way?

Observation

Observation research studies are concerned with behaviour rather than attitudes and motives. You may for instance observe behaviour and analyse and interpret the meaning of that behaviour for your firm or its products and service offerings. It is through observing behaviour that you may identify a customer or consumer requirement that your company can translate into a product or service that will profitably satisfy the need. Interviews and questionnaires depend on respondents answering questions about their behaviour, beliefs, motives and attitudes truthfully.

It may be necessary to observe behaviour not just because respondents are unwilling to answer questions truthfully but because they do not record their own behaviour effectively and are therefore unable to provide the researcher with answers. For instance, can you truthfully remember where you were on 12 January this year, and can you recall every detail about that day? Unless it was your birthday or a special occasion, it is unlikely that you remember. Supposing you want to track the route taken by customers walking around your store, with the aim of locating particular high value items in a particular aisle that they are likely to visit more than once, the easiest way to achieve your research aim is probably to observe behaviour. Data could be recorded on a computer map of the store or you could use string diagrams, electronic measuring devices, surveillance cameras and so on. Electronic meters may be used for flow counts of all sorts if the question is quantitative in nature. For example, as people pass certain points in the store where a meter is located it is triggered and records the traffic flow round the store. Sometimes observation panels are convened as in the case of measuring TV habits and sets are metered with the aim of observing TV watching behaviour.

Audience measurement

The system for measuring audiences is based on a development of the JICTAR system, i.e. electronic meters fixed to a sample of television sets. The first step in selecting the sample or panel of homes which will have these meters is the Establishment Survey. The Establishment Survey is based on a random sample of over 43,000 interviews conducted continuously throughout the year, and structured by post code areas within ITV areas. The questions are designed to determine patterns of television usage across the country and to ensure that the audience measurement panel is fully representative and up to date. The results of the survey, together with Government census data, are used to select a fully representative sample of homes in terms of viewing habits, TV equipment ownership, family composition, demographics and so on to take part in the audience measurement panel.

4,435 homes take part in the audience measurement panel and the Establishment Survey provides a pool of names and addresses of households which can replace those who drop out for one reason or another. (Panel members are given a nominal incentive payment for their services.) Each panel household continues to provide information to BARB for as long as it remains representative. If the circumstances of the household change, perhaps by the birth of another child, or a grandparent coming to live with the family, it will be picked up by an updating interview. If the change makes the household statistically unrepresentative it will be dropped from the panel and replaced by a new representative from within that area.

The electronic meters attached to the television sets of the panel households have developed considerably since the days of JICTAR. The householder no longer has to remember to post the tape back to the company, or to complete a questionnaire. The meter registers when the set is switched on and off, and which channel it is tuned to. In addition, each household has a gadget like a television remote control with numbered buttons on it, and each member of the household has their own number. Each person presses the appropriate button on when they start to view, and off when they stop, and the data is fed into the electronic meter. In case the panel members forget, a signal flashes on the meter if the television set is on, but no buttons have been pressed. Guest viewers are allotted special buttons with a facility for registering their age and sex. All the information about what channel the set is tuned to and who is watching is retrieved overnight automatically by a computer using the telephone system.

Retail audits

Retail audits are used to gather data in the files for trade research. EPOS systems have enabled many firms to observe stock positions (stock on hand, inflows, outflows) and the speed at which stock items are moving through the retail stores.

Panel research

A panel is really a form of longitudinal survey from which comparative data are drawn from sampling units on a number of occasions. Panels might be drawn from individuals, firms or households. They are a useful means of providing continuous data. Information revealed from panel survey techniques may be general or specific in nature. For example, general trends in the market place or the industry or specific television viewing habits or specific purchasing information. Panels may also be used to evaluate promotional messages on a regular frequency. Panels of this type may be particularly useful in the identification of shifting attitudes over time. For example, maybe the panel reflects society's wider concerns about the environment, when viewing a particular motor vehicle advertisement. This is important for marketing and sales managers in the car firms to understand, because changes in attitude, may lead to changes in behaviour. If it is known that there is this shift in attitude, maybe the promotional campaigns can be adapted to accommodate the change, or maybe the product needs refinement and so on.

Diary panels

A panel is an important source of continuous research data. One such technique is a diary panel. A representative sample of respondents is selected from the population under consideration and respondents are asked to keep a diary. The diary is provided by the researcher, and respondents are asked to record specific data in accordance with the specific research criteria. Inferences can then be drawn from diary data when it is collected and analysed.

Diary panels are usually run by an independent market research agency that will sell the results to interested companies. It is a useful method of research when a marketing researcher wants to discover the effects of various decisions on a larger audience, for example, the effects of promotional messages or price changes. Panel research data is most effective for consumer research. *BARB* is a form of diary panel.

Audience appreciation

BARB also manage an audience appreciation service, which is totally confidential to the subscribing broadcaster (BBC, Channel 4 and the ITV companies).

RSL run the current service which began in August 1994. It consists of a regional panel of 3,000 adults (individuals over 16 years of age). There is also a children's panel of 1,000 children aged 4 to 15. The adult panel operates weekly whilst the children's panel covers one week in every four.

The basic operation requires panellists to complete weekly booklets. The programme diary requires respondents to rate on a scale from 0–11 each programme they watch. (The children's panel only covers broadcasts up to 9 pm.) This data is used to produce an Appreciation Index (AI) for each programme which is expressed as an average mark out of 100. Top line data is also collected for viewing to the satellite channels (where appropriate). A second booklet consists of questions which can be asked by the broadcasters about any aspect of a particular programme on a particular day. They might wish to know, for example, what the public thinks about a presenter of a programme. More general questions about series or serials are also asked, usually at the end of the run.

Audience appreciation is a valuable tool by which broadcasters evaluate the performance of programmes, and assists in the planning of future schedules. As such the data remains confidential to the subscribing broadcasters.

Home audits

Home audits are another means of gathering consumer data. With permission of the householder the researcher visits the household at specified intervals and investigates the cupboards to see what items the householder stores. This is to check on buying habits. The packaging from some goods is sometimes taken away to provide further information about dates of purchase and consumption times, promotional offer information and so on. The respondent may also be asked to complete a brief questionnaire.

Question 10.8

(a) List the major types of observational research.
(b) Observation may have benefits over survey techniques for marketing researchers wanting to analyse behaviour – why is this the case?

Experimental research in marketing

Experimental research designs require careful selection of respondents. For instance matched groups may be selected and then subjected to different treatments. There will normally be a control group against which the experiment may be measured, with the aim of identifying any significant factors. The main purpose of experimental research design is to identify cause and effect relationships by eliminating competing explanations of the observed findings.

For example in a retail environment maybe you could identify two almost identical stores, with identical layouts, staffing, systems, procedures and stock. The two stores would both have an almost identical customer base. In one store you may decide to test the effect of charging different prices for specific categories of goods over a set time period. Alternatively, you may decide to test for the store location of different goods and the sales volumes achieved.

Exam Hint

When discussing experimental marketing research design, it is important to be aware of the major shortcoming which is the assumption that you can identify and select a matched pair and isolate variables. You may note that the key word is **almost** when referring to experiments in business situations. An experiment in the truly scientific sense of the physical sciences is not possible, since you will never have completely identical stores in completely identical locations with a completely identical customer base. This does not invalidate this type of research but it may limit findings. Careful design is very important.

In-store testing

Product testing is a relatively quick and inexpensive method of gathering information about consumer attitudes towards a particular product. In-store testing can be a useful convenient way to gain insights into expected consumer behaviour before a full product launch is implemented. It can provide managers with relatively low cost, fairly accurate information, and a big advantage is that it can be done quickly. Selected stores can be chosen to test a particular product and to gather information about likely buyer behaviour before a product is launched. In-store testing is also a useful way of promoting the product before, during and after a launch. All in all in-store testing may provide marketing and sales managers with an important low cost source of qualitative data about a specific product or brand. Test marketing may also provide quantitative data for sales forecasting.

Question 10.9

Examination style part B
When planning a consumer promotional campaign it is important to have an understanding of attitude and behaviour. Explain how this type of information could be obtained by marketing managers and discuss how the results could be used.

Answers

Answer 10.1

Primary and secondary.

Answer 10.2

Survey, observation, experiment or simulation.

Activity Debrief 10.3

Third person
Word association
Sentence completion
Story completion
Thematic apperception
Cartoon completion
Psychodrama
Ink blot tests

Any two of these techniques could be selected and then two chosen to explain how the technique may be applied. Examples of application are given in the unit, but you may provide your own examples.

Activity Debrief 10.4

A focus group is a discussion group of between 6 to 12 people drawn from a population, with the aim of being representative of that target group. Attitudes, opinions, motives and behaviours should reflect the wider population. Sometimes time and cost constraints mean that the group is not selected particularly scientifically and sampling techniques are not used but they could be. This is often the case because the research is only a pilot for a much larger study, and the aim of the group is to identify key issues that could be explored more thoroughly and more scientifically later using survey techniques. For example the focus group research may have the aim of establishing a battery of questions related to customer service or customer satisfaction for use in a survey using scaling techniques to a much wider audience. The steps involved would be the same as those described for undertaking any marketing research, i.e. define the issues to research, decide on who will collect the data and how to collect the data. Apply appropriate techniques, in this case focus group, process the data, analyse the findings, and finally report the findings.

Answer 10.3

Scaling techniques such as a Likert scale, rating scales, semantic differential scales, Kelly grids. Open style questions may also provide qualitative data whereas closed questions will provide quantitative data.

Answer 10.4

- Attitudes are important because they determine behaviour.
- Marketing researchers often need to understand behaviour to adapt the marketing mix elements of price, product, promotion and place.
- Motives are important to understand because they lead to behaviour. For example, a basic need such as shelter or clothing will lead to a purchase of accommodation or clothing items. Motives derived from lifestyles and reinforced through advertising may lead to the purchase of specific products or services.

Answer 10.5

Closed questions are dichotomous giving only two choices, e.g. yes/no. Open questions give respondents a free choice limited only by the amount of space in which to answer the question.

Answer 10.6

Computer assisted telephone interviews are conducted by the researcher having a questionnaire on screen that responses can be entered on to while speaking to the respondent via a telephone.

Answer 10.7

This is a survey conducted in a shopping mall or hall using sampling, quota or judgement to select appropriate respondents who are used to provide data about shopping behaviour and consumer attitudes.

The major advantages are time and cost since a great deal of data may be collected quickly from a single location (shopping mall/hall) or from a number of locations where the foot traffic is high. Costs of data collection can therefore be very low when expressed in terms of cost per respondent.

Answer 10.8

(a) Visual, audits (retail/home), panel research (diaries), electronic metering.

(b) It is often assumed that you need only ask people to tell you how they behave and that will inform you about behaviour. This view, however, is somewhat naive since respondents will have their own reasons for providing information in a particular way which may not be an accurate reflection of their behaviour. Observation techniques overcome this imperfection since they observe actual behaviour. Observation studies will therefore provide more accurate measures of behaviour than survey predictions. Sometimes observation studies combined with other marketing research may be conducted with the intention of attempting to make predictions about future behaviour.

Answer 10.9

A study of attitude is important since it will affect behaviour. The exact causal links are, however, extremely complex. Attitude is a *predisposition* to behave in a particular way. There are three components to attitude: cognitive (what is known or believed), affective (feelings toward the subject) and conative (likely behaviour). Studying attitudes is important for marketing and sales managers who want to make predictions about customer or consumer behaviour. Attitude research may reveal patterns of behaviour in market segments or in specific types of customer or consumer groupings. From the patterns of behaviour it may be possible to make predictions about future trends. When making low level decisions people often act first and form an attitude later. People taking important decisions will make them according to attitudes they hold. For example, if you are out shopping and decide that you want to buy a cup of tea in a strange town, then you will probably go into any café selling tea. Once you have left that café you may form an opinion about it, and if you visit again a judgement may now be based upon opinion (i.e. your attitude towards the café). More significant purchasing decisions like buying a car or a house will almost definitely be based on attitudes that you hold to a variety of important factors that affect the decision.

Information about attitudes and behaviour may be gathered in a number of ways. There may be some secondary research that was conducted for another purpose by someone else that may provide you with sufficient information for your needs. For example, published research about consumer attitudes. If this is not sufficient then you may want to join in some syndicated research study into attitudes held that is being conducted in your industry. It may be possible to use omnibus research studies that are regularly conducted if they provide information to meet your requirements.

Depending upon specific research objectives, time and cost, we may decide to conduct a number of depth interviews rather than conducting a survey or before conducting a survey, the main focus of depth interviews being to establish attitudes for respondents that are representative of a larger population that we are seeking to influence. It may be enough to complete the depth interviews or we may want to explore further some of the findings from this research by testing them on a larger population using survey techniques. Marketing managers could investigate attitude, using survey methods. Surveys may be conducted using primary data to identify attitudes held by particular consumer groups. The survey questionnaire may employ specific questioning techniques such as scaling techniques (e.g. Likert scales, rating scales and semantic differential scales), with the intention of exploring attitude. If we are concerned to find out how attitudes affect behaviour, we may then need to proceed to a second stage of marketing research using observation techniques, the intention being to establish what particular attitudes cause certain behaviour. In other words are there any causal links we can identify for particular types of consumer (i.e. behaviour patterns)?

The results from the research may be used to inform a promotional campaign by adapting the communication towards the target audience, to provide stimuli that the audience will respond to. For instance, research could inform the promotional campaign about any strongly held beliefs and attitudes that need to be reinforced.

Unit 11 Management and technology

Objectives

After studying this unit you should:

- ❑ Know how information technology is affecting the way in which management information systems are designed and used to support marketing and sales decisions.
- ❑ Know about some of the major developments that are taking place in IT.
- ❑ Know and understand the importance of database management in a marketing and sales environment.
- ❑ Know and understand key terms:

  Databases
  Information technologies
  Modems
  On-line
  Internet/World Wide Web
  CD ROM
  Multimedia
  Smart cards
  EPOS
  EFTPOS
  Decision support systems
  Expert systems
  Neural networks

Study Guide

You should work through this unit carefully and reflect back to other units where you have been introduced to some of the important concepts in other contexts. It is essential that you keep up to date in this rapidly changing area.

You will be provided with a discussion of the most important IT aspects and how they are impacting upon Marketing Information Systems.

You should supplement this unit with additional wider reading that will keep you informed about the latest developments. The *Financial Times* is a particularly good newspaper for reporting technology and innovation and has a section devoted to it every day. Thursday is marketing and advertising day on the management page of the *FT*, and they very often have snippets that are directly applicable to your studies. Other broadsheet newspapers and contemporary magazines will have relevant articles sometimes. *Marketing* (CIM Magazine) often devotes space to IT and how it affects marketing and sales information, and there may from time to time be useful short pieces in *Marketing Success*.

Exam Hint

Many of the concepts introduced in this unit have been mentioned in other units and some of them may not be completely new to you. This is important because in an examination you may well be expected to discuss the developments taking place in information technology and how they can affect the marketing information system. Information technology should not be seen as being in a box but should be seen as an integral part of any information system. Candidates will be rewarded for their up-to-date knowledge of IT and MIS applied in the context of a mini case or question that allows the candidate to demonstrate knowledge and practical understanding of the application.

Developments in information technology

The developments in three key areas have led to the establishment of the information society. The areas are communication, computer and information technologies. These areas have converged during the last few years to give rise to powerful management tools. Below you are provided with a table showing the major developments since the 1940s.

Decade	Communication technology	Computer technology	Information technology
1940s	Radio Military mobile radio	Single function General purpose	
1950s	Tape recording Cable TV Microwave links Crossbar switching Direct distance calling Video tape recording	Commercial computers Programming languages Transistors	
1960s	Satellite communication Digital communication Electronic switching	Integrated circuits Minicomputers Structured programming	
1970s	Facsimile transmission Mobile radio Packet switching Videotext	Database management systems LSI Application generators Microprocessors Relational databases Spreadsheets VLSI	On line enquiry Professional databases Management information systems Integrated text and data processing Transaction clearing systems Professional problem solving Materials planning Stock control

1980s	Teleconferencing Local area networks (LANs) Cellular radio Wide area networks (WANs) Private satellites Integrated service digital networks Personal telephones	Portable computers Logic languages Optical disk storage Expert systems Transputer Voice recognition Dataflow processors Wafer scale integration	Scheduling Electronic mail Teleconferencing Computer aided design (CAD) Computer aided manufacture (CAM) Computer aided diagnostics Remote sensing devices
1990s	Switched wideband services Value added networks (VANs)	Gallium arsenide chips Parallel processing Learning capability Natural language recognition Optical chips Biochips	
2000	Personal mobile communication via satellites	Ultra-intelligent machines	

New technologies supporting the marketing information system

New technology together with new approaches to marketing and selling has enabled organizations to collect, analyse and use information about their customers in a more strategic way. Research by Hines (1996) has shown that many retail organizations in the UK are beginning to recognize customers as a strategic asset in gaining competitive advantage. For example, in the UK clothing market, retail chains account for over 60 per cent of sales and the top two retail groups have around 28 per cent of the total market. In recent times the trend has been to reduce the supplier base and to build better quality links with the remaining supply chain partners. One noticeable catalyst has been the ability of retailers to link information systems with key suppliers to gain greater control of the supply chain. EPOS has given retail stores better quality data about stock movements and a greater insight into consumer behaviour. EFTPOS has given the retailer the ability to deliver customer service whilst maintaining cash flows by allowing flexible payment methods. EDI links with suppliers is enabling just-in-time stock replenishment to take place painlessly for the retail stores.

A typical product line held in stock by a supplier can be replaced in a matter of hours rather than the weeks or months it used to once take. This speed of order fulfilment is also placing demands on manufacturers in clothing and textiles to offer quick response through the use of flexible manufacturing systems. The speed at which information travels, places demands on the supply chain to move the physical goods more quickly to take advantage of the accuracy and timeliness of knowing the customers' demands. Customers too have become more demanding as their expectations are raised by the new information technologies and what can be achieved.

Schmittlein (*Financial Times*: Mastering Management – Part 8 (5), 15 December 1995) comments that for customers to be considered strategic assets four conditions must apply:

1 The customer base must be stable and a predictable source of future sales.
2 Individual customers must be able to be segmented very effectively in terms of future sales potential based on their historical purchase record.
3 Customers are subject to depreciation just like other assets, i.e. customers wear out.
4 Customers can be bought and sold.

It is interesting for marketing managers considering the importance of information systems and what the implications for each condition might be. For example, in the financial services market it has long been recognized that retaining existing customers and extending the range of products sold to customers is a profitable way to develop new business. The development of this new business is, however, dependent upon having an accurate database. Some companies have been successful for this reason whereas others have failed to grow new business, not through a failure to recognize opportunity but through a failure to be able to exploit the opportunity through inadequate information about their existing customers or through an inability to extract customer data effectively to provide appropriate information. Retail loyalty schemes are an attempt to develop effective data capture systems about customer buying habits that the retailers may be able to exploit at a later date by segmenting the customer base and target marketing. The fact that customers wear out may be a function of changing habits, growing older, changing incomes, changing tastes, changing lifestyles, geographical movement and so on. Tracking systems that are able to identify customer groups and significant changes in behaviour may enable organizations to minimize risks in this particular area so that all customers do not disappear at once. Finally, the fact that customers can be bought and sold is self-evident. Mergers and acquisitions take place often because a competitor is keen to gain access to particular customers. In many cases a strong customer database may be the very substance of the purchase. For example, one catalogue retailer buying another is in fact buying itself an expanded customer database amongst other things.

New technology and customer service

The customer is becoming more discerning and is the driver for change in many industries, the engine being new technology. Today's customers expect a high service level as well as a quality product.

> Consumers are becoming more technology-literate, and young customers in particular will know what can be done to improve service. If they are not satisfied, they will go elsewhere.
>
> Warwick Morgan, ICL Retail Systems, 1994.

Current technology provides the customer with speedy service, knowledge of availability, ease of payment, speed of transaction and speed in delivery through the use of EPOS, EFTPOS, EDI and IT.

Marketing information technology is changing the way markets are structured and the way in which firms communicate with each other. The competitive environment is rapidly changing, and boundaries are being redrawn. The way in which suppliers, distributors and customers correspond, and how they organize their working relationships is constantly shifting as a result of new technologies. Take the clothing industry as an example. It is now possible for a retail organization in England to develop designs which may be transmitted to a remote manufacturer offshore with production specifications and for the manufacturer to action production via an expert system, organize transportation, inform the customer, invoice the customer and despatch the goods within a matter of days rather than weeks or months as was the case not so long ago. This not only opens up new market opportunities but may also present competitor threats. Markets no longer need to remain fixed to a particular locality but new technologies increase the opportunities to develop global markets for what once may only have been local products or services.

Information technology has created new marketing techniques and new marketing channels. Database marketing allows vast amounts of customer data to be stored cheaply and to be used to target more accurate and hence cost effective mailshots and other marketing tactics. This is only strategically important if a firm is able to gain an advantage over competitors by accessing and applying technologies that a competitor is unable to develop. Alternatively, it is a threat if a competitor is able to use it and we are not. Computer links to suppliers and customers are common in some industries whereby the firm is able to place orders regularly via a computer link to replenish stock from a supplier or a customer is able to order from the firm directly. For example, in the motor-vehicle industry some distributing garages for particular marques are able to satisfy customer demand by entering the precise specification of the vehicle and placing the order via computer link to the factory where the vehicle will be manufactured. On placing the order, the manufacturer is able to provide the distributor with a production schedule and advise a firm delivery date which can be communicated to the customer.

Communication technology

The developments in the area of communications have enabled people to communicate effectively over much greater distances. Although the telephone itself is an important development, fibre optics and satellite technology have enabled people to communicate in pictures, text and speech. Linking communication technology to computing technology means that large volumes of data can be transmitted anywhere in the world where they have receiving technology. For example, one is able to communicate in video picture and speech, or one can send text in a variety of forms over great distances at relatively low cost using say electronic mail.

Modem

A modem is a device that enables your computer to send and receive information through a telephone line. There are both internal and external modems. In communications, you can use a modem to call an information service, bulletin board, personal computer, or to automatically answer an incoming call from another computer. In some software packages using a communication link you can dial a phone number so that you can call and communicate to another person via a wordprocessor. If you are using an external modem, after plugging it into your computer through an available *COM* port, you must plug in one or two standard telephone cords. Once you connect to an information service or another computer, you can exchange information either by sending or receiving text interactively (like having a conversation), or by transferring entire files. You send text to another computer by typing in the communications window. Typing is used to make menu choices or to send messages to another personal computer user. When sending and receiving text, any typing by either party appears on the screens of both computers. You need not do the typing on-line. You can transfer an existing file that you typed off-line. It is expensive to type on-line. It is much quicker and cheaper to transfer files. During a file transfer, however, the contents of the file are not displayed on either computer's screen. After the transfer is complete, the contents of the file can be viewed and edited by the party that received it. If the transferred file is an application, it can be used when the transfer is complete.

Information services and bulletin boards

Information services and electronic bulletin boards usually use mainframes or minicomputers to store and distribute information.

A bulletin board stores messages, files, and programs. Users can upload information to the bulletin board, and view and download information put on the bulletin board by other users. An electronic mail system is a type of bulletin board. An information service is also a type of bulletin board, because the service's computer contains databases of information that you can view and download. Information services usually offer a variety of services, such as news, airline schedules and fares, and stock market quotes. Examples are CompuServe and Prodigy. To subscribe to an information service or bulletin board, contact the service and ask them to set up an account for you. They will send you instructions which typically include the communication and terminal settings to use with their service, a local phone number for the service, and a password that allows you to sign on to the service or bulletin board. Information services charge a fee for connect time, but many bulletin boards do not charge a fee.

Exam Hint

Questions will not be asked on technological developments alone, but you will be expected to be aware of their impact upon marketing and sales information systems. You need to be able to demonstrate to the examiner an understanding of how technological solutions could be applied to particular marketing and sales information problems.

On line catalogues

On line means simply that once you dial a number and your modem links you to a receiving computer system you may access the databases on the line. If you use on-line database systems it is important to use them as effectively as possible. This often means being able to communicate and retrieve data from the remote system on-line and transmitting it back to a local system where the data may be examined off-line. Reading data off-line is cheaper. It is not always possible to retrieve data in this way and some systems may only be read on-line. This is always more expensive.

Many manufacturers and retailers are exploring ways to use the Internet to display their wares. For example, the Sears Clothing Catalogue is available in the US and accessible on-line. These types of catalogue are sometimes multi-media. This means that they use video, text and graphics. Graphic images are always much slower to access and can be problematical given the non-standard linking technologies. However, you can see the possibilities that this technology is opening up for marketing and sales opportunities. For example, you can choose a particular item of clothing, see a picture, either a still graphical image or a video, and read text. Price and availability can be checked on-line and an order can be placed. Payment could also be transmitted electronically simultaneously. Nevertheless, many banks are still nervous about transmitting money in this way until security is made less breachable by hackers. Computer theft is still a worry.

Publishers have also experimented with on-line services charging fees to access journals and book catalogues.

CD ROM – Compact Disk Read Only Memory

CD ROM catalogues are widely available, storing vast amounts of data, and again these can hold text or can be multi-media. Many services are using or thinking of using CD ROM systems to sell information. Data compression and transmission techniques are making it possible for sound, pictures and text to be transmitted around the globe using phone lines and satellite links. These converging technologies are transforming the way firms, industries, markets and individuals interact. The full impact of such technological developments is not yet certain. However, one thing we can be certain about is the fact that they will give rise to new marketing and sales techniques and opportunities and that for those who do not fully understand the impact they pose a great threat.

Smart cards

Smart card/Electronic wallet – is moving us towards a cashless society. The smart card is a fairly simple concept. The smart card either debits direct from your account or is credited with an amount which allows purchases within that limit. The card can then be replenished for further use. The card will be unique to an individual customer just like your bank cheque card or credit card and is a substitute for money. The card will have so many credit units logged in its memory and may from time to time be replenished rather like your bank account. A report in the *Financial Times* (14 July 1994) discussed the introduction of smart cards in Hong Kong for use by customers in a range of stores and on the transport systems. The customer carrying these cards will pass by a scanner that will read the card on entry to the transport system and once again on exit at which point a charge for the journey will be made. Your smart card will then have the appropriate units deducted from the card. In future people carrying smart cards may not even physically have to offer the card for payment but rather passing a particular signal point, cards will be read and transactions recorded even when the card is located in your pocket or in a bag. Security is a concern and designers of smart card systems are aware that there may be some consumer resistance to the introduction of cards that may be located on the person being read by unauthorized persons. Consumers may still prefer to tender their cards in completing a transaction even though it is not necessary.

The smart card offers marketing and sales opportunities to firms buying into the networks. They also offer customers a convenient and safe way to pay for goods and services. Consider approaching a supermarket checkout with your goods in your trolley and passing them over a barcode scanner yourself, or a world where merely lifting the item out of the basket triggers the recording of the sales transaction because there is a reading device on the trolley. Your smart card could then be scanned and the appropriate value of units deducted to match the goods taken. The secure checkout gate would then open to allow you to exit with your goods. Supermarket checkouts as we now know them with rows of people at the checkout and lining up to be served would be a thing of the past. When you get home, before watching your favourite television programme, you can contact your *virtual bank* on screen and obtain a statement of account and top up your smart card ready for tomorrow's transactions.

Many people believe the smart card will make sales promotions easier and more effective. The smart card is a card embedded with computer chips that can store reams of data about a person and that person's buying habits. Over the past few years, more companies – mostly supermarket chains – have been testing smart cards in their frequent-shopper programmes. Many companies already run loyalty programmes, and smart cards are expected to make them more effective. When it comes to running such programmes, some marketers believe that a smart card has several advantages over a magnetic stripe card, both for the consumer and the marketer, including:

- ease of use,
- greater flexibility,
- enhanced ability for cross promotions,
- ability for multiple applications,
- long-term financial gains, and
- improved security.

There are signs that some major card issuers are starting to wake up to the smart card's potential. The smart card, or chip card, combines on one piece of plastic multiple payment applications, fraud-fighting security devices, and a portable marketing database that can be tapped at the point-of-sale (POS) to create on-the-spot promotions. Despite their advantages, smart cards still cost more than magnetic strip cards, and there is no infrastructure to support them. However, for all the difficulties the technology presents, many experts believe that now is the time to begin tapping the potential of smart cards. Benefits for banks from smart cards lie in their potential to replace cash transactions in marketing strategies, and in the ability to put multiple applications on a single card.

The technology may offer opportunities to provide increased levels of customer service while at the same time releasing human resources to deal with specific customer enquiries.

Television shopping

People have been introduced to buying goods directly from their domestic television set for a number of years. Experienced direct marketers such as K-Tel have used the TV to sell their records and other household products for many years, offering the customer flexible payment methods such as VISA and Master Card. The more recent phenomenon has been a TV channel dedicated to home shopping (QVC). Convenience is the most important factor in the marketing mix for customers choosing to buy goods and services in this way. Next time you are away on business and bored in your hotel room take a look at QVC (if you are not already an avid follower!). It is an interesting experience and you can become very knowledgeable about the most unusual products in a short space of time. Marketing and sales policies, systems and procedures have to be adapted to deal with this different way of doing business. However, as novel as it might seem to us today remember that supermarkets were once novel, as were high street stores, as indeed were markets themselves in the middle ages. Merging technologies may mean that we simply buy many goods and services in the next millennium using TV or Virtual Reality Computer Systems. It will be extremely important for delivery systems and the logistics functions of organizations to ensure that the right goods get to the right place on time.

Multimedia

Multimedia is a term that describes the variety of approaches mixing text, pictures and sound. Multimedia products are widely available as a substitute to the printed media, e.g. encyclopaedia or other book-based materials can be enhanced by incorporating a multimedia approach. CD ROM (Computer Disk Read Only Memory) products are available from a number of publishers, book and record stores. Many of these CD ROMs are either educational or informational in nature. There is a marketing multimedia project using sound, text and video graphics that has developed materials for learning marketing. London Guildhall University, Manchester Metropolitan University and the University of Central Lancashire have cooperated on the development of materials for this.

Multimedia products are also widely available and growing on the World Wide Web (WWW). Hardware requirements to use multimedia effectively have to have fast central processing units, e.g. 486 or Pentium computers running at speeds of 90 MHz-plus together with at least 16 Mb of Random Access Memory (RAM). If you are accessing multimedia information via the Internet (WWW) then you really require a fast modem (modulator–demodulator) to transfer data quickly, 28 bps or more. Fast data transmission means reduced on-line costs. This is particularly important for the transmission of graphic files that require many bytes of data. It can take minutes rather than seconds to 'download' graphic files so the better the hardware specification, including the fastest possible modem speed, will ensure cost minimization.

With regard to CD ROM hardware, again it will pay the user to consider buying the fastest possible speed (usually quad or six speed CD ROM drives) since this allows much faster access to data.

One of the major benefits of using multimedia information is the ability to see and hear as well as to read. This is particularly useful in a variety of information applications and also extremely useful for transmitting training material or information which is more suited to audio or visual presentation. For example, micro surgeons have been able to access multimedia information about performing specific operations from experts at other hospitals throughout the globe before performing a similar operation. A further example where multimedia is usefully applied is to enable claim assessors in the insurance world to transmit accident reports back to the head office from a remote site with a spoken, written and visual report of the accident. One can easily see how multimedia could be used to inform managers in a variety of technical and managerial situations, e.g. engineers, scientists, sales managers, teachers, lecturers, trainers, management consultants etc.

The combination of information and telecommunication technology employing fibre optics, whereby greater volumes of data can be transmitted more easily down very thin wires, has enabled telecommunication companies to take advantage of 'opportunities of scope' rather than merely scale. These companies such as British Telecom Plc, AT&T and Northern Telecom amongst others, have been able to transmit graphics in the form of video pictures in addition to sound. In the case of home entertainment, feature films and other audiovisual entertainment may be purchased via a telephone line linked to a domestic television set. Billing may be processed as an additional charge to the usual telephone bill. The multimedia market world wide was estimated to be worth around £380 million in 1992 but is expected to increase to around £20 billion by the year 2000. Telecommunication companies have the existing networks that can carry far more data than is currently being transmitted and so they will be able to add income without necessarily adding to cost, hence achieving economies of scope.

There are in existence a number of shops, banks and shopping malls where one is able to buy particular products or services at the touch of a button on an electronic screen. Sometimes there are facilities to speak into the screen via a microphone or handset and a video picture may appear in the corner of the screen to talk you through available alternative choices. Such systems have been used to sell financial services such as mortgages, insurance and bank services.

CD ROM (Compact Disk Read Only Memory) drives added to personal computers allow pictures, sound and text to be accessed. Data compression and transmission techniques make it possible for sound, pictures and text to be transmitted around the globe using phone lines and satellite links. Converging technologies are transforming the way firms, industries, markets and individuals interact.

Video conferencing enables managers at a number of remote locations to meet face to face to discuss important issues without the need or cost to drive a car, ride a train or a plane. Think of the opportunities and implications for sales and marketing managers?

Virtual reality banking 'a case in point'. It was reported in *The Times* in December 1994 that virtual reality was stepping out of the games arcade and into the building society. Early in 1995 Nationwide Building Society unveiled its first virtual reality branch, bringing normal building society services, combined with the latest interactive video technology. The system will imitate the experience of walking into a normal branch, but instead of talking to someone behind the counter, you will press buttons on the screen for information, to open accounts and to arrange mortgages. The first system was a branch in the south of England, later to be introduced into other branches. The eventual aim of the project, codenamed Blue Sky, is to provide banking in the home, the workplace, at shops and at railway stations. The system uses a mixture of text, full colour video, sound, photographs, pre-recorded presentations and video telephone conferencing. The aim is to give you sufficient data to make an informed choice and speed up the time taken to process applications for new accounts and mortgage applications. Paying in and withdrawing cash will be carried out in the traditional way. On touching the screen, the doors of the virtual branch open. You will enter what seems, at first sight, to be a normal Nationwide branch. However, instead of approaching a receptionist for guidance, you simply touch the box marked receptionist, activating a video. The video presenter will then explain all the services on offer and how to access them. Initially, information on mortgages, savings and investments will be available, but this will be extended to include all Nationwide products, including insurance. Quotations for mortgages will be available, plus information to help you to compare savings and investment products. Once you make your choice, you can fill in the form. A printout copy will be given. If you need more help, all you do is pick up the video conferencing telephone and talk to one of Nationwide's staff. Legal requirements mean that it will not be possible to complete all transactions because signatures with witnesses are needed for some transactions. Presently, services that require security will not be offered. For example, you will not be able to transfer funds to another account. Banking is moving away from the branch to outlets such as the home or workplace, through the personal computer or television, and to other locations, including airports and shopping areas. It is envisaged that five years from now, financial organizations will be delivering their services in the home through the computer or television. However, before your bank can move into the home, you will need to have access to cable or a special telecommunication line. It is estimated that 50 per cent of homes will have access to cable and 25 to 30 per cent of homes will have multimedia personal computers by the end of the decade. Customer reaction to Blue Sky has been positive. 'I have seen the future, when can I have it?' was one of the comments from customers.

Home banking

The National Westminster Bank is currently piloting an interactive home banking system. It is conducting a home shopping experiment with British Telecom, Safeway and W.H. Smith. This involves testing a multimedia system at 2,500 homes in the Ipswich and Colchester areas. The service will be delivered through the television and will be similar to Nationwide's virtual branch except it will not have a video conferencing facility.

A number of major banks have already developed home banking services for customers. Access is gained to banking services 24 hours a day to execute simple transactions. These systems are still in their infancy. The systems work by using communication technology. All that is required is a modem, telephone link and/or a video/computer terminal link depending on which options you choose and which banking system you connect to. Commonly provided services are bank balances, standing orders, direct debits and the issue of cheques. Services for commercial company banking systems are more sophisticated offering higher levels of service. Home banking offers increased levels of customer service at a price and presents the banks with an opportunity to provide additional services to customers (e.g. insurance, mortgages, loans, brokerage, taxation). It is envisaged that this type of service will reduce the necessity to invest in high street retailing branches and the numerous paper communications to offer services to customers. From the bank's point of view these services enable promotional efforts to customers to be better targeted, and present the bank with the opportunity to add value by providing the customer with additional products that earn a higher return for a given promotional spend.

In the future the combined power of the smart card and home banking may replace paper transactions such as cheques and anyone who has a bank will be able to transfer money without even a visit to the retail branch except in *virtual reality*.

Technophobia and consumer resistance

There is, however, still some managerial and consumer resistance to the introduction of new technology, and the downside to all the excitement and opportunity presented by the new information technology revolution. Frequently when overexcited and enthused, talking about the future technologies, colleagues and friends take time and delight in reminding me that consumers like to shop. It is a social experience, customers like to physically touch what they buy. They like to see and touch the clothes they buy. Many people are still resistant and afraid of using new technology. Systems designers are aware of many of the problems and have tried to develop systems that appear familiar, for example just like a domestic TV set.

What do consumers think about technology?

Research from the Henley Centre (reported in *FT* 30.03.1995, p. 14) has identified four different groups of consumers:

- *Technophiles (24 per cent)* are people who are enthusiastic about new technology in a general sense and are interested in their application. These people are most likely to be male rather than female, aged under 35, and more likely to belong to social class C1 than AB.
- *Aspirational technophiles (22 per cent)* are generally excited by new technology but much less interested in its application. More likely males and concentrated in social class AB.
- *Functionals (26 per cent)* are people who claim no interest in the technological developments. They are not hostile to it especially if it enhances customer service. They are most likely female and over 45 years of age.
- *Technophobes (28 per cent)* are those people openly hostile to technology at all levels and sceptical as to the value of technology. People over 60 years of age, more likely female and distributed evenly through the social classes.

The future adapted from Media 2004

E-mail common for technology users. Personalized newspaper sent via E-mail to your address on the Internet. The newspaper selection is taken from a worldwide press network and downloaded to your computer E-mail address. Your interests have been noted by the subscription agency from information you provided and from known information about your personal likes and dislikes through an electronic observation system that has tracked your interests including purchases made through computer and other sources. Shopping is done over the TV and through the Internet. Communication to family and friends is via the videophone. Test driving cars, testing machines for the home and holiday purchase choices may all be made via *virtual reality* without leaving home. If you decide to buy, that too can be done within virtual reality.

Security

Security is a very important consideration for firms investing in new technologies, it is essential to develop customer confidence in the use of new systems. The last thing any organization wants is to invest in new computer systems and to find the integrity of the system breached by a third party. It is not merely payment systems and the transmission of money that must be secure; you also do not want confidential information relating to customers, products or markets to be obtained by third parties, particularly your competitors.

Retail markets and new technology

In retailing MIS provide an opportunity for the retailer to:

- Gain control over the supply chain.
- Utilize in-store space more efficiently by stocking only those lines that are moving quickly.
- Identify effective in-store sales locations for particular goods.
- Electronic Point Of Sale (EPOS) systems allow low stock-holding.
- EPOS means rapid replenishment of fast moving stock items.
- EPOS allows the identification of slow moving stocks.
- Electronic Funds Transfer at Point Of Sale (EFTPOS) allows the rapid exchange of goods for funds from the customer (e.g. switch cards; smart cards etc).

Electronic point of sale (EPOS)

Retailing businesses have been revolutionized by EPOS systems. Next time you enter a supermarket or visit the high street stores observe the way in which your purchasing transactions are dealt with. Goods will usually have a barcode on them and that barcode is passed over a scanner by the sales assistant. The barcode holds information on stock item identification, price and store location, amongst other things. When your purchase is complete the stock account for the store will be updated, the difference between the selling price and cost price will be recorded to furnish profit on the item and if needs be the item will be automatically replenished by the EPOS system triggering a re-order. Further consider the types of marketing and sales information such systems can provide instantly:

Sales by stock item (stock code)
Sales by department
Sales by store
Sales by in-store area location
Fast moving stock items
Slow moving stock items (items to delete)
Hourly or daily or weekly sales
Sales by customer
Sales by staff or till location
Overs and shorts reports
Inventory analysis
Analysis of exception reporting
Profitability/contribution by stock item
Transaction type: cash, credit card, switch card, cheque etc.

Extending Activity 11.1

Next time you go to a retail store, observe carefully the way in which goods are displayed and priced on the shelves. Note down any electronic pricing methods in the store. Observe the point of sale transaction and the technology used. Ask about the store system and what information it is able to provide. How is data transmitted? What data is collected? What do the management use the data for? Be inquisitive – find out. If you happen to work in retailing you have an advantage!

Computers allow a company to locate a product in its warehouse, to devise a delivery schedule which makes the most efficient use of its vehicle fleet, and to track a consignment on its way to its final destination. Managing the supply chain can lead to considerable reductions in the amounts of stock which have to be held. This efficiency enables firms to save money tied up in working capital. Concentrating all of a company's delivery activities in one centre not only reduces the levels of stock which have to be held. It means that a wider range of stock is available to customers and allows the distribution centre to add extra services.

Technology and information for marketing managers

Scanner data, point-of-sale data, and single-source data supply a wealth of information to the consumer packaged-goods industry about consumer buying patterns. The information systems challenge is to find new ways to analyse this data to help businesses uncover new market opportunities. The key problem facing today's marketing and sales managers is not a lack of data but a lack of systems that transform voluminous scanner data into decisions that may achieve a competitive advantage. Three different system approaches – expert systems, neural networks, and decision support systems – are being pursued to better mine and use the data that businesses routinely collect on consumers. These alternatives are examined in terms of decision support advantages they offer marketers and managers of consumer packaged goods. As scanner data continues to intrigue the consumer packaged-goods industry, the use of information systems to analyse this data and identify the marketing opportunities hidden within it becomes paramount.

Database marketing

Database marketing involves the use of computer software to maintain detailed customer information for marketing purposes. More and more companies are turning to database marketing as a means of competing for market share and profits. Four factors have led to database marketing's increasing popularity:

1 Technological improvements
2 Diversification of products and markets
3 Rising cost of postal services, labour and media costs
4 The expanding use of credit cards and free-phone telephone numbers.

As early as 1990, an industry survey in the US conducted by *Direct Marketing* magazine showed that more than a half-million businesses were significantly relying on database marketing techniques. Companies can benefit from database marketing in several ways. It can help increase response rates, steer product development efforts, forecast sales more accurately, test various marketing mixes, and improve mass marketing decisions.

Companies are collecting mountains of data about individuals, processing it to predict how likely they are to buy a product, and using that knowledge to hone a marketing message precisely measured to get them to do so. New generations of faster, more powerful computers are enabling marketers to home in on ever-smaller niches of the population, ultimately aiming for the smallest consumer segment of all – the individual. A growing number of marketers are investing millions of pounds to build databases that enable them to find out who their customers are and what it takes to secure their loyalty. Marketers are increasingly recognizing that past customer behaviour, as recorded in actual business transactions, is by far the best indicator of future buying patterns. By weaving relationships with its customers, a company can make it inconvenient for consumers to switch to a competitor. Using neural-network software, computers can plough through masses of data and determine how specific variables may be dependent on one another.

Database marketing has evolved from the use of mailing lists to a system to gather and use information on individual prospects and customers. With a database of all customers and prospects, companies are studying the ways and means to increase their abilities to better communicate with the individuals that compose that market. Database development should be approached as a sales, marketing and distribution opportunity that brings the customer and prospect into direct linkage with a company's marketing and sales efforts. Advertising, sales promotion, public relations, direct mail and sales calling are moving into an interactive relationship with marketing databases.

Who is using database marketing?

CIC Video, distributor of Universal and Paramount films on video, uses a database as its essential tool to keep tabs on the video market and influence it. The data drives direct mail, telesales, field sales force, and merchandising activities. It enables analysis not only of existing consumers and retail outlets, but is also used to identify potential new market sectors.

Neural networks

Artificial Neural Networks (ANN) are distributed and parallel information processing systems composed of many simple computational elements that interact across weighted connections. ANNs exhibit certain features such as the ability to learn, recognize trends, and mimic human thought processes. ANNs attempt to model the architecture and processing capabilities of biological neural systems. The ability of neural networks to identify patterns in data could be utilized in many areas of marketing management: retail sales forecasting, direct marketing, and target marketing.

Neural-network software can automatically learn from large sets of data on its own. The software can build a strong statistical model describing important relationships and patterns in the data. Parallel processing systems devote dozens or even hundreds of microprocessors to scouring a giant database for records that meet a complex set of criteria.

Available software?

There are more than 300 sales and marketing computer packages available in the UK and another 200 in the US according to a recent survey in *Marketing*. In order to choose from among marketing software packages, it is necessary to:

1. Identify and prioritize needs.
2. Identify possible software solutions.
3. Shortlist a small number of packages.
4. Evaluate each software package according to needs.
5. Evaluate each package in detail with a focus on functions, cost, and benefits.

For direct marketing, the following should be considered when selecting a marketing database:

1. Approach prompting.
2. Campaign management/administration.
3. Campaign planning.
4. Campaign execution.
5. Campaign monitoring.
6. Tracking.

To ensure that the right data are collected, marketers should review data used in the business environment and develop a picture of what is needed. Any data issues that will be faced when developing a consistent marketing information base should be determined. By building statistical models, marketers can gain a clearer understanding of sales drivers.

An example of how retailers use data

Retailers are major users of marketing information systems and have invested heavily in a number of technologies to capture and manipulate data. One system that many retailers have found advantageous is marketed by Retail Merchandising Service Automation (RMSA). RMSA sales forecasts are built based on customer demand, not management initiatives. The two systems most frequently used by apparel and footwear retailers are the Merchandise Planning System and the Unit Management approach. Merchandise Planning reports provide sales forecasts and merchandising data, including projected inventory levels and markdowns, for a period of 6 to 10 months into the future. The information is sorted by classification for each store that a buyer oversees. The key component of RMSA's system is a rolling 12-month planning and forecasting module. This rolling or dynamic plan is based on location, customer demographics, seasonal factors and merchandise, and allows the buyer maximum flexibility in tailoring a custom plan for each classification.

Definition 11.1

An *expert system* is one that is self contained and when data is entered into the system the system will automatically update the appropriate information files and take a decision based upon an algorithm (a series of conditional statements) stored somewhere in the system.

A *marketing decision support system* may be defined as a co-ordinated collection of data, systems, tools and techniques with supporting software and hardware. Decision support systems are used for gathering and interpreting relevant information from the business and about the organization's environment. The information is used as a basis for marketing decisions and action.

Unit 12 Specimen papers

THE FINAL EXAMINATION TIP

Rationale behind the examination

Managers need to have the capability to manage the future, especially for marketing and sales. This capability is developed by collecting and classifying data that may be analysed to provide information on which to plan, control and decide, Data is collected from a variety of sources. Sources are twofold: first, external, and secondly, data is also collected internally for other purposes as well as for marketing and sales but may nevertheless be applied to marketing and sales problems and activities.

The CIM Management Information syllabus reflects the diverse nature of information and the variety of analytical tools that are available to managers. Students need to develop a wide understanding of the nature of information sources and an ability to apply knowledge to specific marketing and sales problems. In approaching your study you may need to study the key elements of the syllabus separately but you should always be looking at problems and issues from the wider perspective and developing your skills in applying techniques and knowledge from across the syllabus as appropriate. The following diagram shows how the syllabus is related to management information for marketing decisions.

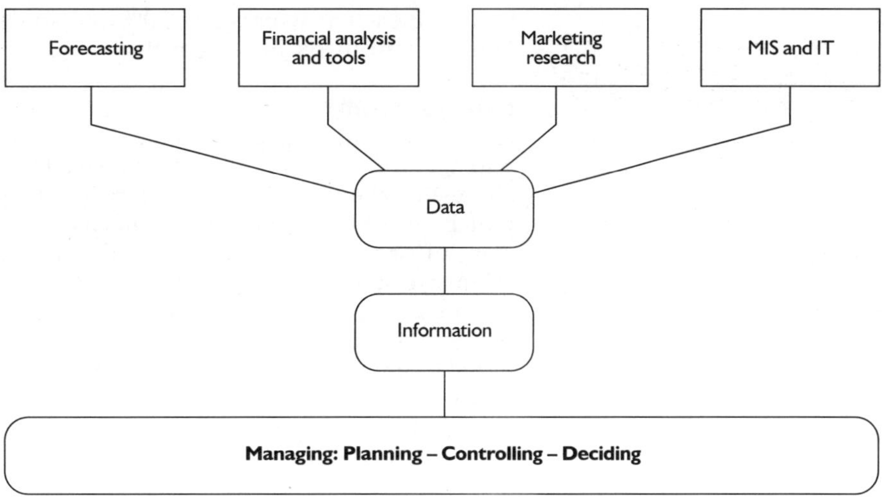

The examination

The examination is divided into two parts. Section A is a mini-case presenting you with specific issues and problems that need to be resolved using data provided and by applying your knowledge from across the syllabus. Answers need to go beyond description, and better candidates will develop the ability to analyse and evaluate data given to provide informed judgements, decisions and recommendations. Candidates must use the numerical data given in the case and select and apply the data as necessary. It is pure folly to ignore numerical data when it is provided. Choosing and using the appropriate numbers and having the ability to apply relevant tools and techniques can provide quantitative analysis on which to base your conclusions and evaluations. Qualitative issues must also be considered where appropriate.

Students also need to make sure that they answer the questions in the context in which they are set. If a question asks you to outline the steps necessary to research a particular overseas market then you should provide an answer that focuses on the particular overseas market and the steps necessary. You should avoid merely regurgitating what you have read in a textbook at the expense of ignoring the context. If you merely provide a general answer giving the research steps but ignore context it demonstrates a lack of understanding of the real issues. Take time to plan your answers in the examination; it is time well spent. If you are asked for a report then provide your answer in report form. Be careful to follow the instructions given in the question. Structure your answers clearly, do not waffle and do not wander off the point. Answer the question and nothing but the question.

Section B provides students with a choice of question. These questions tend to be straightforward, testing a specific part or parts of the syllabus. For example, a question may focus on forecasting and the distinction between forecasting and budgeting. Alternatively, a question in this section may focus on a specific marketing research technique, such as focus groups.

Reading

You should read as widely as time permits and always attempt to keep yourself up to date with developments in technology by reading the broadsheet newspapers and other appropriate material. The reading list is comprehensive and reflects the diverse nature of the underpinning knowledge areas. This Workbook will provide a comprehensive study guide with many worked examples and relevant questions and answers at the required standard.

Important change to the examination structure

Since June 1996 the exam structure has been revised as follows:

Section A worth 40%
Section B each answer worth 20% and students will be required to do three questions from six in section B.

Plan your time

It is important that you spend some time reading the questions on the paper before attempting any answer. Jot down points that occur to you alongside the question as you read the paper. Then consider carefully which questions you think you will attempt. Remember section A is compulsory and worth 40% and you then need to select your three strongest questions from section B worth 20% each. Do attempt the required number of questions otherwise you will simply lose marks for a whole question. Do the questions you feel most comfortable with first in order to gain confidence. It is surprising what a good answer will do for your confidence. The examination is for three hours and the marks awarded to each part of the question are given on the paper, so allocate your time accordingly. There are 180 minutes and 100 marks available. You have 1.8 minutes in which to earn each mark not allowing for reading time.

If a question is worth 20 marks you should allow 36 minutes maximum. The mini-case should take you no longer than 72 minutes. Parts of questions worth 10 marks allow 18 minutes and for 5 marks allow only nine minutes. Good time-keeping is essential in helping you to achieve your objective, i.e. to *pass the exam.*

Common exam errors and omissions to avoid

The following list will give you some indication of common errors and omissions that cost marks in the exam.

1 Repeating the question in the answer

Students often repeat the question and spend far too long – often as much as a page or two – doing so before getting to the point, or offering any analysis, if they ever do. Sometimes in Section B students have been known to address the point of the question only in list form at the end. This is foolish and very costly.

Action

You should recognize the importance of answering the question set by the examiner and avoid repetition.

2 Failure to analyse data given in the question

Students often ignore relevant numbers either because they do not know how to deal with the data presented or because they are fearful of numbers. This is folly and a good grasp of all the tools and techniques listed in the syllabus is essential for confidence in dealing with the problems presented.

Action

Candidates should make sure that they build and develop the necessary numerical skills to analyse and evaluate data to reveal appropriate information pertinent to the situation. There are now probably enough past questions and answers around (including the pilot paper) to give a strong indication of the type of numerical skills required. Furthermore, this Workbook contains many further activities and questions at the required standard that should allow skills development to take place.

3 Failure to answer the question

Some students simply ignore the examiner's question and answer all they know about a related topic. For example, on the June 1995 paper there were a number of scripts where the candidates attempted a question requiring a discussion of marketing research methods appropriate to a given situation but not only did they ignore the context, they decided the question was about primary and secondary data. Whilst they described this very well, they failed to give an answer that addressed methodologies. This is an extremely good way to score *zero.*

Action

Students need to have these points reinforced at every opportunity when they present work for marking by their tutors. Remember, examiners want to give credit to students for their efforts but are only able to do so on the evidence presented.

4 Ignoring the context of the question

Some students fail to shape their answer to take account of the given situation and merely regurgitate some rote-learned points in answer to the problem. These students do not focus on the context.

Action

Students must learn to be sensitive to the context of the case or the question. It simply requires *common sense* and a bit of *thought* before starting to compose an answer.

Advice from the senior examiner

Remember the appropriate acronym – **PASS.**

Presentation
Good presentation is often the hallmark of a good candidate. Write legibly in black ink and make the layout clear and easy to read. Major headings should be underlined with a ruler and tabular data clearly presented.

Analysis
Data in the question should be analysed using any appropriate financial tools. Alternatively, where the question does not have numbers it may still present data that can be analysed or discussion points that need to be evaluated to achieve a balanced case.

Structure
It is very important to structure answers clearly and in line with the parts of the question so that examiners can clearly pick up points students are making and give credit. If a question has sections (a), (b) and (c) then the answer should clearly indicate (a), (b) or (c).

Sense
Students should always make certain that they have answered the question and nothing but the question, providing evidence and analysis in such a way that the answer is sensible.

If you have put in the work and you follow these instructions to the letter you should be in a good position to demonstrate your knowledge, skill and understanding to the examiner. It only remains to wish you Good Luck!

Specimen exam paper 1 June 1997

Advanced Certificate in Marketing

Advanced Certificate in Sales Management

Management Information for Marketing and Sales 3 Hours' Duration

This examination is in two sections.

Part A is compulsory and worth 40 per cent of the total marks.

Part B has six questions, select three. Each answer will be worth 20 per cent of the total marks.

DO NOT repeat the question in your answer but show clearly the number of the question attempted on appropriate pages of the answer book.

Rough workings should be included in the answer book and ruled through after use.

PART A

Global Plc

You are a Product Group Marketing Manager for Global Plc responsible for three products A, B and C.

Global Plc budgeted profit and loss statement for the year ending 30th June 1997

PRODUCT GROUPS	A	B	C
Sales	£1,500,000	£1,440,000	£900,000
Cost of Sales	£600,000	£720,000	£270,000
Gross Profit	£900,000	£720,000	£630,000
Overheads apportioned	£100,000	£100,000	£100,000
Net Profit	£800,000	£620,000	£530,000

The table above is a budgeted profit and loss statement for the three product groups within your control. In recent weeks it has become evident that the sales forecasts on which the budgets are based are over-optimistic. As a result stock/turnover has declined from 40 days to 60 days during the year. Cash flow is also significantly lower than predicted. The forecasts produced in March 1996 on which the Sales Budgets were based were as follows: Product A 100,000 units, Product B 120,000 units and Product C 90,000 units. In the past these sales forecasts have been compiled from a number of sources that include the following:

- Sales director and sales team estimates of forward orders.
- Percentage increases over the current financial period budgeted sales figures.
- Percentage increases over current financial period actual results.

You are apportioned with £300,000 of fixed overheads for your area of responsibility from the Global group accountant and you have flexibility to decide how the overheads are apportioned to each of the products within your control. In your role as Product Group Marketing Manager you have been given the task of commenting upon the issues raised by the management team.

PART A

Question 1

You are asked to write a report to the Managing Director and members of the management team that addresses the issues and gives clear recommendations. You should provide calculations and any tables you consider important in supporting your analysis and recommendations.

(a) Why are the sales forecasts so important to the budgeting process and what do you consider the main weaknesses to be in the compilation of the current sales forecasts? **(5 marks)**

(b) What steps can be taken in future to achieve more accurate sales forecasts and what additional sources of data can be used? **(10 marks)**

(c) How sensitive is overall profitability of your three product groups to a 10% and a 20% fall in forecast sales? **(15 marks)**

(d) Comment on the treatment of fixed overheads and suggest ways in which overheads may be fairly apportioned to each of the product groups in your control. **(10 marks)**

(40 marks in total)

PART B – Answer THREE Questions Only

Question 2

Consider an organization of your choice wanting to introduce a comprehensive marketing information system to achieve the following objectives:

- To improve customer service levels.
- To provide marketing and sales managers with more accurate information.

You have been asked in your role as Project Manager to prepare a preliminary statement that outlines:

(a) The key elements of such a marketing information system. **(5 marks)**
(b) What technology can support the system. **(5 marks)**
(c) An outline plan of how you propose to investigate and design such a system. **(10 marks)**
(20 marks in total)

Question 3

You are a newly appointed Sales and Marketing Manager for an industrial products group. As part of your job description you are required to make effective use of existing distribution channels and to increase the effectiveness of the sales team. The sales team currently consists of six sales people who are assigned territories. In your new role you are asked for a short report addressed to the Sales Director covering the following points:

(a) How you intend to acquire performance data about the sales force. **(5 marks)**
(b) What type of data you intend to collect giving specific examples. **(5 marks)**
(c) How you intend to use the data to help you plan and control both distribution channels and the sales team. **(10 marks)**
(20 marks in total)

Question 4

As a retail marketing manager it is part of your brief to evaluate price and in-store promotions on a regular basis. Looking through a recent EPOS report you have noticed one particular product group with a current selling price £5 per unit which is not achieving the required profit margin of 25%. Instead according to your quick calculations it appears to have a profit margin of only 20%. The product group is also under-performing in volume terms by 200 units per week against target. You need to consider and evaluate the following suggestion providing appropriate calculations in support of your recommendations. Your answer should be written in report style as a proposal to your Area Manager.

(a) How much would the retail selling price need to increase by in order to achieve the 25% profit margin required? **(10 marks)**
(b) It has been estimated that a reduction in price of 10% would increase weekly volumes by 500 units based on an analysis of similar products. How would this reduction affect the current position in terms of both profit and volume? **(10 marks)**
(20 marks in total)

Question 5

You have been given the task of attracting new customers in your role as Business Development Manager for an advertising agency. In this role you have been asked to write a report to your Marketing Director covering the following points:

(a) How you intend to search and find initial leads for new business and what data sources you will use. **(10 marks)**
(b) How you intend to minimize the risk of bad debts with new business development ensuring that cash flow and profitability are maintained at adequate levels. **(10 marks)**

(20 marks in total)

Question 6

You are the Marketing Manager with responsibility for a newly created marketing department having seven full-time staff whose responsibilities include sales, promotion and customer services. You have been asked to write a memorandum to the Managing Director that gives an indication of how you propose to prepare a departmental budget. This should give proposed budget headings and an indication of how you intend to control expenditure under each heading. More particularly you are asked for detailed suggestions of the report formats and control information you require. **(20 marks)**

Question 7

Information Technology (IT) and in particular 'the Internet' has created new communication and information opportunities for many organizations. You have recently been given the important responsibility of investigating marketing possibilities using IT. You have been asked to prepare a report to present to marketing staff to make them aware of the range of possibilities. You should illustrate your report with appropriate examples. **(20 marks)**

Specimen answers June 1997

Answer – Question 1

To: The Managing Director
From: A Student
cc: Management Team
Date: 10th June 1997
Subject: Product Group Performance

Terms of reference

The following report will address four specific areas as requested:

(a) The Importance of Accurate Sales Forecasts
(b) Improving Future Sales Forecasts and Widening Data Sources
(c) Sensitivity of the Three Product Groups to Volume Changes
(d) Equitable Apportionment of Overheads to Product Groups

(a) The importance of accurate sales forecasts

Sales forecasts are important to the budgeting process since all subsidiary budgets are based upon the sales budgets that are derived from the sales forecasts. Cost of goods sold, production, purchasing and all expense overheads will be planned on the level of sales that the business has forecast for the financial period. The major weaknesses with the way in which the sales forecasts have been used are:

(i) The budget was prepared in March 1996 for the financial year from 1st July 1996 until 30th June 1997 and there appears to have been no updating to the forecast prior to the financial period commencing nor during the budget period.

(ii) Data gathered for the sales forecast seems to have relied heavily on limited sources:

Sales director and sales team estimates
Percentage increases over the current budget
Percentage increases over current actuals

Therefore, no account has been given to external changes impacting upon the business nor to the changes that may have occurred in the current sales mix, product mix, channel mix, new products introduced, old products deleted from the range, investment in plant that may have achieved efficiency gains or changes in working practices that may affect the forecasts.

(b) Improving future sales forecasts and widening data sources

In order to improve the accuracy of sales forecasts the following matters need to be addressed:

- Effective external data gathering in relation to the macro economy and those political, economic, social and technological factors that have an impact upon the business. For example, any legislative changes that affect demand or supply; social policy in relation to environmental matters or economic measures that cause a shift in demand by changing the propensity to consume the products that Global supply.
- A wider choice of internal data sources may also help forecast sales more accurately. For example, monitoring sales records, inventory movements, customer enquiries and customer comments on the existing product ranges together with any internally or externally gathered intelligence about competitor products and developments.
- More systematic gathering of in-house data with the aim of generating a better understanding of our customers and their preferences may lead to better sales forecasting. This is a fairly low cost option that can make an immediate return.

The use of externally published market reports (e.g. Euromonitor, Mintel, Keynote, DTI, Nielson, Taylor Nelson) may also be helpful data for achieving more accuracy in sales forecasting. This data will be useful to place any internal sales forecasts in the context of the wider market. It may also alert the company to changes in the external markets that may impact upon the company's product range.

Occasionally it may be appropriate to use external experts particularly if a new product launch is taking place either for Global or one of our major competitors to assess the effect on sales.

The closer the forecasts are to the time period the more accurate they should be. Furthermore, continuous or rolling forecasts would help accuracy and would allow budgets to be updated as and when required. In this context the preparation of a flexible budget would be more useful and should enable managers to obtain better quality information about product performance. Therefore, as volumes change the effect on cost and profit can be seen immediately.

(c) Sensitivity of the three product groups to volume changes

The three product groups are listed in the tables below:

Product Group A	**£'000 100%**	**£'000 90%**	**£'000 80%**
Sales	1,500	1,350	1,200
Cost of Sales	600	540	480
Gross Profit	900	810	720
Overheads	100	100	100
Net Profit	800	710	620

Product Group B	£'000 100%	£'000 90%	£'000 80%
Sales	1,440	1,296	1,152
Cost of Sales	720	648	576
Gross Profit	720	648	576
Overheads	100	100	100
Net Profit	620	548	476

Product Group C	£'000 100%	£'000 90%	£'000 80%
Sales	900	810	720
Cost of Sales	270	243	216
Gross Profit	630	567	504
Overheads	100	100	100
Net Profit	530	467	404

The flexed budgets in the tables reveal the following sensitivities:

(i) Each 1% fall in volume for product group A results in a fall in the contribution by £9.00.
(ii) Each 1% fall in volume for product group B results in a fall in the contribution by £7.20.
(iii) Each 1% fall in volume for product group C results in a fall in the contribution by £6.30.

Hence for each 1% fall in volume profits are reduced by the amount of the lost contribution given for each product group.

(d) Equitable apportionment of overheads to product groups

Overheads are currently simply apportioned equally across the three product groups without any particular reference to the way in which the products consume resources. There are a number of more equitable ways in which the overheads could be apportioned using either absorption costing or activity based costing.

If absorption based costing was applied then given the data it would be reasonable to use a unit cost basis as a starting point for a more equitable distribution of the overheads. This would at least take account of the fact that the different products have different cost structures and consume resources differently. To ensure that this is the most appropriate method would require gathering further cost data detailing labour and material costs consumed in each product together with data about the specific overhead costs and how they contribute to each product. This may lead to a different apportionment of overheads and another more appropriate absorption rate being chosen, e.g. £ per direct labour hour; % direct labour; £ per unit of direct material; % direct material; £ per machine hour; Standard Costing. The particular chosen basis should reflect the major cause of overhead costs in each of the products produced.

Alternatively Activity Based Costing identifying cost pools and the cost drivers for each product group may provide a more accurate costing. Overheads being attributed to product groups more equitably using the specific cost drivers identified.

It should be remembered that the informative benefits of having more accurate costings must exceed the costs of designing and implementing the costing system.

Answer – Question 2

(a)

The diagram below illustrates the key elements in any marketing information system (MkIS). The key elements are:

The Internal Database – this may consist of a number of different subsidiary databases that are used for other purposes such as: accounting records; costing records; customer accounts; customer history records; production records; marketing records and so on.
External Databases – these may consist of any externally accessible databases, e.g. Government agencies accessible through the Internet (inflation forecasts; GDP forecasts; DTI records; Inland Revenue Statistics and other government statistical data; Subscriber services such as Dunn and Bradstreet; Mintel Reports; Trade and Industry Databases held by professional or trade groupings.
Marketing Research – this could consist of specially commissioned marketing research reports conducted on behalf of the organization. It could also consist of syndicated research or general industry research that has been conducted by an external agency, e.g. Nielson or Keynote. An organization may wish to use these pieces of marketing research as part of its overall MkIS.

Decision Support Systems are internally designed systems that can aid decision-making. Data from any or all of the databases may be combined and manipulated to reveal information.

(b)

Information and communication technologies are those most likely to be of use in supporting any MkIS. The key technological support being a suitable computer to gather data, store data, process data and retrieve data. An internally networked system – an Intranet will be needed if a number of people inside the organization are to have access to data. For example, to improve customer service levels it may be necessary to allow front line sales staff to have access to customer accounting records, details from production schedules and delivery dates from despatch and distribution records. Furthermore, in order to provide marketing and sales managers with more accurate information it is essential that they have rapid access to changed data in the system. These managers may also require access to external databases relevant to their industry that may be contacted via the

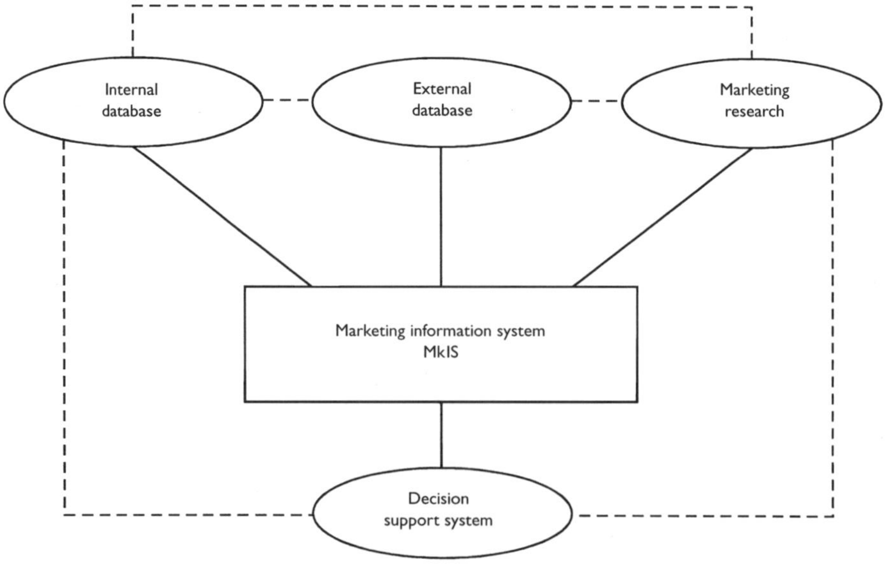

Source: Hines, T (1997), *Management Information for Marketing and Sales*, Butterworth-Heinemann: Oxford

Internet or on an internal file server where subscribed CD-ROM data sources can be accessed, e.g. Mintel Reports. A MODEM or an ISDN connection would be needed to communicate externally via the Internet. Managers in split site organizations may want to have access to electronic mail to exchange data files with other managers at other sites.

(c)

- The first step in investigating and designing any MkIS must be to decide upon the objectives of the system. What is the system needed for and what is it intended to do?
- Having established the needs and the intended objectives the next step is to identify the appropriate data sources that will make up the system. These will usually be subdivided into the key elements: Internal Databases; External Databases; Marketing Research; Decision Support Systems.
- Considerations regarding data capture need to be made.
- Costs and Benefits of the Information must also be carefully considered.
- Any system should be flexible to allow for growth and adaptation as needs change.

Answer – Question 3

REPORT ON SALES TEAM PERFORMANCE

To: Sales Director
From: Sales and Marketing Manager – Industrial Products
Date: 10th June 1997

The following short report covers the three key areas discussed in our recent meeting:

(a) Acquiring performance data about the sales force
(b) Specific examples of the types of data
(c) How the data may be used to plan and control both the sales force and the distribution channels

(a)

Performance data about the sales force may be acquired in a number of ways that may include: regular sales reports from salesmen themselves both written and verbal; observation; sales data and internal records relating to sales performance and sales territories; annual performance may be monitored through a formal appraisal system. Sales team meetings, communications with customers, diary records and questionnaires may also be used for acquiring data on performance.

(b)

Types of data that may be collected could include:

- Sales revenue per order (this could also be segmented by channel).
- Sales revenue per call (this could also be segmented by channel).
- Sales revenue per new accounts (by channel).
- Sales expenses/sales revenue per customer (by channel).
- No. of new accounts per period (by channel).
- % New accounts/total accounts (by channel).
- No. of orders per sales representative (by channel).
- Order per call ratio (by channel).
- Average order value per sales representative (by channel).
- No. of calls per period (by channel).
- No. of sales/no. of calls (by channel).
- Profit per call (by channel).
- Contribution per call (by channel).

(c)

Data such as that indicated in part (b) above may be used to plan and control both the distribution channels and the sales team. For example, looking at the number of calls made and the number of orders gained may lead to more effective call planning and timing of calls. Comparing monthly data it may be possible to identify a trend when a similar number of calls in a particular month has led to more sales that month and the identification of possible reasons for this. Using these types of data it may be possible to plan calls with maximum effect to miss out calls in months when there is little sales activity and simply maintain contact more cost effectively by phone, e-mail or letter.

In response to how effective sales channels are it may be appropriate to use performance measures that indicate channel profitability. For example, industrial products may be sold direct to customers mail order, to wholesale customers and to retail outlets. This being the case it would be important to have performance measures that indicate the proportion of sales and profitability for each segment and to use the data gathered on how sales representatives use their time and apportion it between each segment. Measures such as: profit by channel; contribution by channel; expenses by channel would start to build a picture of how effective each particular sales channel is.

Answer – Question 4

To: The Area Manager
From: Retail Marketing Manager
Date: 10th June 1997
Subject: Price Changes

Scanning some recent EPOS data it came to my attention that Product Group A seems to be underperforming our agreed targets. To remedy the situation with regard to achieving the required 25% profit margin I have given a detailed calculation in (a) below:

(a)

If the current selling price £5 earns a margin of 20% the cost structure must be:

Selling Price	£5	100%
Cost of Sale	£4	80%
Profit	£1	20%

Margin = Profit/SP, i.e. 1/5

To ensure a margin of 25% the structure needs to be:

Selling Price	100%
Cost of Sale	75%
Profit	25%

Mark-Up = Profit/Cost of Sales, i.e. 25%/75% = 1/3
1/3 on cost of £4 = £1.33
Hence the revised selling price needs to be £5.33 (cost £4 + profit £1.33)

(b)

A recent internal report indicated that a reduction in selling price by 10% would lead to an increase in weekly volumes by 10%. It must be emphasized that this increase in sales volume is only an estimated figure and there is no guarantee that it will be achieved if we lower prices. The volume relationship is always important to the total profitability of any decision. Given the data in this situation and assuming that the selling price reduced by 10% we are able to estimate the position as follows:

The current selling price being £5 and a reduction of 10% leading to a fall in price to £4.50 cost remaining at £4

	Current Position		10% Fall in Selling Price	
Selling Price	£5	100%	£4.50	100%
Cost of Sale	£4	80%	£4.00	88.89%
Profit	£1	20%	£0.50	11.11%

Profit per unit would fall to 11.11% at £0.50 per unit.

Volumes would increase by 500 units leading to an increase of £250 (500 × £0.50).

However, the critical factor is how many full price sales are lost to earn this increase?

For example, if current sales at full price are 500 units at £5 this would result in a loss of 500 × £0.50 = £250 and there would be no advantage in achieving the increased volumes. If of course existing sales were already higher than 500 units lowering the price to achieve an additional 500 unit sales would result in throwing profit away.

Recommendation

It is recommended that we raise the selling price to 33.33% higher than current cost of sale price to achieve the required margin and reject the suggestion of reducing prices for the reasons stated in part (b) of this report. It is also recommended that we monitor the effect on volumes daily as a result of this decision.

Answer – Question 5

To: Marketing Director
From: Business Development Manager
Date: 10th June 1997
Subject: New Leads Without Risk?

(a)

There are a number of ways in which I intend to find initial leads for new business. First of all it is important to recognize that not all new business means that it is necessary to attract new customers but rather it is important to attract new orders from existing customers, i.e. new custom rather than new customers. There are a number of advantages in following this approach:

(i) We already know something about the needs of our existing customers and should be able to gather data from our existing customer database, internal records, the sales team and by contacting them to talk about their future requirements and how we can help them.

(ii) Furthermore, we also know about the customer's payment track record which should help in avoiding bad debts or at least help us to minimize any risk in that area.

It is recognized that we may in addition want to attract some new customers. In our search for new business whether from existing customers or completely new business there are a number of data sources that can help. These data may be usefully classified as secondary and primary sources and they are listed below:

Secondary data sources:
- Trade press.
- Market survey reports.
- Newspaper reports on firms in the fields that you specialize in.

Primary data sources:
- Discussions with the sales team.
- Discussions with existing customers.
- Examining sales records for existing customers.
- Examining potential customer enquiries.

The list is not exhaustive but will give an indication of how we can begin our search.

(b)
I have already explained one way in which bad debts can be minimized by attracting new business from our existing customer base. In terms of any new business it is important that we have a clear policy and detailed procedure for cash collection from our customers. For example, it is important to have the following steps in place:

1 Take up credit references – two trade references and a bank reference usually suffice.
2 Ensure invoices are issued promptly.
3 Regular statements and reminders are sent.
4 Salesperson responsible for the sale monitors payment and encourages the customer to honour their payment terms.
5 Consider incentives for early or prompt payment.

The effect upon cash flow and profitability of some of these measures is indicated in the table below:

Policy	Cash Flow	Profit
Invoice on time	Get the cash quicker	Reduces cost of chasing debt and increases profit on the order
Regular reminders	Get cash quicker than you otherwise would	Reduce the time you would have to have funded the debtor, e.g. every month taken as credit by a customer beyond their agreed terms could be costing you profit. Supposing an order worth £12,000 at invoiced sale is delayed by an extra month beyond agreed terms and the firm's cost of capital is 12% per annum it will cost 1% of the order value to fund the debtor and your cost of sale has increased by £120

Answer – Question 6

To: Managing Director
From: Marketing Manager
Date: 10th June 1997
Subject: Departmental Budgets

The newly created marketing department has seven full-time staff whose responsibilities include: sales, promotion and customer services. The first decision to be taken centres around the status of the department in budgeting terms. By this I mean is it to be a cost centre and simply responsible for costs associated with the activities within its remit or is it to be a profit centre having responsibility for both costs and revenue attributable to the departmental activities? My recommendation would be to create a profit centre since the activities undertaken by the department contribute to revenue as well as cause cost. It will provide motivation to the individuals in the department if they can see the connection between costs and revenues within their control. As a result it is more likely that they will feel ownership of the budget and hence accept responsibility rather than see it merely as a financial imposition.

The marketing department budget should be a plan expressed in financial terms and as such budget headings need to be chosen to reflect the activities that cause cost and generate revenue. The budget should have headings for each category of revenue attributable to the department. Similarly each expense heading may be related to specific revenue streams to show the profit generated by each activity. It is also important to identify fixed and variable costs since the latter will be affected by any changes in volume whereas fixed costs will not change.

The main budget headings should reflect the key activities undertaken by the department which are sales, promotion and customer services. Within each of the major headings there will need to be subsidiary revenue and expense headings. For example:

Salaries
- Sales Team
- Promotion Team
- Customer Service Personnel
- Marketing Support Staff

Staff Training
- Sales Team
- Promotion Team
- Customer Service Personnel
- Marketing Support Staff

Travel Expenses
- Sales Team
- Promotion Team
- Customer Service Personnel
- Marketing Support Staff

Sales Commissions

Telephone Expenses
- Sales Team
- Promotion Team
- Customer Service Personnel
- Marketing Support Staff

Promotion and Advertising Expenses
- Sales Promotions (detailed)
- PR Expenses
- Print Advertising
- TV Advertising
- Radio
- Other Media
- Coupon Offers
- Design and Print

Revenue budgets will be prepared from sales forecasts and expense budgets will be prepared assuming the accuracy of the sales forecasts. Zero based budgets will be developed since we are a new department and have no constraints in terms of past history. Expenses will need to be justified by each manager responsible for a specific budget area.

It is necessary to ensure that the plan can be controlled. The usual budgetary control mechanisms are sufficient to achieve this such as variance reports detailing the difference between actual and budgeted expenditure for each budget heading broken down into specific time periods (e.g. Weekly, Monthly, Quarterly and Annual Variance Reports). When variances are identified action can be taken to keep the plan on target. Flexible rather than fixed budgets are more meaningful in this context and it is important to adjust budgeted costs in line with budgeted volumes. For example, if we budget to sell 1,000 units and the variable cost of selling 1,000 units is £1,000 it would be necessary to adjust the budgeted figures in line with any actual sales to identify a cost variance rather than a volume variance.

Report formats could take the form of budgeted and actual profit and loss accounts for the marketing department. Sales Revenue attributable to marketing will need to be segmented by each revenue stream and costs attributable to each segment will need to be shown. An Example is given below:

Marketing Department Profit Centre
Profit and Loss for Month Ending xx.xx.xx
REPORT FORMAT #1

Heading	£ BUDGET	£ ACTUAL	£ VARIANCE
SALES REVENUE By Product By Service Other TOTAL REVENUE			
EXPENDITURE Salaries Staff Training Costs Selling Expenses etc.			
PROFIT/(LOSS)			

REPORT FORMAT #2

	PRODUCT 1	PRODUCT 2	SERVICE 1	SERVICE 2	OTHER
SALES COSTS EXPENSES PROFIT/(LOSS)					

This memorandum has given a brief summary of my proposals. I would be pleased to clarify or discuss any aspect of the Marketing Department Budget in more detail at our budget meeting next week. I will be presenting the proposed report formats with exemplars at the meeting.

Answer – Question 7

REPORT TO MARKETING STAFF
Marketing Opportunities Created by Information and Communication Technologies (in particular – Internet)

Prepared by: A Smith
Date: 10th June 1997

Information and communication technology developments have created new opportunities for marketeers and the way in which markets are researched, accessed and structured. Computer technology and particularly computer networks allow individuals to communicate inside an organization (often called an INTRANET) and across organizational boundaries (using the INTERNET). Networked computers allow the exchange of data and information in text, graphic or digital form. For example, it is possible to gain access to information stored on a computer database that can be on the other side of the world and in a matter of seconds to transfer that stored information to your own desktop computer to work on or read off-line. To access the data you will need to have access to the INTERNET either directly with a modem attached to a telephone on which you can dial a local point of presence (POP) and a subscription to a network provider such as PIPEX, Compuserve, BT, Demon etc. or via an internal network having access through a provider. Network connections to the INTERNET will usually have an ISDN link rather than a modem because ISDNs can handle more than one machine at a time, are faster downloading data and hence on-line costs should be lower. Browser software such as that supplied by Mosaic, Netcape and Microsoft Explorer are needed to investigate the INTERNET effectively. Most new computers purchased come with software that includes some browser software. Alternatively, a network provider will supply it.

Although the picture painted is about how useful the INTERNET can be it is worth commenting on some of the problems and frustrations, e.g. time it takes to do a search; key word searches often throw up strange results and do not find what you want; systems are slow at particular times of the day; initial enthusiasm can turn to boredom and if your site is dull you are unlikely to get a repeat visit even when you have updated it later; problems with browser compatibility and the time it can take to download graphics files with varying modem speeds and even with ISDN links; Data security and secure payment systems; Virus transmission via the Internet.

Possibilities for using ICT and in particular the INTERNET fall into six specific areas:

1 Marketing Research
2 Competitor Research
3 Electronic Mail
4 Establishing a Website
5 Video Conferencing
6 Still Photographic Transmission

1 Marketing research

It has already been indicated that external databases created by other organizations may be accessed using the INTERNET. Some of these data sources are free for example in the UK some government statistics may be accessed (using http://www.emap.co.uk/cso/) whereas other sources may be listed and only obtained on payment of a fee to the supplier, much in the same way one would purchase a subscription to quarterly statistics in book form; you can obtain them in CD ROM formats or directly using the INTERNET and down loading the statistics to your own desktop computer. Commercial organizations such as Mintel, FT Profile, MAID, Various Newspapers, Magazines and Journals are now accessible via the INTERNET. It is possible, therefore, to compile marketing reports and include up-to-date market research statistics without leaving your desk. It is also possible to access professional bodies such as The Chartered Institute of Marketing (using http://www.cim.co.uk) and use various services if you are a member, including the library.

2 Competitor research

It is possible to conduct some competitor research using the INTERNET particularly if your competitors have their own Websites. Many organizations have now established their own sites using HTML formats scripted using JAVA. A list of our competitor sites with their INTERNET addresses will be available on the INTRANET from next week.

Many organizations give a history of their organization, recent developments, annual reports, press releases and product information. It is therefore possible to gather a great deal of information about competitors. Data gathered can be digital sound recordings, graphic or text. Text is easy and fast to download whereas digital sound may be a little slower and graphics slower still. The speed at which files can be downloaded will depend on their type and on the capability of your desktop or networked machines. New products are often highlighted and some organizations offer the opportunity to purchase their products or services over the INTERNET. For example, when studying for my marketing examinations for the Chartered Institute of Marketing I visited the INTERNET Book store (using http://www.bookshop.co.uk) and placed an order for Management Information for Marketing and Sales by Tony Hines simply by keying the title and author name and then entering my payment details. I was a little concerned about giving my credit card details over the INTERNET because I had read about breaches in security. However, when I e-mailed the bookstore with my concern they advised me of their secure payment system by opening an account which I did. The book was delivered to my home in a few days from placing the order.

3 Electronic mail

E-mail is available to anyone who is connected to the INTERNET and has appropriate software such as that supplied by Microsoft or proprietary software. E-mail is simply the facility to exchange text between remote computers. For example, one could send several pages of text including spreadsheet data and graphics from London to Singapore. This type of exchange could be particularly useful to transmit promotional material, catalogue data, purchase orders, sales orders, store layouts, designs and messages that would be sent by conventional 'snail' mail. The advantage is speed and cost. E-mail is sent at the cost of a local telephone call and a great deal of data can be sent in a very short time. For instance if you have a fast modem 33,000 bits per second (bps)can be sent and you are only charged for the time you are connected to the external line. To give you some idea of comparability you could send a two page facsimile using conventional technology to someone else with a fax and depending upon where you were to send it the cost would be the cost of that call. Two pages would take about one minute to transmit and if you sent it to Hong Kong it would cost you the price of a one minute call to Hong Kong. An e-mail transmission could send many pages in a minute and cost only a local call rate to the POP. I recently sent a 30 page Marketing Report to an associate in Sydney in less than one minute.

4 Establishing a website

As mentioned many organizations have already established sites. A Website provides a useful marketing opportunity but only for people who have access to the INTERNET. A recent survey in the USA showed that the most likely users are children at High School, College Students and Universities all of whom have low cost access. Home users tend to be middle aged professional males. It is important that we know who are the likely users and to establish whether or not they match our target market.

A site can be established at a reasonably low cost but we need to be certain what our specific objectives are to be. Competitor sites record all visits and ask the visitor to complete a form giving their personal contact details to add to a database of potential customers. They also ask whether the visitor is an existing customer and some brief data about what they mostly buy and from whom. It may be useful to do this for a test period and to monitor the results carefully before deciding to launch a permanent site. Sites do need to be attractively designed, easy to find your way around, provide visitors with useful information so they come back, be updated regularly and possibly provide an opportunity to purchase products directly.

5 Internet video phone calls and conferences

It is also possible to conduct sight and sound conversations between two or more people using the INTERNET and video conferencing software. This could be useful for the International Marketing Team to meet without the need to travel. Additional hardware in the form of a video camera attached to the computer and video conferencing software is needed.

6 Still photographic transmission

Finally it is worth noting that digital cameras that are able to store still pictures are now relatively inexpensive and can be obtained from £250 upwards depending on pixel quality required and the number of pictures it is able to store. These cameras could be useful for our buying team and our marketing teams when visiting overseas centres. They would be able to take photographs and transmit them back immediately from anywhere in the world at any time to our UK Head Office with a text commentary via the Internet using a laptop, mobile phone and fax/modem card. This could help us gather market information, competitor information regarding new or existing products, review prospective purchases and new designs. It could also enable the decision-making cycle to be shortened by not having to wait for a buyer to return from overseas before decisions are taken and it could help with tactical marketing decisions being taken more quickly.

Specimen exam paper 2 December 1998

Advanced Certificate in Marketing

Advanced Certificate in Sales Management

Management Information for Marketing and Sales 3 Hours' Duration

This examination is in two sections.

Part A is compulsory and worth 40 per cent of the total marks.

Part B has six questions, select three. Each answer will be worth 20 per cent of the total marks.

DO NOT repeat the question in your answer but show clearly the number of the question attempted on appropriate pages of the answer book.

Rough workings should be included in the answer book and ruled through after use.

Part A

The Big Event Marketing Group Plc

You have joined the Big Event Marketing (BEM) Group from the Marketing Department of a national newspaper where you have been involved with promotional and marketing activities similar to those that the BEM Group organize. The group are currently bidding to secure a number of major contracts for 1999 and 2000. You have been asked to lead one of the teams bidding for the contract to run four high-profile seminars with the title 'Managing in the New Millennium'. There are a number of aspects to the organization of the tender for the contract that the client has specifically requested in their brief:

1 It is important that an Internet Website is established to publicize and inform prospective delegates about the event.
2 The whole event must make a profit and this has been set at a minimum of 25%.

You have already done some preliminary market research and established the following facts:

- Demand is likely to be high for such seminars providing you are able to attract high quality speakers. You hope to attract 150 delegates to each event. In this context it is likely that the daily cost for a small number of speakers of reasonable repute will be in the region of £20,000. In addition it will be necessary to attract other speakers with a small expense budget who may be prepared to come to publicize their own organization (e.g. management consultancy firms, high technology providers and the like).
- In order to keep costs down and to maximize profitability you have already decided to hold a series of four one-day events with optional overnight accommodation. You have negotiated a special rate with a five star hotel group at £60 per person per night. The normal rate is more than double this. It is your intention to achieve the required rate of profit that still offers the room at a discount to the delegate. However you will have to offer speakers their rooms free on the night before the event. It is expected that you will need to keep six rooms for use by speakers at each daily seminar and two rooms for your own BEM Group staff.
- Other costs include: cost per delegate per day rate £100; conference proceedings and delegate bags £10 per head; incidental costs allowed for at £5 per delegate; your preliminary preparation costs amounting to £3,000 will need to be recovered against the event; you will also need to budget for staffing the event at £2,500 per event; you have allowed a budget of £2,000 for development and maintenance of the Internet site.

Part A

Question 1

You now need to prepare a short report for an internal briefing of Senior Managers that covers the following points:

(a) A budget that clearly shows the expected income and expenditure for the four planned events.

(16 marks)

(b) The price you will need to set for the event given that you need to achieve a 25% profit margin as a minimum.

(8 marks)

(c) An explanation of how your price and profit margins could be affected if you achieve only 80% of the planned number of delegates at the event.

(8 marks)

(d) Suggestions on how the Internet Website will be used by both your own company in establishing the event and by the delegates before, during and after the event.

(8 marks) (40 marks in total)

Part B – Answer THREE Questions Only

Question 2

You have recently been appointed as a Marketing Manager for a marketing consultancy firm, and you have been asked to conduct a review of operations in your firm with a view to attracting new clients. In this context you have been asked to produce a brief report that gives details of:

(a) Possible sources of data that you will refer to in your review of operations. Internal and external sources should be identified. **(10 marks)**

(b) What types of information each data source will provide. Give specific examples of how the data will be used in the review. **(10 marks) (20 marks in total)**

Question 3

The company you work for has the following performance indicators for the last financial year:

i) Stock Turnover four times per annum.
ii) Return on Investment 6% per annum.
iii) Gross Margin 50%.
iv) Net Margin 10%.
v) Debtor Turnover three times per annum.

Your current Marketing Manager has asked you to prepare a memorandum to explain to team members what each of the performance measures means and why they are important indicators of performance. **(20 marks)**

Question 4

Your organization or an organization of your choice has indicated that they would like to find out more about the possibility of exploiting new information and communication technologies within the company's marketing mix. You have been asked to write a short report that outlines possibilities and explains in detail any benefits that could accrue both immediately and in the longer-term. **(20 marks)**

Question 5

You have been asked to work with the Finance Department in your organization to prepare the sales and marketing departmental budget.

Write a report that covers the following points:

(a) An explanation outlining the ways in which such a budget might be prepared. **(10 marks)**

(b) An explanation of the key objectives that such a budget should achieve. **(10 marks) (20 marks in total)**

Question 6

List and describe the features that you would expect to find in any organization's Marketing Information System (MkIS). Explain the importance of each feature identified in providing key information giving specific examples from your own organization or any organization of your choice. **(20 marks)**

Question 7

You are newly appointed as a Marketing Manager in a publishing company and have been given specific responsibility for a new product launch. Your organization want to introduce a new magazine aimed at the teenage female market as identified as part of last year's strategic review.

In this respect you have been given a budget of £30,000 to conduct further market research prior to the launch. Explain how you would plan and conduct this research. You are required to give the specific stages in your research plan and evaluate and justify each of your chosen options.

(20 marks)

Answer – question 1

To: **Senior Managers**
From: **Marketing Manager**
Date: **8th December 1998**
Subject: **Managing in the new Millennium**

Terms of reference

The following report follows your request for an internal briefing on the following areas:

(a) A budget of the expected income and expected expenditure for the four planned events.
(b) The price needed to achieve a minimum 25% profit margin.
(c) An explanation of the effect on selling price and profit margin of achieving only 80% of the planned activity.
(d) Suggestion on how the Internet website will be used by the company and the delegates before, during and after the event.

a.

Big Event Marketing Group Plc

Income and expenditure budget – Managing in the new Millennium

	Per Delegate	Per Event		Total (4 Events)	
Variable Costs					
Daily Cost	£100	£15,000		£60,000	
Conference Proceedings and Bags	£10	£1,500		£6,000	
Incidental Costs	£5	£750	£17,250	£3,000	£69,000
Accommodation					
Delegates (150) (I)	£60		£9,000		£36,000
Subtotal			**£26,250**		**£105,000**
Fixed Costs					
Speakers' Accommodation (6)	£60	£360		£1,440	
BEM Group Staff Accommodation (2)	£60	£120		£480	
Speakers		£20,000		£80,000	
Preliminary Costs (ii)		£750		£3,000	
Staffing Costs		£2,500		£10,000	
Development and Maintenance of Website (ii)		£500	**£24,230**	£2,000	**£96,920**
Total expenditure			**£50,480**		**£201,920**
Income (iii)			£67,500		£270,000

Notes

(i) The accommodation is optional, therefore these figures may be excluded from the calculations. If these costs are excluded, the total costs are £165,920 and the Income £221,227, rounded to £222,000.
(ii) The preliminary costs and the development of the website are assumed to be incurred for every event.
(iii) Given that a 25% margin is required the total costs have been multiplied by 100/75 i.e. £201,920*100/75 = £269,227 rounded to £270,000.

b. Price needed to achieve a margin of 25%

As shown in the above budget, given the total costs of £201,920, the selling price needed to achieve a margin of 25% would be calculated as £201,920*100/75 which is £269,227 rounded to £270,000. As there are expected to be 150 delegates per event, this would mean 600 delegates for the four events and therefore the price charged per delegate would be £450 (£270,000/600).

Based on the assumption that the accommodation is optional, the price per delegate would be £370 (£222,000/600) and if accommodation were required this would be charged to delegates at £80 (£60*100/75).

As with any price based on cost plus, there is a significant assumption that the market will accept this price. The acceptance would depend on a number of factors, including demand, competitor prices, the market, the customers' attitude and so on. These factors would need to be borne in mind in setting the price per delegate. However, it is not the purpose of these briefing notes to give a detailed discussion of these issues.

c. Effect of achieving only 80% of target

Many of the figures used in the above budget are based on assumptions; many of these assumptions are valid, such as the costs per delegate etc., which are the figures quoted by the hotel. Other figures are not as valid and are subjective. The validity of the selling price has been mentioned but the other major figure in the budget is the level of activity. This is assumed to be 150 delegates per event. However it would be useful to review the effect on prices and margins if these figures were not achieved. It has been proposed that the figures are assessed on the basis that only 80% (120 per event) of the planned numbers were achieved.

There are two main ways that the effect can be calculated, by maintaining the planned margin or maintaining the planned selling price. The following figures, (based on four events) illustrate the options:

i) Maintaining the planned margin

The variable costs would stay the same at £175 per delegate, the total variable cost would be £84,000 (600*0.8*£175), the fixed costs would remain the same at £96,920 (including the speakers and staff accommodation costs), the total costs would be £180,920, the sales value would be £241,227 and the selling price would be £503, an increased of 12%.

ii) Maintaining the selling price

The total costs would be the same as those in 'I' but the sales value would be £216,000, resulting in a profit of £35,080 and a margin of 16%, a fall of 36% on the planned margin of 25%.

Several significant assumptions have been made in the above figures, namely that the variable costs are linear, that the fixed costs are fixed for the relevant range of 480 to 600 delegates and there are no minimum bookings for the hotel. It may be that some of the variable costs are dependent on a minimum order quantity and that the fixed costs may be stepped and therefore reduce at certain delegate levels. For this briefing the above assumption has been made, however this may require further investigation.

d. Using. The internet website

Both the company and the delegates could use the Internet website, before, during and after the event. The following briefing is focused on the how the Internet website would be used, and the suggestions are considered under the two headings of (i) the company and (ii) the delegates.

i) The company

Before

Advertising the event.
Targeting the audience.
Detailing costs per delegate and accommodation costs.
Providing an event contact person.
Providing registration information (booking forms, payment details).

Collecting information about visitors to the website; they could be mailed information about the event.
Details of other facilities offered by the company.
Company information.
Setting up a hyper link to other BEM sites.
Providing up-to-the-minute information.
Providing a promotional tool for direct marketing through e-mail.

During
The programme and agendas could be shown.
Details of speakers (CVs).
Timetables.
List of all the delegates.
Last minute changes.
For issuing press releases.
Enabling delegates to ask questions of the speakers.
Providing multimedia options.
Detailing the agenda for the following day.

After
Contact details for follow-up events.
Gaining feedback on the event.
Providing copies of papers presented.
Relationship marketing.
Database information.
Electronic conferencing.

ii) Delegates
Before
To learn about the plans for the event.
Register attendance, send for more information.
Find out which companies are sending delegates.

During
To confirm the daily schedule.
View information about the speakers.

After
Provide feedback on the event.
Provide ideas for future events.
Obtain copies of papers for seminars they could not attend.
Obtain list of delegates and their company details.

Answer – question 2.

To: **Marketing Director**
From: **Marketing Manager**
Date: **8th December 1998**
Subject: **Review of Operations Regarding New Clients**

Terms of reference

To conduct a review of operations, with a view to attracting new clients to our marketing consultancy service.

When conducting the review it is prudent to examine the existing data available, both internally and externally, in order to establish the current position of the company and the proposed future position.

The report comprises two sections:

(a) The possible sources of data, both internal and external, which will be used in the review of operations.
(b) The types of information that each data source will provide.

a. Sources of data

There are several sources of data, these are listed below under internal and external.

Internal sources of data

Sales invoices.
Debtor lists.
Sales records.
Client databases; current and historic.
Customer complaints.
Internal management reports.
Sales personnel.
Management accounts, e.g. budget/actual/variances.
Enquiries.
Personnel details.
Job costings of consultancy projects.
Details of unsuccessful quotations.
Responses to direct mail or previous advertising.

External sources of data

Bought-in mailing lists.
Trade directories, Kelly's, Kompass.
Trade associations.
Government reports and statistics.
External databases on prospective clients.
Internet searches.
Newspaper and magazine articles.
Externally published segment reports.
Yellow pages.
Local directories.

b. Types of information each data source will provide to attract new clients

- The management accounts will provide us with information on which segments provide the highest contribution. This will enable us to be more focused on those areas. They will also show whether the company is proceeding according to plan.
- The list of customer complaints will inform us on which areas we need to improve on and on which to avoid in dealing with new clients in the future.
- The debtor lists will enable us to select clients who are better payers and more financially reliable.
- Sales records will provide information on how efficient and effective the company has been in delivering the consultancy; it will also enable us to assess trends in sales by client and by market.
- Records of previous consultancy projects will help us in determining which types of project are attractive to clients.
- Sales personnel would be a useful source of information on potential clients and growth areas, this may come from discussions with customers.
- The job cost details will enable us to establish if it takes too long to complete a project and whether this would deter new clients.
- What would clients expect of our staff: are they suitably trained, do they project the correct image of the company.
- For direct mailing and advertising, what type of client responded to this approach and how did the company approach them. Have details been retained of the responses and the notes on them.
- As regards external sources, mailing lists, the Internet, trade directories and trade associations, may provide possible new clients. The latter two would be more closely focused on the potential clients who may want to use our consultancy service.
- Other external sources which would be useful; would be articles in newspapers and magazines; new groups of customers may be identified, and new developments in the market may be identified.

- Information on competitors would be of significant help, such as the type of clients they have, the size of the company, any parameters for selecting clients, the kind of service they offer, their profitability, what kind of image do they project and so on.
- Government reports and statistics would be useful, particularly if changes were about to be made in certain markets, e.g. the lifting of the beef ban. Market trends might be revealed in the statistical reports.
- Information on market share would be useful, how large the market is, the coverage of the areas in the market, whether the market is growing, declining, or reached saturation point.
- As regards databases, they would provide the company with the latest information on potential customers and their profiles.
- Any technological changes would need to be identified, as this may help in gaining new customers, e.g. via the use of the Internet.

Answer – question 3.

Internal Memorandum

To: Management Team
From: Marketing Assistant
Date: 8th December 1998
Subject: Performance Indicators

I have been requested to prepare an explanation of the meaning and importance of the current performance indicators used by the company. The current performance indicators and the figures for the company are:

Performance Indicator	Company Results – Last Financial Year
Stock Turnover	Four Times per Annum
Return on Investment	6% per Annum
Gross Margin	50%
Net Margin	10%
Debtor Turnover	Three Times per Annum

It is proposed to review each performance indicator in turn.

Stock turnover

This is calculated by the cost of sales/average stock expressed as the number of times or months or days. It provides an indication of how many times the stock figures has been replaced during the year. The cost of sales figure is used because it is valued on a similar basis to the stock value, therefore the comparison is on a like for like basis.

Stock is a critical figure for a company and the objective of most companies is to sell it as soon as possible. However there is no universal target which can be applied to every industry and each industry and company should be assessed on its own merits. For example, the stock turnover for a supermarket would be expected to be high since most goods are perishable – for some a target of three times per week is realistic. For a shipbuilder the figure may be two times per annum, depending on the size of the ship.

A high (or higher) turnover figure is generally the objective. However what is acceptable will depend on the industry, the company, the economy, the company strategy and so on. A useful comparison would be made against the budget for the company or previous figures, to try to establish a trend.

For this company, the stock is turned over four times per year, meaning that stock is replaced, on average, every three months. It is difficult to assess if this is acceptable or not.

The ratio is important since it is focused on one of the key components of working capital. If the stock is not turning over, it means that difficulties are being experienced in selling it – because it is out of fashion, it is obsolete, it is deteriorating and so on. This will also have an impact on cash flow; if the goods are not sold, cash is tied up in stock and it costs money to store and maintain.

Return on investment

This is calculated by the operating profit/capital employed expressed as a percentage.

Operating profit is before interest and tax; capital employed is share capital and long-term loans. It is important in making an assessment to establish which figures are being used, as there are several alternatives e.g. (profit after interest, profit after interest and tax, investors capital, net assets and so on.

ROI is a primary measure from which all other financial performance measures flow.

It means the return, which has been achieved on the money invested in the business by the shareholders and long-term lenders. It is comparable with the returns from a bank account or building society; however, there is little risk in lending to these organizations, but there is a risk in investing in other organizations, therefore the returns should be higher.

At present in the UK, the low risk rate of return from a bank is around 6%, which is the same as that for the company. This is quite poor since there is no premium for risk, i.e. a higher rate of return should be made, which allows for the risks being taken. Having said that, the poor return may be due to certain circumstances within the company of which we are not fully aware. Return on investment is a primary ratio, two secondary ratios are net margin and asset turnover. Given the net margin is 10%, this means that the asset turnover ratio must be 0.6 times, a very poor return, suggesting that insufficient sales are being generated from the capital employed.

Gross margin

This is calculated by gross profit/sales and it is expressed as a percentage. This means that the percentage is an indication of the mark-up on direct costs. In this case the mark-up was 100% on cost. Different industries have different norms for mark-ups. For example, a jewellery business will tend to mark-up goods by 100%, and a greengrocer may mark-up only 50%.

It is a good indicator of financial performance, as is a measure of the pricing strategy. Whatever the percentage margin, it should increase or stay the same; a lower margin would tend to suggest a worsening of the company's financial position. In this case there is no comparison available, but it could be compared with budget or previous figures or other companies.

The ratio is also an indicator of whether enough gross profit is being made to cover the fixed overheads and achieve a positive net margin.

Net margin

This is calculated by net margin (operating profit)/sales, expressed as a percentage. This is a secondary ratio and is a significant component of the ROI. As mentioned under ROI, if the net margin is multiplied by the asset turnover ratio, the result is the ROI.

Net margin is the balance which is left after deducting overheads from the gross margin value. As well as a component of the ROI, when compared with the gross margin percentage, it is an indicator of the proportion of overheads to sales. In this case overheads are 40% of the sales value.

It is an important indicator for several reasons, but mainly because it is a significant component of ROI.

Debtor turnover

This is calculated by sales/debtors expressed as the number of times. It is an indicator of how long customers who have been sold goods on credit take to pay their debts. As with stock turnover, it is a working capital ratio.

This is important since if customers do not pay their debts on time, there may be a problem with cash flow.

For this company, the debtors have turned over three times per annum. This means that debtors pay for their goods four months after purchasing them; a significantly long time. Linking this ratio to the stock turnover ratio, stock is being held for three months before it is sold, then customers wait four months to pay for it. In the meantime it is likely that suppliers of the goods will not wait seven months to be paid so the cash flow of the company will be under pressure.

Conclusion

Ratios are an essential measure of whether the objectives of the company are being met. Management select ratios which they consider to be crucial measures of financial performance.

It would appear that the management has selected these ratios, as they are crucial to the success of the company. Other ratios could have been used but management must consider that these five are crucial.

All the indicators would be more meaningful if they were compared with the budgeted measures, with the industry ratios possibly, competitors measures, or with historic ratios for the company. All the above would lead to more meaningful comparisons and enable the company to assess whether the ratios are improving or declining.

Answer – question 4

To:	**Marketing Director**
From:	**Marketing Assistant**
Date:	**8th December 1998**
Subject:	**Exploitation of New Information and Communication Technologies**
Remit:	**To outline the possibilities of exploiting new information and communication technologies within the company's marketing mix, and the benefits that could accrue both immediately and in the longer-term.**

The following report has been prepared in response to the above remit, using a bank as the main focus for the ICTs. There are several ICTs and it is proposed to consider each one in turn. The target audience is technophiles and aspiring technophiles, who between them make up approximately 50% of consumers.

Internet

A website could be developed for the bank that would include details of the full product range of the bank. The range might include mortgages, insurance, current and deposit accounts, currency exchange, cards, etc. It could be updated with new products. Any person logging on to the site could be entered on the database and contacted later. The design of the site should be particularly focused on the above mentioned groups. School and university students should be a particular focus group since the Government is committed to increase the number of computers in education and their ICTs. The reasoning being that once a customer has chosen a bank they tend to stay with the same one.

Modems

This is used to convert digital data into audio signals suitable for phone transmission. The device allows computers to communicate with each other. There are many uses from using it to call an information service, personal computer, bulletin board and so on. They could be used to send or receive documents and files to printers. The document could be typed off-line and then sent. The transferred document could then be edited, printed, or incorporated into another report. Management reports could be circulated by this technology with significant savings. A variation of hot design can be used where the bank staff can view customer's details from anywhere in the country.

Video conferencing

This is another ICT that could be used once the above reports had been circulated for a management meeting. The meeting could take place using video conferencing. It would also enable more flexible working patterns. Time wasted in travelling to meetings, travelling abroad, would be minimalized by this technology. This could also be developed into virtual banking, as in virtual reality games. The customer does not need to enter a bank physically to obtain details of the services provided or use the service. It could be carried out using virtual banking. A combination of menu choices, supported by video conferencing would enable any customer linked up to the system to carry out any banking task without moving from their computer.

Smart cards (electronic purse)

These cards allow purchase of items up to a predetermined limit – a value of credits. They are another step towards the cashless society. Some banks are already using them to pay for meals and refreshments within the bank. The cards would be of benefit to the bank's customers as they would be supplying a service for paying for many purchases, such as shopping, parking, drinks, books, meals, etc. Many banks are supplying smart cards to university students to enhance the service to them.

The benefits for banks from smart cards come from the replacement of cash and cheque transactions, and in the ability to put multiple applications on the same card. This would enable the cash dispensing service to be reduced, thus freeing staff to deal with specific customer enquiries.

CD-ROM

These can be used to store significant amounts of data, both text and multimedia. Sound, pictures and text can be transmitted using modems, phone lines and satellite links. This means that they could be used for marketing the services of the bank, for training the staff and so on.

Database marketing

With new software available, the possibilities of holding extensive information on the bank's customers and using it intelligently are limitless. As a bank, detailed information on customers is already being stored; details such as address, earnings, where they purchase goods and services, when they pay them, how they pay their debts, their buying preferences. By using appropriate software, the market could be segmented more accurately, customers targeted specifically and products positioned accordingly. Gaps in the market could be identified and filled. Retaining existing customers and extending the range of products sold to customers is the most profitable means of developing new business.

Home banking

Some banks are already experimenting with home banking. The service can be effected through a modem, phone, and video conferencing links, depending on the provider. Currently home banking provides most of the services of the bank without the use of letters or the usual communication forms. Cheques can be issued, standing orders and direct debits set-up, bank balances known, etc. This service allows more sophisticated targeting of the market and facilitates the opportunity to promote additional services (mortgages etc.) to the customer. Partly as a result of this the number of high street banks is declining, thus the savings are significant. The savings in paper both for the bank and the customer are also worthwhile. Home banking also enables the bank to add value to the service provided to customers, by promoting other services which the customer has not yet requested.

Voice recognition computers

Security within the banking sector is a continual problem. The use of signatures and photographs to ensure security of the customer's and bank's information is very low technology. The use of fingerprints and possibly voice recognition would enhance the security of many bank transactions and be another added value product for the bank to sell on.

Mobile phones

A recent report on ICTs in the office environment highlighted the fact that that mobile phones were equated with e-mail, local and wide area networks, and were seen as critical factors to the success of the surveyed companies. The advanced features now becoming available on mobile phones suggest that this is another ICT that the banking sector should not ignore. Displays are being incorporated into the mobile phone, which could be used by both bank staff and customers alike to exchange information.

EPOS, EFPTOS and EDI

These are also ICTs. Organizations such as retail stores and manufacturers have reaped significant benefits through EPOS, by being provided with more information about stock control and consumer behaviour. EFTPOS has facilitated the delivery of customer service and allows more flexible payment methods. EDI links with suppliers allow just-in-time stock replenishment and improved production planning by suppliers to take place through a phone line, ISDN or other communication medium.

Conclusion

There are significant benefits in using ICTs to the banking and other industries. Some of the benefits will be immediate and can be secured in the short-term with minimal cost. Database management, modems, the Internet and mobile phones fall into this category.

Other benefits are long-term requiring considerable discussion in deciding whether to implement them or not. This is because they are very expensive and time-consuming to install and may soon become out of date and out of fashion. Home banking, video conferencing and smart cards fall into this category.

Answer – question 5.

To: **Marketing Director**
From: **Marketing Assistant**
Date: **8th December 1998**
Subject: **Preparation of the Sales and Marketing Departmental Budget**

Terms of reference

The following report follows a request to prepare the Sales and Marketing departmental budget, working in conjunction with the Finance Department. The report follows the sequence of your request, namely:

(a) An explanation outlining the way in which a budget may be prepared.
(b) An explanation of the key objectives that such a budget should achieve.

a. An explanation outlining the way in which a budget may be prepared

The budgeting process may be approached from several directions; the standard approach is to commence with the setting of the company's objectives. These are determined in conjunction with the assessment of the environment; the resources within and without the company; the situations audit; and so on. The next step would be to determine the principal budget (constraining) factor, which is usually sales. Once the sales budget has been prepared, this would be followed by the finished goods, production, materials usage, materials purchases, marketing, selling, administration, capital, research and development, profit and loss, balance sheet and cash budgets and finally the master budget.

Once the budget had been prepared it would be submitted to the Board of Directors for approval. If it were not approved the budgeting exercise would begin again. If it were approved, it would be published before the year commenced and used for control purposes by comparing actual against budget.

Three types of budget may be used to construct the above budget for the Sales and Marketing Department. Two types are linked together, fixed and flexible budgets. Fixed budgets are set for a function, based on a specific level of activity for a year, and usually remain unchanged until the following year. The budget is compared with actual figures on a monthly or annual basis and variances calculated. However, since the actual activity may be higher or lower than the budgeted activity, the variances are generally meaningless. It is not conducive to control, but it may be useful for planning. This type of budgeting may be used for the sales and marketing budget.

If the actual activity is generally different form the budgeted activity, the company may turn to flexible budgeting for improving the control of the organization. In flexible budgeting the costs are flexed according to the actual level of activity, so that cost comparisons are made on a realistic basis. The costs, which are flexed, are usually the variable costs. More realistic comparisons are made when actual figures are compared with budget.

Another type of budget, which might be used for service departments, is zero based budgeting. As hinted in the title, the budget is based on a zero base or green field site and uses decision packages to determine what the level of activity is and the cost of that level. This is in contrast with the incremental approach where a percentage is added every year. It may be that a basic marketing function would cost £x, a more sophisticated level would cost £x1 and a very sophisticated marketing would cost £x2. This process is followed throughout the organization, and once the decision packages have been determined, choices are made through discussions across the organization as to the level of activity needed to achieve the organization's objectives. As both Marketing and Sales Departments are service functions, the technique could be applied here.

Rolling budgets may also be employed, once the initial budgets have been prepared. With this approach, a budget or forecast is made for the first quarter (or month) of the following year, the first quarter (or month) of the first year is then deleted. Thus the budget is rolled forward so that a more up-to-date annual budget is available. This type of budgeting resulted from criticism that towards the end of the budget year, the budgets for the final months were likely to be significantly out of date.

b. Explanation of the key objectives of budgeting

A budget is a financial plan of action prepared in advance of the period to which it relates. It should be prepared in-line with corporate objectives. A budget has several objectives, namely planning, control, decision-making, motivation, co-ordination, co-operation and so on.

Planning is important for without it control would not be possible. Planning also forces management to address the major issues facing the organization and to quantify the plans to resolve them. For the Sales and Marketing Department several projects may be planned for the year ahead, these would be incorporated into the budget.

Control is also important, as the plan would be worthless without control. It is necessary to determine whether the plan is being achieved. This is carried out by comparing actual figures against budget and calculating variances. If the plan is not being achieved, it may be that the plan needs to be revised or action needs to be taken that will influence the actual figures.

Decision-making is also a key objective that budgeting should achieve, as it is involved in all the areas of planning and control. Decisions have to be made regarding which products to make or which services to provide. Once variances are calculated, decisions are required on how to resolve any problems highlighted, i.e. where is the problem, what is the solution, can it be implemented. Decision-making only exists when choices need to be made. It may be that one of the projects in a series has not been successful. A decision needs to be taken as to whether to continue with the series or not. If the decision is no, further decisions would have to be taken regarding the funds released.

Motivation is a key objective of budgeting, i.e. motivating the staff to achieve the budget by taking responsibility for their functional department. Managers tend to be demotivated when they have not been involved in the preparation of the budget and they cannot influence it. For example, the Sales and Marketing Department Manager may have been apportioned a value for rent and rates to their budget; this value cannot be influenced by them.

Co-ordination is fundamental to budgeting, each functional area will discuss and agree the budget across their departments, sales will discuss the budget with marketing, and indeed all the functional area will be involved with the preparation. Ultimately all the budget managers will be focused on achieving the company budget. If there is no co-ordination each budget will be prepared independently and the result will lack focus. Budgeting is one of the few techniques that encourage co-ordination, there are few others, hence its importance.

Co-operation is similar to co-ordination; sales need to co-operate with production and with marketing. It would be meaningless if the Marketing Department were to start a promotional campaign, and not liaise with sales or production. It is likely that production would be unable to meet the demand, sales would be unaware that the campaign was running and therefore would not focus their resources accordingly.

Evaluating performance is another objective of budgeting. The performance of the manager is an obvious one but also the performance of the department is another. Performance can be assessed on whether the budget has been achieved. Unfortunately, this may result in managers inflating their budgets by building slack into them. This generally results in the actual figures being below budget and apparently saving money.

Answer – question 6.

The following diagram lists and describes the features of a Marketing Information System (MkIS). The diagram is that developed by Kotler.

The MkIS consists of people, equipment, and procedures, to gather, sort, analyse, evaluate and distribute, needed, timely, and accurate information

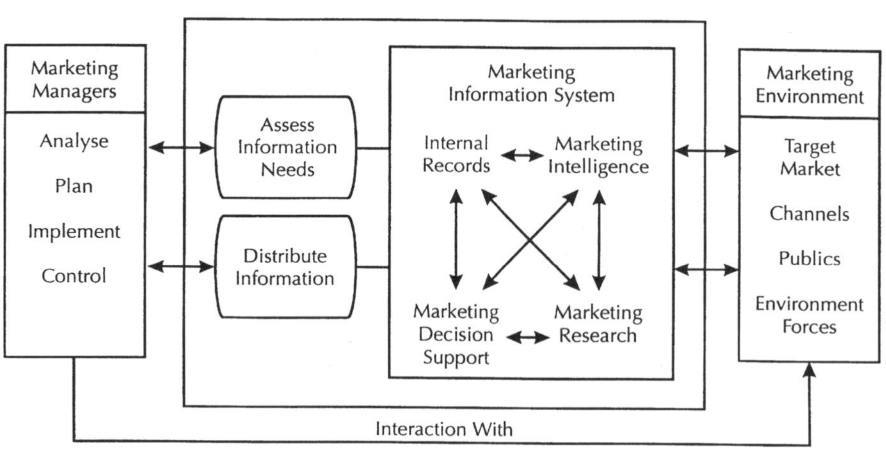

to marketing decision-makers. It is part of a wider management information system that focuses on the marketing element.

It can be seen from the diagram that there are four main elements of the marketing information system, namely, internal records, marketing intelligence, marketing decision support and marketing research. These four areas interact with the marketing environment on the one hand and the marketing managers on the other. The marketing environment is focused on the target market, the channels of distribution, the public and the environmental forces. Marketing managers analyse, plan, implement and control, using the information drawn from the marketing information system and the marketing environment.

Internal records are very important to marketing decision-makers. The data from internal records can be analysed into information if the database is sufficiently. Data from internal records is generally easily accessible, of low cost, can be arranged and rearranged depending on the decision which needs to be made, is accurate and subject to misinterpretation less.

A specific example comes from an organization involved in the manufacture and sale of cutlery and kitchen implements, who include monthly sales reports by product and customer. From these it is possible to track which products are selling well and through which channel, e.g. retail, wholesale, direct mail. This information assists in the development of new products that will hopefully provide high earnings. The production and development departments are responsible for developing and testing new products. Proposed selling prices are calculated and assessed for their viability. If the costs are too high, e.g. if the steel used is expensive because of the strength needed, the product may not be developed further.

Marketing intelligence data is gathered in many forms, and can be classified under competitor intelligence, customer intelligence and market intelligence. Competitor intelligence is the systematic gathering of data that provides information on competitors. It answers such questions as, who are the competitors; what are their objectives; what are their strategies; what are their strengths and weaknesses; where are they vulnerable; what strategy are they following that will affect our company.

The sales team may be used by the organization for gathering competitor data. Their reports from visits to exhibitions and customers provide us with competitor activity intelligence on products, service, etc. For example, from a chance remark by a customer who also buys from our competitor, it was discovered that they were about to produce a complete range of barbecue products and use racks to display their product in shops. Only their products would be displayed on the racks, so other competitor products would be marginalized.

Customer intelligence may be gathered through environmental scanning, trade exhibitions, trade press, trade associations, field sales force, etc. This would include, who the customers are; what they buy and where from; the importance of price; where they are located; how they can be reached, etc. The organization has a very good relationship with a number of key accounts. The managers of these companies show the sales force the sales data for all products sold. This includes sales of our competitors. By viewing this data, we can assess how we are performing, and what benefits we provide to our customers over our competitors. This data assists us in boosting our relationship with the customer, by suggesting ways in which the retailer can improve their sales and by fully understanding what they are currently doing and trying to do. For example, instead of selling each product as an individual kitchen utensil, they could be grouped in sets. From discussions with our customers, it was felt that products could be grouped into sets, such as pasta, cheese, etc. so that instead of selling the products individually, several products were combined into a set. This resulted in a perceived improvement in service to the end user and benefited the customer and us.

Marketing research is the systematic gathering, recording and analysis of data relating to the sale and transfer of goods. It includes market research, product research, price research, communication research, distribution research, and consumer research and buyer behaviour.

The research can be conducted using primary or secondary sources. Primary data may be collected using surveys, focus groups, observation and experimentation. Secondary data may be collected from published data sources, such as market research reports, historical marketing research, internal databases, etc.

One of the ideas of the marketing department of the company was to sell the cutlery on racks in non-traditional areas such as garages. Market research was carried out on a sample to establish if this was a suitable channel.

Marketing decision-making or Decision Support Systems comprise the elements that enable particular decisions to be taken. DSS systems rely on databases and information. The data and information is systematically collected, stored and retrieved using tools and techniques, with supporting software and hardware. The software used may be databases, (on customers, products, suppliers, competitors, financial and non-financial), spreadsheets, (forecasts, budgets, cash flows, actual/budget comparisons,) hardware using networked computer systems, technology using ISDN lines (for updating website and contacting suppliers and customers). Statistical packages may also be used for forecasting and trend extrapolation.

Focusing on spreadsheets, the company uses the most up-to-date financial and non-financial information to update the forecasts of profit and loss statements, cash flows and balance sheets. This is used to assess whether the targets are likely to be met, and if not what the consequences of not doing so are.

Each of the above elements is integrated with the marketing environment and the marketing managers. The marketing environment is focused on the macro- and micro-environment whilst the marketing managers are focused on analysing, planning, implementing and controlling the marketing function.

In conclusion, the whole rationale of a MkIS is to reduce the risk and uncertainty surrounding decision-making, so that decision-makers are enabled to make the optimum decision.

Answer – question 7.

To:	**Board of Management**
From:	**Marketing Manager**
Date:	**8th December 1998**
Subject:	**Product Launch**
Remit:	**To conduct further market research into the launch of a new magazine aimed at the teenage female market.**

At the outset, it would be necessary to decide who should carry out the research; in-house staff or an external agency, or a combination of both. The use of in-house staff would depend on their expertise in the market and their workload. If an agency were used our organization may benefit from their expertise in up-to-date techniques; their research would be more objective and impartial; they would have a greater depth of experience; and the staff of this organization may benefit from liaising with them. All the issues of timing, cost, expertise, confidentiality, knowledge of sector, independence, etc., would need to be considered in this decision.

Once the decision regarding who will carry out the research has been made, the following plan has been drafted, which would be used to conduct further research in order to launch the new magazine. It is assumed that the previous research is not being duplicated. The steps in the sequence of the plan are as follows:

i) Establish research objectives.
ii) Identify research problems.
iii) Conduct cost/benefit analysis.
iv) Draft research proposal.
v) Identify data collection methods.
vi) Identify means of measuring performance.
vii) Collecting the data; selecting an appropriate sample.
viii) Analysing the data.
ix) Presenting the data.
x) Recommendations and conclusions.

The steps are now considered in more detail.

i) **Establish research objectives.** Clear research objectives would have to be established and should have the qualities of being specific, measurable, achievable, realistic, and time based. This stage is very important, since it would give direction to the research and would be used later to evaluate whether the objectives had been achieved. For example, the objective might be 'to conduct research of the reading habits and leisure time of teenage females using a sample of 1,000 within the age range of 13–19 years, and to complete the research within six months.'

ii) **The identification of the research problem** may require the carrying out of exploratory research to determine which information is significant. In this case it could be how to identify the target market and what their preferences would be on the content of the magazine.

iii) **Cost/benefit analysis** is also important, as the budget is £30,000. This budget would be broken down into its constituent parts, and an assessment would need to be made on what benefits would accrue from spending money on each part. This could be carried out by decision tree analysis, to determine the value of achieving perfect information, i.e. to establish the incremental sales from conducting the research and targeting the market properly.

iv) **The drafting of the research proposal** would be the main document explaining the methodology of carrying out the research; what kind of research would be carried out; the problems that might be encountered; and how the budget would be allocated. Decisions on exploratory or in-depth research would be addressed.

v) **Data collection methods** would then have to be determined from a list of survey, interview, questionnaire and shopping mall tests.

vi) **Performance measurement.** It is important that the research should be assessed through measuring the success rate. Performance measurers need to be determined. One measure might be the achievement of the objectives (in step 1).

vii) **The selection of the correct sample** is important. The sample size would depend on the accuracy of the results required and the company resources e.g. budget and staff. For this purpose it is felt that a sample of 1,000 females from our target group (A, B groups) would be appropriate. Sample selection would need to be addressed, from the alternatives of quota, random, non-random, etc. The accuracy of the data could be tested using statistical methods.

viii) **The collection of the data** would involve the design of the questionnaires and the questions for interview etc., and should be focused on the objectives. Both qualitative and quantitative data could be collected. The importance of this stage cannot be over-emphasized, for if the correct technique is not used and accurate collection of data is not carried out, the validity of the research would be put in jeopardy.

ix) **The analysis of the data** would be carried out using both manual (for closed questions) and computer (for open-ended questions) methods. The data could then be entered into various models to establish and interpret the findings. Z charts, moving averages, simulations, etc. could be used to process the data into information. Qualitative data might also be provided on trends, preferences, etc.

x) **The presentation of the report** would be the final step, which would include the recommendations and conclusions.

As the launch of the new magazine is important, the research must be carried out in an organized manner, in order to provide the company with valid, accurate and reliable findings. This will minimize the risks involved with such a large project.

Finally, it is proposed that a meeting should be organized in the near future to discuss the report and facilitate a decision on the project launch, including the time-tabling of the process.

Appendix A Approaching the module for continuous assessment*

Objectives

In this appendix you will:

- ❑ Be introduced to a structure that will help you put together a Continuous Assessment Portfolio.
- ❑ Consider all issues that may arise as you work through the module.
- ❑ Consider aspects of team working which might apply to this module.

By the end of this unit you will be able to:

- ❑ Put together a well-structured portfolio for assessment.
- ❑ Manage your time effectively in preparing for assessment.
- ❑ Work productively in a team and as an individual to achieve results.

Study Guide

In this appendix you will be introduced to all you need to know and do to achieve a good result in the assessment of this module. There are no 'activities' in this appendix, as all the work it suggests relates to the assembling of your actual portfolio. In the first unit of the book, we suggested that you read this appendix before you progress too far into your course of study, as much of the work can be done on an ongoing basis. If this is your first reading of this appendix, you will find that it makes more sense as you start to work on your assignments. You should return to this section as a final check before your folder is submitted for assessment.

Introduction

The Chartered Institute of Marketing has traditionally used professional externally set examinations as the means of assessment for the Certificate, Advanced Certificate and Postgraduate Diploma in Marketing. In 1995, at the request of industry, students and tutors it introduced a continuously

* This appendix written by Gill Kelley.

assessed route to two modules, one at Certificate level, and one at Advanced Certificate.

With the revision of the syllabus for 1999/2000, the decision was taken to offer this route to assessment on four modules, two at each level.

Management Information for Marketing Decisions is highly suited to assessment through Projects and assignments, and this appendix is written to assist students whose tuition centres are running this means of assessment.

Carrying out a skills self-assessment

Students studying for the CIM Advanced Certificate in Marketing come from widely diverse backgrounds; some work in marketing, some are looking to move into marketing, some work in large organizations and carry out very focused roles, and some work in small organizations and carry out a wide range of activities. Some students are not currently working and are looking to acquire a new range of skills to help them find work in the future.

The 'Personal Development Assignment', which may be referred to as a 'Learning Log', gives you the opportunity to develop skills covered by the syllabus for this module which are very relevant to your personal situation.

You are encouraged to consider the following questions:

- *How important is this topic in my current work role? (or how important will it become in the future?)* You will have several sources of information to help you consider the answer to this question. If you are working, look at your job description, your last appraisal or performance review, and talk to your manager. You also have your own existing knowledge of your job to refer to – how is your role changing? Are you being asked to do certain things on a more regular basis? What is your organization doing? Is it introducing new products, or new computer systems or packages?
- If you are not working, look at advertisements for jobs that interest you and talk to other students about what their jobs involve.
- *How well do I do this aspect of the syllabus now?* It may be that you have not been involved with using this particular skill in the past, or perhaps it has just been introduced as part of your job.

A self-assessment checklist is shown in Figure A1. It consists of a list of marketing tasks which relate to the syllabus for Management Information for Marketing Decisions. You should assess yourself against the list, marking (1) when the task is very important in your current role, or is likely to be in the near future, and along the scale to (5) where your job does not involve a particular task. You should then assess your current skill level in each area. It will help you arrive at a rating if you are able to talk to colleagues who you trust, as well as your own manager or tutor, and get their confirmation of your current skill level. When you have completed both columns you will find that the biggest 'skill gap' is shown by the widest gap between the numbers you have circled e.g. An 'importance rating' of (1) and a 'skill level' of (5) is a key area for improvement.

Completing a Personal Development Log

When you have carried out your self-assessment tests and have arrived at an appropriate number of areas for improvement, your next step is to develop a plan to make these improvements. You may have come across

CIM Advanced Certificate – Management Information for Marketing Decisions			
Task	*Done now?*	*Important in current role**	*Current skill level***
Use I.C.T. to:			
Manage customers	Y/N	1–2–3–4–5	1–2–3–4–5
Support marketing decisions	Y/N	1–2–3–4–5	1–2–3–4–5
Improve a marketing process	Y/N	1–2–3–4–5	1–2–3–4–5
Develop customer relationships	Y/N	1–2–3–4–5	1–2–3–4–5
Re-structure a market	Y/N	1–2–3–4–5	1–2–3–4–5
Undertake a:			
Financial forecast based on sales ata	Y/N	1–2–3–4–5	1–2–3–4–5
Decision tree analysis	Y/N	1–2–3–4–5	1–2–3–4–5
Critical path analysis	Y/N	1–2–3–4–5	1–2–3–4–5
Work related break even analysis	Y/N	1–2–3–4–5	1–2–3–4–5
Show the application of:			
CPV decision to budgeting/sales promotion/promotional decisions	Y/N	1–2–3–4–5	1–2–3–4–5
NPV or Internal Rates of Return to an investment decision	Y/N	1–2–3–4–5	1–2–3–4–5
Activity based costing in improving marketing decisions	Y/N	1–2–3–4–5	1–2–3–4–5
Demonstrate the effect of overheads on:			
Pricing/Promotion/Distribution/Product Development/Market Entry	Y/N	1–2–3–4–5	1–2–3–4–5
Make pricing decisions	Y/N	1–2–3–4–5	1–2–3–4–5
Apply ratio analysis to inform marketing decisions	Y/N	1–2–3–4–5	1–2–3–4–5
Prepare a marketing budget	Y/N	1–2–3–4–5	1–2–3–4–5
Generate marketing research information to:			
Develop a promotional campaign	Y/N	1–2–3–4–5	1–2–3–4–5
Develop a new product or service	Y/N	1–2–3–4–5	1–2–3–4–5
Develop a new market	Y/N	1–2–3–4–5	1–2–3–4–5
Develop existing markets	Y/N	1–2–3–4–5	1–2–3–4–5
Develop customer relationships	Y/N	1–2–3–4–5	1–2–3–4–5
Improve customer serv ice	Y/N	1–2–3–4–5	1–2–3–4–5
Improve channel efficiency	Y/N	1–2–3–4–5	1–2–3–4–5
Improve category management	Y/N	1–2–3–4–5	1–2–3–4–5
Informa a pricing decision	Y/N	1–2–3–4–5	1–2–3–4–5
Inform a sales decision	Y/N	1–2–3–4–5	1–2–3–4–5

* Where 1 = very important and 5 = of little importance.
** Where 1 = excellent and 5 = poor.

Figure A1 Decision skills audit checklist

the planning structure that follows in your earlier studies. It will also be useful in a personal development context:

Situation This is the result of your self-assessment.

Objectives Set some objectives for what you want to achieve, e.g. to improve research and decision making skills with particular emphasis on developing existing customer relationships, within the next four months.

Strategy This is how you are going to meet your objectives. In the example given above you may decide that you have to improve your knowledge first, then carry out some research, and finally, ask a colleague for feedback.

Tactics The details involved in your strategy. Again, using the example given above you might decide to look at the relevant chapters of textbooks which cover this topic, attend the session at college which covers 'conducting primary and secondary research', and spend some time in the marketing research department at work to see live examples of research being carried out. Your next step may be to ask to get involved with carrying out some customer satisfaction research for you organization. This might involve the development of an appropriate questionnaire, or the use of an existing one to generate some information for analysis.

'Men' Who else is involved? The colleagues at work that you have identified to help you.

'Money' Do you need a budget? This is not necessary. You may decide to buy a book – but the library is also a useful source of information.

'Machines' If you need to analyse your data on a particular piece of software, then you need to find out how you can get access to the necessary equipment. Can your employer or the college help. Does anything need to be photocopied?

'Materials' You may decide to present your findings in Report format, in which case you will need paper and a binder of some sort.

'Minutes' When do you have to complete your assignment? It is useful to work backwards, in stages, from your deadline, allowing some time for contingencies.

'Measurement' Against what criteria will you measure your progress/ success? You will make the decision when you have completed your background study – reading, work shadowing, etc. Remember that you are looking to achieve, or make progress towards your objective, which should be SMART.

Now your plan is in place. Make a note of the 'milestones' it involves in your diary. By when do you need to have found an appropriate book to read (don't forget to write up your record of background reading!), and arranged to spend some time in another department? By when do you need to have completed all of the preparation for your data analysis? When will you write up your Report?

Now put your plan into action. There are too many plans that are lists of good intentions. You will achieve nothing unless you act on these intentions and see the plan through to the finish.

While you are completing this part of the exercise you should write up your Learning Log. Everything you do will form part of this 'log' – the plan itself, the notes you make about the reading you undertake and the work shadowing, the questionnaire you used and the data you have gathered and other associated material, the analysis of the data and the recommendations you make as a result of the exercise and, most importantly, your own reflective statement of what you have achieved and what you still need to work on. What was the most difficult part? How did you feel at the start of the exercise and how do you feel at the end? Did you achieve your objectives? If not, why not?

A learning log is a useful way to track your own development. The stages involved are recording:

- a description of an incident that has happened in the work place;
- your observations from the incident;
- a plan for what you would do differently or what you would change in the future;
- how it links it to underpinning knowledge gained on the programme.

You are making a commitment to change your behaviour. You should 'reflect' about the application of your learning in your own work context. An example is shown in Figure A2.

This assignment has other benefits, as it helps you to develop skills that are useful in tackling case studies in your examined modules. Your reflections represent your analysis of situations that you have encountered at work, and also you will be recommending realistic action plans for the future.

When you have made your plan for the first area for improvement, then you need to extend this to the other areas which you have identified and follow the above suggestions for each.

Learning Log	**Date: 12 April 1999**
Learning experience Visit to Head Office.	
What happened While I was talking to our Management Accountant today I mentioned to him that I was studying financial aspects of marketing as part of my course, and that I was really struggling to get to grips with the difference between fixed and variable costs. As we were talking through some of those which apply to our organization I suddenly realised what had been getting in my way – as a 'service' company rather than a manufacturer, we do not have variable costs; all are fixed. We employ all out staff on permanent contracts, don't pay overtime, and don't have stock or components to buy in.	
Conclusions I need to do some analysis of costs and figures of different types of industry so that I get a real understanding of the terminology used and how it works. I have realized that focusing just on my own organization gives me too narrow a view to understand the new information I am studying – I need to take a broader view.	
Actions Spend half a day with our Management Accountant going through the figures which are used within our organization – budgets, financial accounts, marketing (and other) expenditure. He has put me in touch with a colleague in a local engineering firm who is happy to go through the same process (and my manager has said that I can do this in works time!)	
When Early next month when all the 'month end' figures are completed.	

Figure A2
Example learning log reflective statement

Working as a team on assignments

Working within a team on assignments can be an area of concern for many students who are being assessed in this way for the first time. However, many students who have gone through the process state that this has been the most useful area of learning for them. It is very relevant to today's workplace, as many of us now work in a team, or in more than one team, on a variety of projects. Areas of concern include – what if I can't keep up with the rest of the team? What if I let the others down? What if one of the others on the team lets us all down? Will it affect my marks if someone else does badly? In fact, most assignments are structured so that some of the marks are awarded for an individual's contribution and some awarded for the work of the team. Also, only one or two of the assignments are 'team' based – other assignments will be undertaken by you as an individual, and so the majority of marks you achieve are on your efforts alone.

An important part of teamwork is working together to ensure that all are able to contribute on an equal basis – you will learn a lot about yourself and others through working closely on a piece of work which is to be assessed.

Dr Meredith Belbin, a British researcher, studied hundreds of managers working to solve exercises in teams.

He established that, in order to achieve their goals, individuals in teams have to recognize their differences. Imagine a football team made up of eleven strikers, or eleven goalkeepers! Many organizations think that by putting all their brightest people together, the team will consistently outperform other teams. This is not always the case, and Belbin realized that a successful team needed to be made up of a number of different 'roles' which related to different processes. For example, while there is a need for someone to take a strategic view, who is stable and controlled – there is equally a need for someone to pay attention to the detail of completing the task, and these people tend to be more anxious and introvert.

Belbin devised a questionnaire which identifies the role(s) which individuals are most comfortable in when working in a team. The roles are described as follows:

- *Implementer* – is stable and controlled and perceived by other team members as a practical organizer. They turn concepts and plans into practical working processes systematically. They can be thrown easily by sudden changes or too much uncertainty, and function through knowledge and expertise.
- *Coordinator* – controls the way in which a team moves towards the objectives using the team resources. They are intelligent without being intellectual, disciplined and have natural authority. They recognize the team's strengths and weaknesses and are good at setting priorities.
- *Shaper* – gets things done, is outgoing but can become anxious. They seek to impose some shape or pattern to group discussions. They have a high control need and can become impatient, impulsive and easily frustrated. Their outward confidence often conceals self-doubt.
- *Plant* – brings new ideas and strategies to the group through bright intellect. These ideas can inspire but a plant can sulk if these ideas are not accepted. The plant stays detached when team members get bogged down with problems and can then give a spark to move forwards.
- *Resource investigator* – is popular with team members and wonderful at networking outside the team. They build useful external contacts and resources for the team. They communicate, collect ideas, and adapt to find solutions from an outside view, preventing the team from stagnating.
- *Monitor evaluator* – analyses problems using their intellect. They can be perceived as cold, but their objectivity can prevent the team from making a mistake. They can be negative to change but their judgement is worth listening to.

- *Team worker* – cares about the team members as people and fosters team spirit. They are sensitive and loyal and don't like confrontation. The team worker likes harmony and works to develop this in team members.
- *Completer finisher* – is an anxious introvert who is particular about getting things done properly. They have personal discipline and give tasks more than the usual degree of attention. This can be perceived either as compulsive perfectionism or paying attention to detail. They also have a sense of urgency.
- *Specialist* – is someone who has a particular knowledge or skill. This individual is often more comfortable working alone than in a team. However, their contribution of specialist knowledge can often overcome a problem that is delaying progress.

You may not have the opportunity to identify your own team role, or those of others in your team. However, the key point to remember is that we are all different, and all have various strengths and weaknesses which can be used to best effect when working with others. It is up to everyone within a team to 'manage' the situation so that all are able to contribute, and that one person's strength is used to overcome another's weakness. Perhaps those of us who are most impatient with others when looking to make progress towards a goal have the most learning to do – it is part of everyone's role in a team to encourage, help and support the less experienced and less confident so that all achieve together.

There are a variety of issues that may arise when you are working with a team from your tuition centre. For example, most of you will be in demanding full-time employment which may involve working away from home from time to time. A member of your team may be ill, or have family commitments which make it difficult to attend meetings outside of tuition sessions. Again, it is part of teamworking to use the individual parts of the team to overcome such difficulties. Perhaps there are parts of the work that can be shared out and undertaken between meetings to minimize the time taken working as a group. How are you going to communicate? Is everyone on e-mail at work or home? Will contact be made by telephone or fax?

Teamworking can be very rewarding, and can forge strong bonds. Teams formed at Certificate level for continuous assessment work often stay together when they move on to the Advanced Certificate, and are still supporting each other when they tackle the case study at Diploma level.

Managing your time

What is time management? It's wisely using one of your most precious resources – *time* – to achieve your key goals. You need to be aware of how you spend your time each day, set priorities so you know what's important to you, and what isn't. You need to establish goals for your study, work and family life and plan to meet those goals. Through developing these habits you will be better able to achieve the things you want to achieve. When study becomes one of your key goals you may find that, temporarily, something has to be sacrificed in favour of time needed for reading, writing notes, writing up assignments, preparing for group assessment, etc. It will help to 'get people on your side'. Tell people that you are studying and ask for their support – these include direct family, close friends and colleagues at work.

Time can just slip through your fingers if you don't manage it – and that's wasteful! When you are trying to balance the needs of family, social life, working life and study there is a temptation to leave assignments until the deadline is near. Don't give in to this temptation! Many students have been heard to complain about the heavy workload towards the end of the course, when, in fact, they have had several months to work on assignments and they have created this heavy workload themselves.

By knowing how to manage your time wisely you can:

- Reduce pressure when you're faced with deadlines or a heavy schedule.
- Be more in control of your life by making better decisions about how to use your time.
- Feel better about yourself because you're using your full potential to achieve.
- Have more energy for things you want or need to accomplish.
- Succeed more easily because you'll know what you want to do and what you need to do to achieve it.

Putting together your portfolio for assessment

At last – you have finished all your assignments and your folder needs to be prepared for submission! A question often posed by students is 'How much should be in my portfolio?' There is no simple answer to this and it will depend on many things. Your tutor will have given you a 'Portfolio front sheet' which is shown in Figure A3.

Candidate name: ____________________ **CIM reg. no:** ____________________

Centre: ____

Section 1 (to be completed by the student)

Item	✓
CV and job description (if appropriate)	
Introductory page	
Learning Log	
Assignment 1	
Assignment 2	
Assignment 3 (if appropriate)	
Other relevant paperwork (not course notes)	
Final reflection	

This section to be removed before portfolio is returned to student

Section 2 (to be completed by tutor)

Item	**Mark**
Learning Log	
Assignment 1	
Assignment 2	
Assignment 3	
Total mark	

Tutor comments:

____

____

____

____

Figure A3
Portfolio front sheet

This should be used as a checklist of your folder's contents and guide you through the process of putting it together. The first question you should ask yourself is 'Will this make sense to someone who has not met me?' The folder contents will be looked at by an 'internal moderator' – someone who works in your tuition centre, but has not taught you during this module, and may be looked at by one or more 'external moderators' – people whose job it is to ensure that all students on Chartered Institute of Marketing continuously assessed modules are marked fairly and consistently. This overview is taken as part of a quality control process that looks at the consistency of assessment within tuition centres and across the network of tuition centres.

So, when your folder is chosen, will the moderator get a true picture of who you are and all the hard work you have undertaken within this module? The first way you can help this process along is by including your CV (look back at Unit 6 if you have not yet prepared a CV) and a brief description of your current work role. This will help the moderator put your work 'in context'.

The next thing which is asked for is an 'introductory page'. This again helps the moderator make sense of your portfolio. It does not have to be more than one page, and will be considered the 'starting point' in terms of the skills covered within this module.

For example, you might say:

> When I started this module I had just moved into my first marketing role. I was still uncertain of all that I would be expected to do within my new role, and this is why I decided to study for my CIM Advanced Certificate. When I looked at the skills audit it was quite easy for me to identify my strengths and weaknesses. I studied Finance as part of my degree, and I had also taken part in seminars – so my knowledge of the financial aspects of the syllabus and my personal communication skills were strengths. I was used to gathering information from the Internet and other sources, and I am computer literate. My main weakness was going to be:
>
> - Applying my existing knowledge in a marketing context, and getting involved in primary research.
>
> Once I had looked at this exercise I actually felt better about taking the module – but realized that I still had some way to go. Our tutor encouraged us to select topics from the list that would provide us with a challenge as well as being useful in our current and future work role, and this helped me pick the areas to work on in my 'Learning Log'.

Your folder should now contain all the work you have done within your assignments. Again, it may be necessary to put a few introductory comments to each assignment, and a note of what your main learning points were from going through the exercise. If you have undertaken research for an assignment, then it may be appropriate to include this in the back of your folder as an Appendix. Your course notes should not be in this file.

After your assignment work you should include your 'Record of background reading' which is shown in Figure A4.

There is no limit to the number of sheets you include as a record of background reading – make your record as you are reading and don't leave it until the deadline for submission of your work. By then you will have forgotten where you found a particularly useful piece of information.

Your final reflection should conclude your portfolio and 'look forward'. Look back at your introductory page. What were your expectations at that point? Have they been met? Did the strengths you identified then turn out to be real strengths as you worked through your assignments? What have you learned about yourself as you have worked through the module? Did you dread having to make recomendations about a marketing issue, but, on the day, things went really well and you no longer fear being put into the situation at work? How much of your learning have you been able to apply at work? Have you been able to solve any real work problems

Candidate name: ____________________

This sheet should provide a record of reading you have undertaken in support of this module. It is not just a bibliography – you should list the key learning points from the chapter or article you read, and state whether you would recommend it to another student and why.

1	**Title/publication:** **Chapter/article title:** **Key learning points:** **Recommendation:**	**Author:** **Publisher:**
2	**Title/publication:** **Chapter/article title:** **Key learning points:** **Recommendation:**	**Author:** **Publisher:**
3	**Title/publication:** **Chapter/article title:** **Key learning points:** **Recommendation:**	**Author:** **Publisher:**

Figure A4
Record of background reading

through work you have done in your assignments? How much has your Manager been involved? What do they think?

This statement will be personal to you, and should look forward to points you have identified as needing work in the future. We never stop learning – keep up this process of continuous professional development as you go through your studies and you will have acquired the habit by the time you need to employ it to achieve chartered marketer status!

Summary

In this unit we have looked at all the issues involved in tackling this module by 'continuous assessment'. Like life, you will get out of this process what you are prepared to put in. It is possible to achieve high grades, but you need to balance the work you are putting in to your examined modules with the work you are putting in here. Do not be tempted to neglect one in favour of the other as this will only lead to disappointment. One of the advantages of 'continuous assessment' is the feedback you are given on an ongoing basis to help you improve your practice. Remember, however, that your final 'grade' will be issued with your other examination results. Your tutor will be able to give an indication of how it may be graded, but final grades are awarded at 'moderation' and can be adjusted at this point.

Finally, remember that study and learning must be applied if it is not to be a waste of time, effort and money!

Appendix B Syllabus

Management Information for Marketing Decisions

Aims and objectives

- To develop students' understanding of the need for and place of an integrated management information system in supporting marketing decisions and to be able to develop appropriate MkIS structures by applying basic concepts.
- To emphasize the importance of forecasting in the planning process and to apply forecast information in a variety of contexts relating to marketing decisions.
- To apply financial concepts in order to make effective marketing decisions together with an ability to apply financial analysis to a variety of marketing management problems.
- To explore the sources of marketing research information, how they are obtained (strengths and weaknesses) and be able to apply marketing research information to a range of marketing problems in a variety of contexts.
- To develop a practical and applied understanding of developments in information and communication technologies that impact upon marketing management decisions and how management information is gathered, stored and communicated both within and across organizational boundaries.

Learning outcomes

Students will be able to:

- Apply their understanding of management information systems in designing appropriate marketing information systems (MkIS) and management control systems.
- Recommend appropriate changes to management information systems to achieve specific objectives in a specific context.
- Demonstrate their understanding of the importance of forecasting information in a range of marketing contexts and be able to apply this to forecast at a variety of levels, e.g. organizational, departmental, product level, and service level.
- Apply their knowledge and understanding of financial management to make appropriate marketing decisions and recomendations and to work within predetermined budget limits using appropriate financial controls.
- Apply their knowledge and understanding of management information structures to design and implement appropriate systems to collect a variety of data and market intelligence in order to provide improved decision making. In so doing students will be able to identify benefits to internal and/or external customers.
- Design and implement appropriate marketing control systems through effective use of management information from a variety of sources that will include internal and external data.

- Analyse, evaluate and apply a range of quantitative and qualitative data and make appropriate recommendations that lead to effective marketing decisions in specific marketing contexts.
- Understand the place of information and communication technologies in the process of generating, storing and retrieving a variety of sources of management information for marketing decision making.

Indicative content and weighting

3.1 Management information systems – basic concepts (10%)

The important role that information plays in supporting decision making in marketing.

Specific areas of application will include:

3.1.1 Identification of the component parts of management information systems (MIS) and a marketing information system (MkIS)

3.1.2 Application of basic management information concepts how information is gathered, stored and retrieved to support marketing decisions

3.1.3 Recognizing and recommending improvements to the MIS or MkIS

3.1.4 The importance of context in suggesting system improvements to the MIS or MkIS

3.1.5 The relationship between an organization's management information system and their marketing information system (MkIS)

3.2 Information and communication technology supporting marketing decisions (20%)

- The developing information and communication technologies (ICTs) and how they can be used to support decisions taken in marketing and management. In particular how ICTs are changing the ways in which data sources are accessed, processed, analysed and evaluated.
- The application of information and communication technology solutions in the context of marketing management decisions.

Specific areas of application will include how ICTs assist in:

3.2.1 Managing customers

3.2.2 Supporting managers in their marketing decisions

3.2.3 Improving marketing processes

3.2.4 Improving the effectiveness of marketing information

3.2.5 ICT's role in changing customer relationships and restructuring markets

3.3 Forcasting information for marketing decisions (10%)

The range of forecasting methods and tools that are available to develop forecasts, e.g. time series analysis, econometric forecasting, sales forecasts, decision trees, delphi technique, critical path analysis.

Specific areas of application of underpinning knowledge include:

3.3.1 Financial forecasts based on sales forecast data

3.3.2 Decision trees to analyse the marketing options available

3.3.3 A critical path based upon forecast data

3.3.4 Financial plans based upon forecast data

3.3.5 Distinguishing between a forecast and a budget

3.4 Financial information to support marketing decsions (40%)

Students will need to demonstrate their understanding of basic financial concepts through their application to marketing management decisions in a variety of contexts.

Specific areas of application will include:

3.4.1 Contribution and break-even analysis

3.4.2 Cost, profit and volume decisions in a variety of contexts, e.g. budgeting, promotional decisions, sales promotions

3.4.3 Effect of overheads on a variety of marketing decisions, e.g. pricing, output, promotions, distribution, product development, market entry or expansion

3.4.4 Activity based costing/activity based management and their significant role in improving marketing decisions

3.4.5 Pricing decisions in a variety of marketing contexts, e.g. setting appropriate selling prices to achieve required margins or mark-ups, setting appropriate transfer prices for internal and external movement of goods and services

3.4.6 Direct product profitability (DPP), channel, category, product and market profit and cost analysis

3.4.7 Application of ratio analysis in a variety of contexts

3.4.8 The financial impact of marketing decisions (including financial implications of marketing plans) and the sources of information required

3.4.9 Budget preparation and control in relation to marketing decisions, e.g. budgeted profit and loss statements for a specific product range

3.4.10 Application of financial information required to improve customer service or enhance product quality

3.4.11 Identification of appropriate variances and ability to draw implications from them, e.g. between budgeted and actual figures

3.4.12 Investment decisions in a marketing context using payback and discounted cash flow techniques such as net present value or internal rates of return

3.5 Marketing research information applied to marketing decisions (20%)

Choosing and using a range of marketing research information to make decisions in a variety of contexts.

It will be necessary to have an understanding of appropriate marketing research methods and tools that generate information in order to apply them to a specific context.

Specific areas of application would include:

3.5.1 Developing promotional campaigns

3.5.2 Developing new products or services

3.5.3 Developing new or existing markets

3.5.4 Establishing or developing customer relationships

3.5.5 Improving customer service

3.5.6 Changing channels or improving channel efficiency

3.5.7 Improving category management

3.5.8 Pricing decisions

3.5.9 Sales decisions

Further reading

Bolt, G. J. (1994) *Market Sales Forecasting – A Total Approach*. Kogan Page

Bromwich and Bhimani (1989) *Evolution not Revolution*. CIMA

Chisnall, P. M. (1992) *Marketing Research*. McGraw-Hill

Clifton, P., Nguyen, H. and Nutt, S. (1992) *Market Research: Using Forecasting in Business*. Butterworth-Heinemann

Crimp, M. (1990) *Marketing Research Process*. Prentice-Hall

Crouch, S. (1996) *Marketing Research for Managers*. CIM/Butterworth-Heinemann

Davidson, J. H. (1987) *Offensive Marketing*. Penguin

Dyer, R. E. and Forman, E. H. (1991) *An Analytical Approach to Marketing Decisions*. Prentice-Hall

Green, P. E. and Tull, D. S. (1978) *Research for Marketing Decisions*. Prentice-Hall

Hines, T. (1990) *Foundation Accounting*. Checkmate Gold

Hines, T. (1995) Brief review of competencies required for marketing management posts, working paper. Manchester Metropolitan University

Hines, T. (1996) Strategies for supply chain management in global markets – the downstream implications for small manufacturing firms. *Journal of Clothing Management and Technology*, January

Kelly, G. A. (1955) *The Psychology of Personal Constructs*, Norton

Kent, R. A. (1993) *Marketing Research in Action*. Routledge

Kotler, P. (1994) *Marketing Management, Analysis, Planning, Implementation and Control*. Prentice-Hall

Kotler, P. and Armstrong, E.(1996) *Principles of Marketing*. Prentice-Hall

McDaniel, C. D. and Gates, R. (1993) *Contemporary Market Research*. West Publishing

Oliver, G. (1995) *Marketing Today*. Prentice-Hall

Parkinson, L. K. and Parkinson, S. T. (1987) *Using the Microcomputer in Marketing*. McGraw-Hill

Piercy, N. (1992) *Market-led Strategic Change*. Butterworth-Heinemann

Porter, M. E. (1980) *Competitive Strategy*. Free Press

Sizer, J. *An Insight into Management Accounting*. Penguin

Van Maanen, J. (1983) *Qualitative Methodology*. Sage

Webb, J. R. *Understanding and Designing Marketing Research*. Academic Press

Wilson, R. M. S. and Gilligan, C. (1997) *Strategic Marketing Management, Planning, Implementation and Control*. CIM/Butterworth-Heinemann

Glossary

Absorption costing A method of costing that takes into account a proportion of overheads using an appropriate rate (also called full-costing).

Accounting *Financial* accounting records historical transactions to determine profit and loss. *Management* accounting is concerned with control, budgeting and future costs.

Accounting Standards Board (ASB) Comprises representatives from all major UK professional accounting bodies.

Accrual Sums set aside out of profit for known expenses not yet invoiced.

ACORN A lifestyle profiling technique using neighbourhood addresses to segment the population into groups, e.g. A = Thriving; B = Expanding; C = Rising, the purpose being to use the profiling for targeting and segmentation.

Activity Describes the way in which resources are consumed.

Activity based costing (ABC) A form of costing that is concerned with estimating the cost of activities associated with events to determine a causal cost relationship. ABC is able to deal with volume-related and transactional costs.

Activity ratio A measure of performance based on inputs and outputs or measures related to units of time. Examples include: average debtor collection; stock turnover; fixed asset turnover etc.

Advertising research Research conducted to determine the effectiveness of advertising; for example, recall tests.

ANSI American National Standards Institute.

Archie A searching system to find computer files available using FTP.

Arithmetic mean A statistical measure of central tendency. It is commonly referred to as the *average*. It is subject to distortion by high values in a particular range.

Artificial Neural Network (ANN) Distributed and parallel information processing systems made up of simple computational elements that interact across weighted connections.

Asset Something owned by an individual or company over which they exert rights. Assets have a long-term value and are consumed over a number of financial periods. Depreciation is the charge for using assets. Assets are fixed or current.

Attitude A disposition that a respondent holds towards something. Attitudes often lead to behaviours.

Attribute A characteristic such as size, age, weight, height. Marketing research is often concerned with identifying attributes and assessing attitudes towards them. It is also a feature of a product or service that adds value for the customer.

Audience measurement Marketing research, usually conducted through observation techniques that may be electronic, to measure audiences. It is important for advertisers to know how many people are likely to see their message. See BARB.

Average collection period The measure of how quickly debtors are turning over and hence how quickly cash is collected. Sales turnover/ Debtors will tell you how many times debtors turn over in a period if you use averaged balance sheet figure for debtors and average sales. A type of activity ratio.

Average payment period The measure of how quickly creditors are being paid. Cost of sales/Creditors will tell you how many times creditors turn over in a period. A type of activity ratio.

Bad debt risk The risk associated with the uncertainty of allowing credit to people you make sales to. This risk is often provided for using a doubtful debtor provision.

Balance sheet A statement of assets and liabilities at a specific point in time. It usually takes a form specified in the Companies Act.

BARB Broadcasters Audience Research Board.

Baud rate The number of state changes on an electronic communications line per second. Baud rate is used to describe speed.

Benchmarking A means of performance measurement comparing specific activities with those activities across time periods or against other organizations.

bps Bits per second: modems are usually quoted as being, say, 28,200 bps; the faster the bps the less time you need to spend on line.

BRAD British Rates and Data.

Brand research Research associated with finding out about the intangible values and attributes of the brand: a trade mark, an image, a company, a product may constitute a brand.

Break-even The point at which sales revenue and costs (fixed and variable) are equal. There is no profit and no loss at this point.

Budgetary control A budget is a financial plan for a specific period of time. Budgetary controls are designed with the purpose of assessing variances and putting plans back on course should they deviate.

Budgeting The process of preparing the budget, i.e. the financial plan for a specific period.

Business processes A network of related activities linked by the outputs they exchange.

Capital The amount of money subscribes by the owners of a business. In the case of companies this will take the form of share capital. Profit is added to capital. It is hoped that capital will grow through time as a result of engaging in business.

Capital employed The total funds used by an organization. It includes share capital, reserves (e.g. profit) and loans.

Cash flow The cash receipts minus the cash payments in a period.

Category management This is a term used by retailers (and marketers) to group particular products into categories based for example on customer lifestyles. Configuring products or services in a particular grouping to appeal to a particular segment of the market. An example might be to display merchandise in store to appeal to the 'sporty/active' lifestyle segment by having sports shoes, shorts, T shirts, tracksuits, casual clothing, bags, rackets, gloves, sweat-bands, socks, bicycles and balls close together grouped by this category. As a marketer you are targeting a lifestyle rather than an age band, income band or socio-economic grouping. The retailer allocates the stock-keeping units (SKUs) to the category for management purposes, e.g. stock control, store location. Services can be bundled in a similar way and offered to customers whose lifestyles have been identified from marketing research as matching a particular category. For example, if a bank identifies a category as 'active investors' it may decide to target customers that it identifies with related products or services for that category such as ISAs, unit trusts, stockbroking services, various saving and investment products. The development of smart card technology will enhance the retailer's ability to identify categories and target customers better.

CATI Computer assisted telephone interviewing.

CD ROM Compact Disk Read Only Memory.

Competitive advantage Said to be achieved either on the basis of cost or differentiation. An organization is said to gain a competitive advantage if it is able to distinguish offerings from competitors based on cost or differentiation.

Competitor research Research designed to find out what your competitors are doing. It may include feedback from the sales force in the form of soft data or hard data systematically collected in a variety of ways.

Consumer profiling Identifying types of lifestyles with the aim of clustering consumers into groups and targeting them in a specific way.

Consumer research Research concerned with identifying likes and dislikes, wants and needs, attitudes and behaviours of those who use the company's products or services.

Contribution Sales less variable cost is the contribution made towards overheads initially and later towards profit when the break-even point is passed.

Cost Cost is a fact when it is invoiced. Cost is estimated for internal transactions. For example, firms use absorption costing methods or activity based costing to determine product costs. Cost should not be confused with price.

Cost centre A place, group of people, function, department etc. to which costs are allocated or apportioned with the aim of sensibly classifying costs. Cost centres are usually the responsibility of a manager who is given the task to control cost.

Cost driver A factor that causes cost.

Cost pool A grouping of costs by related cost drivers and activities, e.g. order assembly may be designated a cost pool and the activities assigned to the pool could be picking, packing and returns.

Cost elements Labour, materials and overheads are the elements of cost. These may be further split into fixed and variable elements.

Cost of sales Cost price of goods sold. The matching or accruals principle of accounting attempts to match time periods or numbers of units at cost price with sales revenue to determine profit or loss.

Costing That part of accounting that uses a variety of methods and techniques to work out cost. Product costs and period costs, total costs, departmental costs, capital costs, all need to be estimated.

Credit A period of time allowed between the transaction taking place for a sale or purchase and the actual payment date. For example, sales invoiced often allow thirty or sixty days credit.

Credit rating Judgements made about a customer or supplier that measure their credit worthiness, that is to say will they pay and are they able to pay? Assessments are often made by independent agencies like Dunn & Bradstreet.

Creditor Someone your organization owes money to. Usually suppliers for purchases such as stock.

Critical Path Analysis (CPA) A technique to determine the shortest possible time in which a job may be completed. It recognizes tasks may be sequential or parallel. The latter can be done simultaneously whereas the former are done in sequence. Useful for scheduling.

Current asset Stock, debtors, short term investments, money at the bank and cash are the current assets. CA are assets likely to change form within a year.

Current liability Trade creditors, creditors, short term loans and accruals are current liabilities. CLs are liabilities falling due within a year.

Customer research Research conducted with the aim of finding out what customers want. The research can be quantitative or qualitative in nature and may use secondary and primary data.

Data The raw material from which information is deduced. Data may be facts, figures, words, pictures, electronic etc.

Database Where data is held until required. Databases in paper form may simply be a card index or a filing cabinet. More usually nowadays databases are held electronically in computer systems. For example, customer records.

Data-mining This is a term describing the ways in which an organization's data warehouse (stored data) may be accessed (mined). It is referred to as mining because users are able to drill down through various levels of data. For example, depending upon how a database is structured it may be possible to trace a sale (first level) to a customer (second level) and access a variety of data (third level) relating to that customer.

Data warehouse This is a term used to describe data storage. Computers are used to store vast quantities of data and the data warehouse is usually located within the management information system held in computer files.

Debit An entry into a ledger account on the left hand side of the account. It does not mean anything else. Increasing asset or expense accounts will involve debit entries. Reducing a liability, capital or revenue will also require a debit entry.

Debt An amount owed that is legally recognized.

Debtor Usually a customer who owes money for goods supplied on credit and recognized by the issue of a sales invoice. Debtors are shown in total as a current asset on the balance sheet.

Decision support system A system comprising elements that enable particular decisions to be taken. DSS systems rely on databases and information. It is systematic data collection, storage and retrieval using tools and techniques with supporting software and hardware.

Decision tree A branching technique to demonstrate clearly the choices available. Decision trees may simply detail yes/no decisions, more complex algorithms or they may be assigned probability values.

Deductive reasoning Process by which one reaches conclusions about part of a known population from given facts about the population under study. For example, in a group of six people three are male and three female; the chances of choosing a male at random are 1 in 2.

DELPHI A form of expert opinion involving the respondents in refining their decisions by narrowing down the options or the focus in a series of rounds or stages.

Demographic data Data about a population, e.g. age, sex, occupation, religion, income, ethnicity.

Depreciation Charging a proportion of the cost of a fixed asset (i.e. capital expenditure) to a specific time period based on usage or the time the asset has been held, the purpose being to include a charge for using the asset.

Depth interviews A qualitative method of research to investigate feelings, attitudes, beliefs, in the course of a lengthy interview.

Direct cost A cost that varies with a change in output, e.g. direct materials that cost £1 per unit will cost £2 if two units are produced and £5 if five units are produced.

Direct labour The cost of labour consumed in producing a product or service. This cost will vary with output. Factory or manufacturing labour is often treated as a direct cost.

Direct material Materials whose cost is variable with changes in output. Note: indirect materials are the opposite and are costs that bear no relation to output, e.g. cleaning materials.

Direct overheads Overheads that vary directly with output, e.g. a royalty payment.

Direct product profitability This is a method used to determine the total cost of ownership. Revenues and all attributable costs of owning the product are taken into account to determine direct product profitability.

Discounted cash flow (DCF) A technique used to bring future sums of money to a common measure in a current time period. Net present value (NPV) and internal rate of return (IRR) are DCF techniques.

Distribution research Research related to finding out about aspects of the way in which products and services are transported to the place at which they are sold.

Dividend Distribution of profit made to a shareholder.

Double entry A system of bookkeeping used to record financial transactions. There needs to be a debit and credit entry for a single transaction.

Doubtful debt A provision set aside out of profit for those debtors who may not pay. If they do not pay the debt is then said to be a bad debt.

Earnings per share The proportion of profit attributable to a single share.

E-commerce This is a term describing electronic commerce usually conducted over the internet.

EDI Electronic Data Interchange.

EFTPOS Electronic Funds Transfer at Point Of Sale.

Elements of cost Labour, materials and overheads are the elements of cost. These may be further split into fixed and variable elements.

E-mail Electronic mail. This is a communication between remote computers that uses the telephone network via a modem. Memos, letters, documents and whole files may be sent or received.

EPOS Electronic Point Of Sales, usually using bar code technology.

Equity Shareholders' funds or owners' capital.

E-tailing This is a term coined to describe electronic retailing.

Exchange rate The rate at which one unit of currency is exchanged for another, e.g. £1 = $1.54.

Expense A charge against profit, e.g. telephone expenses.

Experimental research Research conducted as an experiment, e.g. testing marketing to evaluate product success.

Expert opinion Leading or influential people who make informed statements about a particular situation.

Expert system A self-contained system that is able to update records and make decisions based on an algorithm held internally within the system.

Exploratory research Research usually undertaken with a view to extending the study at a later stage if the results are satisfactory.

Extranet This is a network linking selected organizations and parts of their own intranet. For example, in business-to-business markets it may be important to link suppliers to their customer allowing access to stock and production records and payment systems.

Factor analysis A statistical technique to isolate and identify important factors affecting an outcome.

Field research Primary data collection and analysis.

Fixed cost A cost that does not change as a result of a change in output.

Flexible budget A budget that recognizes that some costs will change if activity levels change and adjusts those costs accordingly.

Focus group A small group of respondents (6–10) selected with the aim of focusing on key issues and to collect and analyse qualitative data from respondents to draw conclusions. Focus group research is often done to get the key issues before conducting a larger study.

Forecast This may be qualitative and take the form of statements and scenarios about the future *or* more usually it is quantitative in the form of predictions about future events, e.g. sales forecast for the next year.

FTP File Transfer Protocol is a protocol agreed by parties to a communication link to transfer files in either direction without error and if necessary as compressed data to save cost.

Functions Costs are aggregated by common purpose, e.g. marketing, sales, finance, occupancy and procurement.

Gap analysis A technique to identify gaps, e.g. gaps in the market for a particular product or a gap in a product range etc.

Gearing This is the proportion of equity and loan capital in relation to the total capital employed in the organization.

Generally accepted accounting principles (GAAP) Principles on which financial statements are prepared. They include such things as: prudence, consistency and the accrual/matching principle.

Gross profit Sales turnover less cost of sales.

HTML Hyper Text Mark-up Language

HTTP Hyper Text Transfer Protocol used for World Wide Web.

In-store testing A form of market research to test the attractiveness of particular products or services in the place in which they would be sold.

Inductive reasoning Conclusions reached by comparing a specific situation with what is already known about the whole population.

Information technology (IT) That part of computer technology associated with information and communication systems.

Internal rate of return (IRR) An internally set hurdle rate which investment decisions must demonstrate they can exceed if projects are to go ahead.

Internet An international network of computers linked together. See WWW and E-mail, which are two of the most important aspects of the Internet.

Intranet This is an internal organizational network that uses HTML and a web-browsing interface similar to that used on the internet to access various parts of the internal network.

IP Internet Protocol; the data protocol used throughout the net.

IP address A unique identifier of every machine on the net. It usually consists of four numbers separated by dots.

Investment appraisal A set of mathematical techniques enabling judgements to be reached about capital investment decisions, i.e. to invest or not to invest. Payback and discounted cash flow techniques are the most common.

ISDN Integrated services distributed network. Many computer networks are now linked by ISDN which transmits data faster than a modem link.

JICNARS Joint Industry Committee for National Readership Surveys.

JICRAR Joint Industry Committee for Radio Research.

JICTAR Joint Industry Committee Television Audience Research.

Judgement sample A non-scientific means of selecting a sample based upon judgement.

Liability An amount owed to someone outside the organization and recorded as such.

Life cycle The time it takes from birth to death, e.g. time it takes a new product from its introduction to its deletion.

Lifestyles A technique designed to identify attributes of respondents in the form of their lifestyle within the aim of targeting or segmenting a market. See ACORN.

Likert scale A five- or seven-point rating scale designed for use in questionnaires with the aim of differentiating opinions about a particular item.

Liquidity Liquidity of an organization is dependent on cash flows. Timing is important to ensure a company is able to meet its liabilities as they fall due. Working capital cycles and liquidity ratios give important indicators.

Macro-environment The social, economic, political and technological wider environment in which organizations operate (PEST).

Macro-forecast A forecast based upon factors in the wider environment.

Mall intercept interview Survey technique conducted where foot traffic is high and in a place where your products or services are sold; or where the people you need to address are gathered. Shopping hall interviews are a form of mall intercept interview.

Margin The difference between a selling price and cost (gross margin), i.e. Selling price – Cost price; *or* between gross profit (i.e. gross margin) and expenses (net margin).

Mark-up This is the amount by which cost must be increased to arrive at a selling price (SP). SP = Cost + profit margin.

Market research Research about a specific market.

Marketing research The systematic gathering, recording and analysis of data relating to the sale and transfer of goods. It includes: market research; product research; price research; communication research; distribution research; buyer behaviour; consumer research.

Median value A mid-point in a series of numbers or a group.

Micro-environment The immediate environment of the firm. Internal organization and structures; relations with suppliers, customers and employees.

MIS Management information system.

MkIS Marketing information system; that part of the management information system concerned with marketing. Internal databases and external databases supplemented by marketing research will comprise the system.

Mode A measure that indicates the frequency of the variable or range most often observed in a series of data.

Modem Modulator–demodulator; converts digital data into audio signals suitable for telephone transmission. The device that allows a computer to communicate with other computers.

MONICA A form of lifestyle profiling administed by CACI, who administer ACORN.

Net present value (NPV) A discounted cash flow technique designed to bring future values back to the present time period.

Net profit The difference between gross profit and expenses.

Off line Time when a computer is not on line (see On line)

On line Time spent when a computer is hooked up to another over a telephone link.

Ordinal data Identify relative values, e.g. ranking.

Overhead recovery rate The rate at which overheads are recovered in a product or service when an absorption costing system is used. Labour hours, machine hours, standard hours and other means of absorbing the overheads are used.

Overheads Overheads are non-product expenses. Overheads are usually time-based expenses, e.g. rent. They are usually treated as fixed costs but they may be partly variable, e.g. telephone expenses include a rental portion (fixed) and call charges (variable).

Panel research A form of continuous research involving the use of a panel, e.g. television viewing habits.

Payback The time it takes for an investment to generate sufficient revenues to pay back the initial capital outlays.

PERT Project Evaluation Review Technique – similar to Critical Path Analysis (see above).

PoP Point of Presence; the number you dial to access the Internet.

Primary activities Contributes directly to the purpose of the organization or department.

Primary data Data collected by you usually in the field for your own specific research needs.

Prime cost The sum of all the direct costs of production, i.e. Direct labour + Direct material + Direct expenses.

Product cost Direct costs attributable to the product.

Production cost Direct costs plus any production overheads.

Profit and loss account An account for a specific period of time (month, year) that indicates sales income and expenses for the period to show a gross and net profit or loss.

Profit centre Similar to a cost centre but instead of merely being a place where costs are classified appropriate sales income is attributed to a profit centre and the manager responsible has responsibility for income and cost.

Psychographic data Data from research to determine personality types, lifestyles and social class.

PV See Net present value.

Qualitative Applied to data or research that is related to attitudes, behaviour and thoughts rather than numbers. The opposite of quantitative.

Quantitative Applied to numerical data or research involving the collection and analysis of numbers.

Quota A quota is a prescribed number, e.g. in quota sampling if you decide you need ten respondents, 10 is your quota.

Ratio A ratio is a relationship between two variables that may be expressed in numeric form, e.g. 2:1, or as a percentage. Financial ratios measure profitability, liquidity, investment and activity.

Responsibility centre A unit or function headed by a manager responsible for its performance.

Risk An assessment of the likelihood of an event occurring or not occurring. Uncertainty gives rise to risk.

Rolling forecast A forecast that is continuously updated taking account of changing information.

Sales research Marketing research related to the sales function or sale of products.

Sample A smaller number selected from a total population containing characteristics you want to investigate. Samples may be selected at random statistically or qualitatively meeting specific criteria. Samples should be representative of the total.

Secondary activities Supports primary activities, e.g. administration, technical support and training.

Secondary data Data collected by someone else not specifically for your purposes. Secondary data can be inexpensive. It may be relevant, useful and timely to your needs but you should consider how and why it was originally collected.

Segmentation A means of grouping customers or markets with specific characteristics that you can use to differentiate between them.

Selling price The price at which goods and services are exchanged (sold).

Semantic differential A scaling technique designed to differentiate between what respondents mean in answering a specific question in a survey.

Shareholders' funds Equity capital + Reserves.

Standard cost A costing system usually requiring a number of predetermined rates that allow a standard cost to be calculated for any produce or service. Variances from the standard are later analysed.

Statement of Standard Accounting Practice (SSAP) These are standards issued to the profession in the UK by the Accounting Standards Board to attempt consistency of financial statements. SSAPs only apply to financial statements in the UK produced for external consumption (i.e. audited, published financial statements).

Stock Sometimes referred to as *inventory*; an asset held by the firm until a sale is made, when the stock is part of the cost of the sale.

Telnet A system used to log on to other systems remotely.

Total cost The prime cost plus production overheads and other overheads attributable to the product.

Trading account That part of the trading and profit and loss account that deals with sales and cost of sales to arrive at gross profit.

Trading and profit and loss account See Profit and loss account.

Transfer price This is a price at which goods and services are transferred. The term is most often used to describe a situation when there is an internal transfer between two parts of the same organization. For example, a manufacturing division may supply all its output to a retail sales division. In such cases the price at which goods are transferred is set internally. They may be set at a cost price, cost plus price, a market price (if one exists) or at an arbitrary price based on some other logic. Internal markets are often set up to determine transfer prices.

Trend A pattern that exists between data variables.
Turnover Commonly used to mean sales over a period of time.

Uncertainty Uncertainty about future events leads to risk. Financial decisions are often based upon assessing risk and uncertainty.
Unit cost The cost of a single unit of output before any profit is added.

VALS Values and lifestyles: Survivors, Sustainers, Belongers, Emulators, Achievers, I-Am-Me, Experiential, Socially conscious, Integrated.
Variable cost A cost that varies as a result of a change in output quantity.
Variance A difference between a planned or budgeted expense, cost or revenue and an actual figure.
Variance analysis A technique to investigate variances and focus on causes with a view to realigning the plan.

Weighted average cost of capital (WAAC) This is a calculation that attempts to measure a cost of capital used by the firm according to the proportions of each type of finance used, e.g. equity (the shareholders' funds) and loan capitals. For example, if shareholders' funds represented 50 per cent paying annual dividends of 5 per cent and loan capital represented 50 per cent paying interest on the loan annually at 10 per cent the WACC is 7.5 per cent since proportions are equally weighted.
Working capital Current assets – Current liabilities.
Working capital cycle The time it takes for one complete cycle from receiving stock to paying creditors. Stock turns into a debtor who pays and in turn the creditor is paid.
WWW World Wide Web is the distributed collection of pages of text, graphics and animation links using a simple point and click interface, e.g. accessed through a Windows type environment.

Yield This is a measure of output from a given input, e.g. dividend yield measures the real rate of return by dividing the market price per share into the dividend to arrive at a yield.

Zero based budgeting (ZBB) A means of formulating a budget beginning with a zero base and justifying what is required rather than simply referring to last year's budget and building on that.

Index